IMPROVING VOCATIONAL CURRICULUM

Sponsored by the National Association for Trade and Industrial Education

Coordinating Editor .... **Lester G. Duenk**
Virginia Tech
Blacksburg, VA

Managing Editor .... **Howard Bud Smith**
Executive Editor-Technology
The Goodheart-Willcox Company

Editorial Board:

Clifton P. Campbell, The University of Tennessee, Knoxville, TN
Timothy Lawrence, Director, Virginia VICA, Richmond, VA
Sondra Massie, Russel County Vocational Center, Lebanon, VA
John L. Scott, The University of Georgia, Athens, GA
Ethel M. Smith, Executive Director, National Association for Trade and Industrial Education

South Holland, Illinois

THE GOODHEART-WILLCOX COMPANY, INC.

Publishers

Library of Congress Catalog Card Number 92-31261
International Standard Book Number 0-87006-031-7

2 3 4 5 6 7 8 9 10   93   96 95

Library of Congress Cataloging in Publication Data

Lester G. Duenk.
  Improving vocational curriculum / by Lester G. Duenk.

    p. cm.
  Includes index.
  ISBN 0-87006-031-7
    1. Vocational education--United States--Curricula.
    2. Curriculum planning--United States.
I. Duenk, Lester G.
LC1045.I47 1993
375'.0086'0973--dc20   92-31261
                                        CIP

INTRODUCTION

Improving Vocational Curriculum provides guidelines for those responsible for the development of contemporary curriculum for instruction in vocational/technical fields. It is a compendium of the various systems of teaching and testing for students training for a variety of occupations requiring specialized knowledge and skill development.

The guide consists of 12 chapters, each aimed at specific tasks in curriculum development or at a particular method of instruction. Early chapters deal with the nature of vocational curriculum, the role of occupational analysis as a tool in curriculum writing, and resources for writing curriculum. Later chapters concentrate on specific tasks such as preparing an individualized competency record, writing instruction sheets, writing tests, integrating safety into the instructional program, and organizing the components of the curriculum guide.

Improving Vocational Curriculum combines the skills, knowledge, and experience of a number of specialists in the field of vocational technical education. Each has many years of involvement in the many aspects of teacher education. The National Association for Trade and Industrial Education is proud to have sponsored *Improving Vocational Curriculum* for the benefit of the practicing professionals building and training for a brighter tomorrow.

Lester G. Duenk
Howard Bud Smith

TABLE OF CONTENTS

Chapter 1

THE CURRICULUM IN VOCATIONAL EDUCATION

by

Nelson A. Foell, Associate Professor
Trade and Industrial Education
The University of Georgia
Athens, Georgia

INTRODUCTION

The word *curriculum* is used at all levels of education but it is not always clearly understood. A secondary school has a planned curriculum. The same school also has a number of curricula designed for major program thrusts such as the *academic, general,* and *vocational education* curriculum. Each subject area within the school's major program thrusts usually has curricula for each instructional area such as the *welding* curriculum in the vocational program of welding technology. See Figure 1-1.

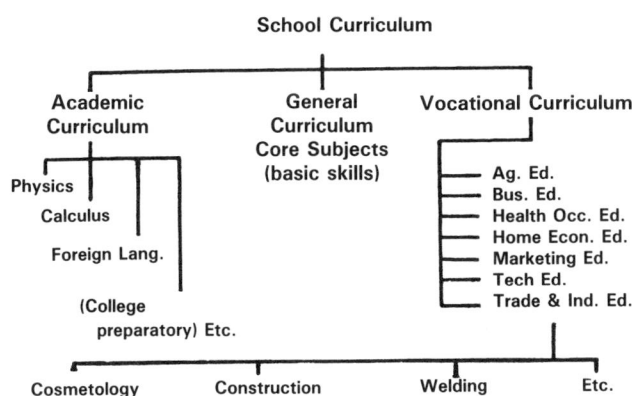

Figure 1-1. Program thrusts in school curriculum.

Does the term curriculum mean the same thing at each vocational level? What does it mean to teachers, to students, or to parents? How does the term curriculum relate to other educational terms used in instruction such as a course of study, curriculum guide, course outline, course syllabus, units of instruction, lesson plans, and others? This chapter will attempt to answer these questions while introducing the remaining 11 other chapters which address various curriculum components comprising a curriculum guide.

CURRICULUM TERMINOLOGY

To understand the structure of the typical school and the school's vocational education curriculum, we must agree on the definitions of several frequently used terms. First of all, a *school* is an institution in which planned and organized learning experiences assist students in attaining predetermined objectives.

Several types of schools offer vocational courses. At the secondary level, those schools having vocational programs are the *comprehensive high school,* the *technical high school,* and the *area vocational technical school.* The *comprehensive high school* is one that offers students academic and general education as well as a moderate range of selected vocational courses. Academic courses are most often designed to prepare students for direct entry into college. Academic courses include study in such courses as calculus, physics, literature, foreign languages, and other collegiate prerequisites. General education courses are those that include core subjects such as basic reading, writing, science, and math skills. General education courses often lack both the rigorous study of the academic curriculum as well as the specialized study and development of technical skills found in the vocational curriculum. Critics of general education believe that it neither prepares students for college nor for entry into the world of work. Vocational programs found in the comprehensive high school usually offer occupational skill development in selected vocational fields. These programs are often limited by budget restraints and student enrollments to four or five occupational areas selected from agricultural, business, trade and industrial, marketing, health occupations, technology, and home economics education. Vocational education curricula found in many comprehensive schools often are further restricted and less occupationally specialized when offered as a cluster concept such as transportation cluster or construction cluster.

The *technical high school,* in contrast to the comprehensive high school, is one in which the main educational objectives are focused either on a wide range of vocational education course offerings with as many as twenty or more choices, or at the extreme opposite, single occupational fields such as marine occupations, commercial graphics, or aviation. Technical high schools offer general and advanced academic courses that support student learning in the specialized occupations. These schools are most often found in larger cities. They were the first "magnet" schools.

The *area vocational technical school* (AVTS) or *area technical institute* is an institution that often offers the student the greatest selection of vocational courses along with career education and employability skills. Students are bused between their regular (home) high schools, which offer few, if any, vocational courses, and the AVTS. The home school provides students with the opportunity to study core subjects as well as advanced academic subjects. The home school also provides opportunities to engage in sports, band, clubs, and other extracurricular activities. In addition to providing secondary level students with vocational education, the area vocational technical school or area technical institute frequently offers post-secondary vocational and technical education to adults.

Educational Programs

Figure 1-2 shows the relationship of the terms school, program classications, vocational educational programs, vocational courses, units, and lessons.

Major Groupings

Each course is made up of several units or major groupings of instructional tasks and concepts best taught together. The words school, programs, courses, units, and lessons are educational terms describing organizational structure of an educational institution. Curriculum, on the other hand, is a broad term that includes all the educational offerings and learning experiences offered under the direction of the school. Using this definition, formal educational experiences such as taking an academic course or participating in a vocational laboratory course are often thought to be the only components of a student's curriculum. However, a student's curriculum also includes participating in such areas as athletic events, clubs, drama, and musical events which are labeled as extracurricular activities. Most students are required to take certain core courses. Vocational students are also required to participate in co-curricular activities through vocational student organizations such as the Vocational Industrial Clubs of America (VICA), National FFA Organization, and Health Occupations Student Association (HOSA). Those student organizations are considered to be an integral part of the curriculum. Students have freedom to elect other courses and to participate in school sponsored activities according to their interest and aspirations. The result is an individual curriculum for each student. Curriculum, then, is an educational term that focuses on learning experiences or subject matter content which are either required or elected by students as part of their formal educational program.

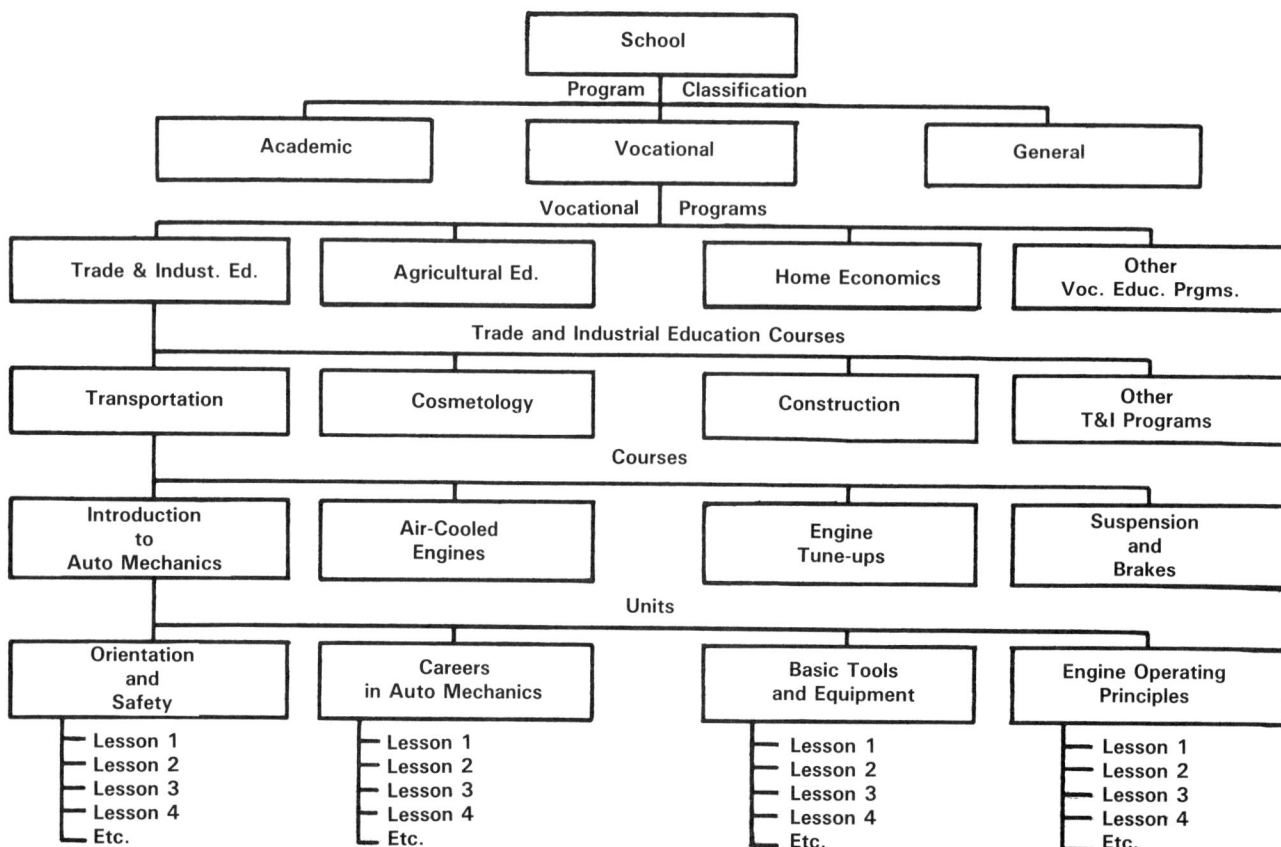

Figure 1-2. School instructional organization.

LEVELS OF CURRICULUM

Each academic or vocational program may also have a stated curriculum such as the mathematics curriculum or the drafting technology curriculum. It is very important that each secondary-level vocational student have a planned curriculum that includes a proper mix of academic and vocational courses as well as noncredit learning experiences to meet individual interests and aspirations. Figure 1-3 illustrates the relationship between an individual student's curriculum and other curricula in the school.

Curriculum Development is a carefully structured process. It consists of identifying educational goals, obtaining school and community related information, and making curriculum decisions such as what content will be included and how the curriculum will be structured. Curriculum development in vocational education usually involves a team of educators and representatives from business and industry working together to develop content for a specific occupational program.

Forms of Documentation

While curriculum development is a process, the terms (a) course of study, (b) curriculum guide, (c) course outline, and (d) course syllabus, refer to forms of documentation of curriculum components used to communicate information about a specific occupational program. The following definitions should be helpful in understanding these terms.

Course of study — This term describes a comprehensive planned program of study that enables the student to complete the curriculum of a specific occupational goal. See Figure 1-3. It includes information about the sequence of courses in the occupation as well as those courses that have a strong relationship to, and support learning in, the occupation to be studied, such as English, science, and math courses. The course of study may also contain some or all of the following types of information:

a. Statement of philosophy and objectives for the school, general program and occupationally specific program areas.
b. A description of jobs for which the occupational program provides instructional preparation.
c. A listing of courses.

Curriculum guide — Although the terms curriculum guide and course of study are sometimes used interchangeably, the term curriculum guide is generally designed for a single course or program. Frequently, curriculum guides are prepared by a curriculum committee composed of educators, curriculum specialists, and business and industry representatives either at the state, regional, or local school system levels. The guides serve as a comprehensive resource to aid school administrators, teachers, and students in understanding and meeting the goals of a particular occupational course or program. The curriculum guide recommended in this book contains the following major categories:

a. Introduction to the guide including information as to how it was developed and description of the community and school setting the program serves.

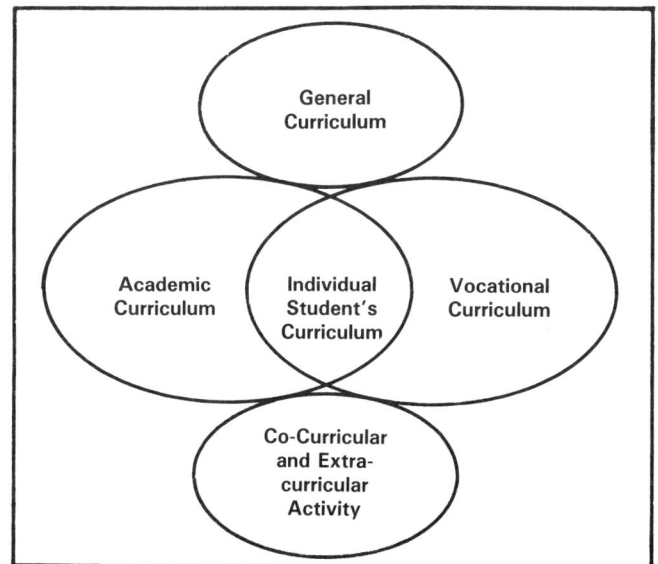

Figure 1-3. Individual student's curriculum within the school curriculum.

b. Philosophical statements for the school, occupational program, and specific occupational program addressed in the guide.
c. Description of how national objectives of education, vocational education objectives, school objectives, occupational program objectives, and specific course objectives are addressed and attained.
d. Description of the occupation(s) for which the program provides preparatory experiences.
e. Listing of written resource materials used to support the program.
f. Listing of audiovisual resource materials used to support instruction.
g. Listing of unit titles.
h. Program and course outlines.
i. Competency records.
j. General safety and conduct rules.
k. Unit guides.
l. Course evaluation procedures and materials.
m. Laboratory management materials.
n. Appendix for the curriculum guide.

Course outline — The course outline is usually that portion of a curriculum guide or course of study that lists the units of instruction and the general content for each unit in the course. Occasionally, the course outline may also include a listing of objectives, methods for delivering instruction, listing of resources, evaluation procedures, and listing of facilities and equipment needed to support the instructional program.

Course syllabus — The course syllabus specifies the content and instructional sequence of a course. It is similar to the course outline except that it generally lists specific course requirements including required readings, exam and test sequence, and other related activities. The course syllabus usually contains information under the following categories:

a. Course description.

b. Course objectives.
c. Unit titles and content outlines of each unit.
d. Instructional sequence and instructional strategies.
e. Reading assignments.
f. Resources needed to support instruction and evaluation practices.
g. Facilities, equipment and materials needed to implement course instruction.
h. The sequence of evaluations and tests.

CURRICULUM FORMATS

Several different formats for organizing curriculum have been developed. Among the most popular are: (a) descriptive, (b) modules of instruction, and (c) units organized by class sessions. This book follows the descriptive approach to curriculum organization. Each of the formats will be addressed in detail in following chapters. A brief outline of the three different formats follows.

Descriptive Method
The *descriptive* method for organizing a curriculum guide is shown in this section. This method works well in those programs of vocational education where the content is developed from an occupational analysis. It provides necessary experiences in course content. Programs in most of the skilled occupational areas are readily organized in this format. Aims, content, methods of instruction, evaluation procedures, and physical facilities are presented as separate chapters or subsections. Any instructional program can follow this organizational approach. The following example shows the basic pattern.
I. Preliminaries.
   A. Table of contents
   B. Introduction
   C. Course philosophy
   D. Course objectives
   E. Occupational description
   F. Curriculum and audiovisual resource materials
   G. Units of instruction
   H. Program/course outline
   I. Individual competency records
   J. General safety and conduct rules
II. Unit Guides.
   A. Task titles and performance objectives
   B. Lesson plan titles
   C. Safety precautions
   D. Laboratory/classroom rules
   E. Manipulative skill lesson plans
   F. Technical information (theory) lesson plans
   G. Unit tests and peformance rating scales
   H. Instruction sheets
   I. Unit safety materials
   J. Unit learning modules
   K. Unit appendix

III. Course evaluation
IV. Laboratory management materials
V. Appendix for curriculum guide
An individual course of study will usually contain all or most of the above information. In fact, many courses of study with the descriptive organization contain additional information about the course, such as descriptions of the teacher's plan for the student directed organization, and examples of the various types of components.

Modules of Instruction
The *modules of instruction* format (self-directed learning) incorporates performance objectives, learning activities, learning aids, and evaluation instruments. Modules are recommended when instruction is to be individualized and delivered in a competency-based, self-paced approach. Modules aid in solving the particular problem of differences in the rate or speed of learning by individual students. The plan for each module includes the terminal and enabling performance objectives for the module and all necessary information to complete activities required by the module. It also includes critique instruments to evaluate the degree of success in meeting the stated performance objectives for the module. This approach is discussed in more detail in Chapter 11.

The module may include a teacher guide comprised of a series of activities which indicates how much might be covered each period, and what points are to be stressed in each activity. The module approach is generally recommended when units of instruction can be designed around major competencies. Other independent content topics are used to provide supplementary instruction that is classified as general, technical, or guidance.

The following outline shows a typical organization pattern for the module method of curriculum development:
1. Table of contents
2. Prerequisites
3. Introduction
4. Directions for students
5. Objectives
6. Learning activities
7. Checkout activities
8. Teacher's final checklist
9. References
The use of the module of instruction approach allows the teacher to integrate the performance objectives, content, methods, and evaluation. Each module should contain all the information, instructions, and criteria necessary to teach and evaluate student progress.

Units Organized for Class Sessions
Another instructional organization approach is referred to as *units organized by class sessions.* Teachers often choose this format for classes which meet only once or twice a week, especially when providing instruction on topics like human relations, or when compressing overview material into survey

classes. The format dictates the use of grouping units for individual class sessions. Each class session covers a *unit* of material. The unit session plan requires advance preparation to fit content into the allotted time. It is most effective when used with students in advanced classes which tend to exhibit less differences in their learning abilities. Experienced teachers often tend to be more successful with this format than beginning teachers. Adult evening classes or apprentice training classes which meet only once per week lend themselves to this pattern.

Considerations for offering this type of organizational pattern include:
1. Beginning teachers may find this format difficult.
2. Careful planning is necessary.
3. Content must be carefully arranged.
   a. If there is too little content, the able student may lose interest.
   b. If there is too much content, the less able student may not be able to keep up.
4. Units usually work best with a homogeneous rather than heterogeneous group.
5. Most regular daytime occupational classes have students with a wide range of abilities.

The following outline describes a typical format:
I. Preliminaries (see descriptive).
II. Introduction (see descriptive).
III. Unit titles for each session.
   Each unit, in turn, is then presented in outline form. Factors to consider in preparing outlines for one or more of these sessions might include:
1. Course goals and student performance objectives.
2. Safety information and safety tests.
3. Classroom management activities, such as:
   a. Tool room procedures.
   b. Student grading system.
4. Lesson plans.
5. Pre- and post-tests.
6. Description of the methods of instruction, teaching aids, and teaching techniques.

GUIDELINES FOR STUDY

In the following chapters, information, guidelines, and specific procedures will be presented for the following kinds of activities which will help the reader develop a curriculum.
1. Occupational analysis. This includes definitions of analysis, writing broad course objectives, identification and selection of tasks, and key point breakdowns.
2. Selecting curriculum sources. Included are sources curriculum materials, business and industrial resources, types of audiovisual materials, and reference materials.
3. Writing the preliminaries for your curriculum guide. Included are the purpose, introduction, philosophy, course objectives, unit titles, and developing the unit guide.
4. Developing individualized competency records. Included are the purpose, examples, and ways of recording the data.
5. Developing unit guides for content, instructional methods, cognitive, psychomotor and affective testing. Also included are different ways of developing examinations and test instruments.
6. Integrating safety in the curriculum.
7. Self-directed learning.

SUMMARY

Curriculum development is an ongoing process. It is subject to frequent modification because of changes in technology, availability of new resources, emerging occupations, and student interests and abilities.

Teachers of an occupational area must update and revise curricula in order to ensure that it remains relevant and valid. The communities served by the educational facility expect the skills, knowledge, and attitudes imparted by the instructor to be those skills that are needed for employment in the real world. Good instruction requires careful and extensive planning. This will result in curriculum guides developed by the instructor that achieve meaningful vocational educational goals.

Chapter 2

THE OCCUPATIONAL ANALYSIS

by

Lester G. Duenk, Professor
Vocational Industrial Education
Virginia Tech
Blacksburg, Virginia

INTRODUCTION

It is generally quite difficult for the new teacher to know how and where to start when there are so many things requiring attention at the beginning of a school year. Equipment must be checked and maintained, safety provisions attended to, student records and school forms completed, and a host of other incidentals must be performed. All require a substantial amount of time.

Most important, the teacher needs to plan what will be taught and then seek to organize instructional materials into some kind of teaching order. Lesson plans are of high priority. Very often the beginning teacher starts preparing lesson plans without much thought about how they might fit into a total program. The result can be a "hodgepodge" of disconnected teaching materials that follow no particular learning sequence.

WHAT IS THE OCCUPATIONAL ANALYSIS?

Occupational analysis is a technique used to break down an occupational teaching area into a manageable approach for instructional purposes. Basically, the occupational analysis is a breakdown, from the simple to the complex, of all teaching content for a particular course or program. The analysis can be likened to an inventory, as it might be taken in a store, or other establishment, which enables one to know the status of stock or equipment at a given time. The inventory is then followed by arranging all materials into a manageable order so that they can be found quickly when needed.

Just as there must be an orderly system for managing a business inventory, there also must be an orderly procedure planned for instructional purposes. Without a planned system of some sort, students will learn in spurts and also at much slower rates.

In most areas of our society, an analysis approach is used to promote time efficiency and quality of a service or product. Engineers and architects have systematic approaches to designing plant organization, planning structural systems, and systematizing approaches to other products and/or service development. The health professional utilizes a system, which is essentially an analysis, to diagnose and treat the human body. The blood tests, urinalysis, and numerous other tests and functions are planned cumulatively so that assessment can be made in an orderly, efficient manner. The same is true in most of the other areas of modern business and industry. Teaching is no different. Teaching must also be done in an orderly, systematic manner in order to be time efficient and quality effective.

ANALYSIS AND INDUSTRY

Industries could not be competitive were it not for the ongoing effort that is placed on analysis of the various jobs in a plant. In order to ensure maximum productivity, industrial analysts are hired to study the jobs that workers perform. They develop very detailed master plans which indicate: (a) the sequential steps to follow, (b) the things to remember about the correct performance of each step, (c) safety to be observed when performing the steps, (d) quality checks to be made at certain intervals, (e) time standards, and (f) other key points which can make the job easier, more efficient and ensure higher quality. Analyses developed for each job are used as guides to train new workers.

The first analysis systems in industry were developed during World War I when there was a shortage of skilled workers in defense industries. Up until this time, the training of workers was largely a "trial and error" situation. With the development of the analysis technique it was found that workers could be trained very quickly and were able to produce more work with less effort. Today the majority of large industries utilize some type of analysis approach in their employee training programs. Many industries employ training directors who supervise a staff of employees to analyze jobs, train workers, and work toward increasing production efficiency.

It is obvious that teaching students in a school laboratory situation also involves efficiency of training similar to that found in industry. The difference is that the end product now becomes student achievement rather than goods or service.

Teachers should plan their instruction so that students can develop to their greatest potential for the time spent in the course or program. Teachers who use a "hit or miss" unplanned approach will find that both teaching efficiency and student development are poor. Furthermore, teacher frustration is heightened when frantic efforts produce minimal results. On the other hand, the teacher who practices an organized system of analyzing and managing instruction will find that teaching can be time efficient, of a high quality, and a pleasurable experience.

Principals indicate that teachers who fail to succeed during their first year very often show a lack of good laboratory management skills. Occupational analysis, when well done, becomes a management technique and makes the teacher's job easier.

Steps in Doing an Occupational Analysis

It is important to follow a logical cumulative system when doing the analysis. The cumulative approach in education is simply starting with small or easy-to-learn basics and gradually combining them into larger concepts. Cumulative learning is continually building upon what was previously learned.

There are various systems for doing an analysis, all of them leading to the same outcome. The approach described here is simple. It involves developing the: (a) course objectives, (b) unit breakdown, (c) task breakdown, (d) lesson title breakdown, (e) step/topic breakdown, (f) key point breakdown, and (g) tools/materials breakdown.

Writing Course Objectives

Before teachers can build an analysis, it is necessary to decide where they are going. The direction to follow is based upon what is expected as student outcomes of the instructional programs. Unless this is done at the start, the teacher is likely to go around in circles, repeating and leaving gaps in teaching because no clear-cut objectives had been established.

There is only a limited amount which can be accomplished in a course; it therefore becomes necessary to select what is most important. Furthermore, the teacher may be limited by the size of the laboratory, equipment available, class size, ability level of students, live work available, and a host of other conditions. It is important to recognize that it is impossible to teach all knowledge, skills, and attitudes about an occupation in the time that has been allotted for a course. Hence, it is necessary to pinpoint the objectives before proceeding with the analysis.

A good way to begin is by checking with local industry to determine what skills are needed in the labor market. Much of this information can be gathered by consulting with the advisory committee. Some commercial materials, particularly Vocational Technical Education Consortium of States (VTECS) catalogs will provide information on current industry needs (see Chapter 3).

Next, list the broad objectives for the entire program. It should be pointed out that broad objectives do not include the conditions and standards that are part of a performance objective. The length of the program may vary from a few weeks for exploratory programs to two or more years for pre-employment and cooperative training programs. Confine broad objectives to a minimal number. With only a few exceptions, it would be possible to list the broad objectives in 25 statements or less. If one gets carried away by listing large numbers of objectives, the analysis system becomes cumbersome. The broad objectives should be confined to the major areas that are included in the program. They should be stated in terms of student outcomes, not teacher goals.

There are two types of broad objectives, technical and nontechnical. Technical objectives are concerned strictly with occupational skills and understandings. Nontechnical objectives relate to goals that are good for all students to achieve without regard for the specifics of one occupational teaching area.

Some examples of technical objectives for drafting follow. The student will:
1. Apply skill in the use of instruments and equipment.
2. Apply principles of engineering geometry to drafting.
3. Perform freehand and template lettering.
4. Draw auxiliary views.
5. Apply the principles of proper dimensioning.
6. Communicate using the vocabulary of the drafter.
7. Apply principles of computer-assisted drafting.

Some of the technical objectives may be of a vocational guidance nature, such as: The student will be able to:
1. Exhibit a knowledge of other occupational areas which are closely related to drafting.
2. Exhibit a knowledge of working conditions and wages in drafting.
3. Exhibit a knowledge of how one may make career advancements in the drafting field.

Some nontechnical objectives are: The student will:
1. Develop habits of responsibility and initiative.
2. Develop good social habits in working with other students.
3. Develop a feeling of pride in the immediate work and in the vocation.
4. Develop the ability to plan, organize, and coordinate jobs.
5. Develop an appreciation and high regard for good quality work.
6. Develop a high degree of safety consciousness.
7. Strive toward gaining recognition as a good citizen as well as a good worker.
8. Develop work habits such as honesty, punctuality, dependability, and cooperation.
9. Learn the rules of professional ethics and abide by these rules to gain public confidence and respect.
10. Develop the ability to solve problems with a minimum amount of teacher help.

There is no point in listing objectives unless the teacher also decides on a definite way of accomplishing those objectives which are considered important. Think through the activities which will help reach the stated objectives, as indicated below.

SELECTED OBJECTIVES FOR A COURSE IN GENERAL DRAWING

Objective No. 1.
The student will gain knowledge and skill in the use of instruments and equipment.

Activities to Achieve Outcomes
1. Plan information lessons on each of the basic instruments used in drawing.
2. Demonstrate their use and have student practice on assigned drawings.

Objective No. 2.
The student will develop an understanding of the place of drafting in the world of work.

Activities to Achieve Outcomes
1. Visit several drafting establishments.
2. Invite an experienced drafter to come to class and address the group.
3. Show the movie "A Career in Drafting."

Objective No. 3.
The student will develop a critical attitude toward personal accomplishments.

Activities to Achieve Outcomes
1. Provide specific standards for each drawing. Discuss these with the students.
2. Provide a clean, organized room that is conducive to good learning.
3. Discuss the importance of good work habits in relation to industrial practice, and job advancement.

A complete listing of objectives for a two year (1/2 day) course in masonry is shown in Figure 2-1.

Unit Breakdown

The main divisions in a course are called units or blocks. Unit is the term that will be used consistently throughout this publication. Units are broad areas of instruction that involve manipulative work and informational instruction. A planned combination of both technical information and manipulative skill development is necessary for learning to take place. Some units will contain more manipulative skill development and less technical information or vice versa.

Entire occupational programs will differ greatly in the "mix" of skill versus knowledge. Masonry, for example, is a skill-oriented occupation. Typically, at least 80 percent of a masonry program will consist of manipulative skill development. An electronics program, on the other hand, will typically be composed of more knowledge development and less manipulative skill development.

Unit titles are arranged so that the content will flow from the simple to the complex throughout the course. There are

The student will:
1. Mix mortar
2. Explain the names and uses of the various masonry hand tools
3. Care for basic tools and equipment
4. Build corner leads and lay brick to a line
5. Construct piers and chimneys
6. Explain the fundamentals of various structural bonds and patterns
7. Gain skill in the use of concrete construction
8. Gain skills in form construction
9. Develop good work habits, such as speed, neatness, and accuracy
10. Develop the knowledge to solve trade problems
11. Practice personal and group safety
12. Develop the manipulative skill needed for handling and spreading mortar
13. Demonstrate the use of masonry tools
14. Estimate materials and labor cost
15. Lay out and build foundations
16. Build and stock a masonry scaffold
17. Develop skill in brick veneer construction
18. Develop skill in fireplace construction
19. Build five different types of composite brick and block walls
20. Build brick walkways

Figure 2-1. Broad objectives for a masonry program.

four basic guidelines to follow in determining whether a body of knowledge can be classified as a unit.

1. **Information and skill must flow.** Work must make sense to the student when combined together. All informational material must be closely related to the manipulative material. Information type and skill type lessons must be coordinated on the same topics.

2. **Difference in function.** The auto body repair student can obviously see that frame alignment, glass installation and painting are different functions within the occupation. Hence, it makes sense that these learning experiences belong in different units. The carpentry student can observe that framing is a function different than exterior trim. Keep like bodies of knowledge and skill together as units.

3. **Gaps between units.** Generally, different types of tools, equipment, materials and/or procedures are used as new units are begun. The cosmetologist will use different implements, chemicals and/or solutions in a unit on shampooing than in a unit on haircoloring.

4. **A logical division point.** Students should gain the feeling at the end of a unit that they have concluded a certain kind of process. Essentially, the teacher terminates the process and begins a new process (which usually requires a knowledge of previous units). The student should feel that there is a logical division in the learning situation.

The first unit is generally called "Orientation" or "Introduction." In this unit the preliminaries are taken care of before entering the basics of the occupational instruction. Some of the items that may be taken care of during the orientation unit are:

1. Greet students, show them where to sit, where to put coats, etc.
2. Introduce self; write name on board.
3. Tell about your background and experience.

4. Have students give names and tell a little about themselves.
5. Explain what will be learned in the course, i.e., major activities, course requirements.
6. Show samples of student work (or pictures).
7. Explain about employment goals, vocational guidance, and opportunities for advanced study.
8. Tell about degree of skill to be developed by students.
9. Explain the importance of working together in the laboratory.
10. Conduct tour of laboratory, tool room, explaining briefly the uses of tools and equipment.
11. Explain use of safety zones around equipment.
12. Go over general safety rules.
13. Fill in enrollment forms.
14. Assign each student a class number.
15. Explain attendance checking-in system, tardiness.
16. Assign lockers; issue keys. Announce regulations concerning key issue, placing on key board, etc.
17. Assign locker superintendent.
18. Pass out a list of general shop rules, post on board. Go over list with class.
19. Show textbooks, workbooks, shop library.
20. Issue tool tags.
21. Explain cost of materials, method of keeping records, paying for materials.
22. Pass out and explain student competency lists.
23. Explain how students will be graded.
24. Explain fire drill procedures.
25. Explain about shop dress, tell what type of clothes to bring.
26. Go over personnel assignments with students.
27. Assign workstations.
28. Give a brief explanation of student group or club activities.
29. Start students doing a manipulative job that they can accomplish in a short time with good results (to motivate).

NOTE: It may be necessary to spread out some of these activities over several days inasmuch as a portion of each period should be spent doing manipulative work which motivates students.

Avoid listing separate units at the beginning of your course for areas like tools, safety, student groups, etc. This type of content should be mentioned during the orientation unit and then taught along with other units as the teacher proceeds through the course. Students are anxious to get started doing active things. Classroom instruction given for several weeks tends to turn off motivation so very little learning retention takes place.

Some instructors list the time that is to be allotted to each unit. There are pros and cons to be considered concerning this practice. Listing of time in hours or weeks enables the teacher to stay on schedule and complete all aspects of a course in the time allotted. Also, students are motivated to keep up with their peers. On the other hand, a time listing for units proves impractical from the standpoint of allowing for individual differences. The newer concept of

mainstreaming disadvantaged and impaired students suggests that some students may take many times longer than others to complete a unit. Consequently, individualizing of instruction is easier to carry out if units of instruction are flexible from a time standpoint.

An example of a unit breakdown that lists instructional time, follows in Figure 2-2. If an administrator prefers that no time limits are set to complete the unit, keep a record of the students' individual time spent at the various unit activities. Remember, however, that the teacher will need some idea of time to spend in the various units when deciding on (a) the number of tasks, and (b) the difficulty of tasks to be included in each unit.

	Length of Program - Two Years			
	1st Year		2nd Year	
Unit Titles	Class Hours	Lab Hours	Class Hours	Lab Hours
1. Orientation	5		5	
2. Mortar	5	45		
3. Brick walls & corners	10	105		40
4. Block walls & corners	10	90		30
5. Foundations & footings	5	20	5	15
6. Piers & pilasters	5	35	5	30
7. Bonding & storing			5	40
8. Leads & walls	10	75		25
9. Bonds	5	10	5	20
10. Paving	5	35		35
11. Fireplaces			5	100
12. Chimney				20
13. Arches				35
14. Ornamental			5	30
15. Concrete	5		5	20
TOTALS	65	415	40	440
TOTAL HOURS FOR TWO YEAR PROGRAM **960**				

Figure 2-2. Unit breakdown for a masonry program.

Task Breakdown

Following the unit breakdown, the next step in the analysis is the task breakdown. Before teachers can plan lessons, tests, instruction sheets, and other needed teaching materials, decisions must be made on a cumulative list of activities that students will perform in each unit. The words *task, job, project, competency,* and *activity* are used interchangeably and cause confusion for the new teacher.

The word "job" was used to describe student activities in trade and industrial education programs for over 70 years, dating back to World War I programs. The original concept was that teachers should converse with students in the same language as that used by supervisors in the real industrial world. The supervisor would assign a *job* to an employee, not a *task, competency,* or *project*. Later when other vocational programs and agencies began publishing commercial materials, the words *task, activity, project,* and *competency* came into use to describe activities that included both manipulative and/or mental student work assignments. For the purpose of this chapter, the word task will be used throughout.

In each unit there should be a list of tasks which proceed in cumulative learning order (a) from the simple to the complex, (b) from the familiar to the unfamiliar, (c) in the sequence performed on the job, and (d) with prerequisite learning first. Later, competency lists for recording student progress can be developed from your task breakdown (see Chapter 5). Also task sheets and other materials will be developed on the basis of the work done so far in the analysis (see Chapter 7).

At this point, begin by making a laundry list of tasks for each unit. Take care that each task is built on previous knowledge and skill. For the purpose of this analysis, list only the manipulative tasks. Even though informational tasks exist, the analysis becomes too cumbersome if informational activities (information and assignment sheets, mathematics problems, print reading exercises, tests, etc.) are included here. Recorded progress on these "written tasks" must be maintained; however, this can be done in the teacher's grade book. Confine the analysis to manipulative tasks, like those found in the industry, on which students' proficiency will be graded. Avoid making the list of tasks too long. Combine smaller, elemental tasks into larger ones if necessary. If too many tasks are listed, student laboratory management and grading present a time and paperwork problem.

Tasks used in occupational classes should be carefully selected by the teacher. Since tasks are vehicles of instruction, and not the end product themselves, they must be selected on the basis of the steps required in their construction and the instructional value of each step.

Some pointers for task selection:

1. Avoid selecting tasks that fit only one specific teaching situation. The selection of tasks, at this time, should not be limited or conditioned by any other specific school or course.
2. Tasks should have real educational value. Refrain from "busy work" as it tends to destroy interest and promotes bad habits and mental laziness. It defeats the very purpose for which the course is offered.
3. Tasks should be useful. Choose work activities that have some utilitarian value in preference to exercises. The instruction will function to a far greater degree if given in connection with something of real worth.
4. Tasks should be representative of the occupation. Select tasks, to the extent possible, that are representative of real occupational practice and that are based on industry needs.
5. Tasks should coincide with the objectives of the curriculum. Keep the objectives of the course in mind so that the tasks assigned will meet these needs.
6. Tasks should offer opportunity for achievement. Remember that all tasks are an opportunity for achievement and not objectives themselves. They are a means to an end — occupational proficiency.
7. Tasks, when combined, should lead to occupational skill. The tasks in every case should be secondary to the skill and knowledge acquired by the student. A task without instructional value has no place in the program.
8. Tasks should represent all phases of the occupation. The tasks should represent a good cross section of the entire occupation.

9. Tasks should offer practice. Each succeeding task should provide opportunities for the further development and application of things learned in preceding tasks. This is particularly necessary for occupational operations that require the development of considerable skill through practice.
10. Tasks should be attractive to students. They should be sufficiently interesting to attract the best efforts of the student. This is a vital point to consider if teachers hope to secure the cooperation of students in the work. Effort and persistence are directly dependent on interest.

A task breakdown for a two-year mine equipment maintenance program is shown in Figure 2-3. Note that this is a laundry list only. Leave one or more blank spaces in each unit listing for additional tasks.

Lesson Title Breakdown

After the task breakdown it becomes necessary to determine what lessons, both informational and manipulative, must be taught to enable the student to perform the tasks selected. This determination is called the lesson title breakdown.

Before beginning, it is appropriate to explain the meaning of the word "lesson" as used in this chapter. A lesson is a presentation given by the teacher that provides new knowledge or skill to students. It can be given to an individual, small group, or entire class. At this point, lesson titles are discussed only as part of the analysis. Lesson plans are described fully in Chapter 6.

A step-by-step description of how to select lesson plan titles to match the task breakdown follows.

1. There are two types of lessons in occupational education, *doing* lessons (psychomotor) and *knowing* lessons (cognitive). Doing lessons may be thought of as demonstrations by the teacher; knowing lessons are related instruction taught in a classroom situation. Instruction in the *affective* domain (attitudes, appreciations, ethics, morals, feelings, etc.) are taught more by example and by good classroom and shop organization than with lessons delivered by a teacher.
2. *Knowing* lessons can be subdivided into three categories: (a) *Technical* (necessary to know), (b) *General* (nice to know), and (c) *Guidance* (for the purpose of guidance in entering, maintaining, and advancing on the job).
3. Doing lessons will last from 10 to 45 minutes, exclusive of practice time. Practice time, which follows, may take several hours or days.
4. Each *doing* lesson (demonstration lesson) must have a broad enough title so that it can be broken down into (1) an outline of the main instructional steps and (2) key points (things to remember to do or say).
5. Each *knowing* lesson must be comprehensive enough so that it can be broken down into an outline of (1) main instructional topics and (2) key points (things to remember to do or say about each topic). Knowing lessons will generally run from 20 to 45 minutes.
6. Plan a series of *knowing* and *doing* lessons which will enable the student to do the *tasks* that you have

Unit 1.	**Orientation and Safety**	Unit 9.	**Oxyacetylene Welding**

Unit 1. **Orientation and Safety**
1-1 Demonstrate the ability to work safely
1-2 Demonstrate the ability to keep a clean, orderly, and safe work area
1-3 Operate a fire extinguisher
1-4 Demonstrate the safe use of hand and power equipment
1-5 _____

Unit 2. **Nature of Electricity**
2-1 Construct an electromagnet
2-2 Build battery banks
2-3 Build circuits on the trainer
2-4 Measure electrical quantities on the trainer with a meter
2-5 Troubleshoot circuits on the trainer
2-6 _____

Unit 3. **Shop Equipment Operation**
3-1 Cut predetermined sizes of metal with the metal shear
3-2 Punch predetermined holes in metal with the metal shear
3-3 Cut predetermined lengths of metal with the band saw
3-4 Drill predetermined holes in metal with the drill press
3-5 _____

Unit 4. **Flat Welding**
4-1 Weld stringer beads
4-2 Weld a lap joint
4-3 Weld square butt joint
4-4 Weld multi-fillet "T"
4-5 _____

Unit 5. **DC Electrical Circuits**
5-1 Prepare a permissible underground splice
5-2 Perform maintenance on a Joy DC Contactor
5-3 Check mercury tubes with a meter
5-4 Troubleshoot panel trainer
5-5 _____

Unit 6. **Horizontal Welding**
6-1 Weld stringer beads
6-2 Weld lap joint
6-3 Weld square butt joint
6-4 Weld multi-fillet "T"
6-5 _____

Unit 7. **Basic Hydraulics**
7-1 Build a basic hydraulic circuit on trainer
7-2 Calculate pressures in a circuit pressure gauge
7-3 Calculate flow rates in a circuit with a flow meter
7-4 _____

Unit 8. **Vertical Up Welding**
8-1 Weld stringer beads
8-2 Weld lap joint
8-3 Weld square butt joint
8-4 Weld multi-fillet "T"
8-5 _____

Unit 9. **Oxyacetylene Welding**
9-1 Cut predetermined sizes of metal with torch
9-2 Weld flat bead
9-3 Produce corner weld
9-4 Produce lap weld
9-5 Produce fillet weld
9-6 Braze flat bead
9-7 Braze lap weld
9-8 _____

Unit 10. **DC Prints and Panels**
10-1 Trace current flow on a 15 S.C. panel
10-2 Explain electrical sequence on a 15 S.C. panel
10-3 Troubleshoot 15 S.C. panel
10-4 _____

Unit 11. **DC Motors**
11-1 Connect a shunt motor
11-2 Connect a series motor
11-3 Connect a compound motor
11-4 Reverse direction of a DC motor
11-5 Change brushes on a DC motor
11-6 _____

Unit 12. **AC Circuits**
12-1 Connect circuits on single phase trainer
12-2 Change tips on a three-phase line starter
12-3 Check a timer with an ohm volt meter
12-4 Check N.O. and N.C. auxiliary switches with volt-ohmmeter
12-5 Build circuits on three-phase trainer
12-6 _____

Unit 13. **AC Motors**
13-1 Wire a 6-lead motor for low voltage
13-2 Wire an 8-lead motor for high voltage
13-3 Wire an 8-lead motor for low voltage
13-4 Wire a 6-lead motor for high voltage
13-5 Reverse direction of an AC motor
13-6 _____

Unit 14. **Hydraulic Pumps and Circuits**
14-1 Identify 3 types of pumps
14-2 Install directional control valve in circuit
14-3 Install a relief valve in circuit
14-4 Install a flow control valve in a circuit
14-5 _____

Unit 15. **Transformers**
15-1 Hook up a transformer with multiple hook-ups
15-2 Connect transformers
  WYE-WYE
  DELTA-DELTA
  WYE-DELTA
  DELTA-WYE
15-3 Measure voltages and current output of a transformer
15-4 _____

Unit 16. **Rectification**
16-1 Check a diode
16-2 Check a rectifier's output
16-3 _____

Figure 2-3. Task breakdown for a mine equipment maintenance program.

planned for the unit.

7. *Doing* lessons (demonstration lessons) start with an action verb.

8. *Doing* lessons, *demonstration* lessons, and *manipulative skills* lessons are the same. *Knowing* lessons, *related information* lessons, *classroom* lessons, *theory* lessons and *lecture* lessons are the same. Do not become confused with terminology changes.

9. The beginning orientation unit may not contain doing lessons. In electronics and cosmetology there are several units composed completely of knowing lessons. Usually, however, both types of lessons are needed in each unit.

10. Plan the *lesson sequence* so that students can start on assigned *tasks* as soon as possible. Task assignments motivate students.
11. The lesson titles selected will be the same as those which will appear on the lesson plans later, consequently they should be kept short.

A lesson title breakdown for Unit 4 in a machine tool technology course is shown in Figure 2-4.

Unit Number ____4____ Title____Lathe____

NO.	DOING LESSONS	REF. CODE
D4-1	Take care of lathe	GM 199
D4-2	Grind lathe tools	MS 235
D4-3	Set speed, tool and depth of cut	FT 182
D4-4	Locate (1) and drill center holes (2)	GM 131
D4-5	Rough and finish turn	MS 249
D4-6	Turn between centers	FT 188
D4-7	Face and cut off a workpiece	
D4-8	Bore, drill and ream	FT 204
D4-9	Taper turn	MS 274
D4-10	Knurl a cylinder	FT 215-16
D4-11	File and polish	
D4-12	Cut external threads	MS 277
D4-13	Cut internal threads	MS 280
D4-14	Use accessories	GM 164
D4-15	Use chucks and face plates	MS 258-60

NO.	KNOWING LESSONS	REF. CODE
	Technical Topics	
K4-1	Safety precautions	BA 247
K4-2	Lathe construction and manipulation	BA 239
K4-3	Lathe cutting tools	BA 242
K4-4	Principles of turning	GM 121
K4-5	Importance of oils and lubricants	GM 166
K4-6	Formulas-feed and speeds	GM 178
K4-7	Thread forms and terms	BA 417
K4-8	Different metals	BA 278
K4-9	Calculating a taper	GM 218
K4-10	Work holding devices	BA 370
K4-11	Accessories and usage	MS 253
	General Topics	
K4-12	History of the Lathe	BA 239
	Guidance Topics	
K4-13	Employment Opportunities in Machining Occupations	MS 631

Figure 2-4. Lesson title breakdown for Unit 4 of a machine tool technology program.

Please note in Figure 2-4 that there are two columns of lesson plan titles. The doing lesson titles (demonstrations) are placed at the top and the knowing lesson titles (related technical information) are placed at the bottom. The lessons are numbered in order, i.e., K4-1 (Knowing Lesson, Unit 4, Lesson 1), D4-1 (Demonstration Lesson, Unit 4, Lesson 1). The reference code column is utilized to list an abbreviation for a reference with the accompanying page number. This easy reference allows the teacher to locate resource materials for developing lesson plans on the topic listed.

Technical lesson titles are for instruction which is necessary to know in order to make judgments in perform-

ing on the job. *General* lesson titles are for instructional material that is nice to know but not essential for the worker to succeed on the job. Typically a teacher will know this type of information but a worker can perform beginning level skills without this knowledge. *Guidance* lesson titles are for instruction in getting a job, keeping a job, and advancing on the job. These lessons might also include such topics as areas of employment, job mobility, wages, and benefits. Guidance lessons may also be presented in the area of social and personal guidance as it relates to the work world. The doing and knowing lessons are taught cumulatively. Lessons are taught from both columns as the instructor proceeds through the unit.

A lesson title breakdown sheet must be made for each unit that was listed in the unit breakdown. All lesson plan titles should be planned so that they are coordinated with the tasks listed in the task breakdown.

Step/Topic Breakdown

Following the completion of the lesson title breakdown, the teacher analyzes each listed lesson plan title into the major steps/topics. Doing lesson titles are broken down into steps. Knowing lesson titles are broken down into topics. For example, a doing lesson titled "How To Drape and Prepare a Patron" might be broken down into the following major steps.

1. Seat patron.
2. Select and arrange materials.
3. Wash and sanitize hands.
4. Drape patron.
5. Remove pins and jewelry.
6. Examine hair and scalp.
7. Brush hair.
8. Sanitize shampoo bowl.
9. Adjust water temperature.

A knowing lesson entitled "Styles of Roofs" might be broken down into the following major topics.

1. Architectural features.
2. Flat roofs.
3. Shed roofs.
4. Gable roofs.
5. Hip roofs.
6. Gambrel roofs.
7. Mansard roofs.

Avoid listing too many steps/topics as each one of these will be broken down into further detail in the breakdown that follows. If too many steps/topics are listed, the lesson may become far too long and students will lose interest.

A step breakdown for a lesson entitled "How To Wire With Non-Metallic Sheathed Cable" is shown in Figure 2-5.

Lesson Title: Wire with Non-Metallic Sheathed Cable
Steps:
1. Locate outlets
2. Install outlet boxes
3. Run cables
4. Splice cables in boxes
5. Install electrical devices

Figure 2-5. A step breakdown for an electricity task.

Key Point Breakdown

For most steps/topics in a lesson there are many things which the instructor must remember to do and say. These items are called *key points, sub-steps* or *task elements*. In this chapter *key points* will be used consistently. If a segment of a lesson is worthy of being considered as a step/topic, there are usually a number of explanatory (key) points which the teacher must present in order to make the lesson understandable. These key points are generally do's, don'ts, how's, why's, when's, where's, safety precautions and "tricks of the trade".

For example, the electricity lesson step breakdown in the previous section could be further developed to include the key points which are listed in the right-hand column of Figure 2-6.

Observe that the special details, often difficult for a teacher to remember, are placed across from the steps. Any safety key point should be preceded by the word *CAUTION*. Special bits of information which are very important are prefaced with the word *NOTE*.

Keep the key points short and to the point. Avoid writing down everything to do and say for each step—provide only a brief outline of all the major key points. Eventually teachers will memorize the basic steps and key points for each lesson.

A key point breakdown must be made for each step/topic for each lesson title planned earlier in the analysis. For some steps/topics, there will be many key points; for others, there may be only a few. Avoid listing trivial items; list only key points which the student must know.

Equipment/Tool/Material Breakdown

Following the completion of the key point breakdown, it is necessary to list all equipment, tools, materials, references, and other items that the teacher needs to present the lesson. This list is placed at the top of the sheet. By paying very careful attention to this part of the analysis breakdown, the teacher can eliminate the frustration of finding that certain things are missing as the lesson is presented. An equipment/tool/material breakdown for the lesson title "How To Wire With Non-Metallic Sheathed Cable" is shown at the top of Figure 2-6. Note that the steps, key points and equipment/tool/materials breakdown can all be combined on one sheet.

Title of Demonstration lesson
Wire with Non-metallic Sheathed Cable

No. D12-3

References:
Richter, H.P., *Practical Electrical Wiring*, p. 155
Abbott, R. and Stetka, J., *National Code Handbook*, p. 240

Equipment, tools, materials:

ceiling boxes	cable straps	switch cover plates	lineman's pliers
switch boxes	lampholders	receptacle covers	diagonal cutter
14/2 cable	switches	cable rippers	screw driver
14/3 cable	duplex recps.	skinning knife	hammer
electrical drill	electrician's drill		

Steps:

Key Points (things to remember to do or say):

1. Locate outlets

1. A. Mark outlet location on framing
   B. Base outlets 16'' from floor
   Note: Outlets should be planned to give the best in adequacy, convenience and service

2. Install outlet boxes

2. A. Ceiling boxes
   B. Switch and receptacle boxes
   C. Special outlets
   Note: To obtain a neat finished wire job, care must be taken in the setting of outlet boxes so they will be straight and flush with the finished wall

3. Run cables

3. A. Plan cable runs
   B. Bore holes in framing members
   C. Pull cables
   D. Install cables in cable boxes
   E. Strap or support cables
   CAUTION: When running cable be careful not to damage the sheath on cable by bending it too short or pulling on it too hard.

4. Splice cables in boxes

4. A. Follow the NEC color code
   B. Use mechanical splicing devices
   C. Insulate splices
   CAUTION: Be sure to install all mechanical splicing devices carefully to ensure electrically secure connections

5. Install electrical devices

5. A. Connect wires to terminals
   B. Secure devices in outlet boxes
   C. Install cover plates
   CAUTION: Take care in making connections and do not leave bare wire beyond the screw terminals
   Note: Follow all requirements set up by the National Electrical Code for cable wiring

Figure 2-6. The key point breakdown related to the step breakdown.

THE ANALYSIS BREAKDOWN SYSTEM

If the analysis breakdown system described here is followed for all units in the entire program, the result will be a complete analysis of the segments of the occupation that are to be taught. A complete analysis of the entire occupation will, of course, be far more comprehensive. Remember to develop the analysis only in terms of what aspects of the occupation you plan to teach, depending on time, physical facilities, type of student, budget and other restricting conditions. Most beginning teachers make their analysis far too broad and realize after a short time that they cannot accomplish in a school program, all that they have learned during many years of working in an occupation. An analysis flow chart is shown in Figure 2-7. Note the cumulative breakdown from the general information to very detailed information.

ANALYSIS CHARTS

For some occupational areas it is useful to develop analysis charts which enable the teacher to see graphically which operations (major steps) make up the larger tasks. Follow these steps in making an analysis chart.

1. Make a laundry list of all tasks to be used as vehicles of instruction. Place these along the top of the sheet. Begin with simple tasks and try to arrange them so that tasks become progressively more difficult moving toward the right. Refer to Figure 2-8.

2. Make a laundry list of all the operations (large steps) involved in the tasks listed. Place these in a vertical column, trying to arrange the list so that simple operations are nearest the top. Don't simply list how to use tools and equipment ("Operate a Circular Saw" would not be an operation; "Saw To a Line" is an operation). *NOTE*: Steps one and two are generally done for an entire occupation. However, if units are sufficiently different it is possible to make an analysis chart for each unit.

3. Place an "X" in the space box below each task requiring a particular listed operation.

4. Add to the list of operations and tasks as necessary. Most occupations would involve 50 or more tasks throughout an 18 month instructional course. The number of tasks, of course, depends on the occupation.

5. Count the marks both horizontally and vertically. This will enable the teacher to arrange the operations in instructional order by frequency of occurrence. Arrange tasks from simple to complex.

6. Put auxiliary operations (used in all tasks) either at the top (mark an "X" in all squares) or at the bottom and don't mark.

7. Erase the marks and number the operations. Assign these same numbers to the operation sheets (see Chapter 7).

8. Check for frequency, complexity and difficulty. *NOTE*: The longer the listing of tasks and operations, the greater the possibility of obtaining an imaginary

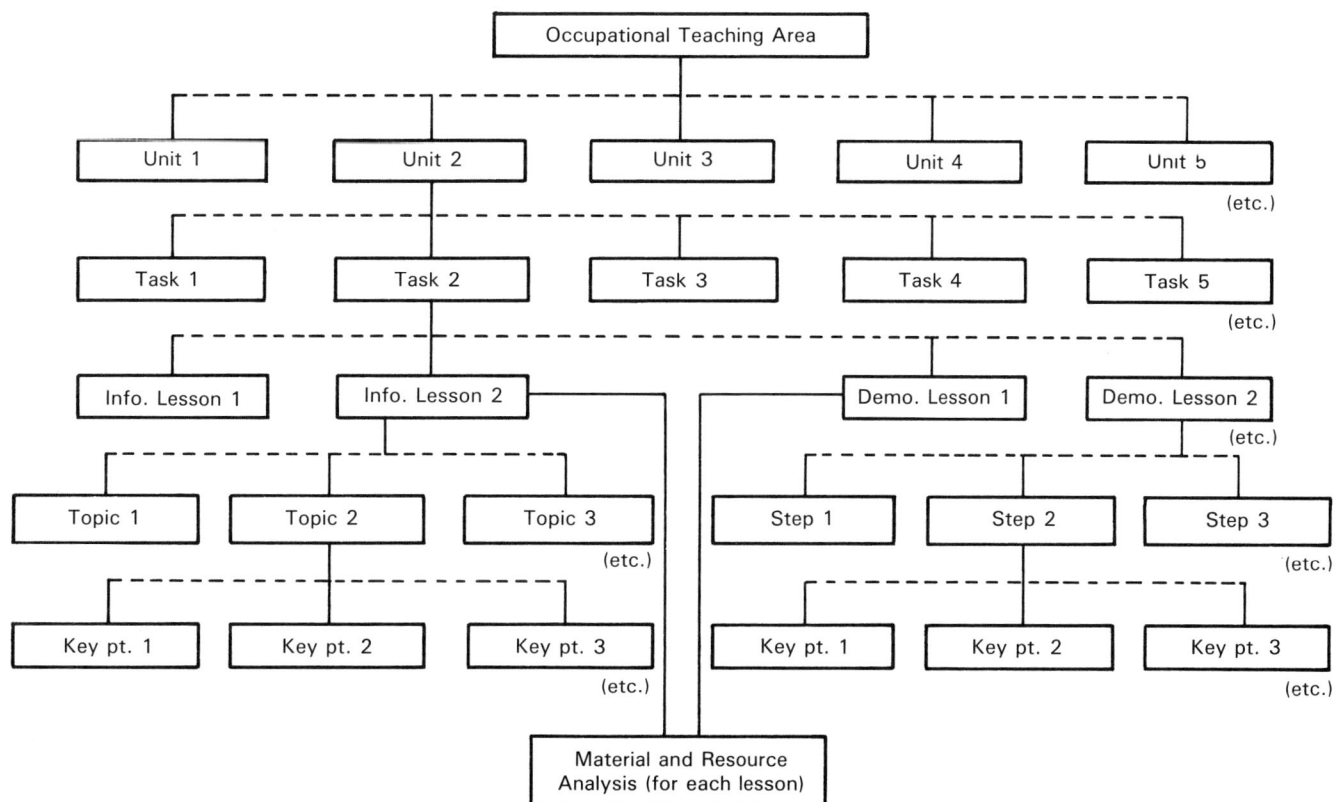

Figure 2-7. Analysis flow chart.

diagonal "cut-off" line across the bottom of the columns.

Some of the advantages in making an analysis chart are:

1. The teacher can determine which operations to teach first.
2. The teacher can use the chart to establish a system of teaching for individual differences.
3. It is possible to plan operations and tasks which proceed from the simple to the complex.
4. If a careful analysis is made, the teacher can be sure that no operations are omitted.
5. Gaps in instruction are minimized.
6. It is possible to determine from the chart which operations should be grouped together for demonstrations.

TASKS

OPERATIONS HOW TO:	Stake out Building	Form Step Footer	Wall Forms	Column Forms	Step Forms	Curved Walk Forms	Erection of Modular Forms	Assemble a Built-up Girder	Install T-Sill	Install L-Sill	Install Joists	Cut & Install Cross Bridging	Cut & Install Solid Bridging	Frame a Stairwell	Frame a Wall Section	Frame a Door Opening	Frame an Arch Opening	Layout & Cut Common Rafter	Layout & Cut Valley Rafter	Layout & Cut Hip Rafter	Layout & Cut Jack Rafter	Frame Chimney Opening	Frame Gable Dormer
	1	2	3	4	5	6	7	8	9	10	11	12	13	14	15	16	17	18	19	20	21	22	23
1 Plan a Procedure	X	X	X	X	X	X	X	X	X	X	X	X	X	X	X	X	X	X	X	X	X	X	X
2 Read a Drawing	X	X	X	X	X	X	X	X	X	X	X	X	X	X	X	X	X	X	X	X	X	X	X
3 Make a Bill of Material	X	X	X	X	X	X	X	X	X	X	X	X	X	X	X	X	X	X	X	X	X	X	X
4 Check Delivered Materials	X	X	X	X	X	X	X	X	X	X	X	X	X	X	X	X	X	X	X	X	X	X	X
5 Make a Plan	X	X	X	X	X	X	X	X	X	X	X	X	X	X	X	X	X	X	X	X	X	X	X
6 Drive & Draw Nails	6	6	6	6	6	6	6	6	6	6	6	6	6	6	6	6	6					6	6
7 Layout Square Cuts	7	7	7	7	7	7	7	7	7	7	7	7	7	7	7	7	7	7				7	7
8 Test for Squareness	8	8	8	8	8	8	8	8	8	8	8	8	8	8	8	8	8		8			8	8
9 Layout Pattern on Stock					9		9			9	9	9	9	9	9	9	9	9	9	9	9	9	9
10 Saw to a Line	10	10	10	10	10	10	10	10	10	10		10	10	10	10	10	10	10	10	10	10	10	10
11 Make a Butt Joint		11	11	11	11	11	11	11	11	11	11			11	11	11	11	11				11	11
12 Test for Level	12	12	12	12	12	12	12	12						12	12	12							12
13 Guide with Pencil		13	13	13	13	13																	
14 Sight for Straightness	14	14	14	14	14	14	14	14	14	14	14			14	14	14	14	14	14	14	14	14	14
15 Snap a Chalk Line	15	15	15			15	15	15	15	15		15	15		15								15
16 Plane Edge Grain																							
17 Plane End Grain																							
18 Saw Curves						18																	
19 Layout & Cut Material				19	19																		
20 Smooth with Sandpaper																							
21 Set a Nail																							
22 Toe Nail					22	22			22	22	22	22	22	22	22	22	22						
23 Trim & Pare with Chisel																							
24 Install Scaffolding			24	24		24															24	24	24
25 Remove Scaffolding			25	25		25															25	25	25
26 Fasten with Screws																							
27 Read Framing Square																		27	27	27	27		27
28 Layout Joints											28												
29 Layout Studs			29												29								
30 Cut & Install Bridging												30	30										
31 Install Termite Shield									31	31													
32 Build Corner Post															32								
33 Layout Floor Opening															33								
34 Build T-Post															34								
35 Install Batter Boards	35																						
36 Cut & Install Fire Stops											36				36								

Figure 2-8. Analysis chart for residential carpentry.

7. It is possible to achieve progression in learning based upon a systematized procedure.
8. Job, operation and information sheets can be developed from the analysis (see Chapter 7).

Shown in Figure 2-8 is an example of an analysis chart, for residential carpentry. It is not a comprehensive chart, inasmuch as over 300 operations would be utilized in the completion of all major carpentry tasks. Furthermore, residential and commercial carpentry would involve different types of tasks. Consequently, an analysis chart should be made for each phase or Dictionary of Occupational Titles (D.O.T.) number.

EXAMPLE LAYOUT OF AN OCCUPATIONAL ANALYSIS

In Appendix 2A are examples of the major elements of an analysis in cosmetology from start to finish. Note that space does not allow for a complete breakdown of *all* the steps/topics and key points for each lesson listed. Use the following breakdown as an example to follow in developing an analysis.

Step 1. Broad Objectives for a Cosmetology Program
Step 2. Unit Breakdown for a Cosmetology Program
Step 3. Task Breakdown for a Cosmetology Program
Step 4. Lesson Title Breakdown for a Cosmetology Program
NOTE. Because breakdowns of each lesson title would be too space consuming, the lesson ***D4-1 Drape and Prepare a Patron*** was selected to illustrate the remainder of the analysis system.
Step 5. Step Breakdown for a Cosmetology Program
Step 6. Key Point Breakdown for a Cosmetology Program
Step 7. Tools/Materials Breakdown for a Cosmetology Program
*Step 8. Step, Key Point and Tools/Materials Breakdown for Lesson D4-1
*Note that Step 8 is a consolidation of steps 5, 6 and 7 for Lesson D4-1, placed on one sheet.

SUMMARY

Occupational analysis is a systematic approach to curriculum development. The analysis is necessary in order to uncover the teaching content and the order of presenting it to students. The analysis will aid in developing a smooth flow of content from the simple to the complex. It aids the teacher in eliminating gaps and duplication in presenting the subject matter.

By teaching competencies and information in an orderly, planned manner, students will be motivated because each new step is built upon something previously learned. Teachers can be more productive because an organized approach is always more efficient from a time standpoint.

The basic system for analyzing your occupation is:
1. Write the course objectives.
2. Develop a unit breakdown.
3. Develop a task breakdown.
4. Develop a lesson title breakdown.
5. Develop a step/topic breakdown.
6. Develop a key point breakdown.
7. Develop an equipment/tool/material breakdown.

It is possible to develop analysis charts like the one shown in Figure 2-8 so the teacher can see which major steps (called operations) must be taught to enable students to perform the various tasks. The analysis chart is made by listing the major tasks horizontally across the top of a chart and the operations vertically along the left side of the chart. Simply check off which operations are involved in the major tasks which make up an occupation.

The chart permits the teacher to see graphically which operations are found in each of the various tasks. This allows the teacher to group students more easily when teaching in the classroom and demonstrating in the laboratory.

Commercial materials are helpful in developing the analysis. It should be remembered, however, that each teaching situation is different and the analysis must be developed so it meets the objectives of an occupational course.

APPENDIX 2A

EXAMPLE LAYOUT OF AN OCCUPATIONAL ANALYSIS
STEP 1
BROAD OBJECTIVES FOR A COSMETOLOGY PROGRAM
(Example)

The overall purpose of this course in cosmetology will be met if the student will realize the following objectives:
1. Apply the principles of professional ethics.
2. Apply principles of hygiene, grooming, poise and personality.
3. Apply principles of bacteriology, sterilization and will be able to keep implements sanitized.
4. Apply principles of shampooing and rinsing.
5. Perform basic hairstyling and fingerwaving.
6. Perform manicuring and become familiar with implements used in manicuring and pedicuring.
7. Apply the principles of massage in relation to scalp and hair treatments.
8. Apply the principles of hair shaping and styling.
9. Perform hair pressing and thermal waving and curling.
10. Perform chemical relaxing.
11. Apply skill in giving permanent waves.
12. Apply skill in care, cleaning, styling, selecting, and quality of wigs.
13. Apply the principles of superfluous hair removal.
14. Apply skill in haircoloring.
15. Apply makeup and give facial treatments.
16. Apply the basics of salon management.
17. Evidence thorough knowledge of cosmetology manufacturers' products.
18. Appreciate and show a high regard for artistic design.
19. Demonstrate a thorough understanding of anatomy and physiology as it applies to beauty culture.
20. Demonstrate a high degree of safety consciousness.

> EXAMPLE FOR ILLUSTRATION PURPOSES ONLY

STEP 2
UNIT BREAKDOWN FOR A COSMETOLOGY PROGRAM
(Example)

Length of program—18 months

UNIT TITLES	Class Hrs.	Lab Hrs.
1. Orientation and Ethics	*10	
2. Hygiene, Grooming, Poise & Personality	10	
3. Bacteriology, Sanitation & Sterilization	20	5
4. Shampooing and Rinsing	20	240
5. Hairstyling & Fingerwaving	20	290
6. Manicuring and Pedicuring	15	100
7. Scalp Treatments & Trichology	15	45
8. Hair Shaping	15	145
9. Hair Pressing, Thermal Waving & Curling	25	115
10. Chemical Hair Relaxing	15	80
11. Massage, Facial Treatments & Make up	15	30
12. Permanent Waving	25	115
13. Hair Coloring & Bleaching	30	180
14. Care & Styling of Wigs	20	130
15. Anatomy & Physiology	40	
16. Hair, Scalp, Skin & Nail Diseases	20	
17. Superfluous Hair Removal	15	25
18. Electricity & Light Therapy	25	30
19. Chemistry	35	
20. Beauty Salon Management & Related Math	30	50
Totals	420	1580

Total hours for program **2000**

*Inclusion of hours is optional in a unit breakdown.

STEP 3
TASK BREAKDOWN FOR A COSMETOLOGY PROGRAM
(Example)

Tasks

Unit No. 1　(10 hrs.) Title: Orientation and Ethics
1.1　Teletrainer, Make Proper Calls

Unit No. 2　(10 hrs.) Title: Hygiene, Grooming, Poise & Personality (no tasks)

Unit No. 3　(25 hrs.) Title: Bacteriology, Sanitation & Sterilization
3.1　Prepare a wet sanitizer
3.2　Prepare a dry sanitizer
3.3　Prepare a fumigant
3.4　Sanitize with wet disinfectant
3.5　Sanitize with a chemical disinfectant
3.6　Sanitize with alcohol
3.7　Sanitize combs and brushes
3.8　Sanitize rollers

Unit No. 4　(260 hrs.) Title: Shampooing & Rinsing
4.1　Seat a patron
4.2　Prepare shampoo
4.3　Prepare cream or conditioner rinse
4.4　Give plain shampoo
4.5　Give non-strip shampoo
4.6　Give medicated shampoo
4.7　Give dandruff shampoo
4.8　Give conditioning shampoo
4.9　Give finishing rinse
4.10　Give dandruff rinse
4.11　Give lemon rinse
4.12　Give vinegar rinse

Unit No. 5　(310 hrs.) Title: Hairstyling & Fingerwaving
5.1　Make sculpture pin curls
5.2　Make cascade curls
5.3　Make ridge curls
5.4　Make directional curls
5.5　Do a skip wave
5.6　Do a style using rollers
5.7　Make roller curls with full stem
5.8　Make roller curls with half stem
5.9　Make roller curls with no stem
5.10　Comb and brush hair
5.11　Tease hair
5.12　Make a "C" shaping
5.13　Give a side part fingerwave
5.14　Give a horseshoe fingerwave
5.15　Style hair in current trend
5.16　Style hair for facial shapes
5.17　Mold finger waves
5.18　Do a style using skip waves
5.19　Do a style using roller curls
5.20　Do State Board style using the required pattern
5.21　Perform current trend for long hair
5.22　Perform current trend for short hair

Unit No. 6　(115 hrs) Title: Manicuring & Pedicuring
6.1　Prepare a manicure table
6.2　Give a plain manicure
6.3　Give an electric manicure
6.4　Give an oil manicure
6.5　Give a men's manicure
6.6　Apply patch to broken nail
6.7　Apply artificial nails
6.8　Give a hand and arm massage
6.9　Give a foot and leg massage
6.10　Give a pedicure

Unit No. 7　(60 hrs) Title: Scalp Treatments & Trichology
7.1　Give the basic scalp manipulations
7.2　Give a treatment for normal and oily hair
7.3　Give an oily and dry treatment
7.4　Give a dandruff treatment

7.5 Use a corrective hair treatment
7.6 Give a treatment for alopecia
7.7 Give a high-frequency treatment
7.8 Give a vibrator treatment
7.9 Give a heating cap treatment
7.10 Give a dandruff treatment
7.11 Give an instant hair conditioner

Unit No. 8 (160 hrs) Title: Hair Shaping
8.1 Analyze hair texture
8.2 Section hair for cut
8.3 Give a razor haircut
8.4 Give a scissor haircut
8.5 Give a blunt cut
8.6 Thin hair with razor
8.7 Thin hair with shears
8.8 Give a shingle cut

Unit No. 9 (140 hrs) Title: Hair Pressing, Thermal Waving & Curling
9.1 Analyze hair and scalp
9.2 Section hair
9.3 Use electric heater
9.4 Give a soft press
9.5 Give a hard press
9.6 Give a touch-up
9.7 Make waves with irons
9.8 Make curls with irons
9.9 Sanitize combs and heaters
9.10 Make shadow waves
9.11 Make croquignole thermal curls
9.12 Make end curls
9.13 Make round curls
9.14 Make poker curls

Unit No. 10 (95 hrs) Title: Chemical Hair Relaxing
10.1 Analyze patron's hair and scalp
10.2 Give skin test (24 hours prior)
10.3 Give strand test
10.4 Select proper strength
10.5 Use chemicals to relax hair
10.6 Use petroleum base on scalp
10.7 Use ammonium thioglycolate
10.8 Use sodium hydroxide
10.9 Use neutralizer
10.10 Apply rinse and conditioner
10.11 Style hair
10.12 Make record card

Unit No. 11 (45 hrs) Title: Massage, Facial Treatments & Makeup
11.1 Give basic massage manipulations
11.2 Give plain facial
11.3 Give dry skin facial
11.4 Give oily skin facial
11.5 Give comedone treatment
11.6 Give acne treatment
11.7 Give facial with contour makeup
11.8 Give facial with corrective makeup
11.9 Give eyebrow arch
11.10 Give muscle toning treatment

Unit No. 12 (140 hrs) Title: Perm Waving
12.1 Make scalp and hair analysis
12.2 Select correct type of permanent wave lotion
12.3 Section and block hair
12.4 Winding and wrapping hair
12.5 Make test curls
12.6 Apply waving lotion
12.7 Apply neutralizers
12.8 Give a perm wave

Unit No. 13 (210 hrs) Title: Hair Coloring & Bleaching
13.1 Give a patch test
13.2 Give a strand test
13.3 Make a release statement
13.4 Keep hair tint records
13.5 Apply a color rinse
13.6 Apply a color shampoo
13.7 Give a semi-permanent tint
13.8 Apply an analine derivative tint
13.9 Remove analine derivative
13.10 Apply an oil shampoo tint

13.11 Give single application tint
13.12 Give double application tint
13.13 Give single application retouch
13.14 Give a double application retouch
13.15 Apply hair toner
13.16 Lighten virgin hair
13.17 Give a tipping
13.18 Frost the hair
13.19 Apply bleach for retouch
13.20 Streak the hair
13.21 Correct dark streaks
13.22 Correct over-bleached hair
13.23 Apply color fillers
13.24 Recondition tinted hair

Unit No. 14 (150 hrs) Title: Care & Styling of Wigs
14.1 Clean a wig or hairpiece
14.2 Shape a wig or hairpiece
14.3 Condition a wig or hairpiece
14.4 Color a wig or hairpiece
14.5 Style a wig or hairpiece
14.6 Attach a wig or hairpiece
14.7 Measure head for a wig

Unit No. 15 (40 hrs) Title: Anatomy & Physiology
(no tasks)

Unit No. 16 (20 hrs) Title: Hair, Scalp, Skin & Nail Diseases
16.1 Give a treatment for alopecia
16.2 Give a dandruff treatment
16.3 Give an oily scalp treatment

Unit No. 17 (40 hrs) Title: Superfluous Hair Removal
17.1 Remove superfluous hair with wax
17.2 Remove superfluous hair with depilatories
17.3 Remove superfluous hair by shaving
17.4 Remove superfluous hair by tweezing

Unit No. 18 (50 hrs) Title: Electricity & Light Therapy
18.1 Give scalp treatment using heat cap
18.2 Use facial and rake electrodes
18.3 Give massage using the electric vibrator
18.4 Use electric hot oil heater
18.5 Use ultra violet ray lamp
18.6 Apply high frequency to scalp

Unit No. 19 (25 hrs) Title: Chemistry
19.1 Test for acidity and alkalinity
19.2 Use pH scale
19.3 Do a test on soaps
19.4 Do a test on shampoos
19.5 Do a test for soft water
19.6 Do a test for hard water

Unit No. 20 (80 hrs) Title: Beauty Salon Management & Related Math
20.1 Organize appointment book and make appointments
20.2 Count money and make change
20.3 Make out work slips and receipts
20.4 Assemble materials for setups
20.5 Dispense materials

STEP 4
LESSON TITLE BREAKDOWN
(Example)

Unit No. 1   Orientation and Ethics

NO.	DOING LESSONS	REF. CODE
D1-1	Use teletrainer	LP-3

NO.	KNOWING LESSONS	REF. CODE
K1-1	Cosmetology as a profession	LP-11
K1-2	Professional ethics	TB-1
K1-3	Classroom policy	FC-17
K1-4	Fire-drill response	FC-21
K1-5	Safety and hygiene	TB-5

NO.	KNOWING LESSONS	REF. CODE
K1-6	State laws	VSB-1
K1-7	Locker assignments	E-1
K1-8	Personal appearance	MG-10
	General Topics	
K1-1	Guide to beauty, charm, and poise	MG-6
	Guidance Topics	
K1-1	Business opportunities	MM-5
K1-2	Wage scales	MM-7
K1-3	Owning a salon	MM-9

Unit No. 2   Hygiene, Grooming, Poise & Personality

NO.	KNOWING LESSONS	REF. CODE
K2-1	Personal and public hygiene	TB-5
K2-2	Care of the feet	TB-15
K2-3	Proper grooming	TB-7
K2-4	Good dietary habits	TB-14
K2-5	Personality development	TB-17
	General Topics	
K2-1	Pleasing personality	TB-17
K2-2	Cosmetic needs	TB-239
	Guidance Topics	
K2-1	Key to success	TB-18
K2-2	Graciousness and friendliness	TB-19

Unit No. 3   Bacteriology & Sterilization

NO.	DOING LESSONS	REF. CODE
D3-1	Sterilize implements	TB-30
D3-2	Mix chemical agents	TB-32

NO.	KNOWING LESSONS	REF. CODE
K3-1	Types of bacteria	TB-24
K3-2	Classification of bacteria	TB-24
K3-3	Reproduction and growth	TB-26
K3-4	Infections and immunity	TB-28
K3-5	Methods of sterilization	TB-30
K3-6	Safety precautions	TB-34
K3-7	Storing chemicals	TB-34
	General Topics	
K3-1	Types of disinfectant	TB-30
K3-2	Types of antiseptic	TB-30
K3-3	Study of bacteria	TB-23
K3-4	State health requirements	SB-2
	Guidance Topics	
K3-1	Prevention of disease	TB-23
K3-2	Ventilation and water supply	TB-36
K3-3	Sanitary use of cosmetics	TB-37

Unit No. 4   Shampooing and Rinsing

NO.	DOING LESSONS	REF. CODE
D4-1	Drape and prepare patron	TB-45
D4-2	Brush hair	TB-44
D4-3	Give scalp manipulations	TB-46
D4-4	Give plain shampoo	TB-45
D4-5	Give liquid dry shampoo	TB-49
D4-6	Powder dry shampoo	TB-49
D4-7	Give color and acid rinse	TB-52
D4-8	Give egg shampoo	TB-50
D4-9	Non-strip shampoo	TB-49
D4-10	Oil shampoo	TB-50
D4-11	Medicated shampoo	TB-50
D4-12	Shampoo twice	TB-47
D4-13	Rinse twice	TB-47

NO.	KNOWING LESSONS	REF. CODE
K4-1	Hair brushing	TB-34
K4-2	Types of shampoos	TB-48
K4-3	Acidity and alkalinity	TB-435
K4-4	Shampooing and rinsing	TB-45
K4-5	Cleaning hairpieces	TB-160
K4-6	Preparation of rinses	TB-48
	General Topics	
K4-1	Chemistry of water	TB-440
K4-2	Water softeners	MD-435
	Guidance Topics	
K4-1	Opportunities for a shampoo person	AD-3

Unit No. 5   Hairstyling and Fingerwaving

NO.	DOING LESSONS	REF. CODE
D5-1	Pin curls, parts mobility, and stem direction	TG-98
D5-2	Style hair with stand up curls	TB-124
D5-3	Ridge curls	TB-230
D5-4	Roller curls	TB-125
D5-5	Style using natural partings	TB-126
D5-6	Style to suit face	TB-126
D5-7	Style hair using basic setting pattern	TB-147
D5-8	Style hair using rollers and pin curls	TB-149
D5-9	Give a side part fingerwave	TB-108
D5-10	Give a horseshoe fingerwave	TB-111
D5-11	Give a shaping	TB-121
D5-12	Do a skip wave	TB-125
D5-13	Tease and comb out hair	TB-128

NO.	KNOWING LESSONS	REF. CODE
K5-1	Various names for pin curls	TB-129
K5-2	Basic pin curl technique	TB-144
K5-3	Roller curl technique	TB-149
K5-4	Basic fingerwaving	TB-106
K5-5	Basic settings and comb outs	TB-147
K5-6	Basic terms used in hairstyling	TB-129
K5-7	Artistry in hairstyling	TB-131
	General Topics	
K5-1	Current and future changes in ''trends''	MBS-35
K5-2	New types of rollers	MBS-5
K5-3	History of ancient styles	TB-354
	Guidance Topics	
K5-1	Trade shows	AH-11
K5-2	Hairdressers Association	AH-11
K5-3	Demand for good hairstylist	MM-20

Unit No. 6   Manicuring and Pedicuring

NO.	DOING LESSONS	REF. CODE
D6-1	Prepare manicure table	TB-69
D6-2	Give plain manicure	TB-70
D6-3	Give lactol manicure	TB-77
D6-4	Give men's manicure	TB-76
D6-5	Repair split nail	TB-75
D6-6	Apply artificial nails	TB-79
D6-7	Give hand and arm massage	TB-74
D6-8	Give pedicure with foot massage	TB-82

NO.	KNOWING LESSONS	REF. CODE
K6-1	Nail structures	TB-397
K6-2	Shapes of nails	TB-68
K6-3	Nail diseases and irregularities	TB-87

NO.		REF. CODE
K6-4	Equipment and cosmetics	TB-165
K6-5	Hand, arm, and massage	TB-74
K6-6	Foot massage	TB-83
K6-7	Safety rules	TB-75
	General Topics	
K6-1	Chemistry of cosmetics	TB-141
	Guidance Topics	
K6-1	Requirements in other states	VSL
K6-2	Your conversation	VTB-130

Unit No. 7   Scalp Treatments and Trichology

NO.	DOING LESSONS	REF. CODE
D7-1	Brush hair	TB-56
D7-2	Give scalp manipulations	TB-57
D7-3	Apply pomade and tonics	TB-59
D7-4	Give dandruff treatments	TB-58
D7-5	Give alopecia treatments	TB-60
D7-6	Use heating cap	TB-80
D7-7	Use vibrator	TB-81
D7-8	Infrared lamp	TB-81
D7-9	Ultraviolet ray	TB-82

NO.	KNOWING LESSONS	REF. CODE
K7-1	Theory of massage	TB-205
K7-2	Scalp manipulations	TB-56
K7-3	Use of electric apparatus	TB-426
K7-4	Benefits of brushing	TB-56
K7-5	Benefits of corrective treatments	TB-60
K7-6	Sanitary and safety measures	TB-55
	General Topics	
K7-1	Structure of hand and arm	TB-206
	Guidance Topics	
K7-1	Build regular patronage	TB-57

Unit No. 8   Hair Shaping

NO.	DOING LESSONS	REF. CODE
D8-1	Section for hairshaping	TB-95
D8-2	Dry scissor haircut	TB-97
D8-3	Thin with thinning shears	TB-97
D8-4	Give a wet razor haircut	TB-98
D8-5	Do razor tapering and thinning	TB-99
D8-6	Give a basic haircut	TB-101
D8-7	Shingle hair	TB-103
D8-8	Shingle hair with electric clippers	TB-103

NO.	KNOWING LESSONS	REF. CODE
K8-1	Methods of haircutting	TB-98
K8-2	Methods of thinning	TB-96
K8-3	Types of hair	TB-93
K8-4	Hairshaping for styling	TB-102
K8-5	Hairshaping terms	TB-104
	General Topics	
K8-1	Current "trend" hairshaping	MB-1
	Guidance Topics	
K8-1	Wages and demand for male and female barbers	AH-5

Unit No. 9   Hair Pressing, Thermal Waving and Curling

NO.	DOING LESSONS	REF. CODE
D9-1	Part hair in sections	TB-306
D9-2	Give a soft press	TB-306
D9-3	Give a hard press	TB-308
D9-4	Give a touch-up	TB-307
D9-5	Wave with marcel irons	TB-314
D9-6	Give thermal curl	TB-317
D9-7	Give round curl	TB-319
D9-8	Give poker curl	TB-319
D9-9	Clean irons	TB-312

NO.	KNOWING LESSONS	REF. CODE
K9-1	Characteristics of hair and scalp	MB-303
K9-2	Types of hair	MB-304
K9-3	Recondition hair	MB-305
K9-4	Holding and handling irons	MB-312
K9-5	Pressing	MB-308
	General Topics	
K9-1	History of marcel irons	TB-311
K9-2	Hair straightening with heat	TB-312
	Guidance Topics	
K9-1	Wage and demand in cosmetology	MM-10

Unit No. 10   Chemical Hair Relaxing

NO.	DOING LESSONS	REF. CODE
D10-1	Give patch test	TB-197
D10-2	Give strand test	TB-197
D10-3	Section hair	TB-195
D10-4	Apply protection cream	TB-198
D10-5	Apply chemical relaxer	TB-199
D10-6	Give test curls	TB-200
D10-7	Apply neutralizer	TB-201
D10-8	Apply conditioner	TB-201
D10-9	Rinse hair	TB-201

NO.	KNOWING LESSONS	REF. CODE
K10-1	Structure of human hair	TB-386
K10-2	Causes of overcurly hair	TB-390
K10-3	Composition of relaxer	TB-195
K10-4	Safety precautions	TB-200
	General Topics	
K10-1	"Trend" for straight hair	MM-21
	Guidance Topics	
K10-1	Demand for beauticians	AH-40

Unit No. 11   Massage, Facial Treatments and Makeup

NO.	DOING LESSONS	REF. CODE
D11-1	Give a plain massage	BC-168
D11-2	Give a high frequency massage	BC-168
D11-3	Give a mask treatment	STC-207
D11-4	Give a pack treatment	BC-169
D11-5	Give acne facial	BC-191
D11-6	Apply facial makeup	STC-217
D11-7	Apply an eyebrow arch	STC-225

NO.	KNOWING LESSONS	REF. CODE
K11-1	Basic manipulation	STC-161
K11-2	Theory of massage	STC-166
K11-3	Physiological effects	STC-190
K11-4	Facial manipulations	STC-196
K11-5	Acne condition	BC-171
K11-6	Corrective makeup	STC-220
K11-7	Cosmetics used in facial makeup	STC-220
K11-8	Method of giving an eyebrow arch	STC-225

NO.		REF. CODE
	General Topics	
K11-1	The eye and art of makeup	MBS-50
K11-2	Current trends in facial makeup	MBS-89
	Guidance Topics	
K11-1	Opportunities for cosmetic technicians	CM-30
K11-2	Merchandising in the beauty salon	STP-111

Unit No. 12   Permanent Waving

NO.	DOING LESSONS	REF. CODE
D12-1	Give pre-permanent test curl	LP-195
D12-2	Section for single halo wrap	STC-169
D12-3	Section for straight back wrap	STC-177
D12-4	Wrap a permanent	STC-93
D12-5	Test curls	STC-174
D12-6	Neutralize a permanent	LP-149
D12-7	Analyze hair for permanent	STC-170

NO.	KNOWING LESSONS	REF. CODE
K12-1	Structure of hair shaft	STC-7
K12-2	Structure associated with hair roots	STC-386
K12-3	Texture of hair	STC-19
K12-4	Composition of hair	STP-25
K12-5	Porosity of hair	STP-310
K12-6	Chemical action of lotion on hair	STP-37
K12-7	3 basic types of hair	RC-43
K12-8	Permanent wave rods	RC-75
K12-9	Sectioning hair before permanent waving	STC-81
K12-10	Application of waving lotion	STP-87
K12-11	Blocking and wrapping	STP-93
K12-12	Neutralizing a permanent wave	RC-39
K12-13	Permanent wave record	WB-17
K12-14	Permanent waving	STP-179
K12-15	Special problems in permanent waving	STC-164
	General Topics	
K12-1	Developments in permanent waving	STC-163
K12-2	History of permanent waving	PWM-89
	Guidance Topics	
K12-1	Merchandising in the beauty salon	RC-16

Unit No. 13   Hair Coloring and Bleaching

NO.	DOING LESSONS	REF. CODE
D13-1	Give a skin test	WB-18
D13-2	Make color selection	STC-245
D13-3	Test for color selection	STC-248
D13-4	Examine scalp and hair	WB-20
D13-5	Give strand test	CB-15
D13-6	Keep hair tint record	WB-19
D13-7	Make a release statement	WB-15
D13-8	Apply aniline derivative tint	STC-251
D13-9	Apply oil shampoo tint	CB-57
D13-10	Apply a color shampoo	CB-127
D13-11	Give a henna pack	MF-151
D13-12	Give a henna pack retouch	MF-152
D13-13	Apply a color rinse	CB-155
D13-14	Recondition tinted hair	CB-163
D13-15	Single application tint for virgin hair	STC-258
D13-16	Single application tint retouch	STC-262
D13-17	Give double application tint and retouch	STC-161
D13-18	Apply semi-permanent tint	STC-267
D13-19	Lighten virgin hair	CB-93
D13-20	Apply a toner	CB-99
D13-21	Give a frosting, tipping, and streaking	CB-127
D13-22	Pre-soften for tint or dye	STC-263
D13-23	Tint bleached hair to it's natural shade	WB-34
D13-24	Remove aniline derivative tint	WB-33
D13-25	Corrective overbleached hair	WB-35
D13-26	Correct dark streaks	WB-38

NO.	KNOWING LESSONS	REF. CODE
K13-1	Classification of hair colorings	WB-15
K13-2	Metallic salt test, analine derivative tints, patch test	LP-197
K13-3	Preparation of hair tinting	LP-96
K13-4	Color selection	WB-17
K13-5	Examining scalp and hair	WB-20
K13-6	Process for oil shampoo tint	WB-21
K13-7	Color shampoos	WB-25
K13-8	Temporary hair color	STC-243
K13-9	Process for single application virgin tint	STC-248
K13-10	Pre-softening	STC-263
K13-11	Process for double application tint retouch	STC-263
K13-12	Semi-permanent tints	CB-224
K13-13	Process for frosting, tipping, and streaking	STC-279
K13-14	Temporary color rinses	CB-269
K13-15	Testing for discoloration or hair breakage	WB-34
K13-16	Tinting bleached hair to natural shade	WB-35
K13-17	Bleaching gray hair	WB-9
K13-18	Remove yellow streaks	WB-8
K13-19	Hair bleaching on eyebrows, lip, arms, and legs	WB-10
K13-20	Reminder and hint for hair bleaching	
	General Topics	
K13-1	How to do better haircoloring	CB-3
K13-2	Principles and practices of beauty culture	MF-239
	Guidance Topics	
K13-1	"How can I speed my growth"	SG-237
K13-2	Opportunity beckons	VD-91

Unit No. 14   Care and Styling of Wigs

NO.	DOING LESSONS	REF. CODE
D14-1	Shape a wig	STC-156
D14-2	Tint a wig	WM-11
D14-3	Clean a wig	WM-9
D14-4	Set and comb a wig	STC-159
D14-5	Attach a wiglet	WM-58
D14-6	Attach a wig	WM-62

NO.	KNOWING LESSONS	REF. CODE
K14-1	History of wigs	WM-3
K14-2	How to measure a patron's head for the correct size wig block	SRC-70
K14-3	How to pin a wig to a canvas wig block	BC-180
K14-4	Fitting and placing a wig	STC-158
K14-5	How to reduce size of wig to fit patron by tucking	WB-7
K14-6	Cleaning a wig	WM-9
K14-7	Wig tinting	STC-157
K14-8	Wig conditioning, color rinsing, and styling	WM-11
K14-9	Wig settings and combouts	STC-159
K14-10	Dry scissor cut on wig	WM-15

NO.	KNOWING LESSONS	REF. CODE
K14-11	Hairpieces	STC-161
	General Topics	
K14-1	Career in wig service	MF-120
K14-2	The difference between mach. wigs and handmade tied wigs	MCP-4
	Guidance Topics	
K14-1	Do's and don'ts for better wig styling	WM-3
K14-2	Retailing of wigs in beauty shops	WB-10

Unit No. 15   Anatomy and Physiology

NO.	KNOWING LESSONS	REF. CODE
K15-1	Cells, tissues, organs, and systems	VD-46
K15-2	Skeleton system	VD-46
K15-3	Muscular system	VD-46
K15-4	Nervous system	VD-58
K15-5	Vascular system	VD-57
K15-6	Respiratory system	VD-76
K15-7	Excretory system	VD-77
K15-8	Glandular system	VD-78
K15-9	Digestive system	VD-78
	General Topics	
K15-1	Physiology and hygiene	RPB-35
	Guidance Topics	
K15-1	Anatomy of beauty	LST-97

Unit No. 16   Hair, Scalp, Skin, and Nail Diseases

NO.	DOING LESSONS	REF. CODE
D16-1	Give dandruff treatment	STC-405

NO.	KNOWING LESSONS	REF. CODE
K16-1	Skin disorders	VD-87
K16-2	The study of hair	VD-97
K16-3	Hair and scalp disorders	VD-104
K16-4	Lesions of the skin	STR-400
K16-5	Nail disorders	TB-85
K16-6	Diseases of the glands	STR-403
K16-7	Diseases of the glands	STR-404
K16-8	Dandruff	STR-405
K16-9	Alopecia	STR-407
K16-10	Ringworm due to vegetable parasites (fungi)	STR-407
	General Topics	
K16-1	Your skin and its care	TB-40
K16-2	Your guide to good health	TGH-70
	Guidance Topics	
K16-1	Art and science of manicuring	ASM-35

Unit No. 17   Superfluous Hair Removal

NO.	DOING LESSONS	REF. CODE
D17-1	Tweeze eyebrows	VD-200
D17-2	Use a wax depilatory	PPBD-505
D17-3	Use a chemical depilatory	STC-301

NO.	KNOWING LESSONS	REF. CODE
K17-1	Temporary methods of hair removal	VD-300
K17-2	Wax type depilatories	VD-300
K17-3	Chemical depilatories	VD-300
K17-4	Care of the eyebrows	PPB-509
K17-5	Electrology	PPB-509
K17-6	History of galvanic electrolysis	VD-323
K17-7	Short wave electrolysis	VD-328
	General Topics	
K17-1	Advantage and disadvantage of depilation	PPB-505
K17-2	Technique of depilatory treatment	PPB-505
	Guidance Topics	
K17-1	When to recommend depilation	PPB-505

Unit No. 18   Electricity and Light Therapy

NO.	DOING LESSONS	REF. CODE
D18-1	Use infrared lamp in a facial	STC-21
D18-2	Use thermal lamp for hot oil mask	STC-22
D18-3	Give scalp treatment with infrared lamp	STC-58
D18-4	Give scalp treatments using glass rake electrode	STC-59
D18-5	Give treatment for alopecia applying indirect high frequency current	STC-61
D18-6	Give a treatment for alopecia aresta applying ultraviolet rays	STC-61

NO.	KNOWING LESSONS	REF. CODE
K18-1	Electricity with facial treatments	VD-194
K18-2	Electricity with scalp treatments	VD-213
K18-3	Results produced by electricity treatments	VD-120
K18-4	Galvanic current	VD-124
K18-5	Faradic current	VD-127
K18-6	Sinusoidal current	VD-128
K18-7	Light therapy	VD-133
K18-8	Ultraviolet rays	VD-133
K18-9	Infrared rays	VD-134
K18-10	Visible lights	VD-134
K18-11	Safety precautions in electricity	VD-128
	General Topics	
K18-1	Composition of light	VD-131
K18-2	Therapeutic effects	VD-132
K18-3	Physiological effects of ultraviolet	PPB-243
	Guidance Topics	
K18-1	Effects of infrared rays	VD-134
K18-2	Effects of ultraviolet rays	VD-134

Unit No. 19   Chemistry

NO.	DOING LESSONS	REF. CODE
D19-1	Test for alkali in soap	PPBC-211
D19-2	Make peroxide shampoo	PPBC-231
D19-3	Make a brightening rinse	PPBC-231
D19-4	Make a shampoo tint	PPBC-228
D19-5	Apply a depilatory	PPBC-212

NO.	KNOWING LESSONS	REF. CODE
K19-1	Introduction to chemistry	VD-137
K19-2	Chemistry as applied to cosmetics	VD-141
K19-3	Chemistry of water	VD-144
K19-4	Composition and uses of cosmetics	STC-441
K19-5	Cosmetics for skin and face	STC-448
K19-6	Cosmetics of scalp and hair	STC-448
	General Topics	
K19-1	Simple chemistry in beauty culture	PPB-39
K19-2	Inorganic chemistry	PPB-393
K19-3	Organic chemistry	PPB-192
	Guidance Topics	
	U.S. Pharmacopoeia (USP)	STG-436
	The pH Scale	STG-435
	Regulations governing hair	PPB-221

NO.	DOING LESSONS	REF. CODE
D20-1	Book appointments	STC-455
D20-2	Disperse supplies	STC-456
D20-3	Plan a layout for beauty salon	STC-454
D20-4	Sell cosmetology service	STC-455
D20-5	Keep supply records	STC-456

NO.	KNOWING LESSONS	REF. CODE
K20-1	Opening beauty salon	STC-453
K20-2	Regulations, business, and insurance	STC-454
K20-3	Planning the physical layout	STC-454
K20-4	Advertising	STC-455
K20-5	Business operation and personnel management	STC-455
K20-6	Booking appointments and patron reception	STC-455
K20-7	Beauty salon salesmanship	STC-453
K20-8	Business records and supplies	STC-450
K20-9	Business law for the beauty salon	STC-250
	General Topics	
K20-1	Business law for the beauty salon	VD-345
K20-2	You as a shop owner	VD-343
	Guidance Topics	
K20-1	Things to consider when going into business	VD-344
K20-2	Opportunities books	VD-335

STEP 5
STEP BREAKDOWN FOR COSMETOLOGY
(Example)
THE STEP BREAKDOWN OF UNIT 4, LESSON D4-1

Lesson Title: Drape and Prepare Patron

Steps:
1. Seat patron
2. Select and arrange materials
3. Wash and sanitize hands
4. Drape patron
5. Remove pins and jewelry
6. Examine hair and scalp
7. Brush hair thoroughly
8. Sanitize shampoo bowl
9. Adjust water temperature

Note. This step or topic breakdown must be done for all lesson titles listed in the previous Lesson Title Breakdowns for all units. This is an example for only one lesson title.

STEP 6
KEY POINT BREAKDOWN FOR COSMETOLOGY
(Example)
THE KEY POINT BREAKDOWN FOR UNIT 4, LESSON D4-1

Lesson Title: Drape and Prepare Patron

References (To follow in next breakdown)
Equipment, Tools and Materials (To follow in next breakdown)

Steps	Key points (things to remember to do or say)
1. Seat patron	
2. Select and arrange materials	2. A. Check to see if all materials are at hand. *NOTE:* Avoid jumping up and down to get supplies after procedure has started.
3. Wash and sanitize hands	3. A. Do this before and after each patron.
4. Drape patron	4. A. Be sure dress collar is smoothed under garment before neck strip is fastened. B. When coloring hair take special precautions. Double-check to be sure patron's clothing is protected.

5. Remove pins and jewelry
6. Examine hair and scalp

7. Brush hair thoroughly
8. Sanitize shampoo bowl
9. Adjust water temperature

6. A. Examine scalp for abrasions. **Caution.** If patron has an infection or contagious skin disorder, refer to a doctor.
7. A. Do not brush if giving a permanent wave or haircolor.
8. A. Use disinfectant or cover neck of bowl with folded towel.
9. A. Make sure water temperature is not too hot or cold. B. Check with patron to be sure.

Note. The key point breakdown must be done to match with the steps for each lesson title which you listed.

STEP 7
EQUIPMENT/TOOLS/MATERIALS BREAKDOWN FOR COSMETOLOGY
(Example)
THE EQUIPMENT/TOOLS/MATERIALS BREAKDOWN FOR UNIT 4, LESSON D4-1
(Add to each task breakdown sheet)

No. _____ D4-1 _____

Title of Demonstration Lesson
Drape and Prepare Patron

References
Kibbe, C. V. *Standard Textbook of Cosmetology*, p. 45

Equipment, tools, materials
shampoo   neck strips   comb   brush
shampoo cape   towels   rinse

STEP 8
STEP, KEY POINT AND EQUIPMENT/TOOLS/MATERIALS BREAKDOWN FOR LESSON D4-1 (Combined)
(Example)

Title of Demonstration Lesson
Drape and Prepare Patron

References
Kibbe, C. V. *Standard Textbook of Cosmetology*, p. 45

Equipment, tools, materials
shampoo   neck strips   comb   brush
shampoo cape   towels   rinse

Steps	Key points (things to remember to do or say)
1. Seat patron	
2. Select and arrange materials	2. A. Check to see if all materials are at hand. *NOTE:* Avoid jumping up and down to get supplies after procedure has started.
3. Wash and sanitize hands	3. A. Do this before and after each patron.
4. Drape patron	4. A. Be sure dress collar is smoothed under garment before neck strip is fastened. B. When coloring hair take special precautions. Double-check to be sure patron's clothing is protected.
5. Remove pins and jewelry	
6. Examine hair and scalp	6. A. Examine scalp for abrasions. **Caution.** If patron has an infection or contagious skin disorder, refer to a doctor.
7. Brush hair thoroughly	7. A. Do not brush if giving a permanent wave or haircolor.
8. Sanitize shampoo bowl	8. A. Use disinfectant or cover neck of bowl with folded towel.
9. Adjust water temperature	9. A. Make sure water temperature is not too hot or cold. B. Check with patron to be sure.

Chapter 3

SOURCES OF CURRICULUM MATERIALS

by

Clifton P. Campbell, Professor
Technological and Adult Education
The University of Tennessee
Knoxville, Tennessee

and

Ethel M. Smith, Professor Emeritus
The University of Michigan

INTRODUCTION

Curriculum materials are tangible resources, with instructional content or function. Their purpose is to (a) organize teaching, (b) support learning experiences, and (c) increase instructional effectiveness so that students acquire the knowledge and skills essential for successful performance.

Curriculum materials were once confined to teacher-developed curriculum guides, a chalkboard, textbook, and physical objects. Today, however, teachers have available a steadily expanding array of materials. They may select and use printed matter, nonprint audiovisual media and manipulative aids. Printed materials include such things as books, workbooks, teacher and student guides, instruction sheets, modules, programmed materials, manuals, and a variety of other documents.

Nonprint audiovisual materials involve seeing and hearing and usually require some type of equipment (hardware) for their use. Such materials include overhead transparencies, slides, audio tapes, video tapes, video disks, 16 mm films, and microcomputer diskettes. Manipulative aids are those things that are physically handled and include such items as objects (hand tools, machines, etc.), mock-ups, models, cutaways, trainers, and simulators.

A vast array of federal and state supported centers and clearinghouses as well as government agencies, multi-state consortia, professional and trade organizations, colleges and universities are involved in developing and disseminating curriculum materials. All these efforts are dedicated, in one way or another, to the improvement of teaching and learning.

This chapter presents an organized listing of sources for existing practitioner-oriented materials. A large number of potential sources were contacted, but only those with free or affordably priced products, of good quality and suitable for use in occupational education, have been included here.

It is seldom necessary to contact more than a few of the appropriate sources, but the effort to locate and obtain materials will be far more productive if the searcher is well informed about the many options available.

LOCATING MATERIALS

The development of curriculum and audiovisual materials is flourishing, both in the public and private sectors. As a result, a wealth of materials is available. These materials are disseminated by a number of sources. Some have been advertised in professional and trade journals as well as information exchanges.

Knowing how and where to locate existing curriculum materials is a matter of identifying clearly and precisely what is being sought and what is available. It is also a matter of using personal contacts as a resource, conducting a manual search and utilizing, where available, a computer database search. Once performance objectives are available, a number of approaches to actually locating materials can be undertaken. One of these is called "networking."

PERSONAL CONTACTS

Networking is the use of personal contacts such as fellow teachers, librarians, and representatives at businesses and industries. These personal contacts can be extremely helpful in locating materials.

In addition to local acquaintances, important contacts can be made while attending conferences, trade shows, seminars, workshops, and meetings. The multiplying effect of beginning with personal contacts, and spreading outward from there, can lead to effective results at minimal cost.

A good starting point is to talk with teachers conducting

a similar course or program at other schools. They can be asked what materials work well with their students, where they got them, and if a copy can be borrowed for review. This is the best strategy for locating what are called "fugitive" materials. These are usually locally developed items that are not listed in catalogs, references or databases and are not advertised for sale. In most cases, they exist only at the local level, yet they may be both valuable and appropriate.

In addition to locating and obtaining materials, discussions may lead to additional contacts that can be approached face-to-face, over the telephone or through correspondence. Specialists with colleges, universities, and government agencies that are involved with occupational education are often good contacts as well.

MANUAL SEARCH

A manual search consists of checking source documents, such as indexes, bibliographies, and publisher or distributor catalogs. These and other documents are available in libraries. Materials are also advertised in professional and trade journals, magazines, and newsletters. One newsletter, "Open Entries," provides for the exchange of materials. It is published by the Center on Education and Training for Employment (CETE) at the Ohio State University in Columbus.

The search usually includes writing letters or telephoning documentation centers for vocational and technical education, curriculum laboratories and clearinghouses, federal and state projects, state departments of education, professional associations, labor unions, trade organizations, branches of the military, commercial publishers, manufacturers of equipment used on the job, and other public and private sources. Sometimes telephone inquiries can greatly reduce the time and effort required to obtain appropriate materials.

In order to avoid copyright problems, it is advisable to search for noncommercial materials that are in the public domain. The vast majority of public domain materials are produced or sponsored by government agencies. Noncommercial sources often provide information on the availability of these materials.

When writing a letter or making a telephone inquiry, it is important to (a) indicate clearly and precisely what is needed and the purpose it will serve, (b) ask about the availability of appropriate materials, (c) request a catalog of available items, and (d) ask for sample copies or the loan of examples of materials for review. Both commercial and noncommercial sources are often willing to send courtesy or loan materials. Complimentary copies may not be available, however, when products are priced on a cost recovery basis.

COMPUTER DATABASE SEARCH

Computers add a new dimension to searching for curriculum and audiovisual materials. What once took days of looking through catalogs, indexes, microfiche, and other sources, can often be accomplished via the computer in minutes. Commercial vendors provide on-line search and

retrieval services from database tapes, or access to these databases can be direct. Direct access requires using a personal computer with a phone link (modem) to the on-line vendor's computer. Computerized database searches are also conducted by specialists at many college, university and public libraries, government agencies, or curriculum centers and clearinghouses.

When the search is done at a library, a reference librarian customarily helps prepare for and conducts the database search. This usually takes about an hour and generally requires an appointment. An on-line printout can be produced during the search session, or off-line prints, which are less expensive, can be requested. Off-line prints are done overnight at some libraries or by a vendor and mailed. For searches run on Dialog, Dial Mail is faster than off-line prints and cheaper than on-line prints. The on-line search vendor sends the search results to an electronic mailbox overnight and they can be picked up on a personal computer disk or in hard copy form the next day.

The charges for a database search vary by database, but are generally based on a connect-hour cost, a citation royalty charge, and a nominal telecommunications fee. Costs vary depending on the database(s) searched and the number of citations printed. Connect-hour costs are based on the amount of time spent on-line. The citation royalty charge is paid for each citation (record) that is printed. For most searches these charges are reasonable and well worth the time and effort saved.

Computerized databases which contain records concerning curriculum materials pertinent to occupational education courses and programs include:
1. Educational Resources Information Center (ERIC)
2. Vocational Education Curriculum Materials (VECM)
3. Resources in Vocational Education (RIVE)
4. National Technical Information Service (NTIS)
5. Training and Development Alert
6. Training Media Database
7. TRAINET
8. LABORDOC
The first three databases ERIC, VECM, and RIVE are sponsored by the U.S. Department of Education.

ERIC Database

ERIC is a large and comprehensive educational information system. It consists of a coordinating staff in Washington, DC and 16 clearinghouses located at universities or with professional organizations across the United States. Each clearinghouse focuses on a specialization in education. For example, the ERIC Clearinghouse on Adult, Career, and Vocational Education (ERIC/ACVE) is located on the Ohio State University campus in Columbus.

Clearinghouses acquire, evaluate, abstract, index, and announce educational products in ERIC publications. Approximately 14,000 of these product records have been entered into the computer database each year since 1966. This database is the best single source for information on curriculum guides and instructional materials. It includes items that often are not available through other sources.

On-line computer searches of the ERIC database can be conducted through:

1. Dialog Information Services
2. Systems Development Corporation (SDC)
3. Biographic Retrieval Services (BRS)
4. Other commercial vendors

Most college and university libraries can access this database and provide descriptive information on documents of interest at a reasonable cost.

In addition to time saved and the reduced level of effort, searching ERIC on-line offers other advantages over the use of its printed indexes. For example, descriptors can be combined to make a search specific. Additionally, the computer searchable fields help locate the type of document desired. Furthermore, a hard copy printout can be obtained for those citations (records) of interest.

Database search for curriculum materials. ERIC document records have computer searchable fields which help make a search for specific types of documents more efficient. These fields include the title, author, sources, language of publication, document type, and the descriptor or subject heading field.

Of particular importance in locating curriculum materials is the document type field. This field indicates the form or organization of the document in contrast to its subject matter. Document types and their computer codes are listed in the front of the *Thesaurus of ERIC Descriptors*. The Thesaurus is also used to locate subject descriptors which index ERIC materials.

The following step-by-step procedure shows how the database can be searched for curriculum materials on welding. The materials, in this example, are needed for a population (students) who speak and read Spanish.

1. The *Thesaurus of ERIC Descriptors* is used to identify the following terms for the computer search.
   Subject Heading Descriptor (DE): Welding/DE (DE defaults to the descriptor field)
   Document Type (DT): Guides—For Teacher, code number = 052
2. After entering these terms in the computer, the search provides the following sets of documents:
   Set 1 Welding/DE found 284 documents
   Set 2 DT = 052 found 29,321 documents (all of which were tagged as Teaching Guides, in addition to their subject orientation).
3. In order to determine those documents that have both the welding descriptor and DT = 052 terms in their records, the sets or terms are combined with special words called "system operators." In this case the 'and' operator is used to narrow the search to only those documents that have both terms present.
   Set 3 combines Set 1 and Set 2 and finds 135 documents with both terms.
4. To restrict the search to recently published teaching guides the publication year (PY) field in the record is used. Set 4 will look for only those documents published in the 1980s. The question mark (?) used in this search

looks for any digit. Thus we can find materials published in any year in the 1980s.
   Set 4 combines Set 3 and PY = 198? and identifies 94 documents described as teaching guides on the subject of welding, and published in the 1980s.
5. Finally, the search is narrowed to only those curriculum materials published in Spanish. This is done by combining the previous results (Set 4) and by searching the language (LA) field for Spanish.
   Set 5 combines Set 4 and LA = Spanish and identifies three documents.

All of these documents have the search criteria (welding/DE, DT = 052 for Teaching Guides, PY = 198? for recent publications, and LA = Spanish for Spanish language publications present in their records).

Using Dialog Information Services, this database search would show:

Set	Items	Description
S1	284	WELDING/DE
S2	29,321	DT = 052
S3	135	S1 and S2
S4	94	S3 and PY = 198?
S5	3	S4 and LA = SPANISH

Following is a reproduction of one of the three citations printed from Set 5. A citation is the content of a record. The fields used in the previous search are printed below in boldfaced type so they can be easily located. They do not, however, appear in bold type on an actual search printout.

EXAMPLE

ED230790   CE036281
   Soldadura (Welding). Spanish Translations for Welding.
   Hohhertz, Durwin
   East Texas State Univ., Commerce. Occupational Curriculum Lab.
   1980
   55p.
   Sponsoring Agency: Texas Education Agency, Austin. Dept. of Occupational Education and Technology.
   Available from: Occupational Curriculum Lab., East Texas State University, Commerce, TX 75428.
   EDRS Price - MF01 Plus Postage. PC Not Available from EDRS.
   Language: English; Spanish
   Document Type: TEACHING GUIDE (052)
   Geographic Source: U.S.; Texas
   Journal Announcement: RIENOV83
   Target Audience: Practitioners
   Thirty transparency masters with Spanish subtitles for key words are provided for a welding/general mechanical repair course. The transparency masters are on such topics as oxyacetylene welding; oxyacetylene welding equipment; welding safety; different types of welds; braze welding; cutting torches; cutting with a torch; protective equipment; arc welding; arc welding equipment; welding positions; joints and welds; piercing, gouging, and beveling; DC polarity; AC welder;

and properly and improperly formed beads. (YLB)
Descriptors: Bilingual Education; *Bilingual Instructional Materials; Metal Working; Postsecondary Education; Repair; Safety; Secondary Education; *Spanish Speaking; *Trade and Industrial Education; *Transparencies; **Welding**

The first heading in this citation is the ERIC accession number. This identification "ED" number is used to locate the microfiche copy of this document. Figure 3-1 shows a document in microfiche form. Other headings include the: Clearinghouse "CE" accession number; title; author; organization where the document originated; sponsoring agency; alternate source for obtaining the document; ERIC Document Reproduction Service (EDRS), MF means microfiche, PC means reproduced paper copy, (in this case a paper copy is not available from EDRS and the alternate source must be contacted if a paper copy is necessary); language of the document; document type; informative abstract; and subject item descriptors which characterize the content. Many of these citation headings provide helpful information when deciding on what curriculum materials to acquire.

As previously indicated, the "ED" number on a database citation is used to locate a microfiche copy of the complete document. Almost all college and university libraries maintain the ERIC microfiche collection. The direct availability of most documents, although in microfiche form, makes the ERIC database especially useful to occupational teachers.

Microfiche readers are used to view the document. Units like the one shown in Figure 3-2 are called reader printers. They can make hard copies of a document from its microfiche form. Libraries often have microfiche duplication equipment and can provide a copy of the microfiche for a nominal fee.

Approximately 50 organizations worldwide purchase the ERIC database tapes and facilitate computerized access to them. Through these primary sources, several hundred

service centers provide computer searches of ERIC. The *Directory of ERIC Search Services* identifies these sources and provides complete entries describing the address, telephone number, contact person, price, turnaround time, services provided, files accessed, and how to submit an inquiry.

ERIC CD-ROM database. In addition to on-line computer searches, the ERIC database is available on Compact Disk Read Only Memory (CD-ROM). The compact disk is a highly durable 4.72 inch circular optical storage medium. A single disk can hold over 500 million characters of information. This is as much information as contained on 1,500 floppy diskettes or 270,000 sheets of paper.

As shown in Figure 3-3 CD-ROM equipment includes a personal computer (PC) and a compact disk drive. A printer is added in order to provide hard copy citations of selected records.

Figure 3-2.

Figure 3-1.

Figure 3-3.

The CD-ROM database used by ERIC is user-friendly with ample "help" information and easily understood commands. Only limited PC skills are necessary to access the database directly. With limited practice, searches can be performed quickly and at reasonable or no cost.

VECM Database

This referral database provides on-line information on print and nonprint curriculum materials. In addition to public domain materials entered through the six regional Curriculum Coordination Centers, VECM contains curriculum materials developed by the U.S. military and products from the: (a) American Vocational Association (AVA), (b) American Association for Vocational Instructional Materials (AAVIM), (c) Vocational-Technical Education Consortium of States (V-TECS), (d) National Center for Research in Vocational Education (NCRVE), and (e) Interstate Distributive Education Curriculum Consortium (IDECC).

Products include printed instructional materials (textbooks, workbooks, modules, and noncommercial guides) and nonprint materials (sound-slide presentations, microcomputer diskettes, etc.). The database is updated annually. In addition to adding new products, those that are no longer available or are more than seven years old are removed.

On-line computer searches are conducted through BRS. A search guide is provided by BRS to help in planning and conducting a search. Those who do not have access to BRS can retrieve information from VECM by contacting NCRVE or one of the six regional Curriculum Coordination Centers. The addresses and telephone numbers for each of the regional centers are provided in this chapter under the heading "Regional Curriculum Coordination Centers." Likewise, contact information for NCRVE appears under the heading "National Organizations."

Search results can be printed on-line or off-line by BRS. Each citation (record) printed contains the item title, developer, sponsoring agency, subject-matter classification, educational level, intended user, student target population, and copyright restrictions. There is also a concise description of the item and information about where it can be borrowed or purchased. If the items selected are not available through a regional Curriculum Coordination Center, they can usually be obtained from the developer or sponsoring agency identified on the search citation printout.

RIVE Database

RIVE provides access through BRS to information on vocational program improvement projects. The database contains brief descriptions of both ongoing and recently completed curriculum development and program implementation projects. For detailed information, project personnel must be contacted. Entries include the name of the project director, the organization doing the work, and the sponsor (source of funding).

NTIS Database

This database is produced by the U.S. Department of Commerce. It contains references with abstracts to unclassified curriculum materials published by the Department of Defense, Department of Energy, and numerous other federal agencies. Items selected for purchase can be ordered through the NTIS sales office in Springfield, Virginia. Contact information is provided under the heading "U.S. Government Agencies."

Training and Development Alert

This database is provided by Advanced Personnel Systems in Roseville, California. It is updated bimonthly and contains over 3700 records. Topics covered include: (a) technical training, (b) training techniques, (c) job skills training, (d) instructional design, (e) training needs analysis, and (f) cost-analysis of training.

Training Media Database

Access Innovations, Inc., of Albuquerque, New Mexico provides this database. It is updated semiannually and contains over 12,000 records. The Training Media Database provides references and contact information on training programs and audiovisual media. Among the topics covered are: (a) career development guidance, (b) computers, (c) job satisfaction, (d) electronics, (e) technology, (f) office procedures, (g) photography, and (h) industrial safety. Each citation (record) includes the title, media type, distributor and address, producer and address, education level of the intended audience, brief descriptors, and an abstract of the content. The records come from over 25,000 catalogs representing more than 8,000 program producers.

TRAINET Database

This database is produced by Timeplace Inc., Waltham, Massachusetts for members of the American Society for Training and Development. It is updated daily and contains records of books, audiovisual media, courseware, assessment instruments, and packaged training programs. Each TRAINET citation provides the product description, target audience, vendor details, cost, and ordering information.

LABORDOC Database

This database is a service of the International Labour Office (ILO) with headquarters in Geneva, Switzerland. It provides worldwide coverage on vocational training and related topics. The database is updated monthly and contains more than 145,000 records collected since 1965.

On-line computer searches are conducted in the U.S. through (a) Human Resource Information Network (HRIN) and (b) ORBIT Information Technologies. Citations (records) contain the language of the document, author, title, source, year of publication, descriptors from the ILO Thesaurus and an abstract.

Another ILO database, LABORINFO, is being included in LABORDOC. This will add more records on training as well as related topics such as employment, safety, and the impact of new technologies.

The remainder of this chapter is organized into 13 headings. Each heading provides a list of sources for existing curriculum and audiovisual materials that were classified according to the heading title (e.g. International Organizations). Complete contact information is included for each source. Additionally, explanatory information about the source and the print as well as audiovisual materials available is provided in most cases.

International Organizations

International Labour Office (ILO)
ILO Publications
CH-1211 Geneva 22, Switzerland
-or-
International Labor Organization Publications Center
49 Sheridan Avenue
Albany, New York 12210
(518) 436-9686

A catalog and lists of publications dealing with vocational training can be obtained from the ILO. In addition to other relevant materials, audiovisual training packages for office skills are available. A series of staff development modules and Modules of Employable Skill (MES) can be purchased. MES learning elements are self-contained modules, each covering a specific learning objective. Approximately 800 MES learning elements have been completed in ten occupational areas.

United Nations Educational, Scientific, and Cultural Organization (UNESCO)
Division of Science, Technical and Environmental Education
Technical and Vocational Education Section
7, place de Fontenoy
75700 Paris, France

Among the many publications dealing with occupational education, UNESCO has printed three workbooks which present a comprehensive course on Graphic Communications. Each of the 18 units consists of an introduction, the objectives, content information, exercises, and a test. There is also a workbook on Graphic Communications for students at the primary level. Another publication is a two-volume document on direct current (D.C.) machines. The first volume (ITIB 6331- 22B) contains a topical course outline, a list of jobs the course content is appropriate to, course prerequisites, objectives and other information as well as a model set of 80 technical illustrations. The second volume (ITIB 6331-22M) is a module on D.C. machines which includes the illustrations from the first volume. A free catalog of documents and publications related to the education sector is available from the Documentation and Computer-Assisted

Management Service, Education Sector, 7, place de Fontenoy, 75700 Paris, France.

British Cement Association (BCA)
Publications Distribution
Wexham Springs, Slough SL3 6PL, United Kingdom
(England) Fulmer (028 16) 2727 or Telex: 848352

Free catalog of publications, sound-slide sets and 16 mm films on masonry and concrete construction.

City and Guilds of London Institute
76 Portland Place
London W1N 4AA, United Kingdom
(England) 01-580-3050 or Telex: 266586

A technical testing and qualifying body. Some booklets, leaflets, and information sheets are free. Skill scheme syllabi, skill test booklets, information technology modules, and other publications are available through the Sales Section. A free list of publications provides cost and other particulars.

Construction Industry Training Board (CITB)
Publications Department
Bircham Newton, King's Lynn
Norfolk PE31 6RH, United Kingdom
(England) 0553 776677 or Telex: 81452 CITB G

Training schemes, illustrated technical data sheets (operation sheets) bound together to form trainee manuals, practical exercises, modules, handbooks, training record books, wall charts, sound-slide sets, interactive video, and skills (performance) tests for the building industry are available. Covers all building trades and topics relevant to construction. Free catalog of materials provides costs and other details.

Coordination, Documentation, and Information Center for Vocational Training in Developing Countries (KODIS)
Wartstrasse 6
CH-8400 Winterthur, Switzerland
(Switzerland) 41 52 22 51 05 or Fax: 41 52 23 5717

Makes available curriculum guides, instructor and trainee guides, books, booklets, instruction sheets, practical exercises, wall charts, illustrations, modules, overhead transparencies, video tapes, and sound-slide sets on vocational and technical training topics. Occupations covered include electricity and electronics, metalworking, building trades, air-conditioning and refrigeration, automotives, woodworking, health, and agriculture. Materials are published in English, German, French, Spanish, and Portuguese. They are available on a cost reimbursement basis.

Engineering Industry Training Board (EITB)
54 Clarendon Road
Watford Herts WD1 1LB, United Kingdom
(England) 0923 38441 or Telex: 265451 MONREF G

Books, instructor handbooks, training guides, fully illustrated training elements (operation sheets) bound into brochures (training manuals), trainee logbooks, learning packages, leaflets, posters, wall charts, sound-slide sets, and video tapes. Covers metalworking, foundry, welding, mechanical maintenance, drafting, and electricity and electronics topics. Free catalogs of publications provide costs and other details.

Inter-American Vocational Training Research and Documentation Center (CINTERFOR)
Casilla de correo 1761
Montevideo, Uruguay
(Uruguay) 98 60 23 or Fax: 92 13 05 or Telex: 22573
CINFOR UY

Develops and makes available a variety of instructional materials in Spanish, including the Colecciones Basicas Cinterfor (CBC) publications which consist of fully illustrated operation and "informacion tecnologica" (job sheets). CBC publications were prepared for most trade and industrial specializations and some agricultural areas. Some of the manuals in the CBC series have been translated into English and Portuguese.

International Telecommunication Union (ITU)
Technical Cooperation Department
Training Division
Place des Nations
CH-1211 Geneva 20, Switzerland
Fax: 41 22 733 72 56 (Gr. 2/3) or Telex: 421 000 UIT CH

A list of currently available instructional materials as well as those under preparation can be obtained. Topics include safety, electricity and electronics technology, fundamentals of digital techniques, technical and engineering drawing, maintenance and repair of telephones, data processing, heating and air-conditioning, magnetism, and a host of others associated with telecommunications. Full details on items selected from the list are available from the ITU training division. This information enables the interested party to contact the materials producer directly and make bilateral arrangements for acquisition.

Road Transport Industry Training Board (RTITB)
Publications Department
High Ercall MOTEC
Telford, Shropshire TF6 6RB, United Kingdom
(England) 0952 770441

Curriculum guides, instructor guides, handouts, exercises, booklets, modules, computer software, audio tapes, video tapes, and sound-slide sets on transportation topics. Topics include vehicle electronics, fork and lift trucks, furniture moving, driving tanker and other trucks, and safety in vehicle maintenance and repair. A free catalog of materials provides costs and other details.

National Organizations

Center on Education and Training for Employment (CETE), and Educational Resources Information Center (ERIC) Clearinghouse on Adult, Career, and Vocational Education
The Ohio State University
1960 Kenny Road
Columbus, Ohio 43210-1090
(614) 292-4353 or 1-800-848-4815 or Fax: 614-292-1260

CETE is a full-service organization that integrates vocational education, training, evaluation, development, information, dissemination, and research. It offers products designed for all levels. CETE publishes *Open Entries,* a newsletter which provides for the exchange of competency-based education information. ERIC distributes free catalogs and brochures on available materials as well as the following publications:
1. Centergram is a monthly newsletter which describes projects, products, and services.
2. ERIC File is a quarterly newsletter on issues relating to adult, career, and vocational education in the ERIC system, one of the most comprehensive national compilations of information available.

Indexes to and summaries of a variety of materials intended primarily for use by vocational educators are prepared by the ERIC Clearinghouse on Adult, Career, and Vocational Education. These are announced bimonthly in Resources in Vocational Education (RIVE). Computer searches of the ERIC database can be run on a cost-recovery basis.

The Center for Occupational Research and Development (CORD)
P.O. Box 21689
Waco, Texas 76702-1689
(817) 772-8756 or 1-800-231-3015

CORD is a nonprofit organization which develops competency-based modular materials for vocational and technical education. Curriculum guides, instructor guides, modules, and books prepared for power plant technical training and the following categories are described in a free catalog of materials.
1. Applied academics including - math, biology, chemistry, and principles of technology.
2. Technical core courses in electro-mechanical devices, electronic devices and systems, electrical power and illumination systems, electronic and pneumatic control elements, fluid power systems, instrumentation, heating and cooling, and graphics.
3. Specialty courses in instrumentation and control technology, building equipment and energy management, laser/electro-optics, and mechanical technology.

National Center for Research in Vocational Education (NCRVE)
University of California at Berkeley
1995 University Avenue, Suite 375
Berkeley, California 94704-1058
(415) 642-4004 or 1-800-762-4093

Maintains a database describing vocational curriculum materials and determines the transferability of military technical training materials to civilian programs.

National Occupational Competency Testing Institute (NOCTI)
Ferris State University
409 Bishop Hall
Big Rapids, Michigan 49307
(616) 796-4695 or 1-800-334-6283 or Fax: 616-592-2990

NOCTI is a nonprofit educational corporation which provides teacher and student occupational competency exams as well as industrial assessments for business and industry. A free information packet and brochure describe the following:
1. Teacher Occupational Competency Tests (TOCTs) for certification and the advancement of teachers. Over 55 examinations containing written and performance tests have been developed and validated.
2. Student Occupational Competency Achievement Tests (SOCATs), consisting of written and performance tests, for the assessment of job skills and program improvement.
3. Industrial Occupational Competency Tests (IOCTs) for determining occupational competence. Written and performance tests in specific jobs and skills.

American Association for Vocational Instructional Materials (AAVIM)
745 Gaines School Road
Athens, Georgia 30605
(404) 543-7557 or 1-800-228-4689

AAVIM was organized by a cooperative effort between education, industry, and government agencies in the United States and Canada to provide vocational and technical materials. The following free catalogs list and describe available instructional materials:
1. Catalog of Vocational Resources which includes computer software, video tapes, curriculum guides, manuals, and other instructional materials for most trade and technical specializations including agriculture, horticulture, automotives, construction, drafting, welding, electricity, graphic arts, metalworking, surveying, business and marketing, health and home economics.
2. Catalog of Performance-Based Teacher Education and Competency-Based Administrator Education materials includes modules, video tapes, instructor guides, and supporting materials for teacher, staff, and administrator training.

3. Brochure on Vocational Competency Measures in the fields of agriculture, business and office, health, home economics, technical, trade and industrial, and distributive education.

Regional Curriculum Coordination Centers

National Network for Curriculum Coordination in Vocational and Technical Education (NNCCVTE)

The National Network is funded through contracts with the U.S. Department of Education. The goal is to improve coordination of curriculum development and dissemination. The network consists of the following six regional Curriculum Coordination Centers which provide free services to those associated with vocational and technical education. Among the services are computer database searches and access to products from NCRVE, V-TECS, MAVCC, IDECC, AAVIM, and NOCTI. Information on these organizations and consortiums is provided under the headings just prior to and after this heading.

East Central Curriculum Coordination Center
Sangamon State University, F2
Springfield, Illinois 62794-9243
(217) 786-6375

Midwest Curriculum Coordination Center - See MAVCC, CIMC, and Oklahoma Department of Vocational and Technical Education.
Oklahoma Department of Vocational and Technical Education
1500 West Seventh Avenue
Stillwater, Oklahoma 74074-4364
(405) 377-2000, ext. 589 or 1-800-654-4502 or Fax: 405-743-5154

Northeast Curriculum Coordination Center
New Jersey State Department of Education
Division of Vocational Education
Crest Way
Aberdeen, New Jersey 07747
(201) 290-1900

Northwest Curriculum Coordination Center
Saint Martin's College
Old Main, Room 478
Lacey, Washington 98503
(206) 438-4456

Southeast Curriculum Coordination Center
Mississippi State University
Research and Curriculum Unit
P.O. Drawer DX
Mississippi State, Mississippi 39762
(601) 325-2510

A maximum of seven items at a time are available on loan for a 30-day period.

Western Curriculum Coordination Center
University of Hawaii
College of Education
1776 University Avenue, West Hall 216
Honolulu, Hawaii 96822
(808) 948-7834

Curriculum Consortiums

National and Regional Consortiums

National and regional consortiums have been organized and supported by various states and/or individual institutions. They develop and make available occupational (job) analyses and/or curriculum materials.

Vocational-Technical Education Consortium of States (V-TECS)
Commission on Occupational Education Institutions
Southern Association of Colleges and Schools
1866 Southern Lane
Decatur, Georgia 30033-4097
(404) 679-4501, ext. 543 or 1-800-248-7701 or Fax: 404-679-4556

A consortium of some 25 states, the U.S. Military and other government agencies joined together to conduct occupational analyses and to publish them in the form of catalogs of performance objectives and guides. The catalogs list duties and tasks, performance objectives, performance guides, the standard and its source, and the tools and equipment used. Nonmembers can purchase the catalogs as well as curriculum guides and criterion-referenced test items. An occupational data analysis system is also available for curriculum development where common tasks from a variety of jobs need to be clustered.

Interstate Distributive Education Curriculum Consortium (IDECC)
The Ohio State University
1375 King Avenue, P.O. Box 12226
Columbus, Ohio 43212-0226
(614) 486-6708

A consortium of states that started in 1972 to develop a competency-based learning system based on task analysis for 69 occupations in marketing and distribution. The consortium sponsored the development of 500 modules, and is continuing to develop more competencies based on occupational analyses for additional occupations.

Marketing Education Resource Center (MarkED)
Division of IDECC (see entry above)
The Ohio State University
1375 King Avenue, P.O. Box 12226
Columbus, Ohio 43212-0226
(614) 486-6708

Field tested, self-contained modules are available on marketing and business, economics, management, math, pricing, selling, human relations, apparel and accessories, as well as other associated topics.

Mid-America Vocational Curriculum Consortium (MAVCC) - See Midwest Curriculum Coordination Center, CIMC, and Oklahoma State Department of Vocational and Technical Education.
Oklahoma Department of Vocational and Technical Education
1500 West Seventh Avenue
Stillwater, Oklahoma 74074-4364
(405) 377-2000 or 1-800-654-3988 (for ordering only)

A consortium of 10 states which develops curriculum and instructional materials in a wide range of occupational areas. Each publication consists of units of instruction which contain performance objectives, teacher and student activities, instruction sheets, overhead transparency masters, and tests.

U.S. Military

Listed below are four documents which identify existing courses and programs offered by each branch of the U.S. Military. Inquiries concerning the availability of curriculum guides and instructional materials can be made directly to the school where the relevant course or program is conducted.

	Course Lists	*Obtain by Writing*
AIR FORCE	Air Force Manual 50-5, USAF Formal Schools Catalog	U.S. Air Force SAF/AADPS Bolling Air Force Base Washington, DC 20322
ARMY	Department of Army Pamphlet 351-4, Formal Schools Catalog	Commander U.S. Army Publications Center 2800 Eastern Boulevard Baltimore, Maryland 21220-2896

Note. Distribution of the Army pamphlet is limited. A local Army base or reserve center may make it available for reference use.

| MARINE CORPS | Marine Corps Order P1500.12, Formal Schools Catalog | Commandant of the Marine Corps Code HQSP HQ U.S. Marine Corps Washington, DC 20380 |

| NAVY | NAVEDTRA 10500 (series) Catalog of Navy Training Courses | Commanding Officer Naval Education and Training Program Management Support Activity Code 0722 Pensacola, Florida 32509-5000 |

In order to determine if an existing course will meet your instructional needs, you may want to verify the acceptability of the job analysis upon which the course was based and the acceptability of the validation documentation. The following sources can provide course development documentation, when it exists.

| AIR FORCE | **USAF Occupational Measurement Center (OMYX)** Chief of Occupational Analysis Division Randolph Air Force Base San Antonio, Texas 78150-5000 (512) 652-6623 |

Source of job analysis information (occupational survey reports) on occupational specialties. Task data is gathered through document reviews, interviews of subject-matter experts, and mailed questionnaires completed by job incumbents.

| ARMY | **U.S. Army Training and Doctrine Command** Director, Training Management Institute ATTN: 6-TMI Fort Eustis, Virginia 23604-5206 (804) 878-5251 |

| MARINE CORPS | **USMC Manpower Utilization Office** MCCED Code MPU Quantico, Virginia 22134 |

| NAVY | **Naval Education and Training Program Development Center** (Code IPD-1) Pensacola, Florida 32509 (904) 452-1640 |

Other points of contact concerning the availability of military-developed curriculum guides and instructional materials, which can be adapted for use in civilian programs, include the following:

Army Correspondence Course Program Catalog
Army UPDATE Publications
800 West Church Road
Mechanicsburg, Pennsylvania 17055-3198

Commander
U.S. Army Training Support Center
Attention AET-PE
Fort Eustis, Virginia 23604-5168
(804) 878-4603

Pamphlet 350-100 contains all exportable training materials available from the Army.

Commanding Officer
Naval Construction Training Center
Gulfport, Mississippi 39501-5003

Curriculum outlines, teacher and student guides on most areas of construction including heavy equipment operation.

Commanding Officer
Naval Publications and Forms Center
Attn: Public Sales Desk
5801 Tabor Avenue
Philadelphia, Pennsylvania 19120-5099

Commanding Officer
U.S. Atlantic Fleet C-1 Welding School
Norfolk Naval Shipyard
Portsmouth, Virginia 23709

Materials on welder training.

Public Affairs
Army Corp of Engineers
Department of the Army
Department of Defense
20 Massachusetts Avenue, NW
Room 8137
Washington, DC 20314

U.S. Air Force
School of Health Care and Sciences
Sheppard Air Force Base
Wichita Falls, Texas 76311
(817) 851-2511

Materials related to technician training in dentistry, medicine, nursing, biomedical science and health services administration.

U.S. Air Force
Technical Training Center, 3700 TTW/TTGXD
Sheppard Air Force Base
Wichita Falls, Texas 76311

Materials related to training in the electrical, electrical power line, and electrical power production specialties.

U.S. Army
School of Health Sciences
Fort Sam Houston
San Antonio, Texas 78234-5000
(512) 221-5905

Materials related to the Health Sciences. Conducts a program for Practical Nurses.

Note. Selected curriculum guides and instructional materials developed for use by all branches of the U.S. Military that were judged applicable to civilian education and training programs have been prepared for dissemination by NCRVE. They are available through ERIC and the regional Curriculum Coordination Centers. These materials include public domain texts, teacher guides, student guides, workbooks, programmed instruction, and various forms of audiovisual media. For further information about U.S. Military Curriculum Materials, write or call the:

National Center for Research in Vocational Education (NCRVE)
University of California at Berkeley
1995 University Avenue, Suite 375
Berkeley, California 94704-1058
(415) 642-4004

U.S. Government Agencies

Consumer Information Center
P.O. Box 100
Pueblo, Colorado 81009
(719) 948-3334

Catalogs of free and inexpensive publications sponsored by various federal agencies are available. Books, pamphlets, wall charts, and booklets, appropriate to various vocational areas, are listed and briefly described in these quarterly catalogs.

Government Printing Office (GPO)
Superintendent of Documents
North Capital and H Streets, NW
Washington, DC 20402
(202) 783-3238

A free catalog contains annotations of over 1,000 publications. Also included is the location of 24 bookstores throughout the U.S.

National Audiovisual Center
Customer Services Section
8700 Edgeworth Drive
Capitol Heights, Maryland 20743-3701
(301) 763-1896

The central information and distribution source for more than 8,000 16mm films, video tapes, filmstrips and soundslide sets produced by the U.S. Government. A variety of inexpensive audiovisual media for auto mechanics, construction, electricity, electronics, machine shop, welding, health, and other occupations are described in five different free catalogs. The publications (a) Media for Vocational/Technical Education, (b) Media Resource Catalog, and (c) Media Resource Catalog Supplement, contain most of the entries. Other free literature, including the Quarterly Update, describes new audiovisual titles available for sale and rent.

National Engineering Laboratory (NEL)
National Bureau of Standards
U.S. Department of Commerce
Gaithersburg, Maryland 20899

Conducts a broad series of technical programs in engineering and applied science. The following centers may be of interest for publications: (a) center for Electronics and Electrical Engineering; (b) center for Manufacturing Engineering, which includes Factory Automated Systems Division, Fabrication Technology Division, Automated Systems Division, Automated Production Technology Division, and Industrial Systems Division (robotics); (c) center for Building Technology, which includes Structures Division, Building Physics Division, and Building Materials Division.

National Technical Information Service (NTIS)
5285 Port Royal Road
Springfield, Virginia 22161
(703) 487-4650

Curriculum guides, manuals, and other documents published by numerous federal government agencies. NTIS subject category 92A is used to index documents in job training and career development. Classroom programs may be categorized in 92D education, law, and humanities.

United States Department of Agriculture (USDA)
Publication Request and Distribution Center
Room 6007, South Building
U.S. Department of Agriculture
Washington, DC 20250

Materials available include pamphlets covering a broad range of topics including farm and home machinery, home maintenance, electrical devices, basic handtools, and plumbing.

U.S. Department of Education
Office of the Assistant Secretary for Vocational and Adult Education
330 C Street, SW
Washington, DC 20202-7322
(202) 732-2433

Information on vocational, apprenticeship, and cooperative education programs as well as computer education. Requests must be specific and referrals to other agencies are common.

Colleges and Universities

The following are projects and instructional materials laboratories, centers and clearinghouses at colleges and universities.

Allied Health Professions Project
University of California
1003 Wilshire Boulevard
Santa Monica, California 90401
(213) 743-2311

This project resulted in the production of a series of task analyses and modules to support individualized instruction in the clinical laboratory occupations. Each module includes directions for student use, performance objectives, a vocabulary list, a general introduction, a skill lesson (specific objective, materials and equipment listing, and step-by-step illustrated procedure), a performance checklist, enrichment activities, and reading assignments.

Arizona Center for Vocational Education
Northern Arizona University
Box 6025
Flagstaff, Arizona 86011
(602) 523-5442

Curriculum guides for subjects in agriculture, business, health occupations, home economics, industrial arts, marketing and trade, and industrial education. Free catalog of materials provides details.

Arkansas Vocational Curriculum Dissemination Center
University of Arkansas
115 Graduate Education Building
Fayetteville, Arkansas 72701
(501) 575-6606

Evaluated and determined the usefulness of available computer software programs and video tapes for agriculture, business, career, home economics, marketing, technical, and trade and industrial education as well as plumbing apprenticeship. Directories of the compiled evaluations are available on a cost recovery basis. Prepared curriculum guides in home economics and agriculture education.

Curriculum Center
Ridge Vocational-Technical Center
7700 State Road 544
Winter Haven, Florida 33881
(813) 422-6402, ext. 236

Task lists and student learning guides for over 50 competency-based programs in business, industrial, and marketing education.

Curriculum Publications Clearinghouse (CPC)
Western Illinois University
46 Horrabin Hall
Macomb, Illinois 61455
(309) 298-1917 or 1-800-322-3905 or Fax: 309-298-2869

Job task analysis information and instructional materials on agriculture, business, marketing, health occupations, industrial occupations and other topics.

Extension Instruction and Materials Center (EIMC)
The University of Texas at Austin
P.O. Box 7218
Austin, Texas 78713-7218
(512) 471-7716 or 1-800-252-3461

Computer software, print and audiovisual media for health occupations, marketing, industrial arts (technology), and trade and industrial education.

Illinois Vocational Curriculum Center (IVCC)
Sangamon State University
Springfield, Illinois 62794-9243
(217) 786-6375

Extensive collection of cataloged items in the major areas of vocational education. Numerous free services to Illinois educators.

Instructional Materials Laboratory
The Ohio State University
842 West Goodale Boulevard
Columbus, Ohio 43212
(614) 422-4950

Free catalog of materials on business, marketing, consumer and homemaking, as well as trade and industrial subjects.

Instructional Materials Laboratory
University of Missouri-Columbia
2316 Industrial Drive
Columbia, Missouri 65202
(314) 882-2883

Instructional materials covering a wide range of vocational areas and subjects including career guidance, agriculture, business, health occupations, home economics, industrial arts, marketing, and industrial education. Curriculum package for auto body repair with objectives, information sheets, overhead transparency masters, handouts, assignment and job sheets, and criterion-referenced tests for seven modules.

Instructional Materials Service
Cornell University
Department of Education
24 Roberts Hall
Ithaca, New York 14853-5901
(607) 255-9252

Publishers and distributors of materials on agriculture, conservation and forestry, ornamental horticulture, and related computer software.

Instructional Materials Service
Texas A&M University
F.E. Box 2588
College Station, Texas 77843-2588
(409) 845-6601

Lesson plans, curriculum guides, student materials, computer software and a variety of audiovisual media for trades related to transportation, construction, manufacturing, and electricity/electronics.

Media Center
State Fair Community College
3201 West 16th Street
Sedalia, Missouri 65301
(816) 826-7100

Modules for the building trades, graphic arts and welding. Each module includes a teacher's guide, student guide, and a video tape.

Occupational Curriculum Laboratory
East Texas State University
Commerce, Texas 75428
(214) 886-5623/5624/5628

Develops and disseminates materials for business and office and trade and industrial occupations.

Ohio Agricultural Education Curriculum Materials Service
The Ohio State University
Room 254, 2120 Fyffe Road
Columbus, Ohio 43210
(614) 292-6321

Produced a number of student manuals, teacher supplements, slide series, cassettes, overhead transparency masters, sample exams, forms, and task sheets for a wide range of agriculture-related courses. The materials are tied to the Agdex Filing System.

South Carolina Vocational Education Media Center
Clemson University
10 Tillman Hall
Clemson, South Carolina 29631
(803) 656-3311

The Center for Instructional Development and Services
Florida State University
Tallahassee, Florida 32306
(904) 487-2054

The DACUM Exchange
Humber College of Applied Arts and Technology
205 Humber College Boulevard
Etobicoke, Ontario, Canada M9W 5L7
(416) 675-5061

Vocational Agriculture Service
University of Illinois
College of Agriculture
1401 South Maryland
Urbana, Illinois 61801
(217) 333-3870

Vocational Curriculum Materials Center
Pittsburg State University
116 Willard Hall
Pittsburg, Kansas 66762
(316) 231-7000 ext. 4629

As part of a Basic Core Curriculum Project, 29 units of instruction were prepared in the area of horticulture. Each unit includes a terminal objective, specific objectives, information sheets, assignment sheets, and a unit test. Offers materials for other agricultural areas as well as for trade and industrial, home economics, and industrial arts.

Wisconsin Vocational Studies Center
University of Wisconsin-Madison
964 Educational Science Building
1025 W. Johnson Street
Madison, Wisconsin 53706
(608) 263-2422

Curriculum guides and resource packets, computer software, and audiovisual media are available.

State Resources

Many state departments of education and state curriculum labs have also developed instructional materials.

Consumer and Home Economics Career Exploration Program
Utah State Board of Education
47 North Main
Logan, Utah 84321
(801) 753-7340

Career exploratory modules in child development, clothing, consumer education, distributive education, foods, interior design and housing, nutrition, and textiles. Includes filmstrips, cassettes, instructor guides, texts, computer software, and charts.

Curriculum and Instructional Materials Center (CIMC) - See Midwest Curriculum Coordination Center, MAVCC, and Oklahoma Department of Vocational and Technical Education.

Oklahoma Department of Vocational and Technical Education
1500 West Seventh Avenue
Stillwater, Oklahoma 74074-4364
(405) 377-2000, ext. 591 or 1-800-654-4502 or Fax: 405-743-5154

Develops and makes available instructional materials for all vocational service areas. Materials are in the form of loose-leaf units of instruction, teacher and student manuals, modules, video tapes, sound-slide sets, audio tapes, and competency profiles. Units contain objectives, suggested activities, information sheets, overhead transparency masters, assignment sheets, job sheets, criterion-referenced tests, and answer sheets. Oklahoma Occupational Testing Center (same address) has prepared criterion-referenced and performance-based tests for 45 jobs as well as duty/task lists for over 150 occupations.

Curriculum Development Center
Office of Vocational Education
2024 Capital Plaza Tower
Frankfort, Kentucky 40601
(502) 564-2890

Over 1500 competency-based modules have been developed in 28 occupations, representing most vocational service areas. Each module is developed based on one performance objective and includes instruction sheets, self-checks, and final checkout activities. The modules are supplemented by sound-slide presentations and instructor manuals.

Curriculum Development Unit
New Mexico State Department of Education
Education Building
Santa Fe, New Mexico 87503
(505) 827-6635

Developed ten mini-manuals on office communication proofreading. Each includes terminal and specific objectives, information, tasks for practice, and a test. Answer keys are provided in teacher manuals.

Instructional Materials
Trade and Industrial Education
202-B Skyland Boulevard
Tuscaloosa, Alabama 35405
(205) 759-5448

Performance-based instructional guides, study guides, answer books, modules, and other materials for most vocational and technical specializations.

The Center for Vocational Studies
2003 Apalachee Parkway
Tallahassee, Florida 32301
(909) 877-3341

Supported by the Florida Division of Vocational Education, this center has produced competency-based instructional materials for a number of programs.

Vocational Curriculum and Resource Center
2200 Mountain Road
Glen Allen, Virginia 23060-2208
(804) 262-7439

Develops and distributes materials for a wide range of vocational and occupational service areas. A catalog of items available for purchase and a catalog of documents that can be borrowed are provided upon request.

Vocational Curriculum Laboratory
Cedar Lakes Conference Center
Ripley, West Virginia 25271
(304) 372-7017

Develops and makes available, on a cost-recovery basis, competency-based curricula for agriculture, business and office, consumer and homemaking, cooperative and marketing, industrial and technical, health, and industrial arts education. Each curriculum package includes a teacher's section, an introduction, student competency sheets and learning activity directions, supplements, and evaluation sheets.

State Departments of Education (Including U.S. Possessions)

Alabama

Chief Curriculum Specialist
Vocational Curriculum Development Unit
Division of Instructional Services
State Office Building, Room 802
Montgomery, Alabama 36130
(205) 261-5225

Alaska

Chief Curriculum Specialist
Vocational Education
Pouch F - Gold Belt Place
Juneau, Alaska 99811
(907) 465-2980

American Samoa

Chief Curriculum Specialist
State Director for Vocational Education
Box 324
Pago Pago, American Samoa 96799
(684) 633-5238

Arizona

Chief Curriculum Specialist
Arizona Center for Vocational Education
Northern Arizona University
P.O. Box 6025
Flagstaff, Arizona 86011
(602) 523-4192/5442

Provides a variety of competency-based curriculum guides.

Arkansas

Chief Curriculum Specialist
Vocational Division
Education Building, West
Little Rock, Arkansas 72201
(501) 371-1855

California

Chief Curriculum Specialist
Vocational Education Support Service
California State Department of Education
721 Capitol Mall, 4th Floor
Sacramento, California 95814
(916) 445-0404

Colorado

Chief Curriculum Specialist
Department of Vocational Education
Room 114, Vocational Building
Colorado State University
Ft. Collins, Colorado 80523
(303) 491-5273

Connecticut

Chief Curriculum Specialist
Connecticut State Department of Education
P.O. Box 2219
165 Connecticut Avenue
Hartford, Connecticut 06145
(203) 566-7418

Delaware

Chief Curriculum Specialist
Department of Public Instruction
J.G. Townsend Building
P.O. Box 1402
Dover, Delaware 19901
(302) 736-4681

District of Columbia

Chief Curriculum Specialist
Brown Junior High School
24th and Benning Road, NE
Washington, DC 20002
(202) 724-3922

Florida

Chief Curriculum Specialist
Vocational Division
State Department of Education
Knott Building
Tallahassee, Florida 32301
(904) 488-3192

Georgia

Chief Curriculum Specialist
State Board of Postsecondary Vocational Education
Georgia Department of Technical and Adult Education
CNN Center, Omni, Suite 635
Atlanta, Georgia 30334
(404) 656-5845

Curriculum guides for a number of trades including auto body.

Guam

Chief Curriculum Specialist
Guam Community College
P.O. Box 23069
Guam Main Facility
Guam, Mariana Islands 96921
(671) 734-4311

Hawaii

Chief Curriculum Specialist
Research Coordinating Unit
University of Hawaii
2327 Dole Street
Honolulu, Hawaii 96822
(808) 948-7461

Idaho

Chief Curriculum Specialist
State Division of Vocational Education
650 West State Street
Boise, Idaho 93720
(208) 334-3871

Illinois

Chief Curriculum Specialist
Research and Development
Illinois State Board of Education
100 N. 1st Street
Springfield, Illinois 62777
(217) 782-4620

Indiana

Chief Curriculum Specialist
State Board of Vocational Technical Education
Room 401, Illinois Building
17 W. Market Street
Indianapolis, Indiana 46204
(317) 232-1823

Iowa

Curriculum Specialist
Career Education Division
Grimes State Office Building
Des Moines, Iowa 50319
(515) 281-4718

Kansas

Chief Curriculum Specialist
Research Coordinating Unit
State Department of Education
120 East 10th Street
Topeka, Kansas 66612
(913) 296-2222

Kentucky

Chief Curriculum Specialist
Curriculum Development Center
Office of Vocational Education
2024 Capitol Plaza Tower
Frankfort, Kentucky 40601
(502) 564-2890

Louisiana

Chief Curriculum Specialist
Vocational Curriculum Development and Research Center
P.O. Box 1159
Natchitoches, Louisiana 71458-1159
(318) 352-5348; 226-7061

Maine

Chief Curriculum Specialist
Bureau of Vocational Education
Department of Education, Station 23
Augusta, Maine 04333
(207) 289-3565

Maryland

Chief Curriculum Specialist
Research Coordinating Unit
Maryland State Department of Education
Division of Vocational-Technical Education
200 W. Baltimore Street, 3rd Floor
Baltimore, Maryland 21201
(301) 659-2566

Massachusetts

Chief Curriculum Specialist
Division of Occupational Education
Massachusetts Department of Education
1385 Hancock Street
Quincy, Massachusetts 02169
(617) 770-7380

Michigan

Chief Curriculum Specialist
State Department of Education
P.O. Box 30009
Lansing, Michigan 48909
(517) 373-0402

Minnesota

Chief Curriculum Specialist
State Department of Education
564 Capitol Square Building
550 Cedar Street
St. Paul, Minnesota 55101
(612) 297-4390

Mississippi

Chief Curriculum Specialist
Research and Curriculum Unit
P.O. Drawer DX
Mississippi State University
Mississippi State, Mississippi 39762
(601) 325-2510

Missouri

Chief Curriculum Specialist
University of Missouri
10 Industrial Education Building
Columbia, Missouri 65211
(314) 882-2883

Montana

Chief Curriculum Specialist
Office of Public Instruction
1300 Eleventh Avenue
Helena, Montana 59620
(406) 444-2410

Nebraska

Chief Curriculum Specialist
Nebraska Department of Education
301 Centennial Mall, South
Box 94987
Lincoln, Nebraska 68509
(402) 471-4805

Nevada

Chief Curriculum Specialist
State Director for Vocational Education and Continuing Education
Nevada Department of Education
400 West King Street
Carson City, Nevada 89710
(702) 885-3144

New Hampshire

Chief Curriculum Specialist
Division of Instructional Services
New Hampshire State Department of Education
101 Pleasant Street
State Office Park, South
Concord, New Hampshire 03301
(603) 271-3186

New Jersey

Chief Curriculum Specialist
Division of Vocational Education
New Jersey Department of Education
225 W. State Street
CN 500
Trenton, New Jersey 08625
(609) 292-5622

New Mexico

Chief Curriculum Specialist
New Mexico State Department of Education
Education Building
Santa Fe, New Mexico 87501-2786
(505) 827-6646

New York

Chief Curriculum Specialist
Occupational Education Program Development
State Department of Education
Room 1623, One Commerce Plaza
Albany, New York 12234
(518) 474-4806

North Carolina

Chief Curriculum Specialist
Division of Vocational Education
Department of Public Instruction
Room 528, Education Building
Edenton and Salisbury Streets
Raleigh, North Carolina 27611
(919) 733-7094

North Dakota

Chief Curriculum Specialist
State Board for Vocational Education
15th Floor, Capitol Tower
Bismark, North Dakota 58505
(701) 224-3195

Northern Marianas

Chief Curriculum Specialist
Department of Education
Commonwealth of the Northern Marianas
Saipan, CM 96950
(670) 9311, 9827

Ohio

Chief Curriculum Specialist
Instructional Materials Lab
154 W. 12th Avenue
Student Services Building
Ohio State University
Columbus, Ohio 43210
(614) 422-5001

Oklahoma

Chief Curriculum Specialist
State Department of Vocational and Technical Education
- See Midwest Curriculum Coordination Center, MAVCC,
and CIMC.
1500 West Seventh Avenue
Stillwater, Oklahoma 74074-4364
(405) 377-2000

Oregon

Chief Curriculum Specialist
State Department of Education
700 Pringle Parkway, SE
Salem, Oregon 97310-0290
(503) 378-2713/3569

Modules, booklets, and guides as well as audiovisual
media.

Pennsylvania

Chief Curriculum Specialist
Vocational Education Program Support Services
State Department of Education
333 Market Street
Harrisburg, Pennsylvania 17126-0333
(717) 783-8506

Puerto Rico

Chief Curriculum Specialist
Division of Vocational Education
Puerto Rico Department of Education
P.O. Box 759
Hato Rey, Puerto Rico 00919
(809) 753-7275

Rhode Island

Chief Curriculum Specialist
State Department of Education
22 Hayes Street
Providence, Rhode Island 02908
(401) 277-2705

South Carolina

Chief Curriculum Specialist
Vocational Curriculum Development Section
1237 Gadsden Street
Columbia, South Carolina 29201
(803) 758-5971

Binder of competencies identified for most trade and industrial education programs.

South Dakota

Chief Curriculum Specialist
Division of Vocational-Technical Education
Richard F. Kneip Building
700 North Illinois
Pierre, South Dakota 57501
(605) 773-3423

Tennessee

Chief Curriculum Specialist
Division of Vocational-Technical Education
200 Cordell Hull Building
Nashville, Tennessee 37219
(615) 741-1819

Texas

Chief Curriculum Specialist
Research Coordinating Unit
Texas Education Agency
1701 North Congress Avenue
Austin, Texas 78701-1494
(512) 463-9310

Trust Territory

Chief Curriculum Specialist
Cooperative Extension Services
College of Micronesia
Drawer F
Kolonia, Ponape
Eastern Caroline Islands 96941

Utah

Chief Curriculum Specialist
Vocational Education Division
State Office of Education
250 East 500 South
Salt Lake City, Utah 84111
(801) 533-5371

Vermont

Chief Curriculum Specialist
Vocational-Technical Education
State Department of Education
State Office Building
Montpelier, Vermont 05602
(802) 828-3101

Virgin Islands

Chief Curriculum Specialist
Department of Education
P.O. Box 6640
Charlotte Amalie, Virgin Islands 00801
(809) 774-3046

Virginia

Virginia Vocational Curriculum and Resource Center
2200 Mountain Rd.
Glen Allen, Virginia 23060-2208
(804) 262-5075

Washington

Chief Curriculum Specialist
Commission for Vocational Education
Building 17 - Airdustrial Park
Olympia, Washington 98504
(206) 753-5673

West Virginia

Chief Curriculum Specialist
Vocational Curriculum Laboratory
Cedar Lakes Conference Center
Ripley, West Virginia 25271
(304) 372-7017

See entry under State Resources.

Wisconsin

Chief Curriculum Specialist
Board of Vocational, Technical and Adult Education
4802 Sheboygan Avenue, 7th Floor
P.O. Box 7874
Madison, Wisconsin 53707
(608) 266-2222

Wyoming

Chief Curriculum Specialist
Department of Education
Hathaway Building
Cheyenne, Wyoming 82002
(307) 777-7415

Professional Associations and Unions

Associations that have supported the development of instructional materials.

American Association of Community and Junior Colleges (AACJC)
National Center for Higher Education
1 Dupont Circle
#410
Washington, DC 20036

American Association of Medical Assistants
20 North Wacker Drive
Suite 1575
Chicago, Illinois 60606
(312) 899-1500 or 1-800-228-2262

DACUM chart for medical assistants, career information, and education components book which includes curriculum design, certification, and continuing education information. Content outline and other information on medical assistant certification exam.

American Dental Association
Division of Education
211 East Chicago Avenue
Chicago, Illinois 60611
(312) 621-8099

American National Red Cross
17th and D Streets, NW
Washington, DC 20006

Books, pamphlets, slide programs, filmstrips and video tapes for health occupations. CPR manikins can be borrowed.

American Registry of Radiologic Technologists (ARRT)
2600 Wayzata Boulevard
Minneapolis, Minnesota 55405
(612) 337-8416

Instructor guides and content specifications documents for courses in Radiography, Nuclear Medicine, and Therapy Technology. Test item writing manual also available.

American Society for Training and Development (ASTD)
1630 Duke Street
Alexandria, Virginia 22313
(703) 683-8129

Books and video tapes on vocational and technical training and human resource development.

American Society of Radiologic Technologists (ASRT)
Educational Foundation
15000 Central Avenue, SE
Albuquerque, New Mexico 87123-4605
(505) 298-4500

Video tapes, audio tapes, instructor guides, sound-slide sets, modules, and books are available for courses in Radiography, Nuclear Medicine, and Therapy Technology.

American Society of Safety Engineers
1800 East Oakton Street
Des Plaines, Illinois 60018-2187
(708) 692-4121

Training programs, books, instructor guides, workbooks, video tapes, and sound-slide sets on a variety of safety and health topics. Free catalog of materials provides details.

American Trucking Association
2200 Mill Road
Alexandria, Virginia 22314-4677
(703) 838-1700 or 1-800-282-5463

Publications and video tapes on truck driving. Free catalog of materials provides details.

American Vocational Association (AVA)
1410 King Street
Alexandria, Virginia 22314
(703) 683-3111 or 1-800-826-9972

Instrument Society of America (ISA)
67 Alexander Drive
P.O. Box 12277
Research Triangle, North Carolina 27709
(919) 549-8411 or Fax: (919) 549-8288

Training programs, books, instructor guides, workbooks, modules, instructional resource packages, standards and recommended practices, interactive videodisc instructions, video tapes, computer software, sound-slide sets, and overhead transparencies for instrumentation and controls. Free catalog of materials provides details.

International Association of Machinists and Aerospace Workers (IAMAW)
1300 Connecticut Avenue, NW
Washington, DC 20036
(202) 857-5200

Curriculum guides and apprenticeship standards for programs in machinist, millwright, maintenance electrician, tool-and-die maker, and all mechanic trades.

National Business Education Association (NBEA)
1914 Association Drive
Reston, Virginia 22091-1596

Curriculum guides, games, and competency tests for business education. Free catalog of materials provides details.

National Cosmetology Association (NCA)
3510 Olive Street
St. Louis, Missouri 63103

Instructional guides, slides, and video tapes on hairstyles, as well as career information on cosmetology.

National Council of Local Administrators of Vocational Education and Practical Arts (NCLA)
Trade and Technical Education
Board of Education, City of New York
66 Rugby Road
Brooklyn, New York 11226

National Education Association (NEA)
1201 16th Street, NW
Washington, DC 20036

National Joint Steamfitter-Pipefitter Apprenticeship Committee
901 Massachusetts Avenue, NW
Washington, DC 20013
(202) 737-5611

Curriculum guide for training steamfitters and pipefitters. Instructor guides, manuals, workbooks and overhead transparencies are available on topics including welding, electricity, air-conditioning, instrumentation and refrigeration. Free catalog of materials provides details.

National Restaurant Association (NRA)
1200 Seventeenth Street, NW
Washington, DC 20036-3097
(202) 331-5900 or 1-800-424-5156

Books, booklets, manuals, charts, posters, and video tapes for food service programs. Free catalog of materials provides details.

National Vocational Agricultural Teachers Association (NVATA)
Box 4498
Lincoln, Nebraska 68504

Vocational Industrial Clubs of America, Inc.
P.O. Box 3000
Leesburg, Virginia 22075
(703) 777-8810

Trade Organizations

Organizations that can provide free or inexpensive instructional materials pertinent to specific technical areas.

American Foundryman's Society
Golf and Wolf Roads
Des Plaines, Illinois 60016
(708) 824-0182

Publishes a number of texts, guides, handbooks, and periodicals on general metal casting of ferrous and non-ferrous metals, molding, and coremaking.

American Iron and Steel Institute
1000 16th Street, NW
Washington, DC 20036
(202) 452-1700

Offers a number of guides and filmstrip combinations free to instructors, including "Science of Steelmaking," "World of Work," and others. Beneficial to all levels are the technical reports on metallurgy and material-testing methods.

Associated Builders and Contractors Inc.
729 15th Street, NW
Washington, DC 20005
(202) 637-8800

Modules, including a student manual and teacher guide, on carpentry, electricity, heating, air conditioning and refrigeration, masonry, drywall, painting, plumbing, sheet metal, welding, instrumentation and control mechanic, and other areas. Free catalog of materials provides details.

Associated General Contractors of America
Manpower and Training Services
1957 E Street, NW
Washington, DC 20006
(202) 393-2040

Instructional units for residential and commercial carpentry, heavy equipment operator and mechanic, bricklaying, cement masonry, industrial mechanical maintenance, and millwright. Units include performance objectives, suggested activities, information sheets, transparency masters, job sheets, assignment sheets, paper and pencil and criterion-referenced performance tests, and test answers. Free catalog of materials provides details.

Brick Institute of America
Manpower Development Division
11490 Commerce Park Drive
Reston, Virginia 22091
(703) 620-0010

Books, manuals, technical notes, video tapes, 16 mm films, slides with a script, and other items on brick and bricklaying. Free catalog of materials provides details.

Computer and Automated Systems Association of the Society of Manufacturing Engineers
Box 930
One SME Drive
Dearborn, Michigan 48128
(313) 271-1500

Provides a variety of publications for computer-integrated manufacturing, introductory booklets on CIM.

Electronic Industries Association
Director of Educational Services
2001 Eye Street, NW
Washington, DC 20006
(202) 457-4900

Curriculum guide for electronics technician as well as books, brochures, training aids and collateral materials on service technician training.

Graphic Arts Technical Foundation
4615 Forbes Avenue
Pittsburgh, Pennsylvania 15213
(412) 621-6941

Provides an extensive publications list which includes textbooks, bibliographies, technical reports, audiovisual materials, and learning modules on numerous graphic arts specializations. Technical service and research reports, quality control devices and aptitute tests are available.

Hand Tools Institute
25 North Broadway
Tarrytown, New York 10591
(914) 322-0040

Booklet, 16 mm film, sound-slide set, and wall charts on hand tools are available.

Material Handling Institute
1326 Freeport Road
Pittsburgh, Pennsylvania 15238
(412) 782-1624

Provides information on equipment and equipment handling useful with industrial automation techniques. Educational materials include information on bar coding, printing procedures, audiovisuals, and a reference guide to literature.

National Association of Metal Finishers (NAMF)
111 East Wacker Drive
Chicago, Illinois 60601
(312) 644-6610

Provides books, films, magazines, and software on such topics as coatings, working metals, aluminum properties, and metallurgy.

National Engineering Laboratory (NEL)
National Bureau of Standards
U.S. Department of Commerce
Gaithersburg, Maryland 20899

Conducts a broad series of technical programs in engineering and applied science. The following centers may be of interest for publications: (a) center for Electronics and Electrical Engineering; (b) center for Manufacturing Engineering, which includes Factory Automated Systems Division, Fabrication Technology Division, Automated Systems Division, Automated Production Technology Division, and Industrial Systems Division (robotics); (c) center for Building Technology, which includes Structures Division, Building Physics Division, and Building Materials Division.

National Forest Products Association (NFPA)
1619 Massachusetts Avenue, NW
Washington, DC 20036
(202) 463-2700

Provides publications which address wood use in building construction. They include structural design data, span tables, fire tests, and wood foundations.

National Safety Council
1121 Spring Lake Drive
Itasca, Illinois 60143
(708) 285-1121 or 1-800-621-7619

Books and manuals on hazard control, occupational health, health care facility safety, and motor transport safety. Free catalog of materials provides details.

National Tooling and Machining Association
9300 Livingston Road
Fort Washington, Maryland 20744
(301) 248-6200

Provides career awareness information for the machining trades, as well as instructional units in measurement, grinding lathe tool bits, necessary mathematics, and other topics. Available curriculum outlines include numerical control, CNC, introduction to machine tools, and metallurgy.

Non-Ferrous Founders Society
455 State Street, Suite 100
Des Plaines, Illinois 60016
(708) 299-0950

Publishes basic handbooks and manuals on copper, brass, and bronze castings.

Portland Cement Association
5420 Old Orchard Road
Skokie, Illinois 60077-1083
(708) 966-9559

Handbooks, films, slides, and other items on masonry, cement, mortars, and concrete. Free catalog of materials.

Powder Metal Industries Federation
Princeton Forrestal Center
105 College Road East
Princeton, New Jersey 08540
(609) 452-7700

Publishes a directory of all available materials, including visual aids, industry standards, technical books, and conference proceedings. The *Design Guidebook* provides an excellent introduction to powder metallurgy.

Robotics International of SME
P.O. Box 930
One SME Drive
Dearborn, Michigan 48121
(313) 271-1500

Offers books on many subjects, including welding, machine vision, finishing, deburring, computer-numerical control, and quality assurance. Video tapes, 16 mm films, and slides are also available.

Society of Manufacturing Engineers (SME)
P.O. Box 930
One SME Drive
Dearborn, Michigan 48121-0930
(313) 271-1500

Free catalog of books on manufacturing topics as well as video tapes on sheet metal, metal machining, forging, casting, welding, heat treating, plating and testing.

Society of Plastics Engineers (SPE)
14 Fairfield Drive
Brookfield, Connecticut 06804-0403
(203) 775-0471

A variety of books, reports, course materials, 16 mm films, video tapes, workbooks, and instructor's guides on plastics. Free catalog of materials provides details.

Manufacturers

This list is less than complete because of the enormous number of manufacturers that exist. Only a representative sample is included here. A comprehensive directory of American manufacturers is provided by the *Thomas Register of American Manufacturers*. This multi-volume directory is available at most libraries. It contains contact information and a summary of products produced by each company included. Manufacturers usually have instructional materials for the users of their products.

Acme Automotive Finishes
P.O. Box 6027
Cleveland, Ohio 44101

Product information. Video tapes and sound-slide sets available on loan.

Allied-Signal Aerospace Company
Kansas City Division
P.O. Box 419159
Kansas City, Missouri 64141-6159
(816) 997-5377

Apprenticeship standards for a tool and die maker.

Caterpillar Incorporated
100 N E Adams Street
Peoria, Illinois 61629
(309) 675-1000

Video tapes and 16 mm films on the operation and maintenance of various types of heavy equipment as well as safety.

Cummins Engine Company
1000 Fifth Street
Columbus, Indiana 47201
(812) 379-8264

Chrysler Motors
Service Training
26001 Lawrence Avenue
Center Line, Michigan 48015
(313) 956-5741

Instructor guides, trainee reference books, technical guides, video tapes, slides, and posters on automotive service training are available. Free catalog of materials provides details.

Edgcomb Metals Company
330 Woodycrest Avenue
Nashville, Tennessee 37201
(615) 244-2801

Literature on aluminum and aluminum products.

Ford Motor Company
Operations Planning and Training Department
P.O. Box 07150
Detroit, Michigan 48207
(313) 865-5000 ext. 267

Instructor guides, student texts and handbooks, wall charts, video tapes, filmstrips, transparencies, 35 mm slides, and posters on automotive service training. Independent (self) study program on automotive concepts and technology. Free catalog of materials provides details.

General Motors Training Material Merchandising
Kent-Moore Tool and Equipment Division
SPX Corporation
28635 Mound Road
Warren, Michigan 48092-9923
1-800-468-6657

Instructor guides, reference manuals, video tapes, overhead transparencies and simulators originally developed for General Motors automotive training provided to dealers. Topics include air conditioning, brakes, steering, suspension, body, electrical and electronic systems, engine, and transmission. Free catalog of materials provides details.

John Deere Company
Distribution Service Center
1400 Third Avenue
Moline, Illinois 61265-1304
(309) 765-8000

Instructor and student guides, workbooks, transparency masters, 35 mm slides, video tapes, and 16 mm films on engines, electrical systems, hydraulics, power trains, welding, and various topics dealing with mechanical technology. Some materials available in Spanish, French, German, Dutch, and Swedish. Free catalog of materials provides details.

Lincoln Electric Company
22801 St. Clair Avenue
Cleveland, Ohio 44117-1199
(216) 481-8100

Instructional materials and audiovisual media on welding and electric motors.

North American Phillips Consumer Electronics Corporation
Product Services (Service Training)
P.O. Box 555, Old Andrew Johnson Highway
Jefferson City, Tennessee 37760
(615) 475-3801

Catalog of training manuals, video tapes, and service aids for television, VCR, videodisc, compact disc, etc. A course in digital technology with instructor and student materials as well as a digital trainer.

PPG Industries, Inc.
Automotive, Aircraft, and Fleet
Rt. 1, Lot 21
Stonebrook 111
Bluff City, Tennessee 37618

An instructor's kit on automotive finishes is available free. Video tapes and slides with cassette tape recordings or scripts dealing with auto body topics can be borrowed or purchased.

Rite-Hite Corporation
9019 North Deerwood Drive
P.O. Box 23043
Milwaukee, Wisconsin 53223-0043
(414) 355-2600

Literature on truck loading dock safety.

Robert Bosch Company
Automotive Equipment Division
Department for Technical Publications
(KH/VDT)
Postfache 50,
D-7000 Stuttgart 1, Germany

Robert Bosch Corporation
Sales Group, Department UA/AMA
P.O. Box 4601
North Suburban, Illinois 60197

Technical Booklets in English, German, Spanish, Portuguese, and French on engine electronics, storage batteries, ignition systems, magnetos, spark plugs, alternators and generators, starters, fuel injection equipment for diesel engines and compressed air brake systems. Modules, workbooks, video tapes, and sound-slide sets in English on gasoline and diesel fuel injection. Wall charts and troubleshooting guides are also available.

The Torrington Company
59 Field Street
Torrington, Connecticut 06790

Document on spherical roller bearing service damage and causes.

Whirlpool Corporation
Home Study Department
1900 Whirlpool Drive
La Porte, Indiana 46350-2585
(219) 325-2345/2359

Illustrated programs including text and quiz books as well as transparencies, and video tapes, used to train company and dealer personnel, on: basic electricity, refrigeration, automatic washers and dryers, dishwashers, compacters, ranges, and microwave ovens. Do-it-yourself and service manuals are also available. A free brochure and catalog of technical training materials provides details.

This list is less than complete because of the enormous number of manufacturers that exist. Only a representative sample is included here. A comprehensive directory of American manufacturers is provided by the *Thomas Register of American Manufacturers*. This multi-volume directory is available at most libraries. It contains contact information and a summary of products produced by each company included. Manufacturers usually have instructional materials for the users of their products.

Commercial Publishers of Books and other Instructional Materials as well as Audiovisual Media

A large volume of materials exists on the commercial market in varying degrees of quality. Most commercial enterprises produce for a mass market, so their material may not be suitable for specific training needs. The following enterprises provide free literature describing their print and audiovisual materials.

Addison-Wesley Training Systems
Route 128
Reading, Massachusetts 01867-9984
(617) 944-3700

Allyn and Bacon, Inc.
160 Gould Street
Needham Heights, Massachusetts 02194-2310
(617) 455-1200 or 1-800-852-8024

American Technical Publishers, Inc.
1155 West 175th Street
Homewood, Illinois 60430
(708) 957-1100 or 1-800-323-3471

Books and teacher guides for most trade and technical specializations.

Appleton & Lange
25 Van Zant Street
East Norwalk, Connecticut 06855
1-800-423-1359

Books, journals, and audiovisual media on medicine, nursing, and allied health specializations.

Arco Publishing, Inc.
One Gulf and Western Plaza
New York, New York 10023
(212) 373-8931

Barr Films
3490 East Foothill Boulevard
P.O. Box 5669
Pasadena, California 91107
(213) 681-6978

Bergwall Productions, Inc.
540 Baltimore Pike
Chadds Ford, Pennsylvania 19317
(215) 388-0400 or 1-800-645-3565

Computer software, video tapes, videodiscs, and filmstrips for most trade and technical specializations.

Bobbs-Merrill Education Publishing
100 Front Street
Riverside, New Jersey 08075
(609) 461-6500 or 1-800-257-5755

Business News Publishing Company
Technical Book Division
P.O. Box 2600
Troy, Michigan 48007-2600
1-800-837-1037 or Fax: 313-362-0317

Books, workbooks, modules, computer software, video tapes, audio tapes, and sound-slide sets for many trade and technical specializations.

Cally Curtis Company
1111 North Las Palmas Avenue
Hollywood, California 90038-1289

Career Aids, Inc.
20417 Nordhoff Street, Department R
Chatsworth, California 91311
(818) 341-2535

Computer software, video tapes, and filmstrips for most trade and technical specializations.

Chilton Book Company
One Chilton Way
Radnor, Pennsylvania 19089
(215) 964-4000/4729

Books and manuals on automotive and various arts and crafts.

Clairol, Inc.
Professional Products Division
345 Park Avenue
New York, New York 10154

Instructional materials on cosmetology and hairdressing only.

Coronet, The Multimedia Company
108 Wilmot Road
Deerfield, Illinois 60015-9990
(708) 940-1260 or 1-800-621-2131
Free catalog of filmstrips and video tapes on health topics.

Dana Corporation
P.O. Box 453
Toledo, Ohio 43692-0453
(419) 535-4500

Books, service guides/manuals, posters, slides and video tapes on all facets of automotive. Free catalog of materials.

DCA Educational Products
Kellers Church Road
P.O. Box 338
Bedminster, Pennsylvania 18910
(215) 795-2841 or 1-800-345-3584

Computer software and audiovisual media on automotive, building trades, woodworking, drafting, electricity, graphic arts, metals, refrigeration and other industrial education specializations.

Delmar Publishers, Inc.
Two Computer Drive, West
Box 15015
Albany, New York 12212-5015
(518) 459-1150 or 1-800-347-7707 or Fax: 518-459-3552
Books, workbooks, manuals, study guides, instructor guides, video tapes and audio tapes for many trade and technical specializations.

EMC Publishing
300 York Avenue
St. Paul, Minnesota 55101
(612) 771-1555

Textbooks and computer software.

Glencoe Publishing Company
Bennett & McKnight Division
3008 West Willow Knolls Drive
Peoria, Illinois 61614
(309) 689-3200 or 1-800-447-0682

Goodheart-Willcox Company
123 West Taft Drive
South Holland, Illinois 60473-2089
(708) 333-7200 or 1-800-323-0440 or Fax: 708-333-9130

Textbooks, student supplements, software, and instructor's resource guides for a wide variety of vocational topics including building trades, drafting and CAD, automotive, electricity/electronics, graphic communications, manufacturing and production, metal trades and metallurgy, print reading, technical writing, welding, technology education, small gas engines, and professional books. Please write, fax, or call for a free full-color catalog describing all of the vocational products.

GP Publishing, Inc.
5727 South Lewis Avenue, Suite 727
Tulsa, Oklahoma 74105
(918) 749-8642 or 1-800-727-6677

Free catalog of materials on construction, industrial, and electrical technologies, as well as safety and technical drawing.

Hobar Publications
1234 Tiller Lane
St. Paul, Minnesota 55112
(612) 633-3170

Holt-Rinehart-Winston
6277 Sea Harbor Drive
Orlando, Florida 32887
(407) 345-2525/2000 or 1-800-782-4479

Houghton-Mifflin Company
College Division
Wayside Road
Burlington, Massachusetts 01802
(617) 270-1000 or 1-800-225-3362

Interstate Printers & Publishers, Inc.
P.O. Box 50
Danville, Illinois 61834-0050
(217) 446-0500 or 1-800-843-4774

John Wiley & Sons, Inc.
Attn: Distribution Center
One Wiley Drive
Somerset, New Jersey 08875
(908) 469-4400 or 1-800-526-5368

Leighton & Kidd, Ltd.
295 Evans Avenue
P.O. Box 940, Station "U"
Toronto, Ontario, Canada M8Z 5P9
(416) 252-6407 or 1-800-668-6064 or Fax: 416-252-8331

Industrial, electrical, and mechanical maintenance training programs (61 video tapes with workbooks).

Little, Brown, & Company, Publishers
200 West Street
P.O. Box 902
Waltham, Massachusetts 02254-9961
1-800-343-9204

McGraw-Hill Book Company
Gregg Division
13311 Monterey Avenue
Blue Ridge Summit, Pennsylvania 17294
(717) 794-2191 or 1-800-722-4726

MacMillan Publishing
See Glencoe and/or McGraw-Hill
Contact information.
Also 1-800-257-5755

Meridian Education Corporation
236 East Front Street
Bloomington, Illinois 61701
1-800-727-5507

Books, computer software, video tapes, and filmstrips for most trade and technical specializations.

Merrill Publishing Co.
See Glencoe and/or McGraw-Hill
Contact information.
Also 1-800-848-1567

Modern Talking Picture Service
5000 Park Street North
St. Petersburg, Florida 33709
(813) 541-7571

A variety of 16 mm films on subjects including business, energy, and health.

NUS Training Corporation
910 Clopper Road
P.O. Box 6032
Gaithersburg, Maryland 20877-0962
(301) 258-2500 or 1-800-848-1717 or Fax: 301-258-1731

Training programs, books, instructor guides, video tapes and computer software. Topics include mechanical, electrical, and instrumentation maintenance, plant operations, and electric utilities.

Penton Publishing Company
1100 Superior Avenue
Cleveland, Ohio 44114
(216) 696-7000 or 1-800-321-7003

Books and manuals on fluid power and manufacturing processes as well as computer software.

Pesco International
21 Paulding Street
Pleasantville, New York 10570
(914) 769-4266 or Fax: 914-769-2970

Skills aptitude testing materials and equipment. System scores, interprets, and matches tested individuals to job profiles and maintains records of the individual. Instructional materials, software, test items, and instructor's guide for basic computer skills.

Power Safety International
3315 Old Forest Road
P.O. Box 11886
Lynchburg, Virginia 24506-1886
1-800-323-2695 or Fax: 804-385-3663

Training courses, manuals, and video tapes for power plant operation and maintenance, equipment operation, hydraulics, process controls, industrial controls, programmable controllers, electricity, electronics, and welding.

Prakken Publications, Inc.
416 Longshore Drive
Ann Arbor, Michigan 48107
(313) 769-1211

Prentice Hall
200 Old Tappan Rd.
Old Tappan, New Jersey 07675-9987
(201) 767-5054

Prentice Hall Press
1 Gulf Western Plaza
New York, New York 10023-7771
(212) 373-8820 or 1-800-524-2349

South-Western Publishing Company
5101 Madison Road
Cincinnati, Ohio 45227
(513) 271-8811 or 1-800-543-0487

Summit Training Sources, Inc.
6504 28th Street, S.E.
Grand Rapids, Michigan 49506
(616) 949-2370

Safety video tapes on a variety of topics. Free catalog.

Teaching Aids, Inc.
P.O. Box 1798
Costa Mesa, California 92628-0798

Instructor and student guides, tests and answer keys, computer software, video tapes, filmstrips and transparencies on automotive, diesel mechanic, truck driving, motorcycles, and small engines.

Tel-A-Train, Inc.
P.O. Box 4752
Chattanooga, Tennessee 37405
(615) 266-0113 or 1-800-251-6018 or Fax: 615-267-2555 or Telex: 533018

Over 150 video tape courses on topics including safety and health, hydraulics, motor controls, programmable controllers, electronics, electricity, pneumatics, welding, machine shop, and mechanical as well as motor maintenance. Study guides and transparency masters are available on some topics.

Telemedia, Inc.
TPC Training Division
750 Lake Cook Road
Buffalo Grove, Illinois 60089
(708) 808-4000 or 1-800-837-8872

Manuals, study guides, and video tapes on courses including welding, automotive and construction technology, machining, air conditioning and refrigeration, plumbing, structural painting, programmable controllers, robotics, mechanical maintenance, waste water treatment, rigging, electricity, electronics, and others.

Video Training Resources, Inc.
7500 W. 78th Street
Edina, Minnesota 55435-2889
(612) 944-8190 or 1-800-828-8190

Video and text programs in machine technology, welding, maintenance and other industrial skills.

West Publishing
College and School Division
610 Opperman Drive
Eagan, Minnesota 55123
(612) 687-7000 or 1-800-328-9424

Westinghouse Learning Corporation
5005 West 110th Street
Oak Lawn, Illinois 60453

Chapter 4

WRITING THE PRELIMINARIES FOR YOUR CURRICULUM GUIDE

Dr. Lester G. Duenk, Professor
Vocational Industrial Education
Virginia Tech
Blacksburg, Virginia 24061

INTRODUCTION

This chapter shows how to write the beginning section of a curriculum guide. The beginning section of the guide, along with the development of the individualized competency record (see Chapter 5), should be completed prior to the development of several *unit guides* which present the actual teaching content for a course or program (see Chapters 6, 7, 8 and 9). The beginning section is called the **Preliminaries** as it includes general information about the learning environment, grade level, type of school, objectives and other information which is vital to understanding the rationale for the curriculum design and content.

One should bear in mind that teachers already know much of what is placed in the preliminaries without a need for writing it down. Writing the preliminaries does, however, aid teachers in thinking through the needs and rationale of their programs before beginning to write the actual course content.

The preliminaries for a curriculum guide serve to orient the readers to a course or program. The entire curriculum guide is generally too cumbersome to understand in its entirety, without spending a great deal of time. Consequently, a basic understanding can be gained by reading certain preliminary information. The basic segments of the preliminaries section are:

1. Table of Contents
2. Introduction
3. School Philosophy
4. Vocational Education Philosophy
5. Program/Course Philosophy
6. Objectives
7. Occupational Description
8. Related Areas of Employment
9. Resource Materials
10. Unit Titles
11. Program/Course Outline
12. Competency List
13. General Safety and Conduct Rules

Some of these segments will be explained in other chapters. However, upon completion, all of them will be placed in the above order in the preliminaries section of this curriculum guide.

TABLE OF CONTENTS FOR THE CURRICULUM GUIDE

The major sections of a curriculum guide are listed in a Table of Contents. It is important to plan the order of contents before beginning the various sections of a guide. Later, when the guide is completed, page numbers can be included in the Table of Contents. However, because it is desirable to add, delete, and revise a guide periodically, the pages may be left out and tabbed dividers placed at the beginning of the various sections. An example of a typical Table of Contents is shown in Figure 4-1.

Introduction to the Curriculum Guide

The introduction is the starting point for planning instruction that fits in with the specific needs of the community, school, and students. There are many ways of writing an introduction and the principal or vocational director may already have a set format to follow. Some topics, which may be included in an introduction follow. These are suggestive only; there may be other topics which can be included.

Type of Community. The type of vocational program in a school is dependent largely on the type of community it serves. Some things that can be included are:

1. The geographic area that the school serves.
2. The types of businesses and industries in the community.

Table of Contents

Figure 4-1. An Example of the Table of Contents for a Welding Course.

3. The employment opportunities available for graduates of a vocational-technical center or comprehensive high school vocational program.
4. Postsecondary education (technical and academic) institutions in the area.
5. Economic status of the community.

It is obvious that a community that has many heavy industries will be served best by an occupational program which is in tune with such local employment needs. In a community where there is a concentration of light industries, such as an electronic assembly component plant or computer manufacturing, the school program emphasis will be quite different.

The economic status of a community will play a role in determining which type of programs are most affordable. A machine tool technology instructional laboratory will cost considerably more than a masonry laboratory, in terms of equipment needs. Graphic arts laboratories are very expensive to equip but, if there are several printing or publishing firms in the area, school authorities should strongly consider expending the necessary resources so that students may gain employment skills in the industry.

Type of School. It follows that the curriculum must be developed so it meets the needs of the school. Some considerations here are:

Organization of school - Comprehensive high school, local (one school district) vocational center, area secondary technical center, vocational rehabilitation center, correctional school, postsecondary school, and private vocational institute are some of the organizational patterns found throughout the country.

Class size - Include average figures plus maximums and minimums. This may be set by the administration and/or determined by the number of seats, amount of equipment, as well as other appropriate considerations.

Facilities available - Needless to say, the program design must fit facility, supply and equipment availability. Size of laboratory, quality, quantity and type of tools and machines available will be factors in determining what can be taught. Rotation of students in areas and supplies available for students to complete required competencies must also be considered.

Personnel structure - Consider here the administrative and supportive roles of personnel. A comprehensive high school may have an academic principal with an assistant principal for vocational education. The large area technical center may have several vocational administrators and other supporting personnel.

Available teaching staff - The extent to which related technical information will be taught depends to some extent on the policy of the school in providing resource personnel. Special teachers are often available to work with students in general areas such as reading, technical mathematics, print reading, personal/vocational guidance and other nonlaboratory subjects. The need for special teachers is especially important if a large number of special needs students are in the classes.

Time schedule - The curriculum guide must be planned so that instruction fits into a time schedule which has already been determined by the administration. Some common block time schedules for occupational education programs are:

A. 11th grade, three hours; 12th grade, three hours
B. 10th grade, one hour exploratory; 11th grade, two hours, 12th grade, three hours
C. One year cluster exploratory, four subjects, nine weeks, each
D. Two year cluster exploratory
   First year, four subjects, nine weeks each
   Second year, two subjects selected from first year, for eighteen weeks each, three hours per day
E. One year full-time exploratory for one occupational area, one hour each day
F. Intact adult community college programs consisting of many related technical and academic courses.

Most schools have cooperative programs where students spend part-time on the job and part-time in school. Common patterns of industrial training are: (a) three hours in school, three hours on-the-job training; (b) in-school laboratory classes the first year, leading to cooperative on-the-job training during the latter portion of the second year; and (c) two weeks in school followed by two weeks on-the-job, continuously throughout a school year.

Type of Students. A local administrator or concerned person from outside of the school district may be interested in noting the relationship between the curriculum content and the type of students enrolled in an occupational program. Several different categories might include:

1. Secondary or postsecondary students
2. Percentage of handicapped and/or disadvantaged students in your classes
3. Special classes composed entirely of special groups such as educable mentally retarded (EMR) or trainable mentally retarded (TMR)
4. Rehabilitation school students
5. Correctional students
6. Exploratory students
7. Adult students enrolled in night classes held in secondary school laboratories
8. Adult students (legally up to age 21, or as specified by the state) who are enrolled in mixed classes with secondary school students

Because the abilities and goals of these different groups will vary, the curriculum design must also vary. The content of a postsecondary curriculum guide will differ in many ways from a secondary curriculum guide. Students are generally more mature and require less remedial work. Also many students may have already completed a secondary school occupational program or may have already worked on the job for a period of time after high school.

A curriculum guide that is planned for exploratory students will usually cover a short duration of time and will deal with a hands-on survey of many occupational areas. On the other hand, a two- or three-year block program operating on a half-day basis will usually be occupational preparatory in nature and go into far greater depth.

A curriculum guide designed for impaired, disadvantaged, or correctional type students must have the flexibility that allows for working with many types of special needs. Furthermore, corrections program students are generally taught on an open-entry/open-exit basis because length of residence varies.

Adult supplementary programs are often narrow in scope and are centered around skill development in certain specialties found in selected occupations. A night course for employed commercial sewing machine operators, for example, may deal with developing skill in sewing several new patterns required for a new line of clothing to be produced. A coal mining company may ask the school to offer a night class in welding to upgrade workers in specific mine equipment maintenance and repair.

Although the introduction for the curriculum guide contains vital information about the community, school and students, there are numerous other explanatory items which can aid readers in understanding the reasons for content selection and the general organization of the curriculum guide. Some of these topics follow.

Philosophy and Objectives. The school philosophy and objectives may be included in the **Type of School** section or placed by itself, following the introduction. The philosophy is a statement of beliefs about the school indicating such aspects as school background and the purposes it serves in the community. The school objectives are specific goal statements which are built upon the stated philosophy. Teachers may not need to write their own school philosophy and objectives because the information is often available from the principal or director. This information should be included, however, either as part of the introduction or on a separate page.

In order to provide clarity for the reader, teachers may include other headings such as the program/course: (a) length, (b) prerequisites, (c) purpose, (d) age limitation, and (e) equipment available. Such information may have been included in the previous sections, however, headings such as these mentioned will aid the reader to quickly locate information before progressing through the remainder of the guide. An example of an introduction for a drafting curriculum guide used at the Arnold R. Burton Vocational-Technical School is shown in Appendix 4A.

PHILOSOPHY

The philosophy, as discussed previously, represents the beliefs and purposes of occupational education. These statements can be written to represent different levels, beginning with the general philosophy of occupational education in the United States down to the teacher's own specific course philosophy.

The occupational education philosophy is a statement of beliefs which is general in nature and encompasses all occupational areas, including, but not limited to: (a) agricultural education, (b) business education, (c) health occupations education, (d) marketing education, (e) technology education (industrial arts), (f) public service education, (g) technical education, and (h) vocational industrial education. It provides a statement of beliefs for all age and grade levels, types of students and educational settings, i.e., public school, private school, military, apprenticeship, etc. An example of a general vocational education philosophy is provided in Figure 4-2.

The school philosophy, previously discussed, describes the purpose, concepts and rationale for the entire school which may be a comprehensive high school, community college, vocational-technical center, or other type of school. If the school is concerned with academics as well as technical learning, the philosophy will differ from that of a school

GENERAL PHILOSOPHY

Although vocational education is not considered a part of general education, nevertheless, it is a vital phase of the total education program for the complete development of youth. Whereas general education is primarily concerned with those activities and experiences essential to successful living, vocational education deals specifically with occupational preparation. It is not to be presumed, however, that vocational education is confined entirely to the mastery of skills and technical knowledge. The nature of society requires individuals to possess, in addition, comprehensive understandings of social, civic, and ethical responsibilities. Workers must be able to do the jobs for which they are trained, but they must also appreciate obligations to the community and fellow workers. The key to preparing individuals for gainful employment is to instill in them dignity and respect for themselves and their skills, offer them realistic goals and provide a sense of self identity.

Figure 4-2. An Example of the General Philosophy of Vocational Education in America.

SCHOOL PHILOSOPHY

The philosophy and purposes of the Smyth County Vocational Center are in accordance with and built upon the philosophy and purposes of the Smyth County Public Schools and the Trade and Industrial Education Programs in Virginia.

A philosophy should be a dynamic system of beliefs and concepts, which is continually being defined and redefined in the light of social, economic, and technological changes in our society. The philosophy of the Smyth County Vocational Center is viewed in this perspective.

The staff at Smyth County Vocational Center believes that all students are entitled to receive an education which affords them effective training in both liberal or general education and/or vocational education. An educational program which is cognizant of the value of both liberal and vocational education should produce the highest quality of education for the youth of Smyth County, for the commonwealth, and for the nation. It is the school's belief that by receiving this type of education, students can more fully develop their individual abilities. Vocational education is a locally developed plan of education that meets realistically the demands of occupations which are available to high school graduates. Vocational education helps prepare many students for entry level jobs and also helps to lead some students into postsecondary programs of advanced vocational and technical education.

Vocational education orients itself towards an occupation or a cluster or group of closely related occupations and prepares high school graduates with a marketable skill at the time they leave high school. Many programs are offered at the center, although they are not the student's total curriculum. Vocational courses are an additional learning experience which makes a balanced and meaningful general education program leading to high school graduation.

The educational process is one of classroom instruction and related shop demonstration by the instructor with repeated practice by the students. Emphasis is made on producing a cooperative, safe, dependable, and skilled worker.

The staff recognizes the value of each individual student and strives to develop in each student a feeling of self-worth. The staff believes every opportunity should be available to students who desire and can benefit by our program offerings, and who have the physical and mental potential for becoming safe employees in their fields of training. The staff believes it is important for students to graduate with marketable skills. In order to do this, teachers at Smyth County Vocational Center feel responsible to identify changes in their respective vocational fields and to adapt the curriculum accordingly. The school shares with parents, community and church in preparing youth to become productive citizens and to possess respect and compassion toward others.

Figure 4-3. Educational Philosophy of Smyth County Vocational Center.

PROGRAM PHILOSOPHY

The Commercial Food Service training program is essential in our American educational system because of the ever increasing demand for skilled food technicians. This program will, hopefully, cause behavioral changes in students, resulting in the acquisition of salable skills. The Commercial Food Service program will promote the development of desirable attitudes with respect to health, safety, and business ethics. The student will develop an increased sensitivity to the dignity of work and will, as a result, impart status to the occupation and the entire food service establishment.

In addition to skill development, learning experiences are provided for students to develop the traits of citizenship and leadership, giving these youths dignity and respect for themselves and their acquired skills. Successful completion of the program provides a definite sense of identity, based upon goals which have been reached.

Figure 4-4. Philosophy for a Commercial Food Service Program At D. J. Howard Vocational Center, Winchester, VA.

which is strictly concerned with occupational education. The school philosophy is important because it reflects the rationale for the education in a community. The philosophy, if well conceived, will protect school boards, administrators, and teachers from the pressures of special interest groups who may seek to influence undesirable curriculum changes. This philosophy, if abbreviated, may appear in the introduction (see Appendix 4A) or if lengthy, may appear as a separate section (see Figure 4-3).

The final philosophy statement would be the one prepared for an occupational program and/or course. A program consists of a grouping of courses which lead to a statement of completion, certificate, diploma, or degree. A course is one segment in that program. *Automotive Transmissions* might be a course in an Associate of Science program in Automotive Technology at a community college or technical institute. *Tenth grade exploratory masonry* would be one course in a three-year secondary school masonry program.

Once again the philosophy of an occupational program/course may be thought of as a series of purposes and beliefs which the teacher, the administration, and advisory committee have formulated to be the foundation for what is to be taught. It need not be lengthy; yet it serves to set the stage for the objectives. A sample philosophy for a commercial food service program is shown in Figure 4-4.

Although the broad vocational education philosophy, school philosophy, and program/course philosophy are typical of what is found in a curriculum guide, there are other philosophies which have already been developed and could be included as well. These might be: (a) national/state philosophy of general education, (b) national/state philosophy of specified areas, i.e., secondary education, post-secondary education, rehabilitation education, etc., and (c) philosophy of your vocational area. It is good to be aware of these philosophies in the event that the administration has a planned format that calls for their inclusion.

OBJECTIVES

Objectives are statements of expected student outcomes based upon the philosophy which has been established. It is necessary to plan a general direction before developing the curriculum guide. Like the philosophy, there are many levels of objectives starting with the broad national educational objectives and moving down to the objectives of a specific course.

National Objectives

Over the years, national education objectives have changed with the needs of society. The Commission on the Reorganization of Secondary Education published the *Cardinal Principles of Secondary Education* in 1918 (see Figure 4-5). This was the first attempt by a national organization to determine the purpose of the secondary school in our society. The commission listed areas of daily living which should be taught in secondary school programs.

In 1944 the Educational Policies Commission suggested that the objectives of the secondary school curriculum were in need of change. Some subjects that had gradually entered the curriculum were not included in the *Cardinal Principles of Secondary Education*. This Commission pro-

1. **Health**
   The secondary school should therefore provide health instruction, inculcate health habits, organize an effective program of physical activities, regard health needs in planning work and play, and cooperate with home and community in safeguarding and promoting health interests.

2. **Command of fundamental processes**
   The facility that a child of 12 or 14 may acquire in the use of these tools is not sufficient for the needs of modern life.

3. **Worthy home-membership**
   Worthy home-membership as an objective calls for the development of those qualities that make the individual a worthy member of a family, both contributing to and deriving benefits from that membership.

4. **Vocation**
   Vocational education should equip the individual to secure a livelihood for himself and those dependent on him, to serve society well through his vocation, to maintain the right relationships toward his fellow workers and society, and, as far as possible, to find in that vocation his own best development.

5. **Civic education**
   Civic education should develop in the individual those qualities whereby he will act well his part as a member of neighborhood, town or city, state, and nation, and give him a basis for understanding international problems.

6. **Worthy use of leisure**
   Education should equip the individual to secure from his leisure the recreation of body, mind, and spirit, and the enrichment and enlargement of his personality.

7. **Ethical character**
   In a democratic society ethical character becomes paramount among the objectives of the secondary school.

Note: From *Cardinal Principles of Education.* Commission on the Reorganization of Secondary Education, U.S. Office of Education (Washington, DC: Government Printing Office, 1918), Bulletin No. 35, p.9.

Figure 4-5. Cardinal Principles of Secondary Education.

1. All youth need to develop salable skills and those understandings and attitudes that make the worker an intelligent and productive participant in economic life. To this end, most youth need supervised work experience as well as education in the skills and knowledge of their occupations.
2. All youth need to develop and maintain good health and physical fitness.
3. All youth need to understand the rights and duties of the citizens of a democratic society, and to be diligent and competent in the performance of their obligations as members of the community and citizens of the state and nation.
4. All youth need to understand the significance of the family for the individual and society and the conditions conducive to successful family life.
5. All youth need to know how to purchase and use goods and services intelligently, understanding both the values received by the consumer and the economic consequences of their acts.
6. All youth need to understand the methods of science, the influence of science on human life, and the main scientific facts concerning the nature of the world and of man.
7. All youth need opportunities to develop their capacities to appreciate beauty in literature, art, music, and nature.
8. All youth need to be able to use their leisure time well and to budget it wisely, balancing activities that yield satisfactions to the individual with those that are socially useful.
9. All youth need to develop respect for other persons, to grow in their insight into ethical values and principles, and to be able to live and work cooperatively with others.
10. All youth need to grow in their ability to think rationally, to express their thoughts clearly, and to read and listen with understanding.

Note: From Educational Policies Commission, *The Purposes of Education in America Democracy*, pp. 50, 72, 100, and 108.

Figure 4-6. The Imperative Needs of Youth.

1. Understand and practice the skills of family living.
2. Learn how to be a good manager of time, money, and property.
3. Gain a general education.
4. Develop good character and self-respect.
5. Develop skills in reading, writing, speaking, and listening.
6. Learn about and try to understand the changes that take place in the world.
7. Learn how to examine and use information.
8. Develop a desire for learning now and in the future.
9. Help students develop a pride in their work and a feeling of self-worth.
10. Prepare students to enter the world of work.
11. Practice and understand the ideas of health and safety.
12. Learn how to respect and get along with people who think, act, and dress differently.
13. Understand and practice democratic ideas and ideals.
14. Learn to respect and get along with people with whom we work and live.
15. Learn how to use leisure-time.
16. Learn how to be a good citizen.
17. Develop the ability to make job selections.
18. Help students appreciate the culture and beauty in their world.

Note: From *Goal Card*. Northern California Program Development Center, Chico, CA: The Center, 1971.

Figure 4-7. General Secondary Education Goals Proposed by the Northern California Program Development Center.

posed a new set of secondary school objectives called *The Imperative Needs of Youth*. These objectives are listed in Figure 4-6. It should be noted that the areas of consumer economics, science, literature, art, and music, which had not been specifically mentioned in the *Cardinal Principles of Secondary Education,* now became objectives of the secondary school curriculum.

In 1971 the Northern California Program Development Center proposed 18 general goals (objectives) for secondary education, which are shown in Figure 4-7. In addition to the overlap of several goals found in the *Imperative Needs of Youth*, there are several new goals. Most of these are attitudinal in nature and include items such as "Help students develop pride in their work and a feeling of selfworth," and "Develop a desire for learning now and in the future."

Over the decades the public has expected the secondary schools to address more and more concerns that were originally considered as family, church, or community responsibilities. It is significant that vocational education, although listed in all of the sets of objectives mentioned here, was at one time considered to be a responsibility of the labor community. Until 1917, relatively few locally supported

vocational education programs existed in this country. At that time the public felt that young persons should learn occupations on the job because public schools were designed primarily for academic learning. This shows how the public perception of educational objectives can and has influenced the curricula of our schools.

National objectives need not be confined to secondary education. Postsecondary education, private school education, correctional education and rehabilitation education will all have objectives that differ somewhat from those of the public school. An example of the broad range of objectives for Rehabilitation Education is shown in Figure 4-8. Note that the list includes a number of items concerned with human relations.

Vocational Education Objectives

The educational objectives for different levels and types of schools are very broad in scope. Teachers need to focus their objectives for vocational and/or technical education in a more specific way.

The words *vocational* and *technical* are similar in meaning; however, vocational education is broader and includes training for any type of employment below the baccalaureate degree level. *Technical Education* refers specifically to occupational training that is more mental and less psychomotor in nature. For example, electronics technology involves a great deal of mental application and a lesser amount of psychomotor application, so it is called technical. To avoid confusion in terminology the term *vocational education* will be used throughout this publication, with the assumption that all technical programs lead to vocational goals.

Objectives, based upon the philosophy of vocational education, identify areas which would be addressed in all types of vocational education programs, including secondary, postsecondary, private school, technical institute, apprenticeship and other settings. The objectives for vocational education, as identified by the American Vocational Association, are shown in Figure 4-9. Note that objective Number 1 deals with occupational skills training.

The other eight objectives are concerned with preparing an individual for life. In this sense the national education objectives and vocational education objectives for secondary education have a number of similarities.

School Objectives

At the school level, objectives are based upon the school philosophy. Often the philosophy and objectives are listed together. A comprehensive high school will have different objectives for all of the programs, courses, and services provided. This list of objectives may be placed in the Introduction under "school" or on a separate page. An example of school objectives is shown in Figure 4-10.

---

1. **OCCUPATIONAL SKILLS AND KNOWLEDGE**
   To develop specific skills and related knowledge associated with an occupation.
2. **LABOR ECONOMICS**
   To develop an understanding of labor and management.
3. **JOB ATTITUDES AND APPRECIATION**
   To develop pride in work and an appreciation of craftsmanship.
4. **SAFETY**
   To develop occupational safety habits and understandings.
5. **RELATIONSHIP WITH OTHERS**
   To develop ability to cooperate with other workers in the occupation involved.
6. **INITIATIVE AND RESPONSIBILITY**
   To develop individual initiative and responsibility as a worker.
7. **PROBLEM SOLVING**
   To develop ability to solve problems.
8. **LEADERSHIP**
   To stimulate the development of leadership qualities.
9. **SELF-RELIANCE**
   To foster the development of self-reliance.

Note: From *Objectives of Vocational Education*, American Vocational Association, Alexandria, VA, 1979.

Figure 4-9. Objectives of Vocational Education

---

1. To develop and/or restore individuals to the fullest physical, mental, social, vocational and economic usefulness of which they are capable.
2. To enable individuals to accept their physical and/or mental limitations and to build on their remaining abilities.
3. To aid in the strengthening of the character of individuals through the development of sound moral values, among which are tolerance, respect of law and order, love of country, and appreciation of the cultural and aesthetic aspects of life.
4. To teach individuals to develop attitudes that will aid them in coping with personal and vocational situations that confront them.
5. To teach individuals to develop respect for other persons and their property, and to teach them to be able to live and work cooperatively with others.
6. To provide the opportunity for individuals to obtain additional academic skills to further their vocational and personal skills.
7. To provide individuals with sufficient salable occupational skills and related knowledge along with personal and social skills so that they can gain competitive employment at the entry level.
8. To teach individuals safety standards enabling them to recognize work hazards.
9. To teach individuals to develop pride in their work and their chosen occupation.

Note: From Woodrow Wilson Rehabilitation Center, Fishersville, VA, 1984.

Figure 4-8. Objectives for Rehabilitation Education.

The objectives are:
1. To prepare students for job entry level skills and/or for further education.
2. To evaluate and promote the students on the basis of their achievement.
3. To create an environment which will attract and motivate students.
4. To be responsive to the community in preparing students to meet the vocational needs of the community and encourage the community to be responsive to the school by support and job offerings.
5. To foster good safety attitudes and habits.
6. To develop a sense of pride and self-worth in students.
7. To develop responsibility and dependability in students.
8. To provide adequate facilities and equipment for good instructional programs.
9. To continually evaluate the program and keep up-to-date instruction.
10. To make training available to adult students through night programs.
11. To communicate our program offerings to the high schools and be responsive to the needs of their students.
12. To develop standards of behavior which would enable one to become a responsible citizen in society.

*Smyth County Vocational Center, Marion, VA.

Figure 4-10. Objectives of Vocational School.

OBJECTIVES

Students should have the opportunity to:

1. develop their maximum intellectual potentials.
   How attained:

1. All academic subjects	5. Media center
2. Forensics	6. Study hall
3. Special education	7. Guidance
4. Assemblies	8. Debate

2. realize the importance of mental, physical, and emotional health.
   How attained:

1. Physical education classes	6. Health services
2. Consumer and homemaking classes	7. Athletic program
	8. Band
3. Biology	9. Individual counseling
4. Cafeteria	10. Special Olympics
5. Health education	

3. develop skill and to acquire knowledge for pursuing further education and/or for entering the world of work.
   How attained:

1. Business education	7. Vocational programs
2. Driver education	8. Adult education
3. Consumer and homemaking classes	9. Art
	10. Career math
4. Marketing education	11. Science classes
5. VICA club	12. Field trips
6. Mechanical drawing	

4. provide opportunities conducive to social adjustment and growth.
   How attained:

1. Student counseling	7. Assembly programs
2. Clubs	8. Media center
3. Vocational education	9. Family living classes
4. Driver education	10. Guidance department
5. Social studies class	11. Foreign language
6. Special education	

5. gain worthwhile attitudes that result in responsible citizenship.
   How attained:

1. Government	3. Consumer and homemaking education
2. World history	

6. participate actively in school activities.
   How attained:

1. Band	9. School paper
2. Art	10. Literary magazine
3. Chorus	11. Athletics
4. Dramatics	12. Clubs
5. English classes	13. Science fair
6. Forensics	14. County and district contests
7. Assemblies	
8. Yearbook	15. Debates

7. discover in selves a sense of individual worth and dignity.
   How attained:

1. All academic subjects	5. Special education
2. Individual counseling	6. Adult education
3. Clubs	7. Special Olympics
4. Athletics	

8. engage in creative activities and develop an appreciation of beauty.
   How attained:

1. Art	6. Media center
2. Dramatics	7. English classes
3. Band	8. Forensics
4. Chorus	9. Literary magazine
5. Consumer and homemaking classes	10. Theatrical trips

Figure 4-11. Objectives for Grundy Senior High School.

Comprehensive high school objectives are generally wide in scope. Some school personnel will write general objectives followed by the ways in which these objectives will be attained. A set of school objectives organized in this manner is included in Figure 4-11.

Program Course Objectives

Chapter 2 indicates that the first breakdown of the occupational analysis is a list of broad objectives for a ***program*** or ***course***. For sake of clarity the term ***course objective*** will be used throughout this section.

Begin by listing from 15 to 25 broad objectives for the specific course. This list should not be overly long because each broad objective will cover a rather large area of instruction. State all objectives in terms of expected student behavior. Think about how a student will gain in knowledge, skill, and attitude throughout the course. The listing will help teachers to define how much content can be addressed with students during the time allotted and in the facilities available.

When satisfied with the broad objectives as completed in the analysis, simply utilize that list and place it in the curriculum guide at this point. An example of broad objectives for a course in auto mechanics appears in Figure 4-12.

The overall purpose of this course in auto mechanics will be met if the student will realize the following objectives:

1. Gain knowledge and skill in the use of hand tools, test equipment and diagnostic equipment.
2. Gain knowledge and skill in the repair and service of the automobile engine.
3. Gain knowledge and skill in maintenance of the lubrication system of the automobile engine.
4. Gain knowledge and skill in the service and repair of the engine ignition system.
5. Gain knowledge and skill in the service and repair of the engine fuel system.
6. Gain knowledge and skill in the service and repair of the engine cooling system.
7. Gain knowledge and skill in computer controls.
8. Gain knowledge and skill in the repair of the manual shift transmission.
9. Gain knowledge and skill in the repair of the automatic transmission.
10. Gain knowledge and skill in the repair of the rear axle assembly.
11. Gain knowledge and skill in the service and repair of the automotive brake system.
12. Gain knowledge and skill in the service and repair of the automotive electrical system.
13. Gain knowledge and skill in the service and repair of the automobile air conditioning system.
14. Gain knowledge and skill in the service and repair of the front end and steering.
15. Gain knowledge of the employment conditions in auto mechanics.
16. Develop safe work habits.
17. Develop a high standard of craftsmanship.
18. Develop qualities of self-reliance, dependability and cooperation.
19. Gain an appreciation of the engineering involved in the manufacture of the modern automobile.

Figure 4-12. Broad Objectives for a Course in Auto Mechanics.

Note that the first 14 objectives are technical, dealing specifically with skills in auto mechanics. The last four objectives are nontechnical in the sense that they do not deal with occupational skill development. Note that these objectives are very broad in scope and are not necessarily measurable as will be the case for performance objectives to be discussed in later chapters.

Clarification of Objectives

The last step in completing the objectives section is to clarify each objective in terms of specific student objectives in the three domains of learning: cognitive, psychomotor, and affective.

The cognitive domain of learning includes all learning activities which are mental in nature. Reading, writing, listening with understanding, and reading prints and diagrams are all common forms of cognitive learning.

The psychomotor domain of learning is concerned with the development of manipulative skill with mind, hands and body. The tasks that students do as work assignments in the occupational laboratory are primarily psychomotor. Although some mental (cognitive) application is needed in order to understand the nature of the task, the work is done primarily as a physical activity.

The affective domain of learning is concerned with attitudes, appreciation, ethics, sensitivity, feelings, values and interests. For example, students who are developing a safety consciousness in the laboratory, as opposed to simply following posted safety rules, are developing in the affective domain.

For each of the broad objectives, think of the student outcomes that hopefully will be achieved in each of the three domains of learning. Write these down, following each objective with the (a) cognitive outcomes, (b) psychomotor outcomes, and (c) affective outcomes. This broad approach, called *Bloom's Taxonomy,* is not to be confused with performance objectives. An example of the first six broad auto mechanics objectives found in Figure 4-12, broken down into student outcomes for these domains of learning, is shown in Appendix 4B. This clarification of objectives will direct teachers to think very specifically about what learning outcomes students should accomplish in a course.

OCCUPATIONAL DESCRIPTION

The next step in developing the preliminaries for a curriculum guide is to describe the nature of the occupational areas which are to be taught. In one page or less, describe what the worker does, the working conditions, qualifications, and any other information that will help students understand the true nature of the occupation.

Next, it will be necessary to list the various job titles and Dictionary of Occupational Titles (DOT) numbers for which students may become qualified in a course. Some students are able to progress further than others and it is the teacher's job to determine the competencies which a student should attain in order to qualify for an entry level position in a

specific occupation. For example, note in Figure 4-13 the state course codes for three courses which make up Auto Mechanics I, II and III. Also listed are the DOT numbers for a variety of *"spin-off"* jobs requiring varying degrees of ability, which may be available to automotive mechanics students.

Name of Program	State Course Code	Required Courses for the Program
Auto Mechanics	8506	Auto Mechanics I
	8507	Auto Mechanics II
	8508	Auto Mechanics III

DOT Number			DOT Job Titles
620	281	-018	Automotive Maintenance
620	281	-026	Brake Repairer
620	281	-030	Bus Inspector
620	281	-034	Carburetor Mechanic
620	281	-038	Front-End Mechanic
620	281	-042	Logging-Equipment Mechanic
620	281	-046	Maintenance Mechanic
620	281	-050	Mechanic, Industrial Truck
620	281	-054	Motorcycle Repairer
620	281	-058	Tractor Mechanic
620	281	-062	Transmission Mechanic
620	281	-066	Tune-Up Mechanic
620	281	-070	Vehicle Fuel Systems Converter
610	364	-010	Squeak, Rattle, and Leak Repairer
620	381	-010	Automobile-Radiator Mechanic
620	381	-018	Mechanical—Unit Repairer
620	381	-022	Repairer, Heavy
620	384	-010	Motorcycle Tester
620	584	-010	Spring-Repairer Helper, Hand
620	664	-010	Construction Equipment—Mechanic Helper
620	664	-014	Maintenance Mechanic Helper
620	682	-010	Brake-Drum Lathe Operator
620	684	-010	Automobile Wrecker
620	684	-014	Automobile-Mechanic Helper
620	684	-018	Brake Adjuster
620	684	-022	Clutch Rebuilder
620	684	-034	Used Car Renovator
807	664	-010	Muffler Installer

Figure 4-13. Automotive Spin-off Jobs with DOT Numbers.

Obviously the student who, after some effort, learns to install mufflers, change tires, install batteries, etc., will have developed skill in fewer tasks than the student who has mastered all the competencies required by the skilled automotive mechanic. Nevertheless, this student is employable.

Some DOT classifications for welding might be:
    819.687.014 Welder helper
    819.684.010 Production line welder
    819.384.010 Combination welder
    816.464.010 Hand thermal cutter
    813.684.010 Brazer assembler
    811.684.010 Gas welder
    810.684.010 Tack welder
    816.364.010 Arc welder

An example of the Occupational Description for Related Areas of Employment for a printing curriculum guide is shown in Figure 4-14.

OCCUPATIONAL DESCRIPTION

Printing is an art, a leading industry, and one of our chief means of communication. It provides employment for more than one million workers in a wide variety of occupations. Although these occupations are found principally in the printing, publishing, and allied industries, they are also found in government agencies and in private firms that do their own printing, such as banks, insurance companies, and manufacturers of paper products and containers. The main occupations are:

Phototypesetting machine operator	DOT 650.582
Lithographic artist	DOT 972.281
Cameraman	DOT 972.382
Stripper	DOT 971.381
Platemaker	DOT 972.781
Lithographic pressman	DOT 651.782
Bookbinder	DOT 977.781

RELATED AREAS OF EMPLOYMENT

Occupations in the pulp and paper products area are:

Chipperman	DOT 668.885
Digester operator	DOT 532.782
Beater engineer	DOT 530.782
Paper machine operator	DOT 539.782
Supercalender operator	DOT 534.782
Paper sorter and counter	DOT 649.687
Envelope machine operator	DOT 641.885
Corrugator operator	DOT 643.782
Die maker	DOT 739.381

Figure 4-14. Occupational Description and Related Areas of Employment.

RESOURCE MATERIAL

The selection of curriculum and audiovisual materials was discussed in the previous chapter. It is essential that teachers build a library of both print and audiovisual materials to work from to assemble the curriculum guide. Such materials include: (a) textbooks, (b) parts guides, (c) collision manuals, (d) flat rate manuals, (e) curriculum guides from state departments of education, industry, and local sources, (f) magazines, (g) transparencies, (h) movies, (i) video tapes, (j) film strips, (k) slide-tapes, and (l) a host of educational and industry developed materials.

The longer an *incumbent* worker is on the job, the more habitual the work becomes. Beginning teachers will need printed materials to work from when developing lesson plans and other instructional materials because it becomes difficult after many years of working on the job to remember the exact steps and many key points which relate to each step. It is essential that teachers refresh their memory by studying and working from resource material; otherwise, students may not be taught important information and skills.

As a teacher builds up a collection of these materials, fit new segments into the curriculum guide to improve missing or weak areas. Students are generally motivated by audiovisual presentations. Place acquired audiovisuals in the curriculum guide and incorporate them with lesson plans.

Teachers must be familiar with each step of every demonstration and information lesson and be sure they are accurate. Check with resource materials to be sure that lesson content is correct in every detail.

An example of a resource listing for cosmetology as identified by the Virginia Department of Education is shown in Appendix 4C.

UNIT TITLES

The unit titles for a course should have been completed during the occupational analysis (see Chapter 2). Units are major divisions in the course. Each unit title listed here will later be developed into a complete unit guide (see Chapters 6, 7, 8, and 9). If unit titles listed in the analysis are accurate, place the information in the curriculum guide at this point. An example of the units for a course in Electricity follows in Figure 4-15.

1st Year
Unit 1.   Orientation
Unit 2.   Nature of Electricity
Unit 3.   Direct Current Resistive Circuits
Unit 4.   Sources of Electricity
Unit 5.   Magnetism and Electromagnetism
Unit 6.   Alternating Current
Unit 7.   Electric Motors
Unit 8.   Transformers and Rectifiers
Unit 9.   Meters
Unit 10. Residential Wiring I

2nd Year
Unit 11. Orientation and Review
Unit 12. Residential Wiring II
Unit 13. Industrial and Commercial Wiring
Unit 14. Residential, Industrial and Commercial Lighting
Unit 15. Appliance Installation and Repair
Unit 16. Electrical Troubleshooting and Maintenance
Unit 17. Electric Heating
Unit 18. Wiring for Motors

Figure 4-15. Unit Titles for a Course in Industrial Electricity at Russell County (VA) Vocational Center.

PROGRAM/COURSE OUTLINE

The school administration generally requires an outline of each program or course to be kept on file in the main office. If teachers have performed the occupational analysis and have completed the preliminaries, there should be little difficulty in developing an outline of subject matter. Under each unit title list the major areas of instruction to include in the unit guides for an occupational curriculum.

The administration may provide teachers with a course outline that was used by a previous teacher and ask for it to be reviewed and perhaps modified if necessary. If teachers are starting a new program, an initial outline will need to be developed. Use textbooks and resource materials at hand as well as information provided by the advisory committee. The course outline becomes a quasi-legal document which defines what content will be covered in a course. Teachers should avoid deviating from the course outline without first consulting with the administration. Always double-check that course outlines are based upon the objectives, units, task lists, lesson titles and other materials developed in the analysis. An example of a course outline in industrial electricity based upon the unit titles from Figure 4-15 is shown in Appendix 4D.

BUILDING TRADES
COMPETENCY PROFILE

Instructor: _____

Student: _____
                Last   First   Middle

School: CHS HHS LHS   Grade: 9 10 11 12 PG   Student Number: _____

SPECIFIC JOB COMPETENCIES

Directions: Evaluate the trainee using the rating scale below and check the appropriate number to indicate the degree of competency achieved. The numerical ratings of 4, 3, 2, 1 and 0 are not intended to represent the traditional school grading system of A, B, C, D, and F. The descriptions associated with each of the numbers focus on level of student performance for each of the tasks listed below.

Rating Scale:
- 4 — Skilled — can perform independently with no additional training.
- 3 — Moderately Skilled — has performed independently during training program, limited additional training may be required.
- 2 — Limited Practice — has practiced during training program, additional training is required to develop skill.
- 1 — Exposure Only — general information provided with no practice time, close supervision needed and additional training required.
- 0 — No Exposure — no information nor practice provided during training program, complete training required.

Date [4][3][2][1][0] 1. Orientation and Safety
- 1-1 Demonstrate the ability to work safely
- 1-2 Demonstrate the ability to keep a clean, orderly and safe work area
- 1-3 Operate a fire extinguisher
- 1-4 Demonstrate the safe use of hand and power equipment
- 1-5 Complete a safety test
- 1-6 _____

Date [4][3][2][1][0] 2. Plumbing
- 2-1 Identify steel and copper pipe and fittings
- 2-2 Cut steel pipe with pipe cutters
- 2-3 Ream steel pipe
- 2-4 Thread steel pipe
- 2-5 Make a 90-degree bend in copper tubing
- 2-6 Identify plastic pipe fittings
- 2-7 Install PVC fittings on pipe
- 2-8 Install insert fitting in PVC pipe
- 2-9 Drain, waste and vent pipe
- 2-10 Make a cast iron pipe joint
- 2-11 Discuss pipe joints, angle & flow
- 2-12 Install a fitting on steel pipe
- 2-13 _____

Date [4][3][2][1][0] 3. Carpentry
- 3-1 Read plans and sketches
- 3-2 Identify materials
- 3-3 Identify components of wall layout
- 3-4 Lay out a wall
- 3-5 Identify types of framing joints
- 3-6 Construct a butt joint
- 3-7 Construct building joints
- 3-8 Identify types of framing
- 3-9 Frame a floor
- 3-10 Lay subflooring
- 3-11 Frame a wall
- 3-12 Frame a ceiling
- 3-13 Frame a roof
- 3-14 Lay roof sub-covering
- 3-15 Lay composition shingles
- 3-16 Lay wood shingles
- 3-17 Lay sheet metal roofing
- 3-18 Identify types of exterior wall covering
- 3-19 Apply exterior siding
- 3-20 Identify types of exterior trim
- 3-21 Construct open cornice
- 3-22 Construct closed cornice
- 3-23 Identify types of hardware
- 3-24 Identify types of doors and windows
- 3-25 Hang a door
- 3-26 Hang a window
- 3-27 Identify types of ceiling tile and wall paneling
- 3-28 Install ceiling tile
- 3-29 Install wall paneling
- 3-30 Select proper insulation and drywall
- 3-31 Install insulation
- 3-32 Install sheetrock
- 3-33 _____

Date [4][3][2][1][0] 4. Electricity
- 4-1 Read pointer dial electric meter
- 4-2 Demonstrate electrical safety
- 4-3 Identify electrical tools and materials
- 4-4 Select proper electrical wiring procedure
- 4-5 Install electrical boxes
- 4-6 Install cable in boxes
- 4-7 Install duples receptacles
- 4-8 Install single pole switch
- 4-9 Install 3-way switch
- 4-10 Plan a wiring layout
- 4-11 Draw a wiring plan
- 4-12 _____

Date [4][3][2][1][0] 5. Masonry
- 5-1 Identify masonry tools and equipment
- 5-2 Demonstrate masonry safety
- 5-3 Identify masonry materials
- 5-4 Prepare and apply mortar
- 5-5 Mix mortar by hand
- 5-6 Mix mortar with power mixer
- 5-7 Supply a mortar stand with mortar
- 5-8 Spread mortar
- 5-9 Construct masonry walls
- 5-10 Lay a 4'' corner lead
- 5-11 Lay a 4'' wall

_____   _____   _____
School Year   Instructor Signature   Date

_____   _____   _____
School Year   Instructor Signature   Date

_____   _____   _____
School Year   Instructor Signature   Date

COMPETENCY LIST

The uses and various formats for the competency list (also called task list) are discussed in detail in Chapter 5. Teachers may not have completed this list when they are writing the preliminaries for the curriculum guide; however, it should be located in this section when completed because it must precede the unit guides. Teachers who have done a careful analysis of their occupation as described in Chapter 2 will find the task breakdown will be the basis for the competency list. Decide if it is necessary to add, delete, combine, or break up any competencies, then place the list in the format which has been approved by the administration. An example of a competency list for building trades is shown in Figure 4-16.

GENERAL SAFETY AND CONDUCT RULES

The general safety rules that will be followed throughout the course should be explained to students initially before they start doing work in the laboratory. This is essential to protect students as well as to minimize problems of teacher liability. After explaining the general safety rules, have each student sign and date a copy of the rules. Co-sign the sheet and keep it on file. Post a copy of the general safety rules on the bulletin board. Teach detailed specific safety rules in the units as progress is made through the course. A complete explanation of safety responsibilities is contained in Chapter 10.

General laboratory conduct rules should also be included in this section; however, it is preferable to place these rules on a separate sheet. Avoid listing too many rules. Combine them so that a list of no more than 20 to 25 rules is developed. Follow the same procedure as discussed for safety rules.

Administrators, educators, officials and others will probably check to see that safety and general laboratory conduct rules are included in the curriculum guide. Furthermore, teachers have an ethical and legal responsibility to present and enforce these rules. Examples of general safety and general laboratory conduct rules are shown in Figures 4-17 and 4-18 and Chapter 10.

SUMMARY

In a curriculum guide the preliminaries set the stage for the unit guide content which follows. This first section enables teachers to plan where they are going. Among it's uses, the preliminaries aid administrators, program evaluators, and other interested persons to become oriented to the program before attempting to examine the actual content.

The typical preliminaries section of the curriculum guide contains (a) Table of Contents, (b) Introduction, (c) School Philosophy, (d) Vocational Education Philosophy, (e) Program/Course Philosophy, (f) Objectives, (g) Occupational Description, (h) Related Areas of Employment, (i) Resource Materials, (j) Unit Titles, (k) Program/Course Outline, (l) Competency List, and (m) General Safety and Conduct Rules.

GENERAL SAFETY PRECAUTIONS

1. Keep work area in a neat and orderly condition.
2. Keep all tools and equipment clean.
3. Store creepers off the floor.
4. Use air hoses safely. Compressed air is dangerous.
5. Replace caps on gasoline cans and store them in a safe place.
6. Put all oily rags in receptacles provided for this purpose.
7. Remove watches or rings while working.
8. Familiarize yourself with location of fire extinguishers.
9. Jacks are for lifting only. After vehicle has been jacked up, place safety stands under frame or suspension.
10. Always check brakes before moving any vehicle.
11. Report all accidents and unsafe conditions.
12. Avoid closing doors or hoods on electrical cords.
13. Avoid standing in front of an automobile with the engine running.
14. Do prohibit individuals from sitting in a vehicle while someone else is working on the vehicle.
15. Do operate any tools or pieces of equipment only after they have been demonstrated by the teacher.
16. Keep your legs straight when lying on a creeper; always lie on your back.
17. Protect your hands by using the right tool for the job.
18. Listen to your safety conscience; it will usually warn you of danger.
19. Everyone must wear safety glasses.

Figure 4-17. General Safety Precautions for Auto Mechanics at Grayson County (VA) Vocational Center.

AUTO MECHANICS GENERAL POLICIES AND CONDUCT

1. Each student must have school insurance or be covered by a home policy in order to enroll in this course.
2. Each student shall be in a clean uniform once a week and more often if needed.
3. Students are required to take notes, and file handouts for future reference.
4. Students must have permission from the instructor to leave the classroom or shop area at any time.
5. The students will perform assigned duties with an attitude of responsibility, striving to do jobs to the best of their ability.
6. No foul language may be used at any time.
7. Horseplay in the shop or classroom will not be tolerated at any time.
8. The instructor's office is off limits to all students.
9. The parts cars will be used for securing parts only. No more than one student may go after parts.
10. Any student who damages the parts cars will be grounded.
11. Students' parts will be billed at cost on personal cars.
12. A daily grade will be given based on all rules, policies and procedures, shop ability, and classroom participation.
13. Students must attend classes regularly in order to pass the course.
14. Field trips are a part of the course. Any misconduct on a field trip by a student will result in a cut in grade.
15. All work missed for any reason must be made up.
16. No students' cars may be parked in the auto mechanics area unless scheduled for work on that day.
17. Any student desiring work on a personal car must make arrangements two days in advance.
18. Fries High School students must have a permission slip signed by the principal to bring car.
19. Only student car owners may occupy a car. No passengers will be allowed.
20. Students without permission slips will not be admitted to class, but must check in at the office.
21. A constant cleanup will be done in the laboratory and classroom.
22. A progress chart will be kept on each student's job participation.
23. In the event of a fire drill, students will stop work IMMEDIATELY and will exit from the building in a planned and orderly manner.

Figure 4-18. General Rules of Conduct for Auto Mechanics Laboratory at Grayson County (VA) Vocational Center.

APPENDIX 4A

An Example of an Introduction for a Drafting Curriculum Guide at Arnold R. Burton Vocational-Technical School, Salem, VA.

INTRODUCTION

Type of Community

The "Greater Roanoke Valley," located in southwestern Virginia, consists of Roanoke County, Roanoke City, and Salem City with a combined total population of approximately 190,000. Three separate public school divisions provide education for approximately 43,000 students, of which 27,000 are enrolled in seven high schools, six intermediate schools, twenty-three elementary schools and two special education centers. In addition, about 700 area students are enrolled in parochial schools. Roanoke College, Hollins College and Virginia Western Community College serve the needs of many students who wish to continue their education beyond high school.

Employment opportunities are good in the Valley. The Norfolk Southern Railroad maintains general offices and shops in the city of Roanoke. Other industries include General Electric Company, Ingersoll Rand Co., steel fabricators, garment manufacturers, power tool and hand tool manufacturers, lumber industries, distribution centers, and a large number of smaller trade establishments. Agriculture is practiced extensively in the valley and there are several large orchards.

There are several public libraries, three newspapers, four radio stations, and four television stations. Several churches conduct kindergarten programs open to any resident in the community.

Type of School

The Arnold R. Burton Vocational-Technical School serves the entire population of Roanoke County. The 425 students attending the Center are bused to and from four county high schools each morning and afternoon. There are three buildings at the Center; one houses regular academic classrooms, offices, library, cosmetology, child-care, health assistant, and data processing. One laboratory building houses machine shop, drafting, carpentry, applied physics, power mechanics, masonry, and auto body repair departments. The third building houses horticulture, auto mechanics, electronics, electricity, commercial arts, food occupations, cafeteria and classrooms.

An active vocational advisory council works cooperatively with the school. Members of this council are volunteers from local industries who periodically evaluate the program of the school and make suggestions for the improvement and upgrading of the vocational programs. Once a year the school sponsors an open house. Potential employers are invited to visit the school, talk to the students and observe them at work. Parents and patrons are invited to an informal tour of the school.

The overall purpose of Arnold R. Burton Vocational-Technical School is to produce well-rounded citizens who are prepared to take their place in a democratic society. This is accomplished by (a) teaching salable skills, and (b) aiding students in developing a sense of responsibility for effective citizenship, good moral character, and an appreciation of worthy life values.

Philosophy and Objectives of Arnold R. Burton Vocational-Technical School

This school, in the light of its distinctive position as a secondary school for young people who are not, for the most part, college bound, accepts the idea that, for the attainment of future goals of the majority of its students, courses in liberal arts education and vocational education are both essential and compatible. We believe that our purpose in helping students to become effective, well-rounded individuals and constructive, contributing citizens, compels us to consider the preparation of the student for living, through our academic program as well as for earning a living, through our vocational program. We believe that our purpose should involve developing the entire individual as well as teaching a salable skill.

In order to implement the philosophy of the school, it is the desire of the faculty and staff to continue to aid the student in developing specific attitudes, knowledge and skills. We believe it our duty to help instill in the student a sense of values, an awareness of responsibilities as an individual and as an American citizen, and an understanding of the problems and challenges of society today. We believe that we must prepare the student to become efficient in an occupation by teaching both the necessary and proper techniques of the profession and the values accompanying it—pride in good workmanship and satisfaction in work well done.

As specific objectives, we list the following:

A. Teaching Personnel
   1. To have thorough preparation in their respective fields of teaching
   2. To keep abreast of the latest developments in their fields
   3. To consider the practicality in subject matter taught as well as its value in other areas
   4. To consider the need for constant evaluation of methods and materials
B. Student Development
   1. To offer leadership training to students through SCA, FBLA and VICA, HERO, HOSA, TSA, and FFA
   2. To offer opportunities for cooperation and group endeavor through student organizations

Type of Students

The students at Arnold R. Burton Vocational-Technical School must be enrolled in Grades 10, 11, or 12 of a county high school. It is the goal of most enrollees, upon graduation, to seek and find employment in the immediate Roanoke Valley area or to continue their education. Students are bused to and from the school from their respective high schools. Seventy percent will pursue careers in their chosen vocation; fifteen percent of the students find that they do not have the aptitude or interest for a particular occupation. They will typically pursue careers in other fields. Typically, fifteen percent will pursue higher education.

Student activities include an active Vocational Industrial Club of America, Future Business Leaders of America, Student Council Association, Future Farmers of America, Health Occupations Students of America, Technology Students of America, and Home Economics Related Occupations Clubs. Membership in these clubs entitles students to participate in annual district and statewide contests.

Adult education classes are offered two nights a week, three hours per night for a total of four semesters over a two-year period. Adult students have the dual goals of upgrading their education and improving their vocational skills. Many adults are promoted to higher paid jobs upon completion of the course.

Length of Course

Drafting is a two-year course which consists of three hours per day, five days per week, for a total of 1080 hours. Adult classes operate for three hours per evening, two nights per week, for a total of 320 clock hours.

Course Level

This course in drafting is designed for students attending Arnold R. Burton Vocational-Technical School. It is desirable for a student to begin this course in the sophomore year and continue for two full years. A student may enroll in a cooperative program for the third year.

Course Prerequisites

Students applying for vocational drafting should have average academic ability, above average mechanical aptitude, and a good background in mathematics.

Purpose of Course

This course is designed to prepare students for entrance level employment in the drafting field. Graduates may accept such positions as layout drafters, detailers, checkers, and tracers. Graduate may specialize in a particular field of work such as mechanical, electrical, electronic, aeronautical, structural or architectural drafting.

Age Limitations

Students enrolling in this school should be at least 15 years old. They may, however, do post-graduate work during the daytime program until they reach the age of 20-1/2 years.

Equipment Available

Arnold R. Burton Vocational-Technical School has modern facilities and equipment. All drafting instruments, equipment and computer-aided drafting facilities are furnished by the school.

APPENDIX 4B

CLARIFICATION OF OBJECTIVES INTO COGNITIVE, PSYCHOMOTOR AND AFFECTIVE OUTCOMES

OBJECTIVE 1:

GAIN KNOWLEDGE AND SKILL IN THE USE OF HAND TOOLS, TEST EQUIPMENT AND DIAGNOSTIC EQUIPMENT.

THE STUDENT, AS A RESULT OF ACCOMPLISHING THIS OBJECTIVE, WILL UNDERSTAND: (cognitive)
A. Names and purposes of the common hand tools
B. Importance of test and diagnostic equipment

WILL BE ABLE TO: (psychomotor)
A. Select and use open-end wrenches, box-end wrenches, screwdrivers and pliers selected for faster and more accurate work
B. Select and use torque wrenches, hones, grinders, rules and gauges properly
C. Operate diagnostic equipment to determine what work is required
D. Operate test equipment to check the quality of work

WILL: (affective)
A. Work in a safe manner using the proper tools for each operation
B. Use the correct equipment for the job
C. Demonstrate a good attitude toward equipment care and maintenance

OBJECTIVE 2:

GAIN KNOWLEDGE AND SKILL IN THE REPAIR AND SERVICE OF THE AUTOMOBILE ENGINE.

THE STUDENT AS A RESULT OF ACCOMPLISHING THIS OBJECTIVE WILL UNDERSTAND:
A. The principle of the automobile engine
B. Types of engines
C. Types of valves
D. Materials in pistons
E. Materials used in block castings
F. Types of engine bearings
G. Types of cylinder sleeves
H. Different timing drives
I. Types of oil seals
J. Engine cycles
K. Types of crankshafts
L. Different valve trains

WILL BE ABLE TO:
A. Remove and replace cylinder heads
B. Reface valves
C. Taper valve stems
D. Grind stem ends
E. Grind valve seat
F. De-carbonize cylinder heads
G. Remove cylinder ridge
H. Hone cylinder bores
I. Remove and replace piston rings
J. Replace bearings and check clearance
K. Replace timing gears or chain
L. Replace camshaft bearings
M. Replace crankshaft bearings
N. Grind rocker arms
O. Grind valve lifters
P. Adjust valves
Q. Check crankshaft wear

WILL:
A. Practice cleanliness in engine repairs
B. Explain the importance of the engine to the total automobile
C. Work cooperatively with others

OBJECTIVE 3:

GAIN KNOWLEDGE AND SKILL IN MAINTENANCE OF THE LUBRICATION SYSTEM OF THE AUTOMOBILE ENGINE.

THE STUDENT AS A RESULT OF ACCOMPLISHING THIS OBJECTIVE WILL UNDERSTAND THE:
A. Various circuits of the lubrication system and their functions
B. Purpose of the oil pump
C. Purpose of the pressure relief valve
D. Various types of lubricating oil

WILL BE ABLE TO:
A. Overhaul oil pumps
B. Clean pressure relief valves
C. Clean oil galleries
D. Replace oil filters
E. Clean breathers
F. Replace oil lines

WILL:
A. Gain an appreciation of the research and labor involved in the manufacture of engine oil
B. Work safely with oil under high pressure
C. Recognize the need for using high quality products

OBJECTIVE 4:

GAIN KNOWLEDGE AND SKILL IN THE SERVICE AND REPAIR OF THE ENGINE IGNITION SYSTEM.

THE STUDENT AS A RESULT OF ACCOMPLISHING THIS OBJECTIVE WILL UNDERSTAND:
A. Basic electrical circuits
B. Construction of ignition coil
C. Types of ignition points
D. Purpose of condenser
E. Materials in cap and rotor
F. Function of distributor
G. Tune-up charts
H. Types of spark plugs

WILL BE ABLE TO:
A. Replace ignition switch
B. Test and replace ignition coil
C. Replace and adjust ignition points
D. Test and replace condenser
E. Test and replace cap and rotor
F. Overhaul distributor
G. Reset ignition timing
H. Clean and replace spark plugs

WILL:

A. Exercise care when working with a running machine
B. Understand the danger of working with high voltage
C. Work in a cooperative manner with other students
D. Develop self-reliance in accomplishing assigned tasks

OBJECTIVE 5:

GAIN KNOWLEDGE AND SKILL IN THE SERVICE AND REPAIR OF THE ENGINE FUEL SYSTEM.

THE STUDENT AS A RESULT OF ACCOMPLISHING THIS OBJECTIVE WILL UNDERSTAND:
A. Safety practices involved with gasoline tank repairs
B. Operation of a fuel pump
C. Circuits of carburetor
D. Importance of clean fuel lines
E. Materials used in air filters
F. Operation of choke thermostat
G. Safety involved in maintenance of exhaust system

WILL BE ABLE TO:
A. Remove and clean gasoline tank
B. Repair or replace fuel pump
C. Overhaul carburetors
D. Clean and repair fuel lines
E. Replace intake manifold gaskets
F. Clean or replace air filters
G. Repair or replace choke thermostats
H. Replace exhaust pipes and mufflers

WILL:
A. Appreciate the value of good leadership
B. Develop a proper safety attitude
C. Develop good work habits of cleanliness and orderliness

OBJECTIVE 6:

GAIN KNOWLEDGE AND SKILL IN THE SERVICE AND REPAIR OF THE ENGINE COOLING SYSTEM.

THE STUDENT AS A RESULT OF ACCOMPLISHING THIS OBJECTIVE WILL UNDERSTAND:
A. Types of antifreeze
B. Care of water pumps
C. Material used in radiator construction
D. Operation of automatic fan hubs.
E. Types of radiator hose
F. Types of thermostats
G. Pressure valves of radiator caps

WILL BE ABLE TO:
A. Clean engine water jacket
B. Replace water pumps
C. Clean and repair radiators
D. Replace automatic fan hubs
E. Check and replace radiator hose
F. Check and replace thermostat
G. Test radiator caps

WILL:
A. Use caution while working with hot radiator
B. Develop insight into the necessity of doing operations sequentially
C. Gain personal satisfaction from doing the best job

APPENDIX 4C

RESOURCE MATERIALS FOR A COSMETOLOGY PROGRAM

BOOKS

Ahorn, J. J. (1981). *West's textbook of cosmetology*. St. Paul, MN: West Publishing Company.

American Red Cross. (1975). *Standard first aid and safety*. New York: Doubleday and Company.

Business Education Service. (1984). *Recordkeeping: Task analysis*. Richmond: Virginia Department of Education.

Clairol, Inc. (1984). *Professional encyclopedia of haircolor*. Stanford, CT: Author.

Dalton, J. W. (1979). *The professional cosmetologist, 2nd edition*. St. Paul, MN: West Publishing Company.

Department of Labor, Employment, and Training Administration. (1989). *Directory of occupational titles, 4th edition*. Washington, DC: Author.

Franco, S., Moore, A. M., & Oakley, G. D. (1984). *The world of cosmetology*. New York: McGraw Hill Book Company.

Jackson, C. (1980). *Color me beautiful*. Washington, DC: Acropolis Books.

Keystone Publications. (1988). *Curriculum for cosmetology*. New York: Author.

Kibbe, C. V. (1985). *Standard textbook of cosmetology*. Bronx, NY: Milady Publishing Corporation.

Matrix Essentials. (1988). *Color education guide*. Solon, OH: Author.

Milady Publishing Company. (1987). *Lectures in hair structure and chemistry for cosmetology teachers*. New York, NY: Author.

Oklahoma Curriculum Instructional Materials Center. (1988). *Professional cosmetology practices*. Stillwater, OK: State Department of Vocational and Technical Education.

Pivot Point International. (1988). *Pivot Point continuing education*. Chicago, IL: Author.

Robert, H. J. (1987). *Robert's rules of order, newly revised*. Glenview, IL: Scott, Foresman and Company.

Ross, C. (1988). *The essentials of hair design*. Bronx, NY: Milady Publishing Corporation.

United States Department of Labor, Bureau of Labor Statistics. (1989). *Occupational outlook handbook*. Washington, DC: Author.

Virginia Department of Education, Trade and Industrial Education Service. (1984). *Trade and industrial education service area resource for cosmetology*. Richmond, VA: Author.

Virginia Department of Commerce. (1989). *State board of examiners of professional hairdressers rules and regulations*. Richmond, VA: Author.

Virginia Department of Education. (1984). *Advanced marketing planning for entrepreneurship—teacher's resource guide*. Richmond, VA: Author.

Virginia Polytechnic Institute & State University. (1987). *Virginia vital information education workshops*. Blacksburg, VA: Author.

Vocational Industrial Clubs of America. (1989). *Leadership Handbook for the Vocational Clubs of America*. Leesburg, VA: Author.

Vocational Industrial Clubs of America. (1989). *VICA United States skill olympics regulations*. Leesburg, VA: Author.

Warmke, R. F., & Wyllie, E. D. (1987). *Consumer economic problems, 9th edition*. Cincinnati, OH: Southwestern Publishing Company.

ADDRESSES OF AUDIOVISUALS SUPPLIERS

Clairol, Inc.
Professional Products Division
345 Park Avenue
New York, NY 10154

Keystone Publications, Inc.
1657 Broadway
New York, NY 10009

Mid-American Vocational Curriculum Consortium
1500 West Seventh Avenue
Stillwater, OK 74074-4364
(405) 377-2000 or 1-800-654-3988

Milady Publishing Corporation
3839 White Plains Road
Bronx, NY 10467

Prentice Hall Media
150 White Plains Road
Tarrytown, NY 10591

Director, Virginia VICA
Virginia Department of Education
P.O. Box 6Q
Richmond, VA 23216

FILMSTRIPS

Cosmetology and Hairdressing. Milady
For the Love of Hair. Milady
VICA, Going all the Way. State VICA
Scalp Treatment and Massage. Milady
One-Length Low Elevation Cut. Prentice Hall
Multi-level Cut. Prentice Hall
Finger-waving Techniques. Prentice Hall
Basic Hair Coloring Techniques. Clairol
Temporary Hair Coloring. Clairol
Semi-permanent Hair Coloring. Clairol
Permanent Hair Coloring. Clairol
Basic Lightening Techniques. Clairol
Sculptured Nails (Acrylic). Milady

TRANSPARENCY MASTERS

Personal Appearance. Keystone
Scalp Disorders (TM 4 & TM 5). Mid-America
Facial Shapes (TM 1 & TM 2). Mid-America
Facial Profiles (TM 3). Mid-America
Body Structures (TM 4). Mid-America
Parts of a Pin Curl (TM 1). Mid-America
Pin Curl Stems (TM 2). Mid-America
Bases Used in Forming Pin Curls (TM 4). Mid-America
Implements Used to Form Pin Curls (TM 5). Mid-America
Implements Used in Roller Sets (TM 1). Mid-America
Parts of a Roller Curl (TM 2). Mid-America
Equipment Used in Thermal Work (TM 1). Mid-America
Structures of the Hair (TM 1). Mid-America
Permanent Wave Wraps (TM 2). Mid-America
Types of Hairpieces (TM 1). Mid-America
Types of Massage Manipulations (TM 1). Mid-America
Implements and Equipment Used in Giving a Facial (TM 2). Mid-America
Bones of the Face and Head (TM 1). Mid-America
Muscles of the Face and Head. (TM 3) Mid-America
Implements Used for Temporary Hair Removal (TM 1). Mid-America
Parts of a Nail (TM 1). Mid-America
Bones of the Arm and Hand (TM 2). Mid-America
Nail Disorders (TM 5). Mid-America
Nail Diseases (TM 6). Mid-America
Common Shapes for Manicuring Women's Nails (TM 1). Mid-America
Common Shapes for Manicuring Men's Nails (TM 2). Mid-America
Implements and Equipment Used in Manicuring and Pedicuring (TM 3 & TM 4). Mid-America

SLIDES AND SLIDE TAPES

Wet-cut with Scissors. Milady
Basic Pin Curling. Milady
Comb Pressing Curly Hair. Milady

Curly Over-curly Hair. Milady
Human Hair. Milady
Chemical Relaxer. Milady
Tint-back to Natural Color. Milady
Massage Techniques for Relaxation and Facial Beauty. Milady
Facial Treatments—An Aid to Skin Beauty. Milady
The Health, Care, and Beauty of Skin. Milady
Makeup as a Fashionable Accessory with Emphasis on Color Coordination. Milady
The Art of Corrective Makeup. Milady

FILMS

Tailored Neckline. Milady

VIDEO CASSETTES

Styling for a New Look. Milady
Slow Waving for Varied Loveliness. Milady
Single Process Tint Application. Milady

APPENDIX 4D

COURSE OUTLINE FOR INDUSTRIAL ELECTRICITY AT RUSSELL COUNTY (VA) VOCATIONAL CENTER

GENERAL ELECTRICITY COURSE OUTLINE

I. Orientation
    A. Registration
    B. Introduction to course
    C. Employment opportunities
    D. School policy
    E. Grading system
    F. General shop rules and policies
    G. Shop safety rules

II. Nature of Electricity
    A. Electron theory
    B. Static and dynamic electricity
    C. Conductors and insulators
    D. Circuit components
    E. Safety
    F. Related math and blueprint

III. Direct Current Resistive Circuits
    A. Electrical symbols and schematic diagrams
    B. Series circuit
    C. Parallel circuit
    D. Meters
    E. Ohm's Law - Watt's Law
    F. Safety
    G. Related math and blueprint

IV. Source of Electricity
    A. Cells and batteries
    B. Thermoelectricity
    C. Photoelectricity
    D. Piezoelectricity
    E. Electromagnetic generators
    F. Safety
    G. Related math and blueprint

V. Magnetism and Electromagnetism
    A. Nature of magnets
    B. Magnetic theory
    C. Electromagnets
    D. Magnetic devices
    E. Safety
    F. Related math and blueprint

VI.   Alternating Current
        A. Characteristics of AC
        B. Single phase AC
        C. Three phase AC
        D. Alternating current circuits
        E. Inductance, capacitance, and impedance
        F. Safety
        G. Related math and blueprint

VII.   Electric Motors
        A. Principles of DC motors
        B. Types and characteristics of DC motors
        C. Principles of AC motors
        D. Types and characteristics of AC motors
        E. Safety
        F. Related math and blueprint

VIII.   Transformers and Rectifiers
        A. Theory of transformers
        B. Types and characteristics of transformers
        C. Single-phase transformers
        D. Three-phase transformers
        E. Autotransformers and regulators
        F. Rectifiers
        G. Safety
        H. Related math and blueprint

IX.   Meters
        A. Basic meter movement
        B. Basic meters
        C. Multimeter
        D. Special meters
        E. Safety
        F. Related math and blueprint

X.   Residential Wiring
        A. Underwriters and codes
        B. Identification of materials
        C. Basic devices and circuits
        D. Type and sizes of wire
        E. Safety
        F. Related math and blueprint
        G. Overcurrent devices
        H. Theory of grounding
        I. Service entrances
        J. Planning an installation
        K. Safety
        L. Related math and blueprint

XI.   Orientation and Review (2nd year)
        A. Registration
        B. School policy
        C. Safety rules
        D. Residential wiring review
        E. Related math and blueprint

XII.   Residential Wiring
        A. Adequate wiring
        B. Load requirements
        C. Remote control wiring
        D. Communications and alarms
        E. Safety
        F. Related math and blueprint

XIII.   Industrial and Commercial Wiring
        A. Identification of materials
        B. Armored cable wiring
        C. Rigid conduit wiring
        D. Thin-wall conduit wiring
        E. Flexible conduit
        F. Special circuits and devices
        G. Wire mold
        H. Safety
        I. Related math and blueprint

XIV.   Residential, Industrial, and Commercial Lighting
        A. Incandescent lighting
        B. Fluorescent lighting
        C. Mercury vapor lighting
        D. Neon lighting
        E. Safety
        F. Related math and blueprint

XV.   Appliance Installation and Repair
        A. Major appliances
        B. Small appliances
        C. Troubleshooting appliances
        D. Safety
        E. Related math and blueprint

XVI.   Electrical Troubleshooting and Maintenance
        A. Open circuits
        B. Short circuits
        C. Grounds
        D. General maintenance
        E. Safety
        F. Related math and blueprint

XVII.   Electric Heating
        A. Ceiling heat
        B. Baseboard and wall heat
        C. Electric furnace
        D. Heat pump
        E. Portable heaters
        F. Safety
        G. Related math and blueprint

XVIII. Wiring for Motors
        A. Single-phase motors
        B. Three-phase motors
        C. DC Motors
        D. Across the line controllers
        E. Resistance start controllers
        F. Autotransformer controllers
        G. General controllers
        H. Safety
        I. Related math and blueprint

Chapter 5

The Individualized Competency Record

by

K. Kurt Eschenmann, Associate Professor
Vocational Industrial Education
Virginia Tech
Blacksburg, Virginia

INTRODUCTION

Occupational teachers have many duties and responsibilities in addition to teaching. They are required to keep records, schedule trips, keep shop areas and machines clean, maintain and inventory tools and equipment, discipline students, calculate and assign grades plus many other duties. It should be obvious that teachers do a lot more than "just teach."

Much of what occupational teachers do is a continuation of applying their knowledge, skills, and occupational experience in their new roles as teachers. However, there are many new skills and practices to learn and apply in becoming an effective teacher.

This chapter is devoted to assisting occupational teachers in developing and using the individualized competency record (ICR). The individualized competency record is a modern version of the progress chart. It will be helpful in understanding the ICR if information is first presented about progress charts.

PROGRESS CHARTS

An important part of the occupational teacher's job is keeping records of student progress. There are many advantages in routinely recording student progress for both the occupational teacher and student. What appears to be added work is really a valuable aid to teaching. The following section examines the history of progress charts. The different types and methods of recording student performance are also discussed. Figure 5-1 lists many of the uses for progress charts.

Evolution and Uses of the Progress Chart

Progress charts have been used by occupational teachers for decades. It would be rare to visit a school laboratory

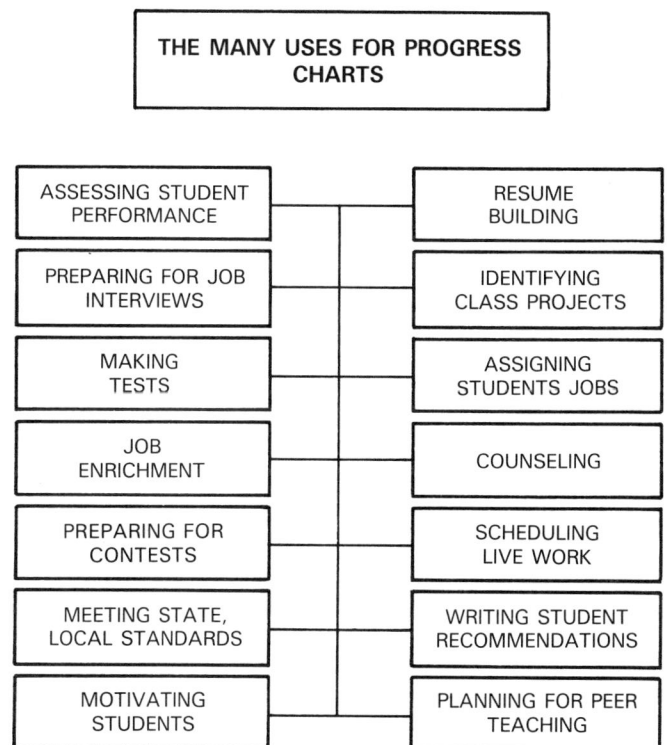

THE MANY USES FOR PROGRESS CHARTS

ASSESSING STUDENT PERFORMANCE	RESUME BUILDING
PREPARING FOR JOB INTERVIEWS	IDENTIFYING CLASS PROJECTS
MAKING TESTS	ASSIGNING STUDENTS JOBS
JOB ENRICHMENT	COUNSELING
PREPARING FOR CONTESTS	SCHEDULING LIVE WORK
MEETING STATE, LOCAL STANDARDS	WRITING STUDENT RECOMMENDATIONS
MOTIVATING STUDENTS	PLANNING FOR PEER TEACHING

Figure 5-1.

program and not see a posted progress chart. The typical chart has the students' names listed, along with competencies, projects, or activities. A blank progress chart is shown in Figure 5-2.

Because the progress chart proved to be an excellent aid to teaching, it was modified to meet individual needs. As a result, numerous versions can be found. Examples of different types of charts are shown on Figures 5-3 through 5-6.

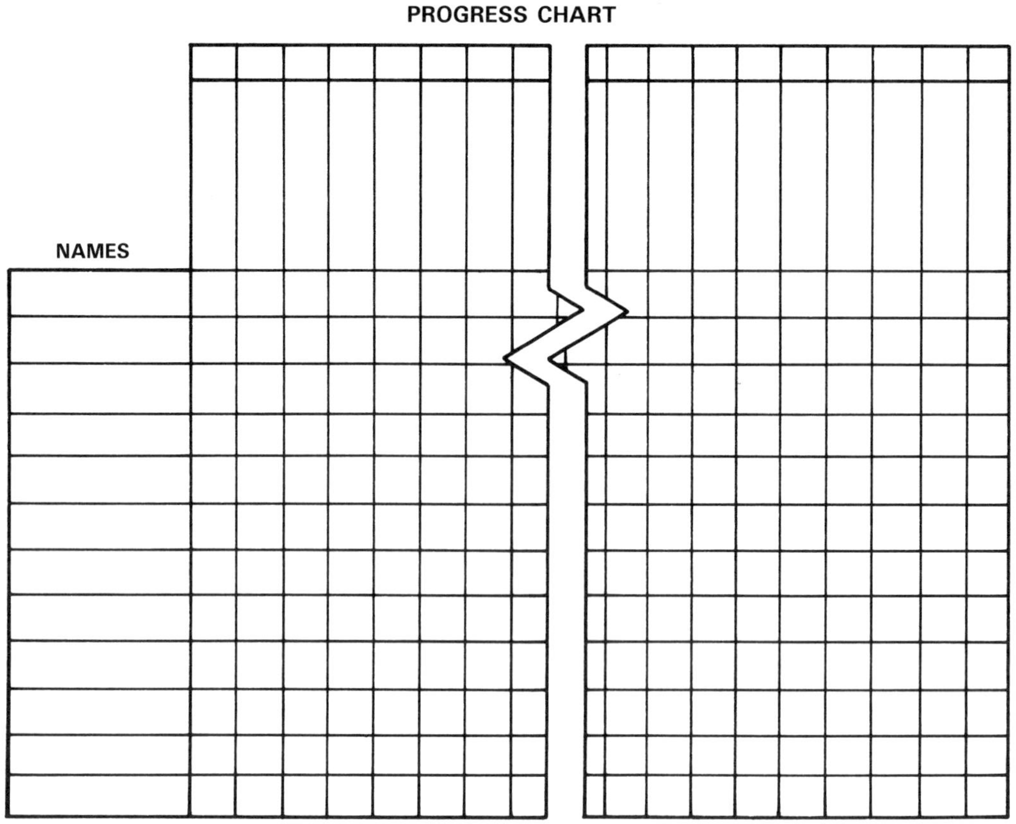

PROGRESS CHART

NAMES

Figure 5-2.

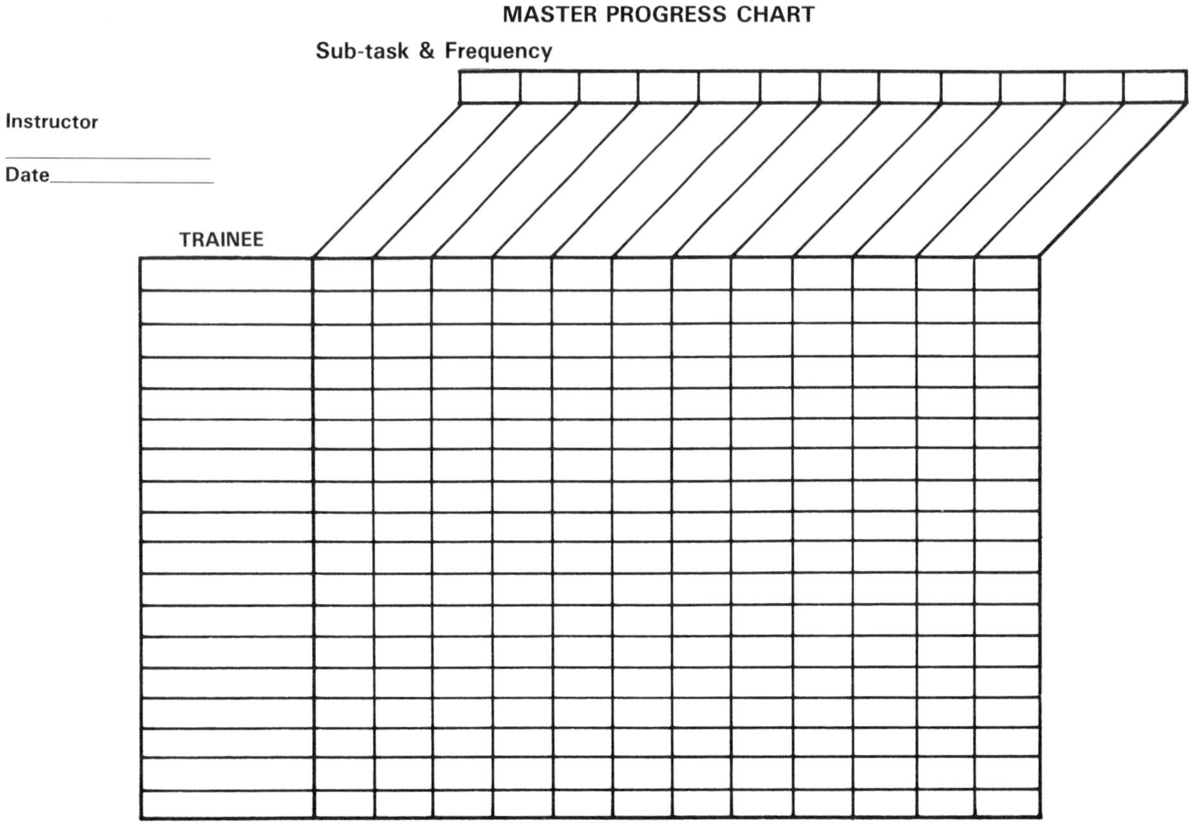

MASTER PROGRESS CHART

Sub-task & Frequency

Instructor

Date_____

TRAINEE

Figure 5-3.

WELDING PROGRESS CHART

MAJOR UNITS	JOBS SKILLS TO BE DEVELOPED
I. Metallic Arc Welding	1. Safety practices in Arc Welding
	2. Operate Arc Welding Equipment
A. Arc Welding Fundamentals	3. The Welding Circuit
	4. Welding Rod Classification
	5. Straight Polarity vs. Reverse
	6. Current setting & Angle of Electrodes
	7. Welding Symbols
	8. Parallel Stringer Beads E6012 Electrodes
	9. Start and Restart Continuous Beads E6012
	10. Single Pass Buildup E6012
	11. Single Pass Square Butt Joint (Closed)
	12. Open Square Butt Joint E6012
	13. Single Pass Lap Joint E6012
	14. Single Pass Fillet Weld E6012
	15. Weave Bead Buildup E6012
	16. Use Numbers 8, 9, 10, 11, 12, 13, 14, 15, 16, 17, with E6012.
	5. Beveled Butt Weld
	6. Outside Corner Weld E6012
	7. Numbers 1, 2, 3, 4, 5, 6, use E6010 and E7018
C. Vertical Position (64 clock hours)	1. Make Stringer Bead E6012
	2. Run Fillet Bead Up Motion
	3. Run Up Butt Weld "Weave Motion" E6012
	4. Down Stringer Beads With E6012
	5. Down Fillet Weld E6012
	6. Numbers 1, 2, 3, 4, 5, use E6010
D. Overhead Position (32 clock hours)	1. Stringer use E6012
	2. Fillet use E6012
	3. Butt weld use E6012
	4. Lapp Weld use E6012
	5. Corner Weld use E6012
	6. Vee Butt Weld use E6012
	7. Perform No. 1, 2, 3, 4, 5, 6, With E6010

Figure 5-4.

ELECTRICITY I	LAB HOURS					LECTURE HOURS				
	M	T	W	TH	F	M	T	W	TH	F
UNIT 1 HOURS_____ ORIENTATION										
1. School Policies										
2. General Shop Rules										
3. General Safety Rules										
4. Identify Tools										
UNIT 2 HOURS_____ BASIC SKILLS										
1. Use Multimeters										
2. Identify Resistor Color Code										
3. Build Series Circuit										
4. Build Parallel Circuit										
5. Explain Conductors										
UNIT 3 HOURS_____ CONNECTION OF CIRCUITS										
1. Make Splices										
2. Solder Wires										
3. Use Wire Nuts										
4. Use Crimp Sleeves										
5. Build a Bell Circuit										
6. Build Circuits, S, S2, S3 & S4										
7. Wire Bedroom										
8. Wire Bathroom										
9. Wire Kitchen										

Figure 5-5.

The use of progress charts increased because of their popularity among teachers. Other factors also promoted their acceptance. In some instances, State Departments of Education (SDE) officials saw their value and recommended that occupational teachers use them in their programs. One of the reasons behind this recommendation was to motivate students to complete assigned work promptly, thereby earning better grades.

School grades are used (a) by some employers to make hiring decisions, (b) by two-year and four-year colleges as an admission requirement, and (c) by other persons to determine an individual's capability for placement in other positions. Grades, however, do not always reveal what students can actually do on the job. The progress chart does not indicate a grade because it is usually posted and serves as an aid to provide an additional record of students' capability in a classroom/laboratory situation.

A second use of the progress chart is to enable teachers to have different students working on various activities and still remember what each has completed. An example of how an auto mechanics teacher uses the progress chart follows.

Mr. Green is an auto mechanics teacher and has 20 students in his class. The laboratory is clean and well organized. The size is adequate and it has four well-equipped bays. While Mr. Green tries to schedule in advance specific tasks for his students to work on, periodically something unexpected

MACHINE TOOL OPERATION	DATE	Job Completed				Unit Completed Grade
		1	2	3	4	
I. BENCH WORK						
A. Layout work						
B. Use & Care of Hand Tools						
C. Blueprint Reading						
D. Use of Measuring Tools						
E. Shop Safety						
II. ENGINE LATHE						
A. Lathe Orientation						
B. Tool Bits & Tool Holders						
C. Chucking Work						
D. Turning Between Centers						
E. Threading						
a. External						
b. Internal						
F. Taper Turning						
G. Lathe Accessories						
III. SHAPER OPERATION						
A. Orientation						
B. Squaring						
C. Shaping Procedures						
D. Angle Shaping						
E. Cutting Special Forms						

Figure 5-6.

occurs. One morning Mr. Green arrived at school and found three cars parked outside his laboratory with notes on them.

The first note read:

"Engine overheated on way to school."
Signed,
Your Principal

The second note read:

"Engine keeps shutting off. I need it by noon!"
Signed,
Your Brother

The third note read:

"It's making a loud, funny noise when stopping."
Signed,
Your Superintendent

Mr. Green had planned to teach an introductory lesson on automatic transmissions and then have students finish previously assigned work. Obviously, he now had a problem! Having worked as a service manager for a local dealership, Mr. Green was familiar with scheduling unexpected work. His solution to the problem was to teach the planned lesson to all students and then select four students to work on the three cars parked outside his laboratory. The remaining students would continue to work on their previously assigned tasks.

A few weeks later when Mr. Green issued report cards a dissatisfied student said, "But Mr. Green, you told me I would get extra credit for doing such a good job on the superintendent's car three weeks ago!" The look on Mr. Green's face indicated that he was confused. Not only was he surprised by the student's question, but he could not remember what the student had done. All he could remember was that two or three weeks ago the students were working on individual projects. Some students did not finish their assigned tasks and received a low report card grade.

A progress chart indicating tasks assigned to individual students would have prevented this problem. Mr. Green could have located two important points of information immediately:

1. Exactly which tasks had been done.
2. The information that the student who didn't finish the task was repairing the superintendent's car.

The main point of the story should be clear. If every student does the same task at the same time, it is easy to remember. However, if all students are doing different tasks at the same time, then an accurate record of individual activities must be kept.

The third use of the progress chart is to help the teacher sequence the learning activities in an organized manner. The learning activities in the form of tasks are taken from the occupational analysis and placed in sequence by such patterns as (a) prerequisite skills, (b) natural job occurrence, (c) simple to complex, (d) progression of skills and knowledge, or (e) some other sequencing method. The sequence of learning activities may, however, need to be different for different students because of facility, equipment or material limitations.

A fourth use of the progress chart is to monitor student achievement. If the progress chart is routinely and accurately maintained, the teacher can use this information to counsel students and increase their levels of motivation toward completing assignments. The progress chart in Figure 5-7 shows a technique for marking assigned, completed, and proficient work.

The progress chart on Figure 5-7 looks quite similar to others depicted previously. The cosmetology teacher has adapted the basic format to meet the students' needs. Across the top, from left to right, are listed the competencies (tasks)

The code symbols shown at top left of the chart are:

- ASSIGNED — a box with a single diagonal line
- COMPLETED — a box with an X
- PROFICIENT — a box divided into six triangles

JOB	CODE	MANICURING						FACIALS					HAIR CUTTING									HAIR BLEACHING					
		Polish Change	Nail Hardening	Equipment	Mending Nails	Eyebrow Arch	Lash & Brow Dye	Cleanup	Blackhead Treat.	Complete Facial	Makeup	Cleanup	Dry Scissor	Dry Thinning	Wet Razor	Shingle	Wet Thinning	Shaping or Trim	Neckline	Clipper-neckline	Other split-ends	Examine Scalp	Release	Preparing Form	Apply Formula	Test for Color	Timing
NUMBER OF TIMES TASK IS REQUIRED		10	10	50	3	50	5	10	6	12	6	45	10	6	10	3	6	10	5	3	3	6	6	6	6	6	6
Blevins, E.										×			×		×		×		×	×	×			×			
Blevins, F.				×								×				×		×		×		×	×				
Boggs, A.																											
Glovier, C.				×	×		×		×						×												
Hess, M.																											
Hess, P.		×		×			×				×				×	×		×				×		×		×	×
Jackson, S.																											
Kilgore, R.		×	×			×	×	×	×	×	×	×	×	×	×												
McGlothlin, B.		×	×	×		×	×	×		×		×		×													
Miller, S.		×	×	×	×	×	×	×	×	×	×	×	×	×						×							
Parrott, S.		×	×	×	×	×	×		×	×	×		×	×		×											
Powers, E.		×	×	×	×	×	×	×	×	×	×	×															

Figure 5-7.

that the student must attain to successfully complete the program. On the left, from top to bottom, student names are listed in alphabetical order. Note that just above the name of the first student is a row titled: "Number of times task is required." This in itself does not establish competence but may be needed (a) because of state licensing regulations or (b) minimum or maximum time to be spent in designated areas of work. Also, the teacher has included in the top left hand corner of the chart the code that is used to record information on the chart. This information can now be used by the teacher to counsel and motivate students.

The progress chart shows that there are 12 students in the class. We can also observe that there are 26 different tasks that each student completes to develop the four required skills shown. A quick look at the progress chart indicates that the majority of the students seem to be progressing at about the same pace. Three students, A. Boggs, M. Hess, and S. Jackson, are noticeably behind their classmates. The teacher can call each of these students into the office for a conference and try to identify the problems which limit their progress. As a result of conferences with these students and observations of their work behavior, decisions can be made that will either lead to improved student performance or eventually reassignment to another program.

THE INDIVIDUALIZED COMPETENCY RECORD

Competency Based Education (CBE) has gained widespread popularity since its initiation in the 1970's. This approach helps ensure that high school graduates are competent in their occupation. The CBE approach is relatively simple in theory. Teachers conduct an occupational analysis to identify the specific skills a job entry level worker needs when hired (see Chapter 2). Since one purpose of secondary occupational education is to teach students entry-level skills, the tasks identified in the occupational analysis are, in fact, taught. As a result, teachers, parents, and employers can be sure that students have the opportunity to attain skills necessary for successful employment.

The number of entry-level skills needed by incumbent workers in different occupations will vary. In some occupational areas the analysis may reveal the need for only 40 or 50 different skills. Other areas may require many more. Because employers hire students primarily based on their skill and attitude levels, teachers need a method to record (a) the number of different skills gained by a student, (b) the level of proficiency attained for each skill, and (c) student attitude toward work in general. While progress charts can be used to maintain a record of activities completed by students, changes are required if the teacher is to record a student's level of performance or competence. Other names used by teachers when referring to these competency charts include (a) competency profile, (b) competency check sheet, (c) individualized vocational plan, and (d) individualized competency plan.

Recording Psychomotor, Cognitive, and Affective Competencies

As a former craftsperson or technician, the occupational teacher knows the importance of gaining a high degree of skill. It is no secret that good technicians will earn more money than those who have marginal skills. Because skill level can determine the future success of workers, occupational teachers must spend considerable class time helping students to become proficient. Obviously, highly proficient students have a better chance of being successful on the job than students who are less proficient. This approach is self-evident. Two questions need to be discussed about skill proficiency, however. They are:

1. Which types of skills are needed by students to be successful in the world of work?
2. Are some particular types of skills more important to students than others?

In answering the first question, three types of skills must be developed in the laboratory and classroom by students to increase their chances of becoming successful workers. Skills must be developed in the psychomotor domain, the cognitive domain, and the affective domain.

Psychomotor domain: A domain used to categorize the skills students develop that involve or require the manipulation of things, objects, tools, and equipment.

Examples of psychomotor domain skills are:
- cut hair
- solder wires
- cut threads
- develop a print
- adjust a machine
- wire a box

Cognitive domain: A domain used to categorize the knowledge of specific information, principles, concepts, and generalizations for problem solving.

Examples of cognitive domain skills are:
- select a hairstyle
- troubleshoot a short circuit
- calculate threads
- critique a layout
- calculate cutting speed
- calculate electrical load

Affective domain: A domain used to categorize the feelings, attitudes, and appreciation toward people, things or ideas.

Examples of affective domain skills are:
- be pleasant to patron
- follow safety
- keeping cutting bit sharp
- keep work free of dirt
- keep machines clean
- remove excess wire

Occupational teachers must teach in all three domains of learning to prepare the student for employment. By using the individual competency records, occupational teachers can record the level of proficiency that each student has achieved

in the occupational skills needed for initial employment.

Some particular types of skills are more important to students than others. The types of skills that are important to students as future workers will vary depending upon the type of occupation for which they are preparing. Students preparing for occupations that require constant contact with the public or fellow workers may need to develop different skills than those preparing for occupations that do not require as much public contact.

The occupational teacher must also know how these tasks are best sequenced. All tasks must be listed in cumulative teaching order. Consequently, after the teacher has identified the tasks and skill levels to be taught, the tasks must be sequenced so students can learn the prerequisite ones first. These tasks are used as "building blocks" to learn the more difficult ones. The listing from simple to more complex skills associated with tasks in each domain is called the *taxonomic level*. Chapter 4 discusses these domains in greater detail.

Recording Student Competencies

The next consideration in understanding the ICR's is the various methods that can be used to record competencies. Three different record keeping methods exist. These three methods are (a) rating scales, (b) grading scales, and (c) indicator scales. While the three scales are somewhat similar, they do have some unique differences.

Rating scales. Rating scales have been used by occupational teachers on ICR's to indicate the level of performance a student has demonstrated on each task listed on the chart. Both numbers and letters can be used to indicate levels of performance. The decision to use either is based on personal

---

USING NUMBERS AND LETTERS TO RATE STUDENT PERFORMANCE

1 — Demonstrates outstanding employment potential
2 — Exceeds minimum employment potential
3 — Meets minimum employment requirements

or

1 — Demonstrates outstanding potential
2 — Exceed minimum potential
3 — Meets minimum potential

or

1 — Skilled, can work independently with no supervision
2 — Moderately skilled, needs limited supervision
3 — Limited skills, requires instruction and close supervision
4 — No experience in this area
A — Demonstrates outstanding employment potential
B — Exceeds minimum employment potential
C — Meets minimum employment requirements

or

A — Demonstrates outstanding potential
B — Exceeds minimum potential
C — Meets minimum potential

or

A — Skilled, can work independently with no supervision
B — Moderately skilled, needs limited supervision
C — Limited skills, requires instruction and close supervision
D — No experience in this area

Figure 5-8.

STUDENT RATING SCALE

TAZEWELL COUNTY VOCATIONAL CENTER
Tazewell, Virginia
STUDENT RATING RECORD

Name _____ Course _____

RATING FACTORS	PERSONAL TRAITS-25% OF TOTAL GRADE				
ATTITUDE	(4) Excellent	(3) Good	(2) Fair	(1) Poor	(0) Unsatisfactory
	SHOP WORK—50% OF TOTAL GRADE				
JOB PERFORMANCE	(8) Excellent	(6) Good	(4) Fair	(2) Poor	(0) Unsatisfactory
CLASSROOM INSTRUCTION	(4) Excellent	(3) Good	(2) Fair	(1) Poor	(0) Unsatisfactory

Grade Period From _____19_____ to _____19_____

TOTAL DAYS ON ROLL _____

TOTAL DAYS ABSENT _____

DAYS MADE UP _____

TOTAL HOURS PRESENT _____

Add scores and divide by four to arrive at total grade.

GRADE _____

POINT SYSTEM
A — 4 points
B — 3 points
C — 2 points
D — 1 point
F — 0 point

Figure 5-9.

preference. Figure 5-8 shows both numbers and letters along with their descriptive statements which give them meaning. Figure 5-9 provides an example of an actual rating scale.

Figures 5-8 and 5-9 illustrate the teacher's creativity in designing rating scales for individualized competency records. In some instances, teachers can use ICR's from commercial publishers. In other cases, they may want to design student rating scales that better meet their program needs. If special rating scales are developed, it is important to remember the following points:

1. Keep them simple.
2. Students must understand the system.
3. Parents and employers must understand the system.
4. The ratings must accurately reflect the student's performance.
5. Account for all student activities in the shop.
6. Use the system consistently and fairly.

Grading scales. Grading scales are also found on some ICR's. As the name infers, grading scales are used by teachers who wish to assign students specific grades on their performance, rather than rate their performance using either a numerical or alphabetical scale. One reason teachers record student performance on ICR's using the grading scale is because they are required to turn in grades for each grading period. This method saves teachers time. Figure 5-10 is an example of an ICR using a grading scale.

Note in Figure 5-10 that the teacher has designed an individualized competency record that contains a wealth of information. This particular ICR records student achievement in the cognitive and affective domains. While student psychomotor skills are not included in the chart, they may be recorded separately. (See Figures 4-16 and 5-11.)

Indicator scales. Indicator scales are the third method that teachers can use to record student competencies. The various codes used by teachers range from the simple check (x) to a more complex code using a variety of symbols and numerical entries. The primary purpose of an indicator scale is to show the teacher which activities the student:

1. Demonstrated.
2. Is currently performing.
3. Completed.
4. Completed and attained a proficiency level.

Regardless of the type of system a teacher selects, it is important to remember that even sophisticated record keeping systems are of little value if the teacher does not routinely use the ICR. Consequently, teachers must design a record keeping system that is adequate for their needs without being so cumbersome that routine information recording becomes a chore.

SCOTT COUNTY VOCATIONAL CENTER
EDUCATIONAL OBJECTIVES PROGRESS
CHART

SCHOOL YEAR 19_____ 19_____

NAME _____

ADDRESS _____   CLASS _____

PARENT'S NAME _____   TELEPHONE NO. ( )_____   HOME SCHOOL_____

TECHNOLOGY: Job knowledge, technical details of the subject or occupation
1 2 3 4 5 6 7 8 9 10 11 12 13 14 15 16 17 18 19 20 21 22 23 24 25 26 27 28 29 30
31 32 33 34 35 36 37 38 39 40

QUANTITY OF WORK: The amount of work performed according to the instruction
given. 0 1 2 3 4 5 6 7 8 9 10 11 12 13 14 15 16 17 18 19 20

QUALITY OF WORK: A degree of excellence; amount of craftsmanship applied to
the work performed. 0 1 2 3 4 5 6 7 8 9 10 11 12 13 14 15 16 17 18 19 20

ATTITUDE AND COOPERATION: Any settled behavior or conduct, a mental position
with regard to facts or a series of facts, a willingness and ability to
work with others; to associate with others for mutal benefit.
0 1 2 3 4 5

LAB MAINTENANCE AND EQUIPMENT MAINTENANCE: The act of maintaining a
positive work area or laboratory equipment. 0 1 2 3 4 5

INITIATIVE AND DEPENDABILITY: Ability to originate or start; the aptitude
to develop or undertake new enterprises and fitness to be relied upon.
0 1 2 3 4 5

SAFETY: The act or practice of keeping oneself and others free from danger, risk
or injury. 0 1 2 3 4 5

(95-100=A) (86-94=B) (75-85=C) (70-74=D) (Below 70=F)

DAYS ABSENT

D -Discipline
DF -Death in Family
L -Educational Leave
SF -Sickness in Family
SS -Sickness -Self
X -Unexcused Absence
T -Unexcused Tardy
ED -Excused (Other)

STUDENTS SIGNATURE _____

	1st 6 wks	2nd 6 wks	3rd 6 wks	1st Sem. Ave.	4th 6 wks	5th 6 wks	6th 6 wks	2nd Sem. Ave.	YR. AVE.

	1st 6wks	2nd 6wks	3rd 6wks	4th 6wks	5th 6wks	6th 6wks
TOTAL POINTS						
LETTER GRADE						
Total Days Absent (6 wks)						
Cumulative Total Absent						
Total Days Tardy						

	1st 6 weeks	2nd 6 weeks	3rd 6 weeks	4th 6 weeks	5th 6 weeks	6th 6 weeks
INSTRUCTORS SIGNATURE						

1)
2)
3)
4)
5)
6)

Figure 5-10.

INDIVIDUALIZED COMPETENCY RECORDS FOR EMPLOYMENT

Many occupational teachers believe that ICR's are only appropriate and necessary in a classroom situation. While the use of ICR's originated for classroom use, occupational teachers use them to assist their students in locating jobs.

Most teachers can remember their first job interview. They were prepared and neat in appearance. They may have even brushed up on company specifics. These types of preparation activities were very worthwhile. Surprisingly many students are still ill prepared to answer the most basic question asked during the interview process, "What can you do?" Research on job interviewing indicates that many students lack good communication skills. Some occupational teachers have modified their ICR's so their students can use them in adequately answering employer's questions concerning their job skills. A sample of one such ICR is shown in Figure 5-11.

NAME ______________ DATE __________ PROGRAM __________

____
INSTRUCTOR'S SIGNATURE

Score	Competency Demonstrated	Kitchen Helper	Cashier	Pantry Helper	Sandwich Maker	Baker Helper	Cake Decorator	Cold	Hot
		SPIN-OFF JOB							
______	Clean work area and equipment	X	X	X	X	X	X	X	X
______	Washes work tables, walls, refrigerator	X	X	X	X	X	X		
______	Sweeps and mop floors	X	X	X	X	X			
______	Carries food and items to and from work stations	X	X	X	X	X	X		
______	Prepares sandwiches to order	X	X	X	X				
______	Know values of featured items and receive money	X	X	X	X	X	X		
______	Weigh and measure designated ingredients	X	X	X	X	X	X		
______	Prepares products	X				X			
______	Bakes products	X				X			
______	Removes bake products from oven & pans		X	X					
______	Breads, food items	X	X		X				
______	Cashes checks	X	X		X				
______	Cuts bread and sandwich buns	X							
______	Set banquet tables	X							

THE STUDENT HAD DEMONSTRATED EMPLOYMENT SKILLS RELATED TO THE FOLLOWING JOBS:

______ Kitchen Helper ______ Sandwich Maker
______ Cashier ______ Baker's Helper
______ Pantry Helper ______ Cook
______ Cake Decorator

Figure 5-11.

In this example, a commercial foods teacher has prepared a document that can be included in the placement file and given to the prospective employer. At first glance, this ICR looks like the others which were discussed. The far left-hand column is titled SCORE and can be used by a teacher to place either an alphabetical or numerical score indicating the student's level of proficiency for each skill. The middle column is titled COMPETENCY DEMONSTRATED and includes all the competencies (tasks) that the teacher includes in the program.

The right-hand portion of this progress chart lists the various "spin-off jobs" for which the student is qualified. "Spin-off jobs" are a new concept to some occupational teachers. Programs organized to explore various allied types of employment are gaining in popularity. If properly identified and used, spin-off jobs can greatly increase a student's opportunity for employment.

This is particularly true for those students seeking employment in a small community or in a community that has a range of diverse industries/businesses. Occupational teachers can identify spin-off jobs for their students by using three criteria. These criteria, stated as questions, are: (a) Does the job actually exist in the local labor market area? (b) Does the teacher have the technical ability to teach students the skills necessary for employment in the job? (c) Does the laboratory have the tools and equipment necessary to teach the student and provide the student with the opportunity for practice? The answer to all three questions must be yes if the spin-off job is to be included on the student's ICR.

At the bottom of the ICR there is a space for the instructor to list tasks for which the student is qualified. By placing checks in the spaces provided, the employer knows immediately the level of competency a student has attained. Students who have a copy of their ICR with them when on a job interview are prepared to provide the employer with specific, documented information concerning their abilities.

It is important to remember that the competencies listed on the ICR should be written in the language of the occupation and not in educational terminology. An example from auto mechanics is used to show the difference between "trade talk" and educational activities.

In Figure 5-12 note that the seven activities which teachers may have their students perform in the laboratory can be

COMPARING EDUCATIONAL ACTIVITIES WITH TRADE ACTIVITIES

EDUCATIONAL ACTIVITIES	TRADE ACTIVITIES
Install spark plugs Replace distributor cap Replace spark plug wires Install and adjust points Set air gap Set timing Adjust carburetor	Perform a tuneup

Figure 5-12.

combined into one, called "Perform a tune-up." Occupational teachers can consolidate tasks in their specialty areas if they ask the question, "What is the task called in the occupation?" The advantage in consolidating tasks where possible is two-fold. First, an employer would not ask auto mechanics students if they can replace a distributor cap, because it is considered to be a simple activity. More importantly, replacing a distributor cap is just one part of the broader activity in tuning an engine. The second reason tasks should be consolidated where possible is that lengthy task lists spread over multiple pages become cumbersome.

STORAGE AND USE OF ICR'S

Need for a System

An important tip to remember about ICR's is to develop a filing system that is both easy to maintain and convenient to use. Unless this is practiced, the occupational teacher will spend time and effort designing competency records for use with each of their students only to have this effort wasted if the ICR is not maintained on a regular basis.

Storing the Individual Competency Records

Occupational teachers should have at least one filing cabinet available to them. If a filing cabinet is not available, there is usually a large desk drawer designed to hold file folders. Teachers need to designate a portion of their filing cabinet, their filing drawer or some other container to store all the ICR's for students in their class.

Once a storage place has been identified, teachers will find that making an individual file folder for each student is the easy way to store ICR's. The advantages of using a file folder for each ICR are that it:

1. Keeps them from being lost.
2. Keeps them from getting dirty.
3. Provides for easy access to record current information.
4. Keeps them from being torn.
5. Provides space for the teacher notes and other important information.

After folders have been prepared for each student, the teacher should develop a method to identify which student's ICR is in each folder.

Alphabetical filing. One widely used method of filing is by alphabetical order of the student's last name. The popularity of alphabetical filing can be seen by the fact that thousands of businesses, libraries and teachers have adopted this method.

Numerical filing. Another method of storing records is by numerical filing. Similar to alphabetical filing, the teacher assigns each student a number and arranges each folder by numerical order. Using the numerical filing system gives occupational teachers more flexibility. In most instances, student numbers are determined by teacher preference. The student's number can be used for other purposes as well. For example, a student may be assigned Number 9, and this number is used to code (a) ICR's, (b) class projects, (c) test scores, (d) personal tools, (e) class assignments, (f) class seating assignments and (g) laboratory clean-up assignments.

Sophisticated numerical codes can provide additional information. An example of a more detailed code could be as follows:

Student Name	Student Code
Code:	1367

1 = Gregg Jones
3 = Morning class student
6 = Senior class standing
7 = Currently employed after school

To use this method of filing, the teacher must use a four-digit code for every student. Also the position of each digit must indicate the same information.

Social security number. Another technique used by teachers to code ICR's is the student's social security number. Similar to the numerical filing system, the social security numbers offer additional advantages. First, teachers are not required to select numbers. Second, students do not have to memorize numbers assigned to them by the teacher. Third, inasmuch as social security numbers are nine digits, the student's file is more secure because it is more difficult to associate a nine-digit number with a particular student's identity.

There are also two potential disadvantages with using social security numbers. First, not all students may have social security numbers. This problem is becoming less frequent. If teachers have students without a social security number, they should assist them to obtain one. Second, teachers must make an effort to remember the social security numbers of all students in their classes. This is difficult to do.

Student rights. Students' rights are particularly evident when it comes to releasing personal records that can include, among other data, confidential information. To protect the rights of students, teachers should consider confidentiality as indicated next.

Confidentiality. Because the information recorded on the student's competency record pertains to only one student, teachers need to be sure that this information is kept confidential. This information should not be shared with other students or teachers without proper permission. Only those individuals who have a need to know information on the ICR should be allowed to look at it. If someone other than the student requests the ICR of a particular student, the administration should first determine if the person is authorized. Only then should this information be shared. Teachers should never release a student's complete folder to another person until all administrative approvals have been made. The issue of confidentiality of student records is so important that all schools have policies concerning proper usage.

Security. One method that a teacher can use to keep ICR's confidential and secure is by keeping them in a filing container, drawer or cabinet that can be locked. If the teacher cannot keep these records secure, they should be kept in the principal's office until proper security has been arranged. Teachers who select an unlocked filing cabinet to store the ICR's can have a bar with hasp and padlock installed.

Do not post. The system that has been described so far in developing and storing ICR's has been based on the concept that teachers keep students' ICR's in a separate file folder. This system makes the ICR different from the progress chart that was discussed at the beginning of the chapter. Remember that progress charts are typically posted in the laboratory and are used primarily by teachers to keep a record of the types of activities that individual students have either previously performed or are currently engaged in. Teachers do not generally include information about an individual student's ability level on these charts. ICR's, on the other hand, contain specific information about an individual student's ability and level of performance. In many instances, grades, tests, personal data sheets and other personal information are also included in the ICR file folder. Because ICR's contain this type of information they should never be posted where anyone can see them.

Preventing altering. Another tip that teachers should consider when developing a method of securing ICR's is to make every effort to prevent students from altering the ICR. In addition to keeping all files locked, the teacher should deny permission to take the original ICR home or away from the classroom. Furthermore, the student should be allowed to look at the ICR only in the presence of the teacher.

In rare instances it may be necessary for the students to take a copy of their ICR's with them and away from the teacher's control. An example of this situation would be when a student is going for a job interview and needs a copy of the ICR to show to the job interviewer. When this happens, the teacher can use techniques that make altering the record almost impossible. One technique would be to place a strip of clear tape over the list of competencies. Students who attempted to "check off" more competencies than they could perform, thus making them look more employable, would first have to peel off the strip of tape. Removing the tape would either remove the printed matter or fray the paper.

Teachers will find that telephoning the job interviewer after the student has completed the interview can provide them with a lot of useful information. This telephone call can also aid teachers in confirming if the information on the ICR was accurate and unaltered.

RELATED USES OF THE INDIVIDUAL COMPETENCY RECORDS

Teacher

Because the ICR has been designed to include information about the student's level or performance, its use for grading is an obvious advantage. In the beginning of this chapter it was indicated that one of the many responsibilities of the occupational teacher is to assign student grades. Whether students receive grades weekly, bi-weekly, every six weeks, every nine weeks, or every semester, grades are an important part of a student's official school record. ICR's designed by teachers to include the type of information needed to calculate a student's grade can make this process easier to manage. As a result, teachers need to review the criteria that are used in determining a student's grade and make sure they are included in the ICR. Teachers who use attendance, attitude, performance, and skill level, must include this information on the ICR. Attempting to track down individual grades that are recorded in different places can make grading an unpleasant responsibility.

If the ICR's are regularly and accurately kept by the teacher, they can also be used when assigning student tasks. An example of this is indicated in the previous discussion of Mr. Green, the auto mechanics instructor. In this situation, Mr. Green could have easily determined which students to assign for repair of the three cars by observing which students had already demonstrated the skill necessary to perform the task. Had Mr. Green wished, he could have assigned a helper to each of the three selected students (or a student who had not developed the necessary skills) who could learn by assisting. This peer teaching technique (buddy system) is very effective and is recommended for occupational teachers.

Occupational teachers can also use the information on a student's ICR to aid in locating employment. Frequently employers will call teachers and ask if there are any qualified students looking for a job. Employers will usually ask teachers to send their best students. This request is understandable but sometimes the best student is not always the right student for the job. If teachers sent their best students for jobs and the employer has the students doing menial activities, boredom and frustration can result. A bored student may soon quit and give the program a bad reputation. By using ICR's, teachers can ask the potential employer for specifics concerning the types of skills desired and send the student who has those skills. The "best student" means the best student for the job, not necessarily the best student in the class.

Student

Students will also find that ICR's can be helpful to them both during their school years and after they have completed their program of study. Those students who have teachers that periodically review the ICR's receive more incentive to learn. This motivation to learn is the result of students knowing what is expected of them in class, the different competencics they will learn, and the teacher's expectation of acceptable achievement.

In addition to increasing their level of motivation, students can also use the ICR to plan and make realistic career decisions. These decisions are possible since it is recommended that occupational teachers include on each student's ICR a list of spin-off jobs or related areas of employment. Furthermore, ICR's should not only include a list of related areas of employment but also the specific skills required by workers in each of the areas. Students who have identified an area of employment they wish to pursue will know the skills which employers require and can use their laboratory time to master them.

Parents

Parents also find the ICR to be an important document. It provides information on (a) their child's performance in school, (b) types of activities performed, (c) and occupations for which they are preparing. Teachers need to be sure that the parent(s) of each student in their classes understand what an ICR is and how it will be used. Sending letters to the parent(s) of each student, telephoning them, or scheduling and conducting parent/teacher conferences are ways in which teachers frequently relay this message.

Parents of students whose performance is unsatisfactory can help teachers to increase the performance by providing direction at home. Parents of students who are performing well can help ensure that this performance continues by properly rewarding or recognizing their child's accomplishment.

Employer

The ICR in the hiring process was discussed in a previous section titled THE TEACHER. Employers can also use ICR's to assign students to a particular job within a selected industry. ICR's aid the employer in knowing what types of skills are required by workers performing the job in question and assigning the student who has these acquired skills.

Another use of the ICR to the employer is in working with supervisory assignments for employees. Effective supervisors get the job done efficiently by getting the most production out of their personnel. Supervisors who are given a copy of the student's ICR can review this document and place students in a job where they are immediately productive. In this type of situation a business gains in productivity and the student gains satisfaction from being recognized as a productive worker. Supervisors can also use the ICR to identify those skills which the student has not attained so that appropriate on-the-job training can be scheduled.

SUMMARY

Individualized Competency Records and progress charts are valuable tools in any classroom. These records can be used by the teacher, student, parent, and employer. They can be developed to meet individual needs. As with any other records that teachers are required to keep, the value of these documents lies in how routinely and accurately they are maintained. No one record keeping system is best for every teacher. The record keeping system must be designed to ensure that the needs of parents, teachers, students, and employers are met. The variations used by teachers in developing ICR's have shown the flexibility they possess.

Properly used and routinely maintained, ICR's can be a valuable aid to any occupational teacher. They can increase not only the teacher's instructional efficiency but their laboratory management procedures as well.

Chapter 6

UNIT GUIDE PRELIMINARIES AND LESSON PLAN DEVELOPMENT

by

Jesse L. Hudson, Professor
Technical Education Department
Pittsburg State University
Pittsburg, Kansas

INTRODUCTION

The purpose of this chapter is to describe the process of preparing the beginning section of a unit guide. This portion of the guide includes objectives, safety rules, lesson plan titles, and lesson plans. The information and examples given here will assist the teacher with the development of lesson plans.

However, before development of instructional material begins, the occupation should be analyzed and organized into a listing of the competencies that a student must develop to be employable. This chapter assumes this has been done and moves on to explain how to develop the initial sections of the unit guide. These sections will help a teacher teach students in a sequential manner. To accomplish this, it will be necessary to describe the relationship of instructional materials, such as a school's curriculum, course of study, unit guide, lesson plan, and the procedures for writing lesson plans.

Examples will be provided of instructional materials with brief descriptions of the basic elements of each. Since there is no one best unit guide format or structure, teachers are encouraged to select the format that will best suit their instructional methods. Lesson content and arrangement of the information needed to teach the students a given competency will vary. Much depends on (a) requirements of the competency, (b) needs of the student, (c) delivery style of the teacher, and (d) curricular requirements of the school.

It is important to note that there are definite basic elements that should be included in every unit guide. Frequently the basic elements listed in the unit guide format will have slightly different names and emphasis will vary. A description of the initial unit guide elements is presented here for the purpose of helping teachers prepare instructional materials that fit the instructional needs of the students and the lesson presentation methods of the teacher.

SETTING THE SCENE

New teachers generally approach their first classroom experience feeling that they urgently need some organizational plan to ensure they will not run out of something to say or do before the dismissal bell rings. Their worst fear is the blank stares of students who, like circus spectators, wait for a tightrope walker to slip and fall.

This feeling drives new teachers to prepare lesson plans based on material they feel most comfortable with or best qualified to teach. Their object is to "wow" the students. Little thought is given to the simplest and best method of presenting organized, sequential instruction.

So strong is the survival instinct that lesson plans are sometimes written without analyzing the occupation. Little attention is given to what needs to be taught, or the sequence in which it is taught. This premature start wastes time and confuses both the teacher and students.

To clearly see the purpose of a lesson title listing (lesson title breakdown chart), the new teacher should be aware of the relationship of instructional materials.

THE RELATIONSHIP OF INSTRUCTIONAL MATERIALS

The relationship of instructional materials has been written in the form of outlines, steps, and organizational charts in an effort to help teachers comprehend these relationships. In general, each method of viewing these relationships involves describing layers of instructional material.

If a school's curriculum is viewed as the top layer, then the second layer is comprised of many courses. Each course is taught by a teacher using a curriculum guide that contains a number of major units. The third layer is comprised of unit guides. Each contains a series of lesson plans and other instructional materials such as tests, job sheets, reference lists, etc.

Each unit guide should be designed to aid the student's mastery of occupational competencies. In looking at the relationship of instructional materials, it is helpful to first consider the school's curriculum.

School Curriculum

A school curriculum is a "group of courses offered by an educational institution or one of its branches." This definition is sufficient when applied to a university, community college, or general education program of a high school. However, vocational-technical schools organize their curriculum around occupational programs, such as air conditioning-refrigeration, electronics, or welding. At a community college, each program area is usually broken into a number of courses. For example, the electronics program at a community college will have a curriculum of its own. The courses will have titles that compare to major unit titles of a vocational-technical school occupational program. This is why it is important to understand the relationship between the school curriculum and the curriculum guide a teacher uses while teaching.

Curriculum Guide

"A curriculum guide is an outline which describes, in broad terms, a particular program or specific course." This scholarly definition does little to help a teacher understand the relationship of the school curriculum to a curriculum guide and the sub-parts of the curriculum guide referred to as unit guides.

The word, *guide,* indicates direction. Like an airplane pilot who is guided by a flight plan from point to point along a planned flight path, a teacher follows a curriculum guide from unit to unit through a planned instructional program. Therefore, the curriculum guide is the teacher's guide through that planned instructional program. It is an important tool for occupational teachers who are responsible for steering students down the path to occupational competency.

Curriculum guides can be very simple or very complex. The degree of complexity is determined by the need for providing information essential to each occupational education instructional program.

Any curriculum guide can be broken into elements. This breakdown often leads to confusion for teachers trying to understand the interrelationship of the various layers of instructional materials. To help eliminate the confusion, it is appropriate to refer to the following curriculum guide components. These components are: (See Chapter 12)
1. Title and Table of Contents
2. Introduction
3. Philosophy and Objectives
4. Occupational Description
5. Resource Materials
6. Unit Titles
7. Course Outline
8. Task List (or Individual Competency Record)
9. Safety and Conduct Rules

10. Unit Guides
11. Evaluation Materials
12. Laboratory Management Materials
13. Appendices

Teachers should see components of this list as major divisions in a curriculum guide. These components may be rearranged in the order that best relates to a school's curriculum and the teachers' instructional needs.

If teachers compare this listing of curriculum guide components and subcomponents with other suggested listings, they will probably find some of the subcomponents listed as major components. This is not a problem as long as the listings do not violate the format of instructional materials established by curriculum development policies.

While a curriculum guide outlines an instructional program in broad terms, the unit guide focuses on one major unit or division of subject matter in a course. The *unit guides* (or major units of instruction) will be listed as *subcomponents* of the *curriculum guide.*

Unit Guide

An occupational education curriculum guide may have few or many unit guides in its instructional program. Generally, there are from five to fifteen units. The typical contents (see Chapter 12) of a unit guide include:
1. Unit Title
2. Unit Objectives
3. Lesson Title Breakdown
4. Safety Precautions and Program Rules
5. Lesson Plans
6. Tests, Including Performance Test Checklists
7. Instruction Sheets
8. Safety Materials
9. Laboratory Management Materials for Unit
10. Learning Modules
11. Resources (references, audio-visuals, etc.)
12. Unit Appendix

Items one through seven, listed above, are considered to be most necessary to an effective and useful unit guide. Items eight through twelve may be optional. These optional sections are included to meet the teacher's instructional needs. This chapter will discuss in detail sections one through five.

A unit guide is a subcomponent of a curriculum guide. It is important to understand the subordinate relationship of the unit guide to the curriculum guide. Without this understanding, the teacher cannot hope to develop coherent, usable instructional materials.

The curriculum guide format listed earlier includes 13 components. Unit guides are listed as the tenth curriculum guide component. Remember, generally there are from five to fifteen units in a curriculum guide. This means that in a curriculum guide there would be from five to fifteen unit guides. Unit guides are placed into the curriculum guide format between the safety and conduct rules component and the evaluation materials component.

A unit guide provides an instructional plan that focuses on one section of subject matter. The instructional contents of the unit guide can be outlined by preparing a lesson title

LESSON TITLE BREAKDOWN CHART

Television and Electronics Products Servicing

Instructional Analysis Chart

MANIPULATIVE LESSONS: What the Students Should Be Able to Do	INFORMATIONAL LESSONS: What the Student Should Know

UNIT II. DC Circuits (45 hours)

	1. Solution of algebraic equations.
	2. Properties of conductors, resistors, and insulators.
3. Measure resistance of given lengths and gauges of copper wire.	
	4. Functions of multiplication and division on hand calculators.
5. Multiply and divide on hand calculators.	
	6. Application of Ohm's Law to series DC circuits.
7. Calculate, construct, measure, and compare measurements to calculated values for a series in DC circuit.	
	8. Review of problems involving fractions and whole numbers.
	9. Application of Ohm's Law to parallel DC circuits.
10. Calculate, construct, measure, and compare measurements to calculated values for a parallel DC circuit.	
	11. Application of Ohm's Law to series-parallel circuits.
12. Calculate, construct, measure, and compare measurements to calculated values for a series-parallel DC circuit.	
	13. Application of Ohm's and Kirchoff's Laws to voltage dividers.
14. Calculate, construct, measure, and compare measurements to calculated values for a voltage divider.	

Figure 6-1. Each of the numbered items requires the development of a lesson plan.

breakdown chart. Figure 6-1 shows a lesson title breakdown chart for a unit guide of an electronics course.

Note that the title of Unit II is "DC Circuits." It specifies 45 clock hours of instruction to teach the eight informational lessons and six manipulative lessons listed. Each lesson title listed indicates the need for the development of a lesson plan.

Lesson Plan

A lesson plan provides the teacher with detailed instructions or directions for teaching a lesson in addition to the technical content. The relationship of lesson plans to the lesson title breakdown chart is simple and direct when a one-to-one ratio of one lesson plan per lesson title listed is maintained.

Each lesson plan will have an array of supporting instructional materials to help students learn the information presented in a lesson. Chapter 7 deals with the instruction sheets used to support the instructional procedure presented by lesson plans. The reader should refer to Chapter 7 for specific information and the various types of instruction sheets.

After a lesson title breakdown chart has been developed for each unit guide, the teacher reviews the unit objective. This unit objective becomes one of the course objectives and should reflect the subjects described by lesson plan titles. There may be more than one objective per major unit because some units are distributed. For example, a safety or guidance unit of instruction may be distributed through a number of lessons in one or more major unit guides. Therefore, a curriculum guide will have at least one program or course objective for each major unit guide developed.

WRITING OBJECTIVES FOR THE UNIT GUIDE

Within the unit guide, a number of lesson plans should be developed. Each of these lessons should have an objective. A few of the plans may have more than one objective, but, as a general rule, multiple lesson objectives tend to confuse students. One clear and concise objective per lesson, on the other hand, will help the student focus on the lesson content. There are two excellent sources of material that can be used in formulating objectives available to occupational education teachers. One source is the Vocational-Technical Education Consortium of State (V-TECS). The other source is the Mid-America Vocational Curriculum Consortium (MAVCC).

V-TECS materials are commonly referred to as V-TECS catalogs. This is because each occupation is represented by a bound listing (catalog) of the duties and tasks required of a competent worker who is employed in that occupation. Each task has an objective listed which can be utilized as a lesson objective. Appendix 6-A is a listing of V-TECS Catalogs by occupational titles.

V-TECS Performance Objectives Matched with Tasks

Teachers should obtain a V-TECS catalog that analyzes their occupational area. Most state departments of education will have the address of the proper curriculum materials laboratory to contact to order the desired V-TECS catalog. Chapter 3 also provides source information.

In some curriculum development situations, the teacher will simply study the catalog and choose major unit subjects they wish to teach their students and make a listing of them and their attending tasks. The teacher then uses the performance objective(s) accompanying each task in the catalog to initiate the writing of each lesson plan. This procedure generates the

```
DUTY: INSTALLING ROUGH FRAMING

PERFORMANCE OBJECTIVE NO. 89

TASK: Install roof sheathing
STANDARD: Ends of roof sheathing must be centered on rafters;
          joints must be nailed every 4 to 6 inches; remainder
          of each sheet must be nailed into the rafters every
          8 to 10 inches; and sheathing must be laid with face
          grain perpendicular to rafters.
SOURCE FOR STANDARD: Writing team of incumbent workers and
                     Modern Carpentry, pages 181.
CONDITIONS FOR PERFORMANCE OF TASK:
    Standard tool kit          Nails
    Circular saw               5/8'' plywood sheathing
    Framed roof                Scaffold
    Ladder
PERFORMANCE GUIDE:
  1. Check roof frame construction and nailing patterns.
  2. Erect scaffold.
  3. Measure and strike chalk line 4 ft. up from end of rafters at
     each end of roof.
  4. Lay top of first row of sheathing on chalk line.
  5. Center end joints on rafters.
  6. Nail sheathing into rafters.
  7. Cut half sheet for second row.
  8. Nail second row, breaking joints.
  9. Continue procedure until roof is sheathed.
 10. Cut excess sheathing along hips.
```

Figure 6-2. Sample of a V-TECS task. (Vocational Technical Education Consortium of States, Decatur, GA)

```
CAKES AND ICINGS
Unit X

UNIT OBJECTIVE

After completion of this unit, the student should be able to list three
types of cakes, complete a list of methods of cake mixing, select
basic types of icings, and prepare and evaluate various cakes and
icings. This knowledge will be evidenced by correctly performing
the procedures outlined in the job sheets and by scoring a minimum
of 85 percent on the unit tests.

SPECIFIC OBJECTIVES

After completion of this unit, the student should be able to:
  1. Match terms related to cakes and icings with their correct
     definitions.
  2. List three types of cakes.
  3. Complete a list of methods of cake mixing.
  4. Select true statements concerning key factors affecting cake
     baking.
  5. Complete a list of standards of quality for shortened cakes.
  6. Select true statements concerning standards of quality for
     foam cakes.
  7. Circle the words which best complete statements concern-
     ing tips for proper cake storage.
  8. Complete a list of purposes of icings.
  9. Select basic types of icings.
 10. Arrange in order the procedure for icing cakes.
 11. Complete a list of statements concerning standards quality
     for icings.
 12. Circle the words which best complete statements concern-
     ing factors affecting portioning of cakes.
 13. Demonstrate the ability to:
     a. Prepare and evaluate a fudge cake.
     b. Prepare and evaluate an angel food cake.
     c. Prepare and evaluate an orange chiffon cake.
     d. Prepare and evaluate a white cake.
     e. Prepare and evaluate boiled icing.
     f. Prepare and evaluate orange icing.
     g. Ice a cake.
```

Figure 6-3. A unit objective is supported by several specific objectives. (Mid America Vocational Curriculum Consortium, Stillwater, OK)

material needed to teach the information outlined by the unit guide lesson title breakdown chart.

An example of a task from a V-TECS carpentry catalog is shown in Figure 6-2. The carpentry task, "Install Roof Sheathing," can become the *performance portion* of a lesson objective. This matches lesson objectives directly to an occupation's tasks.

Teachers are sometimes concerned that occasionally the V-TECS task performance guides contain too little occupational information or manipulations to justify developing a lesson plan. When this occurs, the teacher must combine two or more tasks into a lesson plan that will fit a class period time frame. In some cases it is possible that the committee of incumbent workers, who developed the V-TECS catalog, selected tasks too narrow in scope. Determining what is an occupational duty, task or step of procedure is always subject to the judgment of those developing the list.

Teachers will find curriculum and lesson development less confusing if they use the V-TECS catalogs as a guide, combining tasks as needed to develop competent workers. In some instances, two or more V-TECS tasks may be taught as one lesson. In other cases, one V-TECS task may be divided and taught as two or more lessons. It is for the teacher to decide when to combine or divide.

In developing lesson plans, the teacher should rely upon numerous and varied resource materials. V-TECS catalog sheets can be excellent guidelines but should not stand alone as lesson plans. One reason for this is the fact that the task steps of procedure do not provide key points for each step

of procedure. Furthermore, the application and evaluation components of a lesson plan are not addressed on V-TECS catalog task sheets.

MAVCC System for Writing Performance Objectives

Brief reference has already been made to both unit objectives and lesson objectives. One might ask what is the difference between a unit objective and a lesson objective?

A lesson objective should simply state what the teacher thinks the students should be able to do after the lesson has been taught. After writing the lesson objectives, clearly describing what the students should be able to do, teachers will find it is much easier to write the lesson plan.

The unit objective combines all of a unit's lesson objectives into one general objective. Its purpose is to give direction to the overall instructional process for the unit. A graphic comparison of the unit objective to its supporting specific objectives is shown in Figure 6-3.

Figure 6-3 shows the unit objective and specific objectives for a unit on *Cakes and Icings - Unit X*. This was taken from a MAVCC curriculum guide entitled, *Food Production, Management and Services: Baking*. The important thing to note is that the unit objective is a general statement containing all of the major concepts specified in the objectives. Of course, the specific objectives could and should be used as lesson objectives. MAVCC recommends that teachers develop their own lesson plans that will include each specific objective in a major unit of instructional material.

A final point concerning **specific** objectives: objectives state a performance expected of the student. These expected performances, in turn, make excellent titles for lessons. In some cases, the performances listed in the specific objectives in Figure 6-3 would not constitute enough information to warrant a lesson plan. Then, as with V-TECS, two or more specific objectives should be combined into a lesson plan.

SAFETY RULES

The primary responsibility of occupational education teachers is the preparation of students for the world of work. The students must achieve academic and technical competency levels that will prepare them for eventual employment. Students must also receive instruction which emphasizes safety.

Safety education cannot be compromised. It must be an inherent part of each student's education. Failure in this respect can lead to personal injury and possible lawsuits.

Litigation against school systems and school personnel continues to be a fertile area of activity for some lawyers. In fact, rulings in certain state courts have established the precedent that municipalities are no longer exempt from tort liability. These decisions certainly affect public schools and teachers, especially where school insurance coverage is minimal.

In a school system, the major responsibility for a viable safety program lies with teachers. They, in cooperation with their administrators, must execute administrative recommendations for incorporating and improving safety instruction in the education process. Documentation must be maintained as to who received instruction, and when the instruction was given. Safe working conditions and practices must be maintained in classrooms, laboratories, and shops. Teachers should recommend needed safety improvements to the school's administration. Teachers should also avail themselves of inservice training to stay current on the latest safety practices. Such practices must then be applied to the school setting. Teachers accomplish this through instruction to the students and by setting good examples.

A study of student injury cases shows that when teachers fail to meet their safety instruction responsibilities they can be judged negligent. Teachers so judged failed to:
1. Explain basic safety procedures.
2. Warn of possible dangers.
3. Anticipate unsafe events.
4. Exercise reasonable care.
5. Provide proper supervision to pupils in the selection and handling of hazardous materials.

6. Check that students use safety equipment.
7. Insist on the use of safety guards.
8. Use supplemental safety instructional materials.

Protection from Liability

Teachers can guard against these failures by presenting safety instructions at the beginning of each unit of instruction. To ensure this, they develop safety instruction and safety rules for each unit guide. The instruction and rules become part of the curriculum guide. Another reason for including safety instruction in each unit guide is because safety instruction needs change as students progress through the course. For instance, an auto body unit of instruction on glass has different safety rules than an auto body frame-straightening unit.

To avoid being judged negligent when a student is injured, especially at the secondary level, it is important for teachers to communicate with the students' parents. Parental acknowledgement of student activities and an awareness of the teacher's interest in the safety of the student are important. Teachers should express this interest at every opportunity.

ARC WELDING UNIT
Orientation Lesson and Safety Rules
1. The arc welder must be operated only with the teacher's permission and after instruction has been received.
2. Jewelry must be removed, loose clothing eliminated, and long hair confined.
3. All guards are to be in place and operating correctly.
4. The proper eye protection must always be used.
5. A welding helmet must be worn when welding.
6. Proper ventilation must be available.
7. Goggles must be worn when chipping slag.
8. Others in the area must be warned prior to striking an arc.
9. Gloves and proper clothing must be worn when welding.
10. Closed containers should not be welded without the teacher's permission.
11. Cables, clamps, and electrode holders should be checked and working properly.
12. Screens to protect others must be in place before welding is started.

Figure 6-4. Each unit guide should begin with a safety instruction.

For student's well-being as well as protection of teachers from liability judgments, each unit guide should begin with safety instruction. Only after students receive safety instruction, should teaching in the laboratory or shop start. Teachers must also realize that, as the instructional program progresses, additional safety instruction is needed. For example, when a welding class reaches the orientation lesson in the arc welding unit, the instructor should give each student a set of safety procedures and regulations for study and reference. An example of safety procedures and regulations for arc welding is found in Figure 6-4.

Safety instructional materials for a unit guide should be placed close to the front of the guide. This location will be a reminder that *safety comes first*. Further information on safety in the curriculum guide appears in Chapter 10.

LISTING LESSON PLAN TITLES

All occupations that involve basic procedures can be analyzed for instructional purposes. Most occupations have developed from the adaptation of knowledge and skills based upon past experiences. These occupations can, therefore, be analyzed by listing the tasks performed by a worker. This process is called occupational analysis and is used to list occupational tasks so they may be organized in a systematic and sequential manner.

Use of Occupational Analysis

Teachers should analyze their occupations by preparing occupational analysis charts. In some occupational areas, such charts have already been prepared. They will only require revision. The analysis chart will enable teachers to see graphically which operations make up the larger tasks. The tasks, or competencies, can then be grouped with related tasks to form the major units of a curriculum guide. For each major unit identified by this process, the teacher will need to prepare a lesson title breakdown chart.

Developing Lesson Sequence

The lesson title breakdown chart aids teachers with organizing sequential flow of occupational information. This information will help students learn simple tasks before moving to those more complex. Occupational analysis will also help teachers eliminate gaps and duplications in presenting subject matter. Figure 6-5 shows a sample lesson title

LESSON TITLE BREAKDOWN CHART

Unit No. 2   TITLE: Composition

NO.	DOING LESSON TITLES	REF. CODE
	How to:	
D2-1	Create camera ready copy	G-33
D2-2	Make-up copy	G-51
D2-3	Set typesetter (headliner)	G-62
D2-4	Set typesetter (compositor)	G-64
D2-5	Proofread type copy	G-78
D2-6	Paste-up art work	G-92
D2-7	Use Rub-Down lettering	G-101
D2-8	Proofread (final check)	G-79

NO.	KNOWING LESSON TITLES	REF. CODE
K2-1	Safety	S-36
K2-2	Layout and design fundamental	T-15
K2-3	Final plans	T-7
K2-4	Fundamentals of the typesetter (photo)	T-13
K2-5	Customer's specifications	T-44 R-6
K2-6	Comprehensive layout	T-13 R-19
K2-7	Type size, style, and customer layout	T-28 R-21

Figure 6-5. Lesson breakdown chart is an aid to proper sequencing of the flow of occupational information.

breakdown chart for a graphic arts composition unit of instruction.

The lesson title breakdown chart is similar to the chart shown in Figure 6-1. Both provide for the development of the desired instructional sequencing of occupational information and skill development lessons to be taught.

Developing Lesson Plans

Lesson plan titles should describe, in the simplest and most concise manner, what is going to be taught. To accomplish this, teachers should refer to the task breakdown for the course. They should then include in lesson titles all of the tasks to be learned. There are only two essential elements for all good lesson plans. They are (a) **what** to teach and (b) **how** to teach it. The lesson title describes "what to teach," stating the performance expected of the student. This information is repeated in the lesson objective.

In every presentation the speaker or teacher should:

• Prepare the listener for what is going to be learned in the preparation (introduction).
• Tell and explain to the listeners (presentation).
• Review what was told (summary).
• Provide for application.

SELECTION OF LESSON TITLES FOR UNITS

1. There are two types of lessons in industrial education: **doing** lessons (psychomotor) and **knowing** lessons (cognitive). Doing lessons may be thought of as demonstrations by the teacher; knowing lessons are related instruction taught in a classroom situation. Instruction in the **affective** domain (attitude, appreciations, ethics, morals, feelings, etc.) are taught more by example and by good classroom and shop organization than with definite lessons.
2. **Knowing** lessons are of three types:
   a. **Technical**—necessary to know.
   b. **General**—nice to know.
   c. **Guidance**—for purpose of giving direction for entering and advancing on the job.
3. **Doing** lessons will last from 10 to 45 minutes, exclusive of practice time. Practice time, which follows, may last several hours or days.
4. Each **doing** lesson (demonstration lesson) must have a broad enough title so that it can be broken down into:
   a. An outline of main instructional topics.
   b. Key points (things to remember to do or say). These main topics are called **operation steps**.
5. Each **knowing** lesson must be comprehensive enough so that it can be broken down into an outline of:
   a. Main instructional topics.
   b. Things to remember to do or say. Knowing lessons will generally run from 20 to 45 minutes.
6. Plan a series of **knowing** and **doing** lessons which will enable the student to do the **jobs** which you have planned for the unit.
7. **Doing** lessons (demonstration lessons) start with "How to. . . ."
8. **Doing** lessons, **demonstration** lessons, and **operations** (manipulative skill . . . lessons) are the same. **Knowing** lessons, **related information** lessons, **classroom** lessons, and **lecture** lessons are the same.
9. The beginning orientation unit may not have doing lessons. In practical nursing and cosmetology, there are several units composed completely of knowing lessons. Usually, however, both types are needed in each unit.
10. Plan your **lesson sequence** so that students can start on assigned **jobs** as soon as possible. Job assignments motivate students.
11. The lesson titles which you select will be the same as those which will appear on your lesson plans later on, so keep them short.

Figure 6-6. These titles are guidelines for constructing the occupational instruction program.

The best lesson title is one that best describes what is to be learned from the lesson presentation. These lesson titles are listed, by major unit, on a lesson title breakdown chart as either **doing** or **knowing** type lessons. Select lesson titles for the lesson title breakdown chart by the process outlined in Figure 6-6.

Lessons titled and listed on the lesson title breakdown chart become the blueprint for the detailed construction of an occupational education instructional program. Completion of the unit guide lesson title breakdown chart signals that it is time to begin developing lesson plans. When developing lesson plans, the teacher will need to be aware of the purpose of lesson plans and the basic steps for preparing and presenting a lesson.

Purpose of Lesson Plans

Many teachers feel that because they can perform the occupational competencies (or tasks) required of a skilled employee, no further planning is necessary. In many situations, it is possible to think out and teach a simple task without developing a lesson plan. However, most teachers will find it beneficial to use a written lesson plan. It helps them to cover all the content in a desired sequence without wasting instruction time. The lesson plan allows the teacher to visualize the lesson as it will be taught and mentally practice the presentation. Such visualization also helps the teacher identify and anticipate areas that may confuse students and cause them difficulties. Once they have identified these areas of learning difficulty, teachers can decide on the best way to overcome them and create a more effective learning situation.

Other purposes of the lesson plan involve:
1. Organization of materials, tools, models, and other teaching aids needed to present a lesson.
2. Instilling confidence in the teacher. This confidence will be noticed by students. This perception will, in turn, contribute to the students' learning.

Using Printed Lesson Plans

When writing lesson plans, many teachers find it helpful to use a printed lesson plan format on which to systematically list desired lesson presentation materials. A copy of a printed lesson plan format is shown in Appendix 6B.

This lesson plan format is a fill-in-the-blank type that helps the teacher develop lesson plans in a consistent manner. The lesson objective will always follow the lesson title and precede the lesson introduction.

Teachers should not feel obligated to write something in every space on the lesson plan format but should, instead, realize that the suggested lesson plan element spaces are provided to remind them to list information that may be needed. By listing such items as tools and materials, teaching aids and references when preparing to teach the lesson, the teacher develops an information trail. This trail will be needed when the teacher is called upon to give a repeat performance after the memory grows dim. Further, lesson plans provide evidence of exactly what was taught. This can be legally significant in tort liability cases.

Element of a Lesson Plan

The lesson plan format in Appendix 6B lists elements of a lesson plan. These elements are:
1. Lesson plan heading.
2. Type of lesson (technical or general information and skill demonstration).
3. Lesson title.
4. Lesson objective.
5. Tools and materials.
6. Teaching aids.
7. Informational assignment.
8. Individualized informational assignment.
9. References.
10. Step 1 — Preparation (of the student).
11. Step 2 — Presentation (of the lesson).
12. Step 3 — Application (or tryout).
13. Step 4 — Evaluation (test or checkup).

The first nine elements deal with the teacher's preparation to teach the lesson. Elements 10 through 13 are the steps used in teaching a lesson. These four have traditionally been referred to as the **four-step method** of teaching.

Using the Four-Step Plan

The purpose of these elements is to refresh the teacher's memory and serve as a guide as the teacher gathers those items needed. A two-column lesson plan format, shown in Appendix 6C, is preferred by some teachers. Notice that it has the same basic four steps in the lesson plan body.

Some teachers recognize a five-step method of teaching which includes a preliminary teacher preparation step. The teacher's preparation involves a review of the information listed on the lesson plan. These preliminary review elements extend to, but do not include, the preparation of the students introduction step.

Procedure for Writing Lesson Plans

The following procedure for writing lesson plans follows the format of Appendix 6B. After the lesson title and lesson objective have been determined and written down, the preparation, presentation, application, and evaluation steps follow in set order. (Comments on lesson plan revision problems are reviewed briefly at the end of this section in an effort to prepare the teacher for the reality of how soon new lesson plans become dated and need revision.)

All of the lesson titles for a unit guide should be listed before beginning to write even one lesson plan. This is where many teachers make a major mistake. They often begin to write lesson plans before developing a lesson title breakdown chart. The chart needs to be constructed with consideration of the amount of content to be included in each lesson. Much of the success of student learning depends on the selection and organization of instructional materials.

Lesson titles listed on the lesson title breakdown chart should reflect the performance component of the lesson objective. For example, a lesson in a private pilot flight training course might be titled, *Night Flight Procedures*. A copy of this lesson plan can be found in Appendix 6D. The lesson objectives could be: "Upon completion of this lesson the student should be able to maintain a safe aircraft attitude and position while flying the airport traffic pattern at night and performing takeoffs and landings." The title reflects the performance of flying an aircraft.

After establishing a definite aim for a lesson, the teacher should carefully plan the procedure for attaining the objective.

The lesson objective in Appendix 6D indicates that the aircraft will be flown at a consistently smooth flight path attitude avoiding sharp movement such as steep climbs, turns and dives. Another factor would be the safe position of the aircraft in relation to other aircraft determined by their navigation lights and the recognition of those lights by the student pilot.

Hopefully, this explanation of how a lesson objective can be used to determine lesson presentation content is adequate. The point is this, if students, over a period of time, consistently fail to competently meet a lesson objective during the evaluation step of that lesson, then the teacher is probably using an inadequate instructional process. This would indicate a need for lesson plan revision.

Preparation Step. After the lesson content has been determined with reference to the lesson objective, the teacher is ready to write a lesson introduction. (This is Step 1 of the Four-Step method.) The purpose of the lesson introduction is to prepare the students for their learning tasks and motivate them to learn. In other words, the lesson introduction should pass the **ACID** test, which means the introduction should get the students' **A**ttention, arouse their **C**uriosity, develop their **I**nterest, and create a **D**esire to learn. Does the introduction on the lesson plan Night Flight Procedure in Appendix 6D pass the ACID test? Most student pilots are extremely excited about learning to fly at night. Even without a lesson introduction, they are already attentive, which helps this lesson introduction generate the students' curiosity, interest and desire to learn.

Presentation Step. There are few, if any, hard and fast rules to help the teacher decide exactly what to include in the lesson presentation step. The purpose of this step is to help the teacher present new ideas, information, techniques, skills, and procedures in a step-by-step manner. The most effective instructional method depends on the nature of the things to be taught, number and level of the students in the class, and the equipment and facility available to the teacher.

Note that the presentation of the lesson plan in Appendix 6D is in outline form. There is a note to the teacher that includes directions on how or when to use handout materials. Remember, the lesson presentation step is really an outline of a planned speech which is given extemporaneously while referring to the notes periodically.

Application or Tryout Step. This step of lesson teaching is rather simple. The teacher simply provides an opportunity for the students to apply the new idea, information, techniques, and skills. The student performs the task alone or with the help of the teacher. The application or tryout step should provide experience or practice in meeting the lesson objective. Refer to Step 3 on the lesson plan in Appendix

6D. If a student competently performs the six tryout activities listed, the teacher could probably conclude that the student pilot is able to meet requirements stated in the lesson objective.

Evaluation Step. To evaluate how much the student has learned for a given lesson, the teacher develops questions that help review and/or summarize the major points of a lesson plan. These questions should relate to each of the points of the lesson presentation. The purpose is to check to see that all of the information necessary for a student to competently meet the lesson objective was presented. The number of questions necessary to accomplish this purpose will vary. The exact number should be left to the professional judgment of the teacher. A good rule of thumb is that there should probably be at least one question for each major heading of a lesson presentation outline. The lesson plan in Appendix 6D might appear to violate this rule because the presentation outline had eight major headings and only three questions. However, the questions require multiple answers which provide for evaluation of both the teaching performance and student comprehension and does not violate the rule.

Developing Teaching Aids for the Lesson Plan. After developing a lesson plan like that in Appendix 6D, a teacher may desire to create an informational assignment sheet. It is a simple matter to type the lesson plan elements (minus the content of the presentation) onto a syllabus sheet such as the one found in Appendix 6E.

It should be noted that the questions for Step 4 have not been answered on the student's informational assignment sheet. However, the answers are written on Step 4 of the lesson plan in Appendix 6D.

The information sheet used to supplement a textbook is shown in Appendix 6F.

The information sheet can be used to bring specialized information directly to the students' attention during the lesson presentation. Further explanation of the development of teaching aids will be covered in Chapter 7.

Revising Lesson Plans

Due to the changing nature of occupational education, lesson plans frequently need to be revised in order to keep the instructional program up-to-date. The extent of each revision will then depend on the degree or extent of the technological change. Instructors sometimes develop the attitude that the constant revision of lesson plans takes more effort than it is worth. As a result, some instructional programs soon become technically outdated. Most revision efforts begin as a few simple changes in the lesson presentation, (Step 2). Gradually, these changes will grow into an illegible copy. Then, a total rewrite is in order. This type of rewrite can require more effort than the initial development.

There are other reasons for lesson plan revision. For example, if a teacher is able to purchase commercially prepared lesson plans, these lesson plans seldom meet all of the instructional needs. The teacher is then faced with the modification of the purchased lesson plans. In any event, the lesson plans should be designed or revised to fit the needs for each lesson that the teacher is planning to teach.

Examples of Different Formats for Lesson Plans

Many government agencies run instructional training programs which require the development of lesson plans. Each agency develops its own customized lesson plan format. Notice that the basic elements of each format usually contain the basic elements of the Four-Step method.

The first example is a Federal Aviation Agency lesson plan, "Maneuvering by Reference to Flight Instruments." This lesson plan is shown in Appendix 6G. Note that there is an introduction (preparation) step, development (presentation) step, student's action (application) step, and conclusion (evaluation) step.

The second example is a U.S. Army lesson plan, entitled "Theory of Color." See Appendix 6H.

A quick glance at this lesson plan will show that it is more refined than the example in Appendix 6H. For example, the time element (two hours) is then broken in minute segments, five minutes (5M) for the introduction, 10 minutes (10M) for the presentation, 35 minutes (35M) for the conference. Notice that the 35-minute conference is, in reality, an application step. The student uses new concepts to discuss the information presented in the 10 minute presentation segment of the lesson. This lesson plan then moved to a 10 minute (10M) demonstration of a prism's effect on light followed again by a 35 (35M) conference for the purpose of application. The final five minutes (5M) is the recommended time for the lesson summary or evaluation step. There are 20 minutes that have not been designated; the teacher has the option of varying the pace of the instruction, spending more time in an area that the learners find difficult.

The notes to teachers are particularly helpful. They suggest **how** to present the lesson information as well as remind the teacher **when** to perform certain instructional procedures.

The U.S. Army lesson plan is a very good style for any teacher who has difficulty remembering when to show a transparency, work a math problem, display a model or perform any lesson presentation task. This plan is especially helpful if the group of learners are being presented a difficult concept for the first time. Good lesson plans with a wealth

of detail can save teachers instructional time and embarrassment.

A comparison of the Federal Aviation Agency (FAA) lesson plan and the U.S. Army lesson plan shows that there can be a great deal of difference in lesson plan detail. Nevertheless, the same basic lesson plan elements were used in both.

SUMMARY

Developing the unit guide for a unit of instruction can be a time-consuming but worthwhile task in the performance of teaching duties. The relationship of instructional materials can be shown as a succession of layers or levels. At the top is the school's curriculum. The second layer is made-up of the many courses offered by the school. At the third layer are the unit guides for the individual courses together with lesson plans and other instructional materials.

Any curriculum guide can be broken down into a variety of elements. These could lead to confusion as teachers try to understand the interrelationships of the parts. A set of 13 curriculum guide components were presented to eliminate this confusion. Each of these elements is a major division of a curriculum guide.

Safety should be a significant element in both the curriculum guide and the unit guide. While putting the students' well-being foremost, safety instruction protects the teacher from liability when accidents do occur.

A lesson plan provides the teacher with detailed instructions or directions for teaching a lesson. Great emphasis should be placed on a methodical development of each plan. A four-step method is recommended: preparation, presentation, application, and evaluation. Preprinted lesson formats are useful and worthwhile as they assure consistency and completeness in planning.

A lesson title breakdown chart should be developed for the teacher's occupational education program. Each lesson title in this chart signals a need for a lesson plan. The lesson plan will signal the need for other instructional materials. These instructional materials are necessary if the teacher wishes to be efficient and help students meet the course objectives with a minimal loss of instructional time.

Teachers should not overlook commercial lesson plans. By adopting and customizing them to fit their particular needs, teachers can save hours of preparation time.

APPENDIX 6A

V-TECS CATALOGS

V-TECS Catalogs by Occupation Titles

Vocational Technical Education Consortium of States
Curriculum Publications Clearinghouse
Western Illinois University
Horrabin Hall 46
Macomb, IL 61455

V-TECS Catalogs:
Include the Worker tasks, tools and/or materials; how to perform the tasks; and the standards of competent task performance—all validated by workers in the occupation.

V-TECS Guides:
Include units of instruction that complement the V-TECS catalogs with support knowledge needed for task performance, learning activities, performance evaluation procedures, and student information sheets; developed by instructors and workers in the occupation.

Prices:
Person ordering from the states and agencies listed below will be charged prices in accordance with that state's price structure.

V-TECS Member States:

Alabama	Kansas	Oklahoma
Arizona	Kentucky	Oregon
Arkansas	Maryland	Pennsylvania
Colorado	Massachusetts	South Carolina
Florida	Michigan	Utah
Georgia	Missouri	Virginia
Illinois	New York	Washington
Indiana	North Carolina	West Virginia

V-TECS Member Agencies:

United States Air Force
United States Army
United States Navy
United States Marine Corps
United States Department of Labor (Bureau of International Labor Affairs)

V-TECS CATALOGS
TITLE AND PUBLICATION NUMBER

Accounting Clerk	V-129
Advertising Artist	V-1
Agricultural Equipment Parts Salesman	V-2
Alterationist	V-12
Appliance Repairer	V-74
Architectural Drafter	V-63
Auctioneer	V-136
Audio-Visual Repairer	V-126
Auto Body Repairman	V-3
Automotive Mechanics	V-4
Auto Mechanics:	
Suspension System, Brakes, and Steering	V-149
Auto Parts Clerk	V-5
Automobile Air Conditioning and Electrical System	
Technician	V-150
Automobile Engine Performance Technician	V-151
Automotive Engine and Drive Train Technician	V-137
Baker	V-89
Banking Clerk/Related Occupations	V-7
Bindery Worker/Web Press Operator	V-130
Bookkeeper/Accounting/Payroll Clerk	V-8
Bricklayer	V-36
Building Repairer	V-94
Business Machine Repairer	V-79
Cabinetmaker	V-102
Carpenter (rev.)	V-9
Cashier/Checker	V-10
Caterer	V-144
Cattle Rancher	V-114

Chemical Sales/Chemical Applicator	V-68
Child Care Worker	V-11
Commercial Cook	V-116
Computer Equipment Repair	V-148
Computer Operator (rev.)	V-13
Computer Programmer	V-14
Computerized Numerical Control	V-147
Concrete Worker	V-115
Corrections Officer	V-133
Corrections Sergeant	V-134
Cosmetologist	V-15
Cotton Gin Management and Operation	V-16
County Tax Collector	V-17
Crop Production: Cotton Grower	V-100
Crop Production: Farmer, Cash Grain	V-98
Crop Production: Orchardist	V-96
Crop Production: Tobacco Grower	V-99
Crop Production: Vegetable Grower	V-97
Custom Dressmaker	V-18
Dairy Worker	V-124
Data Entry Operator	V-121
Dental Assistant	V-19
Dental Hygienist	V-113
Dental Laboratory Technician	V-87
Die Designer Jig and Fixture Designer	V-20
Diesel Engine Mechanic (rev.)	V-60
Duplicating Machine Operator	V-128
Electronics Mechanic	V-86
Emergency Medical Technician	V-21
Environmental Control System Installer/Servicer	V-110
Executive Secretary	V-83
Farm Business Manager	V-67
Farm Equipment Mechanic	V-82
Farm Equipment Operator	V-65
Farm Machine Setup Mechanic	V-140
Fashion Salesperson	V-95
Firefighter	V-22
Floriculture Worker, Retail Flower Shop Salesperson,	
and Floral Designer (rev.)	V-154
Food Marketing Manager/Supervisor	V-118
Garden Center Salesperson, Garden Center Worker,	
Landscape Worker, and Landscape Designer	V-92
Gardening/Groundskeeper	V-24
General House Worker	V-26
Hardware Salesperson	V-85
Health Care Worker	V-27
Heavy Equipment Mechanic	V-77
Home Furnishings Worker	V-28
Homemaker: Clothing and Textiles	V-69
Homemaker: Foods	V-70
Homemaker: Housing and Furnishings	V-71
Homemaker: Human Development	V-72
Homemaker: Management and Family Economics	V-73
Hospital Ward Clerk	V-29
Hotel—Motel Management Related Occupations	V-30
House Electrician	V-101
Housing Manager	V-45
Industrial Electrician	V-88
Industrial Maintenance Mechanic	V-93
Industrial Sewing	V-31
Industrial Manager	V-135
Information Processing Specialist (rev.)	V-153
Janitor	V-32
Land Survey Field Technician	V-105
Laser System Technician	V-105
Legal Secretary and Court Reporter	V-33
Licensed Practical Nurse (rev.)	V-34
Logger	V-54
Machine Tool Operator	V-132
Machinist (rev.)	V-35
Meat Cutter	V-37
Mechanical Drafting	V-139

APPENDIX 6B

TEACHER'S LESSON PLAN FORMAT (Type 1)

This lesson plan provides the format only. Adjust the writing space to suit. Lesson plans are usually three to four pages in length.

Lesson Plan # _____

Course Title _____ Course # _____

Unit Title _____ Unit # _____

Technical Information Lesson _____ General/Guidance Information Lesson _____
OR
Job Skill Demonstration Lesson _____

LESSON TITLE

Lesson Objective - Upon Completion of This Lesson the Student Should Be Able To:

Tools and Materials:

Teaching Aids:

Informational Assignment:

Individualized Informational Assignment for Special Students:

References:

STEP 1 - Introduction for Preparation of the Student:

STEP 2 - Presentation Outline:

STEP 3 - Classroom, Laboratory, Shop or Other Activities:

STEP 4 - Lesson Summary and Review Items to be Used to Evaluate the Lesson Against the Lesson Objective:

APPENDIX 6C

TEACHER'S LESSON PLAN FORMAT (Type 2)

TEACHER: Unit _____

LESSON AIM: Lesson _____

TEACHING AIDS:

MATERIALS:

REFERENCES:

_____

_____

I. PREPARATION (of the learner)

_____

_____

II. PRESENTATION (of the information)

Instructional Steps or Topics	Key Points (things to remember to do or say)
(Add sheets as needed)	(Add sheets as needed)

III. APPLICATION (drill, illustrations, analogies, oral questions, or assignments)

_____

IV. CHECK UP or tests (final check on students' comprehension of materials presented)

_____

Suggested reading for students:

The Next Lesson is:

APPENDIX 6D
TEACHER'S LESSON PLAN EXAMPLE

Lesson Plan # _____18_____

Course Title __PRIVATE PILOT FLIGHT TRAINING__   Course # _____IAT-119_____

Unit Title __CROSS-COUNTRY OPERATIONS__   Unit # _____II_____

Technical Information Lesson _____ General /Guidance Information Lesson _____
                                    OR
                   Job Skill Demonstration Lesson ___X___
_____NIGHT FLIGHT PROCEDURES_____

LESSON TITLE

Lesson Objective - Upon Completion of This Lesson the Student Should Be Able To:

1. MAINTAIN A SAFE AIRCRAFT ATTITUDE AND POSITION WHILE FLYING THE AIRPORT TRAFFIC PATTERN AT NIGHT AND PERFORMING TAKEOFFS AND LANDINGS.

Tools and Materials:

1. FLASHLIGHT.

Teaching Aids:

1. 18-119-H1 SYLLABUS SHEET.
2. 18-119-H2 NIGHT FLYING-PILOT EQUIPMENT, PREFLIGHT, AND EMERGENCIES.

Informational Assignment:

1. ANSWER THE QUESTIONS IN STEP 4 ON 18-119-H1.
2. READ HANDOUT 18-119-H2 "NIGHT FLYING".

Individualized Informational Assignment for Special Students:

NONE.

References:

1. FLIGHT INFORMATION HANDBOOK, U.S. DEPT. OF TRANSPORTATION, FEDERAL AVIATION ADMINISTRATION, OKLAHOMA CITY, OK, AC61-21A, REVISED 1980.
2. GLEIM, IRVIN N., PRIVATE PILOT FLIGHT MANEUVERS, AVIATION PUBLICATIONS, INC., GAINSVILLE, FL, 32604 (1986 ED.).

(Continued)

++NOTE: STUDENTS SHOULD REFER TO HANDOUT 18-119-H1 DURING THE LESSON
          PRESENTATION.

Step 1 - Introduction for Preparation of the Student:

NIGHT FLYING IS CONSIDERED TO BE AN IMPORTANT PHASE IN THE COMPLETE
TRAINING OF A PILOT. PROFICIENCY IN NIGHT FLYING NOT ONLY INCREASES
UTILIZATION OF THE AIRPLANE BUT IT PROVIDES IMPORTANT EXPERIENCE IN
CASE AN INTENDED DAY FLIGHT INADVERTENTLY EXTENDS INTO DARKNESS.

NIGHT FLYING IS REALLY NOT DIFFICULT BUT IT DIFFERS FROM DAYLIGHT
OPERATION, IN THAT VISION IS RESTRICTED AT NIGHT. THIS INSTILLS A
CERTAIN AMOUNT OF ANXIETY IN PILOTS WHO LACK NIGHT-FLIGHT EXPERIENCE.
THESE APPREHENSIONS CAN BE OVERCOME ONLY BY ACQUIRING THE NECESSARY
KNOWLEDGE AND EXPERIENCE IN NIGHT OPERATIONS. AS CONFIDENCE IS GAINED
THROUGH EXPERIENCE, MANY PILOTS PREFER NIGHT FLYING OVER DAY FLYING
BECAUSE THE AIR IS USUALLY SMOOTHER AND GENERALLY THERE IS LESS AIR
TRAFFIC.

STEP 2 - Presentation Outline:
  ++NOTE: REFER TO HANDOUT 18-119-H2 AS NEEDED DURING THIS LESSON
            PRESENTATION.
  I.   AIRCRAFT PREFLIGHT AND PILOT EQUIPMENT.
       A.   TAKE A FLASHLIGHT OR BOOK OF MATCHES.
  II. DIFFERENCES IN VISUAL REFERENCES AVAILABLE AT NIGHT. (DEMONSTRATION)
       A.   REDUCED NUMBER OF OBJECTS VISIBLE.
       B.   PERIPHERAL VISION USED AT NIGHT.
       C.   IMPORTANCE OF PRESERVING NIGHT VISION ADAPTATION.
  III. TAKEOFF AND DEPARTURE ALIGNMENT TECHNIQUES. (DIRECTED PERFORMANCE)
       A.   SELECT RELATIVELY DISTANT REFERENCE POINTS.
       B.   ESTABLISH CLIMB ATTITUDE FOLLOWING TAKEOFF WITH POSITIVE
            RATE OF CLIMB.
       C.   OBSERVE FOR OTHER AIRCRAFT LIGHTS.
  IV. POWER APPROACH AND LANDINGS. (DIRECTED PERFORMANCE)
       A.   ATTITUDE AND POWER ADJUSTMENT.
       B.   APPROACH PATH ANGLE.
       C.   AIRSPEED CONTROL.
       D.   TOUCHDOWN AND ROLLOUT.
       E.   BLACKOUT LANDING--MINIMUM ONE PERFORMED AS SIMULATED
            EMERGENCY.

(Continued)

V. USE OF LANDING LIGHTS. (DIRECTED PERFORMANCE)
    A. POWER REQUIRED.
    B. TECHNIQUE IN USING.
    C. COOLING PROBLEM.

VI. INTERPRETATION OF AIRCRAFT AND OBSTRUCTION LIGHTS. (DIRECTED PRACTICE)
    A. RECOGNITION OF AIRCRAFT DIRECTION OF FLIGHT AND RIGHT OF WAY FROM OBSERVED NAVIGATION LIGHTS.
    B. ANGLES AIRCRAFT NAVIGATION LIGHTS ARE VISIBLE.
    C. INTERPRETATION OF OBSTRUCTION LIGHTS.

VII. FLIGHT MANEUVERS OVER DARK AREAS. (WHEN FEASIBLE--DIRECTED PRACTICE)
    A. ABSENCE OF VISUAL REFERENCES.
    B. IMPORTANCE OF INSTRUMENT INTERPRETATION.
    C. LIKLIHOOD OF LOSS OF VFR CONTROL.
++NOTE: REFER TO HANDOUT 18-119-H2, PAGE 2.

VIII. SIMULATED EMERGENCIES. (DIRECTED PERFORMANCE)
    A. ENGINE FAILURE.
    B. ELECTRICAL SYSTEM FAILURE.
    C. RECOVERY FROM UNUSUAL ATTITUDES.

STEP 3 - Classroom, Laboratory, Shop or Other Activities:
++NOTE: DURING IN-FLIGHT INSTRUCTION THE STUDENT SHOULD:
1. PERFORM AT LEAST 10 TAKEOFFS AND LANDINGS.
2. PERFORM A CROSSWIND TAKEOFF AND LANDING.
3. TAKEOFF AND LAND WITHOUT THE LANDING LIGHT TURNED ON.
4. RECOVER FROM AN UNUSUAL FLIGHT ATTITUDE.
5. PRACTICE A SIMULATED ENGINE FAILURE.
6. PRACTICE A SIMULATED ELECTRICAL FAILURE.

STEP 4 - Lesson Summary and Review Items to be Used to Evaluate the Lesson Against the Lesson Objective:
1. WHAT PREPARATION AND EQUIPMENT IS ESSENTIAL FOR NIGHT FLYING?

    A. PREFLIGHT CHECK LIGHT (ADDED TO THE CHECK LIST FOR DAY FLIGHT)
        I.   AIRPLANE POSITION LIGHTS, RED, GREEN, AND WHITE.
        II.   ANTICOLLISION LIGHT--RED ROTATING BEACON.
        III. LANDING LIGHT.
        IV.   COCKPIT AND INSTRUMENT PANEL LIGHTS.

(Continued)

    B. PILOT EQUIPMENT

        I.   FLASH LIGHT.   IV.   EQUIPMENT LAYOUT OR ORGANIZATION PLAN.
        II. NAVIGATION CHARTS.
        III. FUSES.

2. EXPLAIN AIRPLANE, AIRPORT AND NAVIGATION LIGHTING.
            INSTRUCTOR'S JUDGMENT

3. LIST THE ESSENTIAL ELEMENTS RELATING TO NIGHT FLIGHT
    OPERATIONS.

        1. INSPECT THE AIRPLANE BY FOLLOWING THE CHECKLIST WHICH
            INCLUDES ITEMS ESSENTIAL FOR NIGHT FLIGHT OPERATION.
        2. START, TAXI AND PERFORM PRE-TAKEOFF CHECK ADHERING TO
            GOOD OPERATING PRACTICE.
        3. PERFORM TAKEOFFS AND CLIMBS WITH EMPHASIS ON VISUAL
            REFERENCES. (STOP THE LIGHTS FROM MOVING ACROSS THE
            WIND SCREEN BY CORRECTING FOR CROSSWINDS).
        4. NAVIGATE AND MAINTAIN ORIENTATION UNDER VFR CONDITIONS.
        5. APPROACH AND LAND ADHERING TO GOOD OPERATING PRACTICES
            FOR NIGHT FLIGHT OPERATIONS.

APPENDIX 6E

SYLLABUS SHEET FOR LESSON 18
PRIVATE PILOT FLIGHT TRAINING

UNIT #III CROSS-COUNTRY OPERATIONS

NIGHT FLIGHT PROCEDURES

LESSON OBJECTIVE—UPON COMPLETION OF THIS LESSON, THE STUDENT SHOULD BE ABLE TO:
1. MAINTAIN A SAFE AIRCRAFT ATTITUDE AND POSITION WHILE FLYING THE AIRPORT TRAFFIC PATTERN AT NIGHT AND PERFORMING TAKEOFFS AND LANDINGS.

TEACHING AIDS:

1. 18-119-H1 SYLLABUS SHEET.
2. 18-119-H2 NIGHT FLYING-PILOT EQUIPMENT, PREFLIGHT, AND EMERGENCIES.

INFORMATIONAL ASSIGNMENT:

1. ANSWER THE QUESTIONS IN STEP 4 ON 18-119-H1.
2. READ HANDOUT 18-119-H2 ''NIGHT FLYING.''

INDIVIDUALIZED INFORMATIONAL ASSIGNMENT FOR SPECIAL STUDENTS:

NONE.

STEP 1—INTRODUCTION FOR PREPARATION OF THE STUDENT:

NIGHT FLYING IS CONSIDERED TO BE AN IMPORTANT PHASE IN THE COMPLETE TRAINING OF A PILOT. PROFICIENCY IN NIGHT FLYING NOT ONLY INCREASES UTILIZATION OF THE AIRPLANE BUT IT PROVIDES IMPORTANT EXPERIENCE IN CASE AN INTENDED DAY FLIGHT INADVERTENTLY EXTENDS INTO DARKNESS.

NIGHT FLYING IS REALLY NOT DIFFICULT BUT IT DIFFERS FROM DAYLIGHT OPERATION IN THAT VISION IS RESTRICTED AT NIGHT. THIS INSTILLS A CERTAIN AMOUNT OF ANXIETY IN PILOTS WHO LACK NIGHT-FLIGHT EXPERIENCE. THESE APPREHENSIONS CAN BE OVERCOME ONLY BY ACQUIRING THE NECESSARY KNOWLEDGE AND EXPERIENCE IN NIGHT OPERATIONS. AS CONFIDENCE IS GAINED THROUGH EXPERIENCE, MANY PILOTS PREFER NIGHT FLYING OVER DAY FLYING BECAUSE THE AIR IS USUALLY SMOOTHER AND GENERALLY THERE IS LESS AIR TRAFFIC.

STEP 2—INSTRUCTOR'S PRESENTATION:

STEP 3—CLASSROOM, LABORATORY, SHOP OR OTHER ACTIVITIES:

††NOTE: DURING IN-FLIGHT INSTRUCTION, THE STUDENT SHOULD:
1. PERFORM AT LEAST 10 TAKEOFFS AND LANDINGS.
2. PERFORM A CROSSWIND TAKEOFF AND LANDING.
3. TAKEOFF AND LAND WITHOUT THE LANDING LIGHT TURNED ON.
4. RECOVER FROM AN UNUSUAL FLIGHT ATTITUDE.
5. PRACTICE A SIMULATED ENGINE FAILURE.
6. PRACTICE A SIMULATED ELECTRICAL FAILURE.

STEP 4—LESSON SUMMARY AND REVIEW:

1. WHAT PREPARATION AND EQUIPMENT IS ESSENTIAL FOR NIGHT FLYING?

2. EXPLAIN AIRPLANE, AIRPORT AND NAVIGATION LIGHTING.

3. LIST THE ESSENTIAL ELEMENTS RELATING TO NIGHT FLIGHT OPERATIONS.

APPENDIX 6F

INFORMATION SHEET

NIGHT FLYING

Before attempting night operations it is recommended that a complete and thorough checkout by a competent flight instructor be accomplished. This checkout should include a night cross-country flight with landings at airports other than the home field.

Pilot Equipment

The pilot, before beginning a night flight, should carefully consider certain personal equipment that should be readily available during the flight. This equipment may not differ greatly from that needed for a day flight, but the importance of its availability when needed at night cannot be overemphasized.

At least one reliable flashlight is recommended as standard equipment on all night flights. A "D" cell size flashlight with a bulb switching mechanism that can be used to select white or red light, is preferable. The white light is for use while performing the preflight visual inspection of the airplane, and the red light for use in performing cockpit operations. Since the red light is nonglaring, it will not impair night vision. Some pilots prefer two flashlights, one with a white light for preflight, and the other a penlight type with a red light. The latter can be suspended by a string from around the neck to ensure that the light is always readily available during flight. One word of caution, if a red light is used for reading an aeronautical chart the red features of the chart will not show up.

Just as for daylight flights, aeronautical charts are essential for night cross-country flight. If the intended course is near the edge of the chart, and the adjacent chart is not available to identify those landmarks which lie off the primary chart, confusion could result, particularly if the pilot strays off course.

To prevent losing essential items in the dark cockpit, the pilot should have a clipboard or mapboard on which charts, navigation logs, and other essentials can be fastened. Map cases in which to store needed materials should also be considered.

A reliable clock is essential for both day and night flights.

Regardless of what is used, organization of the equipment and materials in the cockpit into a simple well-arranged manner, eases the burden on the pilot and certainly enhances safety.

Preparation and Preflight

Night flying requires that pilots have a complete realization of their abilities and limitations, and observe more caution than during day operations. Although careful planning of any flight is essential for maximum safety and efficiency, night flying demands more attention to all details of preflight preparation and planning.

Preparation for a night flight should include a thorough study of the available weather reports and forecasts, with particular attention given to temperature/dew point spread because of the possibility of formation of ground fog during the night flight. Also, emphasis should be placed on awareness of wind direction and speed, since drifting cannot be detected as readily at night as during the day.

On night cross-country flight pertinent aeronautical charts should be selected, including the appropriate adjacent charts. Course lines should be drawn in black so as to be more distinguishable, and direction, distances, and time estimates accurately recorded. Aeronautical charts should be folded and systematically arranged prior to flight in a manner that they will be convenient to use in the cockpit.

Prominently lighted checkpoints along the prepared course should be noted. Rotating beacons at airports, lighted obstructions, lights of cities or towns, and lights from major highway traffic all provide excellent visual checkpoints. The use of radio navigation aids and communication facilities add significantly to the safety and efficiency of the night flight and should be considered in preflight planning.

All personal equipment should be checked prior to flight to ensure proper functioning. It is very disconcerting to find, at the time of need, that a flashlight, for example, doesn't work.

A thorough preflight check of the airplane and a review of its systems and emergency procedures, is of particular importance for night operations. Since each airplane has its own checklist, it is not intended in this chapter to cover all the specific points. However, there are some general areas, in addition to those involved on all flights, that should be included on the night preflight check.

Night Emergencies

Perhaps the pilot's greatest concern about flying a single-engine airplane at night is complete engine failure, even though adverse weather and poor pilot judgment account for most serious accidents.

All airplane lights should be turned "on" momentarily and checked for loose connections by tapping the light fixture while the light is "on." If the lights blink while being "tapped" further investigation to determine the cause should be initiated.

The parking ramp should be examined prior to entering the airplane. During the day it is quite easy to see stepladders, chuckholes, stray wheel chocks, and other obstructions, but at night it is more difficult, and a check of the area can prevent taxiing mishaps.

If the engine fails at night, the first step is to maintain *positive control* of the airplane—do not panic. A normal glide should be established and maintained and the airplane turned toward an airport or away from congested areas. A check should be made to determine the cause of the engine failure such as the position of magneto switches, fuel selectors, or primer. If possible, the cause of the malfunction should be corrected immediately and the engine restarted. Orientation with the wind direction also should be maintained to avoid a downwind landing. The landing lights should be checked at altitude and turned on in sufficient time to illuminate the terrain or obstacles along the flight path. If the landing lights are unusable and outside visual references are not available, the airplane should be held in level-landing attitude until the ground is contacted. Most important of all, positive control of the airplane must be maintained at all times—do not allow a stall to occur.

APPENDIX 6G

SAMPLE LESSON PLAN FOR A 90-MINUTE GROUND SCHOOL PERIOD

LESSON __MANEUVERING BY REFERENCE TO FLIGHT INSTRUMENTS__ STUDENT _____ DATE____

OBJECTIVE
- TO DEVELOP THE STUDENT'S UNDERSTANDING OF ATTITUDE INSTRUMENT FLYING AS RELATED TO STRAIGHT-AND-LEVEL FLIGHT, TURNS, CLIMBS AND DESCENTS, AND RECOVERY FROM UNUSUAL ATTITUDES

ELEMENTS
- STRAIGHT-AND-LEVEL FLIGHT
- TURNS
- CLIMBS AND DESCENTS
- RECOVERY FROM UNUSUAL ATTITUDES

SCHEDULE
- STRAIGHT-AND-LEVEL FLIGHT   : 25
- TURNS   : 25
- CLIMBS AND DESCENTS   : 25
- RECOVERY FROM UNUSUAL ATTITUDES   : 15

EQUIPMENT
- INSTRUMENT PANEL MOCKUP
- FAA INSTRUMENT FLYING HANDBOOK
- SELECTED SLIDES ON INSTRUMENT FLYING
- CHALKBOARD AND CHALK

INSTRUCTOR'S ACTIONS
- DISCUSS LESSON OBJECTIVE
- DISCUSS CONCEPT OF ATTITUDE INSTRUMENT FLYING
- DISCUSS, AND BY MEANS OF INSTRUMENT PANEL MOCKUP OR CHALKBOARD, DEMONSTRATE STRAIGHT-AND-LEVEL FLIGHT, TURNS, CLIMBS AND DESCENTS AND UNUSUAL ATTITUDE RECOVERIES
- ASSIGN INDIVIDUAL STUDENTS TASK OF DE-SCRIBING, AND DEMONSTRATING BY MEANS OF INSTRUMENT PANEL MOCKUP OR CHALK-BOARD, THE CONTROL OF AN AIRPLANE BY REFERENCE TO FLIGHT INSTRUMENTS
- CRITIQUE STUDENT PRESENTATION AND ASK QUESTIONS

STUDENT'S ACTIONS
- DISCUSS LESSON OBJECTIVE
- LISTEN, TAKE NOTES, ASK PERTINENT QUESTIONS
- VISUALIZE INSTRUMENT MANEUVERS
- PRESENT MANEUVERS AND RESPOND TO INSTRUCTOR'S QUESTIONS

COMPLETION STANDARDS
- THE STUDENT SHOULD DEMONSTRATE, BY MEANS OF AN ORAL QUIZ OR WRITTEN TEST, THAT HE HAS AN UNDERSTANDING OF THE CONCEPT OF ATTITUDE INSTRUMENT FLYING AND OF THE PERFORMANCE OF BASIC FLIGHT MANEUVERS BY REFERENCE TO FLIGHT INSTRUMENTS

(Continued)

APPENDIX 6G—page 2

"INSTRUCTOR'S ACTIONS" EXPANDED AND DETAILED

INSTRUCTIONAL AID	OUTLINE	NOTES
SLIDES ON INSTRUMENT FLYING	1. INTRODUCTION	1. ATTENTION--MAKE A STATEMENT OR ASK A QUESTION THAT RELATES LESSON TO STUDENT GOAL OF BECOMING A PROFICIENT INSTRUMENT PILOT. REVIEW PREVIOUS MATERIAL ON ATTITUDE INSTRUMENT FLYING AND GIVE TIE-IN BETWEEN THIS LESSON AND PREVIOUS LESSONS. 2. MOTIVATION--PROVIDE STUDENTS REASONS FOR NEEDING TO LEARN BASIC INSTRUMENT FLIGHT TECHNIQUE. 3. OVERVIEW--DISCUSS LESSON OBJECTIVE AND KEY IDEAS TO BE PRESENTED.
INSTRUMENT PANEL MOCKUP CHALKBOARD SLIDES ON INSTRUMENT FLYING FAA INSTRUMENT FLYING HANDBOOK	2. DEVELOPMENT	1. DISCUSS CONCEPT OF ATTITUDE INSTRUMENT FLYING. 2. PRESENT STRAIGHT-AND-LEVEL FLIGHT ON MOCKUP FROM STANDPOINT OF PITCH, BANK, POWER, AND TRIM CONTROL. 3. PRESENT TURNS ON MOCKUP FROM STANDPOINT OF PITCH, BANK, POWER, AND TRIM CONTROL. 4. PRESENT CLIMBS AND DESCENTS ON MOCKUP FROM STANDPOINT OF PITCH, BANK, POWER, AND TRIM CONTROL. 5. PRESENT RECOVERY FROM UNUSUAL ATTITUDES ON MOCKUP. 6. ASSIGN INDIVIDUAL STUDENTS TO PRESENT INSTRUMENT MANEUVERS ON MOCKUP MONITOR STUDENT PRESENTATION AND MAKE APPROPRIATE COMMENTS.
FAA INSTRUMENT FLYING HANDBOOK	3. CONCLUSION	1. RETRACE IMPORTANT POINTS RELATED TO ELEMENTS OF KNOWLEDGE PRESENTED AND RELATE THEM TO THE LESSON OBJECTIVE. 2. DETERMINE WHETHER OR NOT STUDENTS HAVE MET OBJECTIVE OF LESSON BY SHORT ORAL QUIZ OR WRITTEN TEST. 3. ASSIGN STUDENTS TO STUDY CHAPTER V OF THE FAA INSTRUMENT FLYING HANDBOOK AS IT RELATES TO MAGNETIC COMPASS, TURNS TO PREDETERMINED HEADINGS AND TIMED TURNS. GIVE TIE-IN BETWEEN THIS LESSON AND NEXT LESSON.

APPENDIX 6H

LESSON PLAN EXAMPLE

DEPARTMENT OF SPECIALIST TRAINING
US ARMY SIGNAL SCHOOL
FORT MONMOUTH, NEW JERSEY

COURSE: Television Equipment Repair

ANNEX: Color Television (Annex P)

LESSON TITLE: Theory of Color

OBJECTIVES: Familarization with the basic principles of light.

REFERENCES: Introduction to Color, Kaufman; Television Engineering, Wentworth; Television Simplified, Kiver

TRAINING AIDS: Color charts, prisms.

METHOD OF
INSTRUCTION: Conference, Demonstration

TIME: 2 Hours

NOTES TO
INSTRUCTOR:

INTRODUCTION:

5M

1. This last phase of instruction is on color television. We will study the theory of light and color, the operation of the TK-41 color television camera chain including the rack mounted accessories, the operation, theory, alignment, maintenance, and repair of color television receivers. This will include the chroma circuit, convergence and purity alignment, and kinescope adjustments.

2. During this lesson we will study the sources of light, the wavelength and frequency of the visible spectrum and the action of the human eye and the prism when stimulated by light.

3. The color television system uses three primary colors to reproduce a televised scene. We will study the characteristics of color, the additive process in color mixing, and the method used to separate scenes into the three colors required for the video signal.

(Continued)

APPENDIX 6H—page 2

PRESENTATION:

10 M

1. Practical Exercise: Students will be given their preventive maintenance assignments for the week. The method of maintenance will be explained for any new equipment.

26 T2-32-(1-2)

   a. Instruct the students to use the correct form and the correct line items.

   b. Instruct the students to report all safety hazards.

35 M

2. Conference: Discuss the nature of light and color applicable to color television.

   a. What is light? There are many definitions from the dictionary, text books, and books on physics.

     (1) Light is an extension of the electromagnetic spectrum.

     (2) Light is a form of radiant energy emitted by, and flowing away from luminous bodies such as the sun or various types of lamps.

     (3) Light is visible radiant energy which causes the visual sensation in the eyes.

     (4) Light is radiant energy which travels through space as electromagnetic waves so short that there are 36,000 to 63,000 per inch depending upon the color of this light.

     (5) The fundamental source of light on the earth is the sun.

   b. How does a person see light?

     (1) The eye is like an antenna circuit of a radio receiver or a television set which is tuned to receive a band of frequencies.

     (2) When the eye is focused on some object emitting or reflecting these frequencies, an electrical impulse is transmitted to the brain. The person then knows that light is present. The amount of light and the frequency of the light tell the brain how bright and what color the light is.

   c. What is white light? White light is not a single color, it is actually all colors shining at the same time.

(Continued)

d. What is color?

    (1) Color is determined by the frequency of the light being emitted or reflected from an object.

    (2) The eye receives a signal from an object of a certain frequency, and the brain is told that the light is red, green, or some other color.

26T2-32-(1-2)

    (3) If the eye is stimulated by two different colors having different frequencies, the sensation of a third color results.

e. The complete electromagnetic spectrum is shown in 26T2-32IS(1-2) Figure 1A.

f. The visible spectrum is shown in detail in diagram 26T2-32IS(1-2) Figure 1B. It is common to speak in terms of wavelengths instead of frequencies at this end of the electromagnetic spectrum. It has been said that there are 30,000 color combinations in the visible spectrum. There are no definite cutoff points between colors.

g. The meter is too large a unit to use in measuring wavelengths as short as the visible light waves. Smaller units are used.

    (1) The MICRON is one millionth of a meter.

    (2) The MILLIMICRON is one-thousandth of a MICRON.

    (3) The ANGSTROM is one-tenth of a MILLIMICRON.

        (a) The ANGSTROM is about 1/250,000,000 of an inch.

        (b) The symbol for an Angstrom is the letter Å.

h. It can be seen from the diagram that the wavelength for green is between 510 and 580 millimicrons. The lower limit of red has a wavelength of 700 millimicrons. This can be expressed as .7 microns. This is equivalent to 1/31,500 of an inch.

i. What is black?

    (1) Black is the absence of light.

    (2) Objects are visible only if they emit or reflect light.

j. The prism.

    (1) Isaac Newton demonstrated that if a white light passed through a prism, a series of colored stripes appeared on a white screen behind the prism. This

(Continued)

occurs because different colors at different frequencies bend at different angles when going from one medium to another. This is the same phenomena that causes color abberations in a lens. (26T2-32IS-Figure 2).

26T2-32-(1-2)

 (2) The reverse action of a prism is similar. If many colors are focused on a prism, a white light will shine out the other side.

 k. Other facts about light.

  (1) Transparent objects can be seen through.
  (2) Opaque objects can not be seen through.
  (3) Translucent objects cannot be seen through clearly.
  (4) A ray of light will be bent if it travels from one medium to another. This is called refraction.

10M

3. Demonstration: Demonstrate the prism. A flashlight or floodlight will be used to project the light through the prism. Throughout the discussion, correlate as many points as possible by demonstrating prism, filter and mirror affects.

35M

4. Conference: Discuss the characteristics of color.

 a. The sensation of white light can be created in the brain of a person by combining three colored lights in proper proportion. These colors are red, blue and green. By combining these three colors in different proportions many other colors can be seen.

 b. It is not necessary for these three colors to be present at the same time for the eye to see the white light. If these colors are made to appear at a fast rate the persistency of the vision of the eye will cause a person to see white.

 c. The screen of a tricolor picture tube contains dots arranged in triangular patterns. Each dot is excited by its own electron beam and emits a red, green or blue light. The intensity of each electron beam determines how bright each dot will glow. The cluster of dots can emit a white light or any other color depending on the strength of the individual beams.

 d. Another method of producing colored light is by holding a colored transparent filter in front of a white light. Only the color which is the same as the filter will pass

(Continued)

26T2-32-(1-2)

through the filter. When this occurs, it is called a transmission or additive filter.

e. Paints, inks, crayon coloring, etc, act as subtractive filters. In the subtractive color process, the filter absorbs the desired color from white light and transmits or passes the other colors. If a person looks at a can of red paint, he sees red light reflected from it. All practical color television systems are based on the additive system.

f. Human eye response to colors.

    (1) The human eye has a greater response to green than it does to blue or red. This means that if all the colored lights were projected with equal power, the green light would seem the brightest to to the eye.

    (2) It is also true that in a white light there is more green present than any other color.

g. Brightness or luminance.

    (1) This is an indication of the quantity of light projected or reflected into the eye or a lens system. Brightness tells how light or dark a scene will be. A red cloth would appear bright red in a lighted room. The same cloth would not be as bright in a darkened hallway. The red cloth would still be the same color but the amount of light reflected would be different.

NOTE: The instructor will demonstrate this principle by holding a piece of red cloth with the room lights on and then with the room lights off.

i. Hue.

    (1) This term identifies the color of an object. The hue indicates whether an object is red, green or blue. The hue is determined by the wavelength. Colors in the same group have the same hue.

    (2) Red, pink, and maroon have the same hue, namely red. The red portion of the spectrum is from 610 to 700 millimicrons. There are many different colors which have a red hue.

26T2-32-(1-2)

j. Saturation.

(Continued)

(1) A 100% saturated color contains no white light. Every pure individual color in the spectrum is a fully saturated color. The degree of saturation determines the shading or tint of a color.

(2) If red becomes diluted with white light it becomes pink, or an unsaturated color. Colors which are diluted are pale or pastel; highly saturated colors are regarded as strong or vivid colors.

k. Luminance and chromaticity.

(1) These two terms refer to aspects of color in a television system.

(2) Luminance is synonomous with brightness; how bright a color will appear.

(3) Chromaticity refers to the hue and saturation aspects of color.

(4) The black and white television signal is the luminance signal.

(5) The color portion is the chrominance signal.

l. How colors are matched in color television.

(1) If red, green, and blue lights are matched in the proper proportion, the eye will see a white light. If there is a different proportion of mixing, the eye will not see a white light, but a light tinted with the color which is predominate

(2) It has been determined by experiment that the following percentages of the three colors will yield a white light.

Red - 30%
Green - 59%
Blue - 11%

(3) These percentages show that the greatest portion of white light is composed of green, a less amount of red, and a lesser amount of blue.

(4) Where green and blue add, the resultant color is greenish-blue called cyan.

(5) Red and blue mix to produce a purple color called magenta.

(6) Red and green produce yellow.

(7) Red and less green produce orange.

(8) Practically all colors can be produced by some combination of red, green and blue.

(Continued)

26 T2-32-(1-2)

m. Color resolution capabilities of the eye.

    (1) The eyes cannot detect color of very small objects or areas. For objects produced by .5 to 1.5 MHz video frequencies the blues and yellows become indistinguishable from gray. For very small objects produced by video frequencies of 1.5 to 4.0 MHz only shades of brightness are seen.

    (2) All that is required in color transmission is a 1.5 MHz band. The remainder of the video picture containing all the fine detail, is reproduced by the luminance signal. This will be explained further in the next two lessons.

SUMMARY:

5M

1. The following information should be in the students notes.

  a. Color television uses three primary colors.

    (1) Red -   615 millimicrons.
    (2) Green -   538 millimicrons.
    (3) Blue -   460 millimicrons.

  b. The following percentages are required to produce white light.

    (1) Red -   30%
    (2) Green -   59%
    (3) Blue -   11%

  c. The eye is more responsive to green light than any other colored light.

  d. The three characteristics of color are; brightness, hue and saturation.

2. Explain the meaning of:

  a. Brightness.
  b. Hue.
  c. Saturation.

3. What percentage of the red, green and blue signals are used in the color television system?

4. Does the normal eye see color equally well in large as well as small areas?

5. How does the subtractive method of color mixing differ from the additive method?

26 T2-32-(1-2)

Chapter 7

INSTRUCTION SHEETS

by

Clifton P. Campbell, Professor
Technological and Adult Education
The University of Tennessee
Knoxville, Tennessee

INTRODUCTION

The nomenclature of instruction sheets can be confusing. Over the years, teachers and curriculum developers have used a variety of titles for different types of sheets. This is partially because of the difficulty in classifying them into clear-cut types with universally accepted names or titles. Most would agree, however, that these sheets, no matter what they are called, are basic to instruction in occupational education. Under the general heading of instruction sheets, there are four common types. Those titles used most often in the literature and by experienced teachers are provided below.

1. *Information sheet* — provides additional, amplifying, or background information of various kinds.
2. *Assignment sheet* — directs students to perform learning activities such as reading, problem solving, observing, or practice. It is often found in student workbooks and study guides where the pages may be perforated for easy removal and submission.
3. *Operation sheet* — provides the instructions necessary to perform each procedural step in a single manipulative operation. (It is called an Operation Chart in Russia.)
4. *Job sheet* — provides directions and sequential steps on how to do a complete job task involving different operations. (It is called a Technological Chart in Germany).

Each of these types is discussed fully in this chapter.

Other types of instruction sheets include the following:

• *Diagram sheet* — supplies schematic and block diagrams, flow charts, or illustrations that do not exist in materials available to the student. It may contain blank portions for students to complete. A diagram sheet is often used in class and for follow-up review during the application phase of instruction.

• *Experiment or laboratory sheet* — a form of assignment sheet. It is used in laboratory courses such as electricity and electronics. It aids students in performing an experiment or trial problem demonstrating the application of a principle. Space is included for recording data and conclusions derived from the experiment. The experiment sheet is somewhat like an operation or a job sheet; it deals with a sequence of procedures to be followed. Its purpose is to develop technical understanding and skill; operation and job sheets are intended to develop manipulative skill.

• *Note-taking sheet* — used for lessons that provide important information to which students must refer from time-to-time or which they must commit to memory. It contains an outline of the subject matter headings and adequate space for the student to write notes appropriate to the headings. Items such as new terms and their definitions are also provided. Frequently, it includes a list of pertinent reference publications. A note-taking sheet may also contain drawings to be labeled or any other "fill-in" activity which optimizes learning.

• *Practice sheet* — a form of assignment sheet. It actively involves students in practicing what was taught by applying their knowledge and skills in various exercises.

• *Problem sheet* — used to pose practical problems such as troubleshooting that require analysis and decision-making in their solution.

• *Procedure sheet* — the title used, particularly by health occupations teachers, for a combination of operation and job sheets.

• *Project sheet* — primarily a listing of operations to be performed in making a project. It usually includes a line drawing of the completed project. While similar in many ways to the job sheet, it differs in that the outcome is a product rather than the performance of a job task. The project sheet and method are limited largely to Industrial Arts courses.

• *Project planning or job plan sheet* — facilitates student participation in planning practical work to be completed in the laboratory or shop. A teacher-prepared form, similar to a blank job sheet, requires the student to supply (a) a working drawing or sketch, (b) a bill of materials, (c) a list of tools and equipment needed, (d) a sequential list of procedural steps and (e) other planning details. It customarily includes a place for the teacher to sign or initial approval before the work is begun.

• *Self-help sheet* — designed for individual study. Information is given, a task assigned, and questions provided to test knowledge of the covered topic.

• *Work or report sheet*—a form completed by students in the process of gathering data or solving problems. It is sometimes used to record the readings or measurements taken in an experiment. Adequate space is provided for writing the required data directly on the form.

These "other types" of instruction sheets are essentially variations or composites of the four types listed earlier. The titles provided, along with a brief description of the sheets, will aid in noting differences between them.

In some courses and programs the types of instruction sheets used fall clearly under the four cited titles. On occasion, however, a sheet may combine content from more than one type. Therefore, it will have no commonly recognized title. For example, a sheet may contain some of the content normally found in an information sheet, together with procedures usually included in an operation sheet. In any case, instruction sheets should fill the needs of the situation. If separate information and operation sheets are appropriate, they should be used. If a combination sheet is better, the practical approach is to develop such a sheet and use it.

When doubt arises as to what title to use for an instruction sheet, it is probable that any title will suffice. Little time should be spent in classifying doubtful cases. It is better to concentrate on adapting or developing the necessary instruction sheets and let the type classification take care of itself.

INDIVIDUAL DIFFERENCES

It is seldom possible or necessary for laboratory- and field-based courses or programs to have sufficient equipment for all students to perform the same operation or job task simultaneously. Differences between students in any group will cause them to progress at varying rates. In short order, they will be working on a variety of tasks. Staggered progress has a side benefit of better equipment utilization. It is not likely that anyone will be idle because the required equipment is in use.

Effective teaching demands recognition that learning is an individual achievement. This is true whether students are assembled in a group learning situation or are trying singly to learn different things at the same time. Variations which distinguish individuals from each other include (a) the wide range of skills and experience, (b) motivation and attitude, (c) aptitude, (d) intelligence, (e) reading grade level, and (f) educational background. Additionally, there is never the same degree of interest or readiness among students. Furthermore, they do not have the same aspirations for the future. These are individual and personal, not group, characteristics.

Accommodating Individual Differences

To accommodate these differences, instruction sheets must provide quality instruction that will permit students to make maximum progress at their own rate. The sheets must be available to the student when needed. A student should not have to wait for instruction until everyone else is ready. Furthermore, others should not be required to

move on before they are ready.

Teachers unfamiliar with the importance of attending to variations in student characteristics largely ignore them. They follow the practice of delaying instruction until a majority of the students are ready. This wastes time and leads to idle and lazy behavior patterns. When required to take instruction before they are ready to apply it, students tend to lose interest and become inattentive.

The full use of well-prepared instruction sheets can help avoid this dilemma. They make it possible to supply the instruction students need at the time they need it. Moreover, they provide structure in the laboratory.

For example, a teacher shows and tells a few students, who are at the same point in their progress, how to perform a job task. Then the job sheet, containing clear step-by-step instructions, is handed out and discussed. The fact that the information is appropriate and usable emphasizes their value. Using the job sheet as a guide, the students work independently as the teacher circulates among the entire group giving individual help where needed. When a few more students are ready, the cycle is repeated. In this way, slower learners get the attention and particular help they need. They are thus able to progress at a rate which is realistic for them, while the more capable move ahead at their own pace.

It is the intent of instruction sheets to sort out difficult content, explaining it in a way that students will understand. Instruction sheets reduce the need to re-explain procedures and repeat directions for each student. Additionally, those who experience difficulty in understanding or remembering verbal instructions have the benefit of clear and explicit directions that can be reviewed as needed. They can be referred to at any time, in or out of class, and as often as necessary.

Instruction sheets are an accurate, permanent record which provides opportunity for intensive study. Oral instructions, however, are but momentary, leaving the student to rely on memory or hastily-taken notes. Because of these features, instruction sheets provide an excellent means of coping with individual differences in learning.

OTHER BENEFITS

In addition to those already mentioned, there are other benefits associated with the proper use of well-prepared instruction sheets. One of the most important is that they represent fully thought out, carefully written, and illustrated instruction. This instruction is based upon performance objectives and is consistent with sound teaching/learning strategies. Unlike bound books and audiovisual media, instruction sheets can be updated at will. Information can be added or revised to suit the needs of a particular target population.

Constructive criticism from fellow teachers, curriculum specialists, incumbent workers, and students will help identify technical inaccuracies, oversights, and deficiencies. The identification and correction of problems reinforces the view that the strength of instruction sheets lies partially in their quality and credibility.

Any instruction that is done repeatedly will be more accurate, more consistent, and briefer if instruction sheets are used. It is all but impossible for a teacher to repeat an oral lesson in exactly the same manner. One method for verifying this is to compare written instructions with tape recordings of several oral presentations on the same content. Teachers are surprised at the repetitions, unrelated matter, and oversights in even their best oral presentations.

Assure Accuracy

Well-prepared instruction sheets provide assurance that complete and accurate information is brought to every student's attention. In addition, the use of written instructions, drawings, and other types of graphic aids that do not have to be copied from a chalkboard is a time-saver. Copying from the chalkboard has little educational value, as well, since the results are seldom complete, accurate, or in usable form.

Indefinite and inexact verbal assignments typically lead to frustrations and problems. Most people have experienced the exasperation that comes from an indefinite assignment. They know that the expectation is to *do what was in the mind* of the teacher. The more exact written instruction sheet corrects this situation.

Instruction sheets are an advantage to both students and teachers. Students benefit by having their attention directed to important information and by having a clear indication of the study, practice, or performance required. They can save time by consulting their instruction sheet rather than always depending on the teacher for assistance. In addition to avoiding a delay, students who use these sheets have a chance to develop self-reliance. They assume responsibility for solving their own problems. Furthermore, the ability to understand and follow written instructions is important on the job.

Save Time, Promote Recall

The teacher benefits by conserving class time otherwise taken up in repeating instructions and answering questions. Instruction sheets are highly useful where attendance is irregular. This is often the case in part-time and night classes. When students miss an assignment or a theory lesson, these sheets provide a means to progress without a great deal of teacher help.

Instruction sheets help students recall earlier instruction. Knowledge and skills that go unused gradually deteriorate; eventually they may be partially forgotten. Because there can be a lapse of time between the initial learning and later practice, students may become confused. Instruction sheets help them recall the details. This eliminates the need for much individual re-teaching. In addition, instruction sheets can:

1. Provide variety in learning.
2. Arouse interest and motivate.
3. Facilitate self-directed and individualized learning.
4. Assure that all students have uniform instructions and information on course requirements.
5. Aid the student in learning and developing new skills

correctly the first time (this is important since an error once made is likely to recur).

6. Enable substitutes, who might not be experts in the occupation, to fill in with a minimum of disruption when the teacher is absent.
7. Be used as a lesson review or for an update briefing before students begin their work.
8. Be collected and stored in a binder for later use, including on-the-job reference.

Instruction sheets help in managing large groups of students, with a range of individual differences, who are working at several tasks. They are not a replacement, however, for a competent teacher. Neither do they eliminate the need for thorough lesson planning. The initial effort in adapting or preparing instruction sheets is substantial, but the work can be spread over time. Ultimately the teacher will be able to handle more students with greater success, higher learning levels, higher student satisfaction, and more efficient use of time. Conserving learning time is a matter of considerable importance in business and industrial training. Is it wrong to insist on the same from education?

LIMITATIONS

Just as there are definite benefits to be realized from the use of instruction sheets, there are limitations as well. For one, time and effort are required to prepare quality instruction sheets. Certainly, it is difficult to develop clear, brief and exact instructions that are adequately illustrated. It is probable, however, that teachers who are unable to write satisfactory instructions are not apt to do any better when attempting it orally.

To be effective, instruction sheets must be easy to read. Many students have difficulty gaining information from the printed page. The sheets must also be brief. Unnecessary words confuse and detract attention from the main points. They must be exact, because they are used to guide considerable effort and the student must have confidence in them. When possible, they should use drawings, flowcharts and other types of illustrations. The importance of illustrations on instruction sheets is underscored in Europe where the word "chart" is used instead of sheet. For example, an operation sheet in Europe is called an operation chart.

Some teachers may depend too much on instruction sheets—even going to the extreme of handing them out and telling the students to "go to work." This is unacceptably poor instruction. If the instructions are too detailed, the opportunity for student problem solving may be lost. Indeed, it is argued that dependence on instruction sheets will "deskill" teachers and interfere with creative instruction. Student progress may even become dependent largely on reading ability.

Once prepared and validated, there is an understandable reluctance to discard instruction sheets. Consequently, there is a danger that outdated sheets will be used year after year regardless of their obsolescence. Other related problems center on duplicating, storing, and managing the sheets.

Some students have difficulty reading and understanding written directions. Furthermore, they may not even be interested in doing so, regardless of ability. It may be difficult to persuade these students to read the appropriate sheets before starting to work. They tend to use a "trial and error" approach, ignoring the instruction sheets.

In response to this problem, it is accepted that success in life increasingly depends upon the ability to read and understand. Consequently, some practice is desirable, if not essential, for all students. In any case, there is an obvious need to keep abreast of technological changes. As a result, experience in acquiring information from printed matter is vitally important.

The practice of "leaning on the teacher" (often unwittingly promoted by teachers) might be effectively discouraged through the judicious use of instruction sheets. Careful laboratory organization and administration can also help minimize this problem.

Some students require outside motivation to induce them to follow printed instructions. In such cases, students should be told not to rely on memory, but to follow the instruction sheet instead. When students continue to ask the teacher for information, they should be courteously shown where the needed information appears. The teacher should not be too willing to give orally what is available in printed form. The student needs to develop competence in the use of printed instructions. Dependence upon the teacher lessens students' ability to become independent learners.

Instruction sheets are not intended to alter program content, replace demonstrations, or reduce personal contact between the teacher and student. They are simply an important aid to the teaching/learning process.

The limitations mentioned here are not the fault of the instruction sheets themselves. They arise when the teacher (a) is uninformed as to their value, (b) does not organize the class, (c) is not favorably inclined toward the possibilities involved, or (d) is using them to avoid work rather than to increase the effectiveness and efficiency of teaching.

GUIDELINES

Ideally, the preparation of instruction sheets should be a cooperative venture among teachers, a curriculum developer and even students. In reality, a curriculum developer is seldom available. Consequently, the best approach may be to involve a group of teachers who have a common interest and wide experience in the particular occupation. This is especially important when unusually high standards are to be met or when considerable effort is necessary. Group efforts pool expertise, judgment, and constructive criticism. Specialized abilities should be considered when forming the group. Some members may be experienced in writing, others in illustrating, another in critiquing the product, and so on. By distributing efforts in terms of specialized interests and abilities, both quality and productivity are increased. In many instances, only minimal training and practice are required to prepare valuable and effective instruction sheets.

Ready-made Materials

Before writing anything, look for "off the shelf" (ready-made) materials. A great deal of material is already available. Vocational and technical programs usually have counterparts somewhere; there may be suitable materials from which to choose.

Instruction sheets can be obtained from (a) vocational and technical schools, (b) trainers in the public and private sectors, (c) curriculum development projects, (d) coordination centers, laboratories, and clearinghouses, as well as, (e) commercial publishers. The availability of such materials is advertised in professional and trade journals, magazines, and newsletters. One newsletter, *Open Entries,* provides for the exchange of materials. It is produced by the Center on Education and Training for Employment (CETE) at the Ohio State University in Columbus.

It is easier and more economical to adopt or adapt available instruction sheets than to "begin from scratch." A word of caution about commercial material, however; be sure the use or adaptation does not violate copyright laws and restrictions. When in doubt, check with a school official or legal advisor.

There will be times when the uniqueness of the (a) performance objective, (b) student population, (c) instructional method being used, or (d) instructional situation, requires instruction sheets which do not already exist. Only then should new ones be prepared. Because teachers have at least a part of the job, it is important that they understand their make-up and how to distinguish good ones from poor ones.

The following general guidelines cover reviewing and preparing instruction sheets. These guidelines can be applied in most cases. Detailed and specific information on preparing and evaluating the (a) information sheet, (b) assignment sheet, (c) operation sheet, and (d) job sheet come later in this chapter.

All types of instruction sheets require careful thought and preparation. Facts, data, specifications, and terminology must be checked for accuracy and currency. Material that is poorly conceived or produced will be ineffective. It may even be subject to criticism resulting in disrespect for the course or program.

Improving Communication

Writing is an important method of communication. It would be difficult, if not impossible, to conduct a course or program without the written word. By inference, the success of any educational venture depends upon the effectiveness of the written materials that are a part of it. Writing that is easy to read is more understandable and improves communication. Every effort must be made to make instruction sheets as readable as USA Today. They are not to be written like a college textbook.

Increasing readability begins with the careful selection and use of easily understood, concrete words that are familiar to students. Considerable time should be spent selecting words that have a specific meaning. This is where a dictionary and thesaurus are important, useful tools. Look for the word that conveys the intended meaning with the least effort for the student. Write for those students who will not understand more complex and abstract words. Remember, students are more likely to quit reading than to reach for a dictionary.

Examples:

Use short, simple, and familiar words when possible. The more syllables there are in a word, the harder it is to read and understand. It is better to over-simplify than to risk misunderstanding. Good writers want to express, not impress.

Poor Choice	Good Choice
consume	eat
facilitate	help
assistance	aid, help

Use concrete, specific words when possible.

Poor Choice	Good Choice
tool	standard screwdriver
majority of readings	seven out of ten readings

Use nontechnical words when possible.

Poor Choice	Good Choice
apiculture	beekeeping
experimentation	test

Some trade or technical terms cannot be replaced by a nontechnical word or phrase; yet the term is unfamiliar to the students. In such instances, a definition needs to be provided at its first use. This is especially helpful if a term has a different meaning to students than that intended by the instructor.

Every occupation has specialized words, phrases, and acronyms that experts use when they communicate with each other. This specialized vocabulary (jargon) can accurately communicate ideas and concepts but is often unfamiliar to the beginning student. Like technical terms, jargon should be avoided unless it improves understanding and prepares students for the workplace. When it is used, define it.

The well-written sentence demands clarity of both thought and expression. It must be short, uncomplicated, and to the point. Strings of phrases and unnecessary words result in hard-to-read, ineffective writing. Students lose interest. Though most words are "workers," some just take up space. It is important to keep sentences short, simple, and easy to read. Get to the point using the fewest words possible.

Examples:

Shorten phrases.

Poor Choice	Good Choice
in view of the fact	since
in the majority of cases	usually
in a manner similar to	like

Avoid wasteful words.

Poor Choice	Good Choice
take appropriate measures	act
is responsible for selecting	selects

Do not use cliches or "buzz words." Worn-out expressions will wear the student's patience thin. Buzz words usually go out of use shortly. Attempts at humor in print are also inappropriate. Facial expressions, posture, and vocal tones are a necessary ingredient of good humor. It is best to save the humor for more appropriate times such as "shop talks." It can be used to relieve tension or anxiety at such times.

To improve the clarity of presentation, and to set a standard for students to match in their writing, attention should be given to: (a) spelling and word meaning (this requires frequent use of a dictionary), (b) sentence structure, subject-verb agreement and use of the proper tense, and (c) punctuation, as well as capitalization. Remember, the weaknesses of spoken words fade with time. The mistakes we put in writing, however, remain for all to see. Consequently, draft material should be put aside for a day or two. Then it should be reviewed for quality of content, and compliance with the guidelines given here. Most teachers find it easier to look for the different kinds of flaws during several readings.

Layout

The makeup of an instruction sheet (arrangement, illustrations, etc.) needs to be visually attractive. The message should also be brief, relating only the essential information. The use of quality illustrations (line drawings, diagrams, tables, or photographs) will clarify and help condense written information. Meaningful illustrations will also assist students in understanding the text. Research and experience show that illustrations, even simple line drawings, are effective in attracting and holding attention. Illustrations make the instruction sheets more interesting. Students are, therefore, more likely to read the accompanying text.

Illustrations should be identified using the word, "Figure," and an Arabic numeral (i.e., Figure 1). Additionally, include a caption using words taken from the accompanying text. Captions serve both as a figure title and as a concise explanation of the figure. Since illustrations get more attention than the text, captions help clarify the content. Figures within each instruction sheet are numbered consecutively. It is important to reference figures in the written text itself.

Illustrations should support the text. They need to be located on the same or facing page, **as close as possible to the related text.** Students can then refer to them with a minimum of page turning. This will prevent students' viewing illustrations as afterthoughts. Illustrations may be detailed, showing only one step at a time, or they may be general, showing the completed work. Both types have advantages and limitations. These should be considered in deciding which to use. As with reading text, students will ignore an illustration that is difficult to understand or too time-consuming.

The various items, points, steps and paragraphs of content in an instruction sheet should be set off from each other. Using numbers, letters or "bullets" (dots) will make each distinct. The pay-off for attending to (a) spacing between lines of text and paragraphs, (b) the balance of textual and illustrative matter, and (c) mass arrangement in general is an easily read and attractive document.

Format

Instruction sheets ought to have a uniform and orderly format. Format has to do with the headings, which function as an outline organizing the content of the sheets. It is best to establish a standard format early in the process of developing instruction sheets. Then use it consistently. This enables students to locate the proper instruction sheet and the content they need.

The heading at the top of the page (first page only), should include important information such as the:
1. Program or course number and title.
2. Subject matter identification.
3. Name of the school and its location.
4. Type of instruction sheet and its number.
5. Title of the sheet.

When longer than one page, they should be numbered "Page 1 of 2," "Page 2 of 2," with the second number indicating the total number of pages. This is the same method that architects and engineers use for numbering their drawings. When this has been done, it will be readily apparent if a page is missing. Proper identification is not only important to students, but also prevents confusion in duplicating and handling the sheets. The use of different colors of paper for different types of instruction sheets can also be an effective aid in identifying and locating sheets.

The effectiveness of instruction sheets is increased by using appropriate headings in a consistent order. Avoid a haphazard sequence, requiring students to look in different places on successive sheets for information of the same type (i.e., references). A clear-cut, orderly form for arranging the content helps students find what they are looking for. This is also useful as students go back to the sheet for review and reference. The format shown in Figure 7-1 provides a complete page heading and an effective content arrangement for part of a job sheet.

The rationale for format standardization is based upon the principle of habit formation. Habit helps make some aspects of instruction sheet use automatic. This frees both developer and user to focus on the more important effort of writing or learning. Detailed format recommendations are provided later in this chapter for each of the four common types of instruction sheets.

Content arrangement is also improved by adding white (blank) space between headings and sections. This distinguishes them from each other.

Horizontal rules (lines), either solid or dashed, also work well for separating sections of an instruction sheet. A carefully worked out format, such as the one shown in Figure 7-1, will have considerable bearing on ease of use.

Techniques for providing emphasis and precautionary information include underlining, boldface type, italics, capitalization, and the use of headings such as "NOTE" and "CAUTION." The word "NOTE" usually precedes important information, which if disregarded, could lead to serious consequences. On both job and operation sheets, it is helpful to insert the word, "CAUTION" where there is a potential for danger to students or damage to equipment or the workpiece. Set in capital letters and boldface type, it precedes a brief statement concerning the hazard and what to do about it. A "boxed" caution statement is, perhaps, even better for focusing attention. The impact of "notes" and

"cautions" is decreased, however, if they are used too often.

Instruction sheets can simplify complex situations and content for student use. Developers should avoid making them so long and detailed that students do not use them to their full advantage. The best instruction sheets cover the subject adequately but are as simple as possible. Unnecessary information, no matter how interesting, is left out. A sound recommendation from experienced teachers is to limit the length of instruction sheets to as few pages as possible. If both the front and back of a page are being used, the word "over" should be placed at the bottom of the front page.

The teacher is well advised to strive for the most learning with the least amount of instruction. Only needed instructional material should be provided, no more. At first, develop instruction sheets which are almost "too lean" for the particular group. Then, during the validation trials (explained later) add the additional explanations, examples, etc., required for students to attain the performance objective. This may reduce the amount of material students need to read and produce interest in the content.

MANAGING THE SHEETS

Instruction sheets can be handled in several ways. It depends largely on whether (a) students are permitted to retain them for study and use, or (b) they remain the property of the course or program and are used by several students. Instruction sheets are usually intended to be consumable, that is, given to the student to keep. When personal copies are provided, they need to be duplicated in predetermined colors if possible. Then they are stored in quantities to be available for hand-out when needed. Sheets more than one page long should be stapled in the top left-hand margin. They may have drilled or punched holes, using the standard three-hole design, so a complete set can be collected in a loose-leaf binder. Stapling eliminates the potential for getting pages out of order and the binder reduces the loss of individual sheets. Tabs or tabbed separator sheets can be added to organize the binder and facilitate ready access to particular sheets.

Experience has shown that when students manage their own sheets they may lose them or forget to bring their binder to class. As a result, some teachers prefer to have individual binders stored in the laboratory or shop even though off-site study is sacrificed.

Another option is to store the instruction sheets either in a filing cabinet or in racks so they are available when needed. The sheets may be handed out separately by the instructor or a student aide. Another possibility is to authorize each student to get the instruction sheets on an "as needed" basis. They can then be stored in a personal file folder, punched and inserted in a ring binder, or fastened together by unit of instruction. Unfortunately, there is a tendency by teachers and students to misplace or mix up loose-leaf sheets.

Yet another option is to assemble and bind the instruction sheets by unit of instruction or for the entire course or program. The bound sets are less likely to be misfiled or lost than individual sheets. Additionally, they can be

Program or Course No. & Title
Subject Matter Identification

School Name & Location
Job Sheet No. _____

HOW TO INSTALL BATTER BOARDS

INTRODUCTION:

Erecting batter boards is a critical step in construction. During excavation the corner stakes are dug out. Batter boards make it possible to reestablish building corners and elevations. If you make sure that the **foundation is square and level**, you will find that framing is much easier.

ACTION STATEMENT:

Install batter boards.

CONDITIONS:

Given a construction site with corner stakes for the building already established, construction prints, lumber and string, measuring tape, carpenter's level, line level, cross-cut handsaw, claw hammer, hatchet, sledge hammer, required nails and a specified starting corner.

STANDARDS:

Batter board posts will be 3 feet to 4 feet outside corner stakes. String and board heights will be within ± 1/8 inch of required elevation, and corners will be within ± 1/16 inch of the diagonal measurement of the 6-8-10 method of determining square.

REFERENCES:

Operation Sheet No. 9 - How to Check for Squareness
Campbell, C.P. (1988). Construction handbook. New York: Builders Press. (pp. 48-51)

PERFORMANCE STEPS:

1. Erect batter boards

   A. Measure and establish batter board locations 3 to 4 feet outside corner stakes as shown in Figure 1.

   B. Lay batter boards out at approximately a 90-degree (right) angle (see

---

G. Transfer batter board elevation to all other batter board corners. Anchor string line to top of installed batter board and extend line to other corners. Use line level to establish elevation and mark batter board posts (see Figure 3).

Checkpoint

Ask the teacher to check your work before proceeding.

Initials: _____

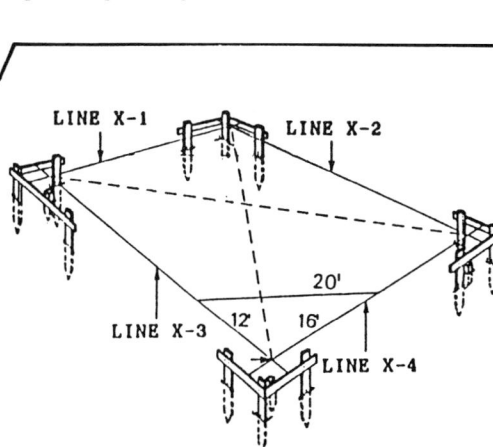

Figure 3
Batter Board Layout

Figure 7-1. Format example.

stored in a bookcase for easy access. Preferably, each student could be given a personal copy. Bound copies of the various types of instruction sheets for a particular course or program are usually referred to as a "student guide" or "manual."

The cover and type of binding will have a bearing on the document usefulness in the hands of the students. A well-bound, attractive guide provides a feeling of quality, and often receives better care than one which is poorly bound. For guides that are to be used repeatedly, good binding and durable cover stock are worth their cost. If the guide is used in a shop or laboratory, its cover should be grease, oil, and stain resistant. Plastic spiral (comb) binding is frequently used for guides up to 1 in. thick. One distinct advantage of spiral bindings is that they permit the guide to lie flat when opened. Another advantage is that the binding can be reopened to insert new or replacement pages. A light-color plastic permits printing on the back, with a permanent marker, for identification when shelved.

Sometimes duplication costs or other practical constraints make it necessary for instruction sheets to remain the property of the course or program. In such cases, they can be laminated or placed in plastic covers (sheet protectors) for repeated use. They can also be assembled and inserted in a heavy-duty binder. While multiple use reduces costs, there are the added problems of worn pages, misfiled materials and time lost while students wait to receive or locate materials. When off-site use or home study is encouraged, a few extra copies of the materials can be made available for individuals to borrow for short periods.

Permanently bound instruction sheets eliminate the problem of lost or out-of-place pages. A distinct disadvantage, however, is the difficulty in updating or replacing pages. The reverse is true with loose-leaf sheets. Pages can be lost, misplaced or misordered, yet a substitute or additional page can be easily inserted.

No single way of managing instruction sheets works best in all situations. Every option has its strengths and weaknesses. Consequently a variety of methods should be tried before favoring one.

Whether instruction sheets are provided to trainees one-by-one, as needed, or in a bound set(s) at the appropriate time, students should keep them, if at all possible. This will facilitate review as necessary and reference use in follow-on courses.

COMMON TYPES OF INSTRUCTION SHEETS

The four most common types of instruction sheets were previously identified. They are the (a) information sheet, (b) assignment sheet, (c) operation sheet, and (d) job sheet. The sections following will examine the main characteristics of each type as well as specific purposes for which each is useful. Examples are provided to clarify the text and illustrate the formats. Flowcharts and checklists are also included to facilitate the review of these four distinct types of instruction sheets.

Teachers should be able to put into written form any

instructions given orally. In most cases, written instructions will be briefer and more accurate. This can be done with minimal time and effort by modifying existing materials. Instructions can be made to meet the special needs of a particular class or program and its students. Even when high quality instructional materials exist, experienced teachers often choose to adapt them or develop their own. In so doing, the teacher expresses creativity rather than being bound by someone else's way of organizing and doing things.

Information Sheet

As the title implies, the purpose of information sheets is to provide explanatory background information on a single topic. These sheets supplement instruction by supplying pertinent, factual information which is (a) current, (b) necessary to have close at hand, or (c) not readily available in any other suitable form. Information sheets present a range of content and examples without unnecessary discussion. This information is essential for reaching knowledge (cognitive) objectives. Information sheets are also used to supply technical, safety, special interest, and career information.

Information sheets can be found with different titles, such as "trade technology sheet," "trade theory sheet," "basic principle sheet," or "reference sheet." The preparation and use of information sheets is recommended when:

1. The necessary information is missing or covered inadequately in available documents.
2. Existing information needs to be condensed, consolidated, and reorganized from several sources.
3. Published information needs to be adapted (simplified) to the level of the students.
4. There is a need to save time and expedite learning.

Information sheets are often concerned with the "why" as contrasted with the "what" and "how" of the operation and job sheets.

Information sheets are needed when important up-to-date information is not available to students. Given this situation, the teacher locates, in source documents, all the needed details. The information is then extracted, consolidated, condensed, and written at the appropriate reading grade level. The elimination of repetitious and unimportant information has been shown to increase the understanding and retention of important facts. The text is then formatted, typed, and illustrated. Information sheets can provide the content students need and still be interesting and pleasant to read. Dull material will not encourage the reading habit.

Information sheet titles should briefly and clearly identify what is covered. The body of an information sheet can be presented in outline or complete sentence form. Flowcharts, pictures, graphs, diagrams, and other illustrations are used where they clarify the text. Illustrations make it easier for students to learn. While the information provided is a condensed version, it should be challenging enough to hold student interest. In any case, simple, easily understood words used in short sentences are best. Further, when the text is double-spaced, illustrated properly, and contains sufficient "white space," the layout will be more conducive to study.

TIRE INFLATION

INTRODUCTION:

An important factor in ensuring long tire life is proper inflation. Tires that are improperly inflated wear out quickly and do not provide proper handling characteristics or optimum fuel economy. Tire pressure and wear characteristics should be checked as regular preventive maintenance.

REFERENCES:

deKryger, W.J., Kovacik, R.T., & Bono, S.G. (1986). Auto mechanics: Theory and service. Cincinnati, OH: South-Western. (pp. 684-685)

Firestone Tire & Rubber Company. (1982). Tire maintenance and warranty manual. Akron, OH: Author.

Geiger, F. W. (1984). Equipment operator 3 & 2 (Naval Education and Training Program Management Support Activity Publication No. NAVEDTRA 10640-J1). Washington, DC: U. S. Government Printing Office. (pp. 2-4 & 2-5)

INFORMATION:

The weight of a vehicle is supported, propelled, and guided by the small amount of tire tread that is in contact with the road at any given time. Improper inflation reduces the amount of tread in contact with the road, resulting in reduced traction. To ensure that the tires on a

Underinflation causes the outer edges of the tire tread to wear quickly. It also causes hard steering, tire squeal, side-to-side wheel vibration, front-end shimmy, and pulling of the vehicle to one side. An underinflated tire flexes in all directions, generating excessive heat. This can result in damage to the sidewalls of the tire, the plies of the tire carcass, and ultimately, tire failure (see Figure 1).

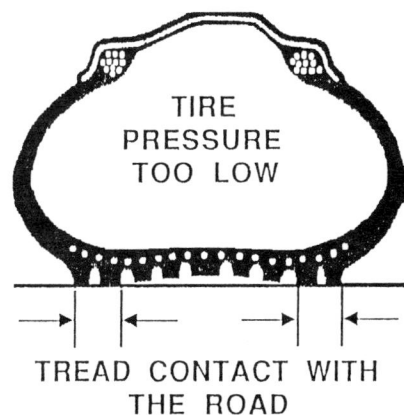

TIRE PRESSURE TOO LOW

TREAD CONTACT WITH THE ROAD

Figure 1
Profile of Underinflated Tire

Figure 7-2. Information sheet.

Information sheets are meant to be studied; they do not direct student activity. For that reason, their format is not as formal as that of other types of instruction sheets. Figure 7-2 shows an example of an information sheet. The format generally includes a page heading, and side headings for the (a) introduction, (b) references, and (c) information. Subheadings are often used to help keep the students on track while reading the information part of the sheet.

An appropriate introduction is short and creates interest. It points out the value of the information, and how it fits in with the rest of the instruction. The introduction provides important motivation to establish readiness for learning.

References are included to credit the sources of information and encourage additional reading. The references should provide for a wide range of student interest and ability. Each reference identifies the author, title, date of publication, other publication information, and page numbers, as well as any other information necessary to locate the document. Style manuals provide details and examples on how to present this information for the various types of publications.

Review questions can be added to determine how well the sheet was understood. Never ask questions that are not answered in the sheet or references. If the student is to write in the answers, provide sufficient space.

Figure 7-3 is a checklist for reviewing information sheets. It contains questions to consider when reviewing the sheets. The checklist is also useful for adapting or preparing information sheets.

Assignment Sheet

Assignment sheets are used to present a new concept, principle, or information. They direct the student to: (a) read and study selected material immediately before or just after the teacher has dealt with it, (b) practice the application of general principles (drilling in mental processes such as mathematical calculations), as well as skills, (c) solve problems, and (d) apply information that has been presented in the class or laboratory. These sheets not only save time but are particularly useful in managing assignments to be done either in class or for homework. Moreover, they help students progress at their own pace.

One of the most important steps toward getting good work from a student is to use directions that state accurately and clearly what is to be done. Vague oral assignments often lead to problems for both the student and the teacher. When given precise and complete assignments in writing, students know exactly what is required. They also know that their work can be held accountable in every detail.

Assignment sheets have a decided advantage over oral assignments. If a student does not understand the assignment at the first reading, it can be re-read. Oral instructions are given once and cannot be reviewed. The understanding of what to do and how becomes less clear as time passes.

Generally, the assignment sheet includes the following parts in a predetermined sequence:

1. Page heading.
2. Introduction.
3. References.
4. Assignment.
5. Study questions.

Figure 7-4 is an example of an assignment sheet containing these components. The following pointers concerning each part of the assignment sheet will help avoid problems.

The page heading includes the assignment sheet title. It should be descriptive yet brief. The introduction explains, in a concise way, the purpose or scope of the assignment and why completing it will be of personal benefit. It arouses interest and motivates the student to complete the assignment. This can be done by relating the assignment to those already completed and those that are to follow. An example can be cited to show the practical application of the knowledge or skill being acquired.

All print and nonprint (audio-visual) reference materials needed to complete the assignment are listed under References. In selected instances, a few optional references may also be included for the more capable and ambitious students to use for supplementary reading. By guiding students to proper sources, the assignment sheet helps to prepare them for future tasks that require locating and using information. The method of citing references should provide complete information including the author's name, title of the document, date of publication, other publication information, and the chapter or page numbers, etc. It is important to include the chapter number or page numbers. Without this information, students may invest a great deal of time without finding the material.

The assignment must be specific and understandable so the student will know what is expected. Directions might identify the pages and paragraphs to be read. When there is a best sequence for studying scattered materials or portions of a book and/or reference document, that sequence is specified. Directions must be carefully and clearly written so that nothing is left to the imagination. Assignments can involve:

1. Preparing a bill of materials.
2. Reading and interpreting drawings.
3. Studying, plotting, and interpreting data.
4. Planning procedures.
5. Observations, investigations or field surveys, and the recording of data.
6. Analysis and decision-making problems similar to those encountered on the job.

When problems are included, provide sufficient examples to show the correct approach to their solution. This serves as a guide to students and helps them succeed. After each problem, allow adequate space for the solution.

Assignment sheets often increase the effectiveness of self-study through a series of thought-provoking questions. These *study questions* direct the student's search for and organization of relevant knowledge. Therefore, they should be stated clearly and concisely. Also, the questions should be difficult enough that students cannot answer them before they have carefully studied the assignment. On the other hand, they should not be so difficult that students cannot answer them correctly. Answers ought to be found within

Title of Sheet Reviewed: _____

Reviewer: _____ Date: _____

Directions: Indicate whether each numbered question is reflected in the **Information Sheet** by placing a check mark in the **YES** or **NO** box. If the question is not applicable, leave the box blank.

YES NO

[ ] [ ]   1. Does the heading at the top of the page provide all the information required?

[ ] [ ]   2. Does the title briefly and clearly identify what is covered?

[ ] [ ]   3. Is there a short motivational introduction?

[ ] [ ]   4. Is a behaviorally written performance objective included? (optional)

[ ] [ ]   5. Are complete reference citations for additional sources of information provided?

[ ] [ ]   6. Is the information up-to-date, accurate, and necessary to have?

[ ] [ ]   7. Is the information presented clearly, logically, and briefly?

[ ] [ ]   8. Is the information challenging enough to hold student interest?

[ ] [ ]   9. Are safety and the appropriate use of tools, equipment, and materials emphasized?

[ ] [ ]   10. Are paragraphs clearly delineated?

[ ] [ ]   11. Are the margins wide enough for binding, filing, etc.?

[ ] [ ]   12. Will the typeface used withstand repeated copying?

[ ] [ ]   13. Are word breaks at the ends of lines avoided?

[ ] [ ]   14. Is the stopping point at the bottom of the page determined by the content?

[ ] [ ]   15. Are appropriate, good quality illustrations used to clarify the text?

[ ] [ ]   16. Are the illustrations referenced in the text and do they have captions?

[ ] [ ]   17. Are the illustrations placed appropriately with the text and in sequence with it?

[ ] [ ]   18. Is the reading level appropriate for most students?

[ ] [ ]   19. Have biases - nationalistic, racial or gender - been avoided?

[ ] [ ]   20. Is the layout visually attractive and the format orderly?

__ __   **Total number of check marks**

<u>Note</u>.   If any question received a **NO** response, determine what modifications are necessary in order to improve that criterion.

Figure 7-3. Information sheet review.

VTE 112, Automotive Mechanics
Tires

Vocational School, Memphis, TN
Assignment Sheet Number 7

TIRE AND WHEEL SPECIFICATIONS

INTRODUCTION:

Shop maintenance manuals contain detailed specifications for vehicles. The ability to use these manuals to determine tire and wheel specifications for automobiles and trucks is necessary on the job. This assignment provides practice in the use of service manuals to determine tire and wheel sizes and inflation pressures.

REFERENCES:

Bennett Garfield. (1989). Tire guide (Vol. 32). Boca Raton, FL: Author.
Chrysler Motors. (1986). Steering, suspension, wheel alignment and balance. Detroit, MI: Author. (pp. 58-61)

ASSIGNMENT:

Read and study the references listed. Using the appropriate reference, determine tire and wheel specifications for designated vehicles. Read the following study questions and write your answers on the lines provided during class time. After completing the assignment ask the teacher for the answer key and check your own work. If your answers do not match the answer key, examine the appropriate reference to locate and correct your error.

STUDY QUESTIONS:

1. What is the standard size tire recommended for a 1986 Ford F-150 two-wheeled drive pickup truck?

   ____

2. What are the recommended tire inflation pressures (front and rear) for a 1982 Chevrolet K20 four-wheeled drive pickup truck?

   Front__________ Rear__________

3. What is the standard wheel rim width for a 1982 Pontiac Grand Prix?

   ____

4. Is a P195/75R14 tire acceptable for use on a 1978 Z28 Chevrolet Camaro?

   Yes________ No________

5. What is the maximum gross vehicle weight of a 1988 Ford F-150 pickup truck with a 117-inch wheelbase?

   ____

Example for illustration purposes only.

Figure 7-4. Assignment sheet.

the content covered. Study questions often constitute an "open-book" test. They permit, and sometimes encourage, students to use information in the references.

Questions can also provide a self-assessment. Students use them to see if they understand the material in the assignment. When used in this way, answers can be supplied so students can check their own work (or the teacher can check it). Adequate space for answers may be provided on the sheet or students may be instructed to use separate paper.

An assignment sheet may also include a written test. The test should be as short as possible while thoroughly covering the material in the assignment. Any kind of test item can be used, but the (a) problem, (b) completion, (c) procedure rearrangement, (d) identification, and (e) multiple-choice types should be emphasized. Test items should require the practical application of information from the assignment to the solution of on-the-job problems. For detailed information on writing test items, see Chapter 8.

If illustrations can be used to advantage, include them. Good illustrations liven up an assignment sheet and clarify what is stated in the text.

A job performance aid for editing assignment sheets is provided in Figure 7-5. This aid can be used to assure that (a) all necessary items (component parts) have been considered when preparing a particular sheet, and (b) all those which are not appropriate or useful have been intentionally omitted.

When the aid is used with the checklist for reviewing assignment sheets (shown in Figure 7-6), the teacher has a tool for critiquing these sheets. The aid and checklist are useful in adapting or preparing assignment sheets.

After the assignment sheet has been completed, it is ready to be tried out with students. The validation tryouts (explained later) may identify problems that should be corrected.

Operation Sheet

An operation is one part of the process of doing a job task. For example, making a wood chair (a job task) includes the performance of manipulative operations such as (a) cutting lumber to size, (b) gluing wood, (c) finishing wood, etc. Each operation requires skill, and is a logical topic for a lesson. For manipulative operations, the lesson includes a demonstration by the teacher. After the demonstration, the operation sheet, with its detailed procedures and precautionary notes, is used by students as an aid in carrying out that operation. This method of presentation, followed by guided skill development, is the accepted practice in occupational education. The operation sheet, sometimes called a "fundamental process sheet," makes it easier for inexperienced students to follow standard procedures and produce acceptable work. It points out hazards and helps eliminate the usual errors some teachers accept as unavoidable. It may also serve as initial instruction for the more capable students who are ready to move ahead of the group.

An operation sheet uses written instructions and illustrations to explain how to perform each procedural step in a manipulative operation. Illustrations are a powerful aid to learning the correct performance of the steps. Appendix 7A presents an effective method of using illustrations and directions for progressive steps to clarify the procedure and simplify the explanations. A capable student, with the proper preparation, will successfully perform the operation when using a sheet such as this.

It is not advisable to include a discussion of why an operation is performed a certain way. The "why" should be taken up in an information sheet or during a "shop talk." The "how to" is a matter of direction; the "why" is a matter of information.

The title of an operation sheet describes, in a few carefully selected words, the name of the operation. It is preceded by the words "How to." See the following examples.

HOW TO FOLD A NAPKIN USING THE TENT METHOD
HOW TO EDGE CONCRETE
HOW TO REMOVE AND INSTALL FUEL INJECTORS IN A DIESEL ENGINE

Certain operations are common to numerous tasks within an occupation. Consequently, the operation sheet will be a useful reference when performing any job tasks that require the same manipulative operation. Because of their potential for multiple use, it is advantageous to first prepare operation sheets covering the basics which occur repeatedly and in various combinations in the different job tasks of the occupation. Instruction in these operations is then available without respect to the job tasks in which they are involved.

Careful judgment is required when determining just how much information should be included in an operation sheet. Perhaps the best advice is to prepare "lean" operation sheets first. Later, based on validation trials, add all that is required to aid the student in performing the operation. Add nothing theoretical or general in nature which would draw attention away from the operation. The introduction is the only appropriate place on the sheet for information that does not deal directly with "how to" perform the operation.

The typical operation sheet has a format much like that of a job sheet. Appendix 7B lists the headings which may be used in formatting these sheets. Not all of the headings listed will be needed in every operation sheet; however, using a definite sequence of the selected headings is recommended. The paragraph under each heading in Appendix 7B briefly explains the content which would be included. With a standardized format, the students quickly learn how to proceed. They need not waste time searching for information.

An important supplement to some operation sheets is a series of exhibits, photographs, or a model for students to study. These examples show the principal steps or stages in the performance, as well as the end product. This approach is particularly valuable for the more important operations, especially when the operation sheet is not well illustrated.

Examples of operation sheets may be found in the instructions that accompany equipment and appliances. Textbooks and maintenance books also contain material on how to perform specific operations. How-to-do-it books and magazines are expert at describing operations in an appealing layout. It would be advantageous for teachers to

ASSIGNMENT SHEET

HEADING AND TITLE STATED ? — NO — SHOULD BE INCLUDED ? — YES — ADD TO SHEET
YES
NO

INTRODUCTION STATED ? — NO — SHOULD BE INCLUDED ? — YES — ADD TO SHEET
YES
NO

PERFORMANCE OBJECTIVE STATED ? — NO — SHOULD BE INCLUDED ? — YES — ADD TO SHEET
YES
NO

REFERENCES STATED ? — NO — SHOULD BE INCLUDED ? — YES — ADD TO SHEET
YES
NO

ASSIGNMENT UNDERSTANDABLE ? — NO — CLARIFY ASSIGNMENT
YES

STUDY QUESTONS STATED ? — NO — SHOULD BE INCLUDED ? — YES — ADD TO SHEET
YES
NO

TEST ITEMS STATED ? — NO — SHOULD BE INCLUDED ? — YES — ADD TO SHEET
YES
NO

REVIEW SHEET USING THE CHECKLIST

ANY REASON TO ADD/ DELETE ANY ITEM ? — YES — REWRITE ADDITIONS/ DELETIONS
NO

ASSIGNMENT SHEET READY FOR VALIDATION PROCESS

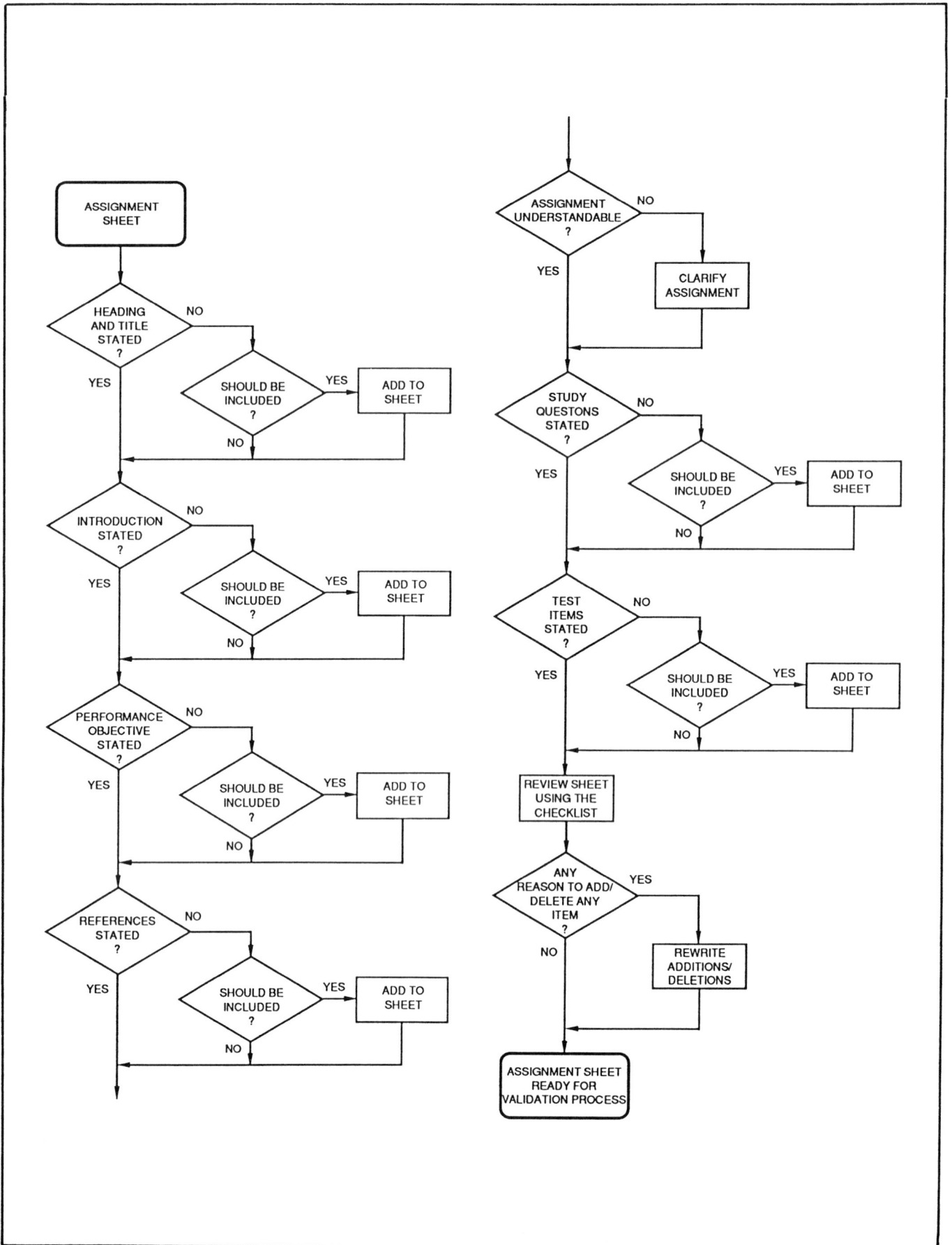

Figure 7-5. Editing assigment sheets.

Title of Sheet Reviewed:_____

Reviewer:_____ **Date:**_____

Directions: Indicate whether each numbered question is reflected in the Assignment Sheet by placing a check mark in the YES or NO box. If the question is not applicable, leave the box blank.

YES NO

[ ]   [ ]   1.   Does the heading at the top of the page provide all the information required?

[ ]   [ ]   2.   Is the title brief and descriptive?

[ ]   [ ]   3.   Is there a short motivational introduction?

[ ]   [ ]   4.   Is a behaviorally written performance objective included? (optional)

[ ]   [ ]   5.   Are complete reference citations for sources of information provided?

[ ]   [ ]   6.   Are the directions accurate and clearly stated?

[ ]   [ ]   7.   Is the assignment specific and understandable?

[ ]   [ ]   8.   Are there examples which show how to solve problems?

[ ]   [ ]   9.   Are the self-study questions stated clearly and concisely?

[ ]   [ ]   10. Are the questions of such difficulty that the assignment must be read and studied before they can be answered?

[ ]   [ ]   11. Are answers to the questions within the content?

[ ]   [ ]   12. Does the sheet include self-assessment answers?

[ ]   [ ]   13. Is adequate space provided for answers?

[ ]   [ ]   14. Is there a test that thoroughly covers the assignment?

[ ]   [ ]   15. Is the reading level appropriate for most students?

[ ]   [ ]   16. Have biases - nationalistic, racial, or gender - been avoided?

[ ]   [ ]   17. Is the layout visually attractive and the format orderly?

___   ___   **Total number of check marks**

Note.   If any question received a **NO** response, determine what modifications are necessary in order to improve that criterion.

Figure 7-6. Assignment sheet review.

consult these types of sources for ideas as they develop or adapt operation sheets.

The job performance aid for editing operation sheets is presented in Figure 7-7. It can be used to assure that (a) all items (headings) which are necessary in a particular operation sheet are in fact included and (b) all those that are not relevant have been omitted.

When the checklist, Figure 7-8, is used along with the editing aid, the teacher has a tool for reviewing operation sheets. This tool is also an effective aid for adapting or preparing operation sheets.

After the editing has been completed, the operation sheet is ready to be examined by others and tried out by students. The validation tryouts will determine the value and effectiveness of an operation sheet. A recommended validation process is provided later.

Job Sheet

The objective of a job sheet is to assist students in the performance of a manipulative job task resulting in a product or service. Job sheets provide a step-by-step sequence of directions on how to do a particular "hands-on" job task involving numerous operations. Although they have much in common, job sheets should not be confused with operation sheets which deal with elements of a job task. Job sheets supplement instruction by providing illustrations and a list of the required performance steps, arranged in sequential order. Sheets of this type have been used for job tasks involving construction, manufacturing, transportation, maintenance and repair, etc.

A job sheet lists the references, tools, equipment, furniture, materials, and supplies needed for doing a complete piece of work or for achieving a certain result. Cited references include the relevant operation and information sheets as well as any other necessary print and nonprint resources. Optional references for the more ambitious students may be included as well.

This sheet is generally used along with operation sheets related to the job task. On occasion, however, a job sheet is used independently, particularly if the job task can be taught in one demonstration. When appropriate, the job sheet may refer to a photograph, exhibit, or model of the acceptable end product. This example can be used for clarification. Students can also compare their work with the example prior to evaluation. This comparison helps ensure success and high standards of performance.

The title of a job sheet should be a brief, but exact, statement of the job task to be done. Like the operation sheet, the title is customarily preceded by the words "how to." For example:

HOW TO INSTALL BATTER BOARDS
HOW TO MIX MORTAR BY HAND
HOW TO THREAD PIPE USING A THREADING MACHINE

Job sheets use essentially the same headings as operation sheets. Appendix 7B shows these headings and provides a brief explanation for each one. All except one of the explanations apply generally to job sheets. This exception is

Procedure. Here, the difference between a job and operation sheet is that job sheets seldom provide the detailed and precise explanation of how to perform each step. Not all of the headings in Appendix 7B will be needed for every job sheet. On occasion, the major performance steps in a job sheet are simply the titles of a series of operation sheets which make up a job task.

A typical job sheet is presented in Appendix 7C. Like most job sheets, this example lists the performance steps without telling precisely how to do them. It assumes that the student (a) can perform the operations involved and (b) has the basic knowledge and skill to use the tools and equipment or will obtain them from appropriate information and operation sheets.

As used in the workplace, a job sheet for an advanced student may take the form of a working drawing, sketch, or work order. However, students in their early training need more detailed instruction and guidance to carry a task through to completion. For that reason, job sheets are typically designed to help the student learn *how to do the task*, as well as to serve as a *job task assignment*.

The amount of detail included in a job sheet can be gradually reduced as students progress through the class or program. At the outset, however, the sheets usually include most, if not all, of the headings listed in Appendix 7B. Also included are line drawings, diagrams, and working drawings to show what is wanted and to clarify any difficulties. When students become more skilled, they should rely less on the job sheet and more on their own resourcefulness.

Some teachers use a prepared form during the advanced stage of instruction, with space for the student to specify the tools, equipment, materials, supplies, and other items required as well as the procedure to be followed. The teacher reviews and approves a completed sheet before the work is begun. This planning experience is viewed as an important learning opportunity.

Adapting Manipulative Performance Tests

One benefit of manipulative performance tests cited in Chapter 9 is their adaptability as "job sheets." A manipulative performance test (MPT), that uses the checklist approach to presenting the necessary performance steps, can be converted to a teaching and learning aid. This is possible because of its content and format. See Appendix 7D for an MPT.

Since the job sheet is used in performing a task and the MPT requires the same performance as that taught, a carefully developed MPT is suited for this additional purpose. Of course, there must be modifications since the checklist portion of an MPT is designed to record observed performance, rather than to help the student learn how to do the task.

It is usually necessary to provide additional instruction and appropriate illustrations to those procedural steps where clarification and elaboration are needed. A good way to identify those areas is to try out the MPT "as is."

Some teachers will use the checklist format while others will decide to modify it. It depends on what proves to be most effective for the students. When the checklist format

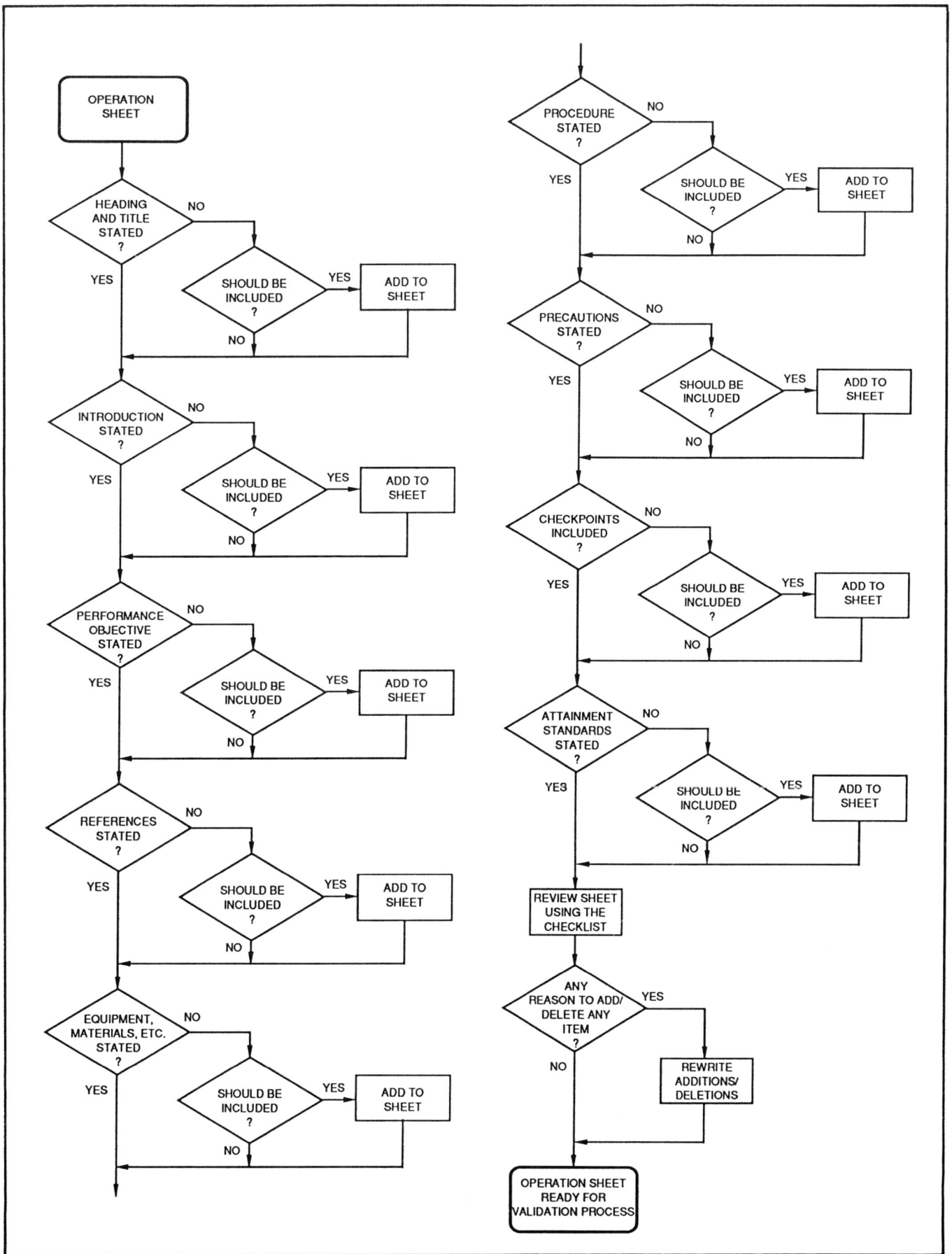

Figure 7-7. Editing operation sheets.

Title of Sheet Reviewed:_____

Reviewer:_____ Date:_____

Directions: Indicate whether each numbered question is reflected in the **Operation Sheet** by placing a check mark in the **YES** or **NO** box. If the question is not applicable, leave the box blank.

YES NO

[ ] [ ] 1. Does the heading at the top of the page provide all the information required?

[ ] [ ] 2. Does the title briefly and clearly identify the name of the operation, preceded by "**HOW TO**"?

[ ] [ ] 3. Is there a short motivational introduction?

[ ] [ ] 4. Is the behaviorally written performance objective included?

[ ] [ ] 5. Are complete reference citations for additional sources of information provided?

[ ] [ ] 6. Are the necessary tools, equipment, furniture, materials, and supplies listed? (not necessary if included in the conditions statement of the performance objective)

[ ] [ ] 7. Are all the necessary performance steps included?

[ ] [ ] 8. Are the steps technically accurate and in the proper sequence?

[ ] [ ] 9. Are the steps written in sufficient detail so students will know how to do the performance?

[ ] [ ] 10. Are appropriate, good quality illustrations used to clarify the text?

[ ] [ ] 11. Are the illustrations referenced in the text and do they have captions?

[ ] [ ] 12. Are the illustrations placed appropriately with the text and in sequence with it?

[ ] [ ] 13. Are safety precautions included at points where there is potential for danger or damage to equipment?

[ ] [ ] 14. Are checkpoints included?

[ ] [ ] 15. Are attainment standards included? (not necessary when included in the standards statement of the performance objective)

[ ] [ ] 16. Is the reading level appropriate for most students?

[ ] [ ] 17. Have biases - nationalistic, racial or gender - been avoided?

[ ] [ ] 18. Is the layout visually attractive and the format orderly?

___ ___ **Total number of check marks**

<u>Note</u>.   If any question received a **NO** response, determine what modifications are necessary in order to improve that criterion.

Figure 7-8. Operation sheet review.

is used, supplemental wording and illustrations are added to the procedural steps as necessary. The "YES-NO" columns are used as a checkpoint by the student or teacher during learning and practice sessions.

A word processor makes modifications relatively easy. For example, the standards can be combined with the task elements/steps. Deleting the standards and the "YES-NO" columns will open up space for illustrations. The result is a balanced, two-column format. Supplemental information, along with a reference to the captioned illustration, can also be added to the combination statement. With computer graphics capability, the illustrations can be inserted while the other modifications are being made.

If a typewriter is used, modifications should be made with a minimum of additional typing by using the existing text. The checklist is cut up, and modified wording along with illustrations, are taped onto a blank sheet. This produces a "cut and paste" job sheet master.

The revised material is next added to the existing behavioral action statement, performance conditions, and attainment standards. The student directions and administrative instructions are deleted. The MPT in Appendix 7D was adapted to produce the job sheet in Appendix 7C.

This adaptation of MPT documentation has the added advantage of providing complete public disclosure on the tasks to be learned and performed. In addition, students who use the job sheet, while learning how to perform a task, can check their own performance capabilities before testing. As a result, they are in a good position to perform the task again for competency certification.

There is no reason to debate the issue of "teaching the test," or "giving the test away" because it is irrelevant in competency-based education. This is true especially when one remembers that the task, its conditions and standards, were identified and described through occupational (job) analysis. Given the need to perform the task successfully on the job, both teaching and testing ought to be performance-oriented. Furthermore, the competency should be based on proper instruction and opportunities for appropriate practice.

Figure 7-9 presents a job performance aid for editing job sheets. It can be used to assure that (a) all of the headings that may be necessary in a particular job sheet have been considered and (b) all those that are not relevant have been intentionally omitted.

When the checklist, shown in Figure 7-10, is used with the editing aid, the teacher has a tool for preparing and reviewing job sheets. The aid and checklist are also effective when evaluating and adapting job sheets prepared by others.

After they are reviewed and edited, job sheets are ready to be examined by others and tried out by students. Validation tryouts determine the need for changes and ultimately prove the value and effectiveness of all types of instruction sheets. A discussion of the validation process follows.

VALIDATION PROCESS

No matter how carefully the instruction sheets were prepared, there is no guarantee that all the time and effort invested will provide effective and efficient instruction. The strongest and most direct evidence of effectiveness is established through an assessment of student performance against behaviorally written performance objectives.

If the instruction sheets help meet performance objectives that provide the criterion-referenced measures, they are said to be valid. If the students cannot do what is called for, the sheets are not valid and must be reworked until they are. Other things being equal, more sources of evidence are better than fewer. Consequently, an ideal validation process also includes information gathered through (a) observations of students using the sheets, (b) questions asked when students have difficulty, and (c) discussions with students after they have taken the criterion-referenced test.

Validation can be compared to the testing process for a new item of equipment. If a component malfunctions repeatedly, there is a problem that must be corrected. By the same token, if the students fail to learn a particular part of the instruction, that portion must be corrected.

Validation implies a "debugging" of instruction sheets. This validation finds where instructions break down and students do not learn effectively or efficiently. A sequence of validation activities begins with a self-evaluation (review) and includes:

1. An examination by constructive critics (quality control examination).
2. Trials with individual students.
3. Trials with small groups of students.

Quality Control

Before trying out instruction sheets on students, have a panel of qualified and constructive critics examine and edit them. These examiners should have expertise and experience in preparing instruction sheets. Their views and opinions are useful in a comprehensive evaluation. The more eyes that scrutinize the sheets, the less chance there is of missing something wrong. Usually, this type of help is not hard to find and it takes little time.

There are three types of quality control examinations to be performed. All are important.

1. An inspection of the accuracy and up-to-dateness of the content. This requires someone with current technical knowledge and skill.
2. A review for readability and composition, and an inspection of the layout and format.
3. An attempt to prejudge the appropriateness of the sheets to the performance objective, as well as to their effectiveness and value.

Examiners should also look for completeness; appropriate use of tools, equipment, and materials; warnings and safety notes. Other important considerations can be taken from the checklists for reviewing each type of instruction sheet. These were presented earlier.

The quality control examination can be done during a panel meeting or when each examiner has the time. A panel meeting has the advantage of group interaction and provides some assurance that the examination is not done superficially. There is sometimes a problem, however, getting all the examiners together.

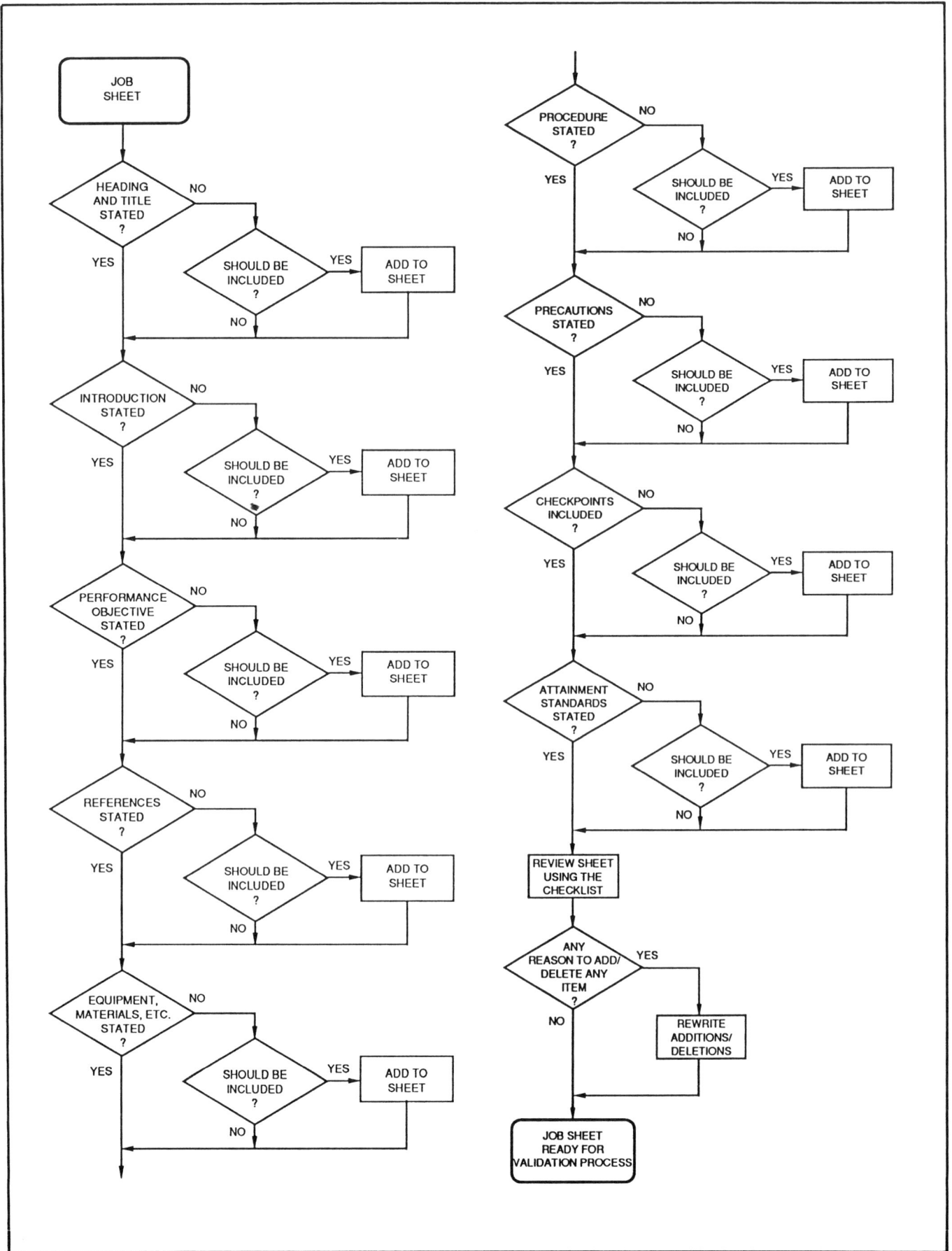

Figure 7-9. Editing job sheets.

Title of Sheet Reviewed:_____

Reviewer:_____ Date:_____

Directions: Indicate whether each numbered question is reflected in the **Job Sheet** by placing a check mark in the **YES** or **NO** box. If the question is not applicable, leave the box blank.

YES NO

[ ]   [ ]   1.   Does the heading at the top of the page provide all the information required?

[ ]   [ ]   2.   Does the title briefly and clearly identify the name of the job task, preceded by "HOW TO"?

[ ]   [ ]   3.   Is there a short motivational introduction?

[ ]   [ ]   4.   Is the behaviorally written performance objective included?

[ ]   [ ]   5.   Are complete reference citations for additional sources of information, including operation sheets, provided?

[ ]   [ ]   6.   Are the necessary tools, equipment, furniture, materials, and supplies listed? (not necessary if included in the conditions statement of the performance objective)

[ ]   [ ]   7.   Are all the necessary performance steps included?

[ ]   [ ]   8.   Are the steps technically accurate and in the proper sequence?

[ ]   [ ]   9.   Are the steps written in sufficient detail so students will know how to do the performance?

[ ]   [ ]   10.   Are existing operation sheets referenced when appropriate?

[ ]   [ ]   11.   Are appropriate, good quality illustrations used to clarify the text?

[ ]   [ ]   12.   Are the illustrations referenced in the text and do they have captions?

[ ]   [ ]   13.   Are the illustrations placed appropriately with the text and in sequence with it?

[ ]   [ ]   14.   Are safety precautions included at points where there is potential for danger or damage to equipment?

[ ]   [ ]   15.   Are checkpoints included?

[ ]   [ ]   16.   Are attainment standards included? (not necessary when included in the standards statement of the performance objective)

[ ]   [ ]   17.   Is the reading level appropriate for most students?

[ ]   [ ]   18.   Have biases - nationalistic, racial or gender - been avoided?

[ ]   [ ]   19.   Is the layout visually attractive and the format orderly?

___ ___   **Total number of check marks**

<u>Note</u>.   If any question received a **NO** response, determine what modifications are necessary in order to improve that criterion.

Figure 7-10. Job sheet review.

When the examination has been completed, it is best to read and consider the editorial comments, then discuss them nondefensively. Examiners often suggest that additional content be added to the instruction sheets. This advice should not be acted upon, however, until student trials confirm that the additional content is needed.

The quality control examination step does not determine validity; nonetheless, it probably will identify oversights, mechanical difficulties, and unforeseen problems that need attention. Only at the tryout stage will there be evidence of the effectiveness of the instruction sheets. While valuable, different points of view are needed, teachers should keep in mind that the examiners' feedback represents their opinion.

Student Sampling

As a part of the validation process, students who are as representative as possible of those who will use the sheets (target population) should be selected to take part in a tryout. These students are called the *sample*. They must fall within the range of: (a) educational background, (b) age, gender, and ethnic composition, (c) skills and experience, (d) motivation and attitude, (e) aptitude, (f) intelligence, and (g) reading grade level, of the user population. If the characteristics of the sample do not match those of the target population, the results will be biased. This means that it will not be possible to generalize from the performance of the sample to that of the target population.

For existing courses and programs that are being revised or upgraded, the sample should be selected from among the current student population. If the course or program is new, the sample is taken from students as representative of the intended target population as can be found.

Where there is no way of getting substitutes for the target population, the only alternative is to observe what the first students who use the sheets do, and listen to what they say. In this case, the first users also serve as the validation population.

While students are not viewed as experts on instruction sheets, those who have tried to learn from the new sheets can be very good observers of their own interactions with the sheets. Consequently, their successes, difficulties, and questions will indicate whether the instruction sheets need modification. For example, if three or four students ask for clarification of the procedure on a job sheet, the procedure needs to be re-examined.

Individual Trials

The validation process itself, begins by trying out instruction sheets on individual students. Those chosen from the sample to participate should have high aptitudes. If they have difficulties, it is reasonable to expect the less capable students to have trouble as well. Moreover, those with the higher aptitudes are generally able to pick out the problems more readily. They are also less reluctant to provide candid feedback.

If the teacher is to gain the full cooperation and active involvement of participating students, the students must be informed of their role in the validation process. It should be explained that they are helping evaluate new instruction sheets. Tell them the learning situation will be somewhat artificial and that if errors are made or difficulties are encountered, it is probably a reflection on the instruction sheets, not on their ability. They should also be told that their help is vitally important. Each participant needs to understand that it is through observations, questioning, test results, and written as well as oral feedback that the value and effectiveness of instruction sheets are determined. Finally, ask them to make notes, on the instruction sheets, wherever they have difficulty or wish to make a suggestion.

During each trial, a single student is closely observed and tactfully questioned while using the instruction sheets. What the student does correctly or incorrectly, where there is trouble, and how much time the student takes are all carefully recorded. Precise records need to be made while the sheets are being used. This can be done efficiently by (a) making notes on a copy of the sheet, (b) using a form designed for this purpose, or (c) dictating into a portable tape recorder.

After using the instruction sheets, which support a performance objective, the criterion-referenced test for that objective is administered. See Chapters 8 and 9 on test construction and validation. This validated or verified test measures whether a student has learned and, if so, how much. This is a particularly important step. The strongest evidence of instruction sheet effectiveness is determined by the student's ability to perform the behavioral action (competency), under the conditions provided and to the standards (criterion) specified by the performance objective. No matter how good instruction sheets might be on other counts, they are of little use if they don't help students reach the performance objective.

Following the test, the students are asked to comment on the strengths and weaknesses of each instruction sheet and to make recommendations for its improvement. The following questions will bring out significant points and aid in-depth probing.

1. Were the directions, contents, and illustrations clear and understandable?
2. Was the content presented in the proper order?
3. Was any part of the material confusing?
4. Were you uncertain about anything?
5. What were the good points?
6. What can be done to make the instruction sheet more interesting and effective?

A discussion centered on these and other related questions will help in maintaining the positive effects of the sheets. At the same time, it will identify any unexpected negative effects. The information collected in this way should be used to supplement the information on whether or not the students were able to attain the performance objective.

Even when one student's performance and feedback indicate weaknesses in an instruction sheet, be slow to make wholesale changes. Only technical inaccuracies and major problems which inhibit attainment of the performance objective should be corrected at this time. As a general rule, **five individual tryouts should be conducted** before any significant changes are made. This ensures that no drastic changes are made based upon the results obtained with an individual student. Only patterns of error and difficulty, which emerge during successive trials, can be trusted to show that a modification is necessary.

A careful analysis of errors made, difficulties observed, test results, and the feedback provided by individual students will lead to the identification of real problems. The analysis also provides the information on which corrective measures are based. Once the necessary modifications are made and the instruction sheets appear to be effective, small-group trials are started.

Small-Group Trials

Validation efforts should now be expanded to a small group of five to ten students. This is done to determine (a) how students will function as a group, given conditions as similar as possible to those under which the instruction normally will be conducted, and (b) if the modified sheets do, in fact, produce the anticipated performance.

There are no rules for deciding how many students should be in the group. Even so, five to ten is probably as good a size as any other reference from which to work. When detailed information is necessary, a smaller group is preferable. On the other hand, a larger group is best if relatively simple, straight forward opinions and group interaction are desired. Of course, the larger the group, the more confidence the teacher can have in the results of this tryout.

The sample of students selected to participate in this stage of the validation process should represent the target population. In an ideal research setting these students would be randomly selected.

Up to this point, the success of the instruction sheets may have been a result of limiting the tryout to those students with high aptitudes. Now it becomes important to determine if the sheets are effective with students of all ability levels.

After the small-group trial, estimates of time requirements based on individual performance need revision to reflect average completion time. Calculate and record the average time. Further modification may be necessary to reduce completion time.

Reduced learning time will increase course or program efficiency; yet, it may decrease effectiveness. Analyzing time data provides guidance when establishing reasonable guidelines on the amount of time to be spent on each performance objective.

An effort should be made to establish the maximum number of trials permitted for a student to reach performance standards. There must be some point at which remedial instruction is specified. Students who are allowed continuous trials, when they cannot attain the learning objective standards, often become frustrated and discouraged. A remedial program with a different approach may well be the alternative.

The method of collecting validation information during small-group trials is much the same as for individual trials. The principal difference is that the instruction sheets are now

being tried out by students (the sample) who are representative of the target population. In any case, each step in the following list will provide valuable information. An analysis and synthesis of the information collected, using this four-step method, will not only identify any remaining problems, but will also help in making beneficial modifications.

1. Unobtrusively observe students using the instruction sheets.
2. Question students who appear to be having difficulties.
3. Administer the criterion-referenced test to assess learning.
4. Conduct an in-depth discussion or "brainstorming" session.

In addition to answering questions and the "brainstorming" session, students can express their views (a) by making notations on the instruction sheets, (b) by completing a questionnaire or checklist, or (c) through any combination of these feedback techniques. As in the individual trials, if the instruction sheets undergo a significant modification, a second small-group trial must be conducted.

The cycle of student use, observation, testing, discussions, analysis of error patterns, and materials modification is repeated until the instruction sheets produce satisfactory results. At this point, continued group trials and modification will most likely result in diminishing returns.

Figure 7-11 provides a job performance aid for conducting the validation process. It would be incorrect to assume that once instruction sheets are validated, duplicated for quantity use, and implemented, they are finished for all time. There will be variations in student characteristics such as aptitude, technological changes, and changes to the performance objectives. Consequently, the sheets must be modified and revalidated periodically to meet changing circumstances.

SUMMARY

Instruction sheets are student-oriented resources with instructional content, used to increase the effectiveness and efficiency of occupational courses or programs. More specifically, they (a) complement or supplement the teaching process, and (b) increase program effectiveness so that students acquire the knowledge and skills essential for successful job performance. Instruction sheets guide students in their interaction with machines, tools, and materials. They assure that all students have the same essential directions for performing practical work and preparing assignments.

The well-written and well-illustrated instruction sheet has significant value, but it cannot be depended upon entirely. This is because problems arise in its use as well as in the development of skills, which require the personal attention of the teacher. Problems such as difficulties in reading and individual learning habits require professional attention.

Among the important benefits to the use of instruction sheets is that students have accurate written information to augment verbal instruction. This written information provides them with the guidance needed. Thus, the teacher has more time to help with the learning process, providing specific assistance to individuals on problems they are experiencing. The use of individual oral instruction and instruction sheets provides motivation which, to a considerable degree, fits the training to individual differences. The problem of providing for individual differences may never be solved with complete satisfaction, but the combination of written and oral instruction is the most satisfactory method yet devised.

The process of preparing instruction sheets is time-consuming and frequently costly. In addition, special abilities are required to prepare sheets having good technical and teaching quality. For these and other reasons, search out "off-the-shelf items" and consider their suitability before committing resources to the preparation of new sheets.

Review relevant instruction sheets from a variety of possible sources to determine their appropriateness. Materials developed elsewhere that are nearly adequate can be adapted (modified) as necessary to suit local needs. After modification, try out the instruction sheets to determine their value and effectiveness.

The true worth of any instruction sheet, whether adopted (accepted in its present form), adapted, or newly prepared, is its effectiveness with students. Only by trying out each sheet on students can the teacher determine its actual effectiveness. This is called validation and the process includes both individual and group trials until the problems identified are corrected. When instructional materials are put into use before they are validated, expect a need for continual revision.

Unfortunately, materials development groups or teams are seldom used to prepare instruction sheets at the local level. As a result, the individual teacher usually adapts or prepares the needed sheets.

Unless the course or program is new or a major revision of an existing one, the number of instruction sheets needed at any one time should not make unmanageable demands on the teacher. On the other hand, the expertise, motivation, and time available for this important and ongoing activity may be inadequate to the task. Even so, the organized approach to developing instruction sheets presented in this chapter will be useful to those who want to improve the effectiveness and efficiency of their course or program.

Finally, there is a tendency to prepare information and assignment sheets instead of operation and job sheets. Student need, not teacher preference, should dictate where to invest the necessary time and effort. The best approach is to prepare the type of instruction sheet that will solve a teaching/learning problem.

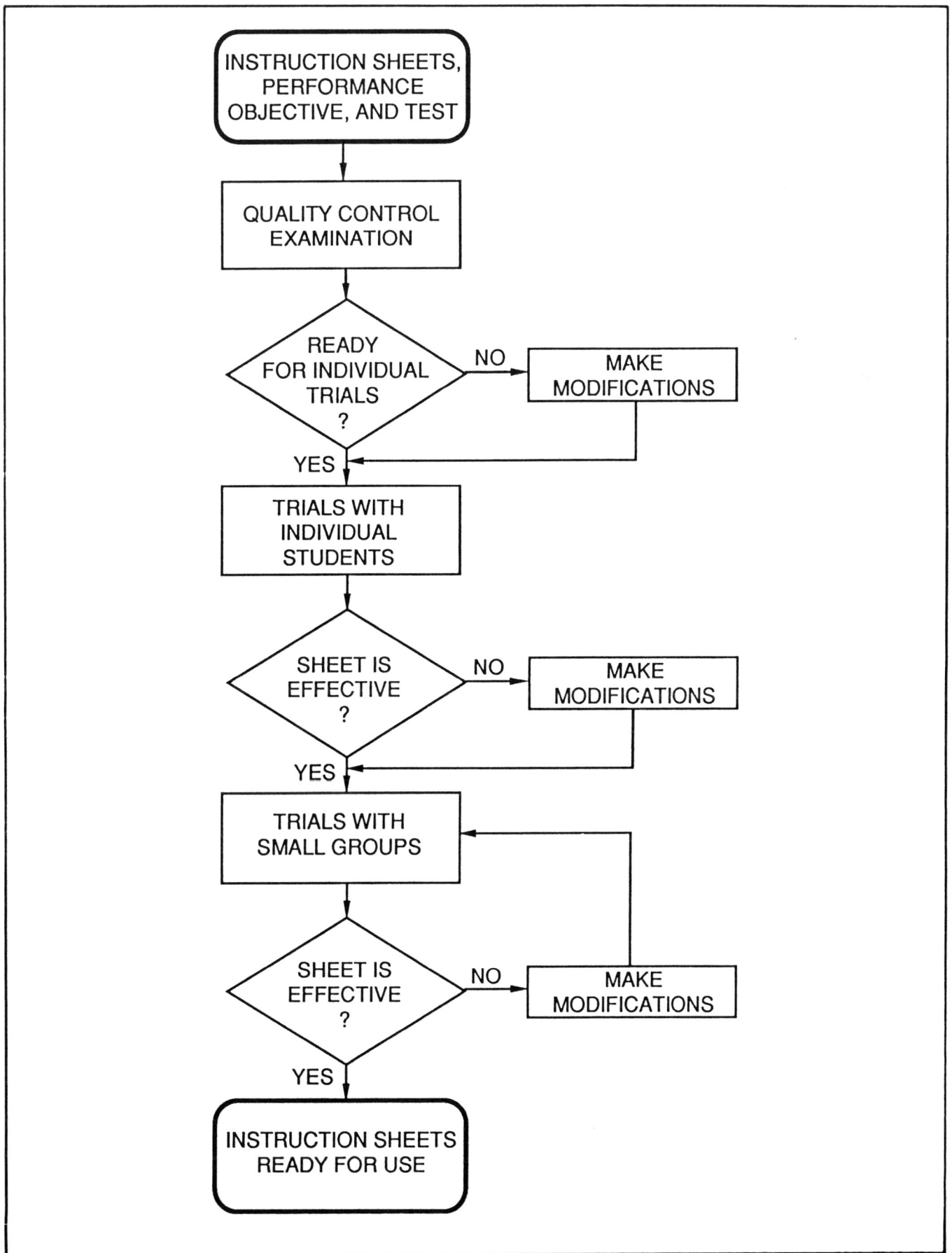

Figure 7-11. Validation process.

APPENDIX 7A

HOW TO OPERATE A HYDRAULIC FLOOR JACK

INTRODUCTION:

Many tasks performed on automobiles and trucks require raising the vehicle to gain access to the underside of the engine and chassis. One of the commonly used devices for raising a vehicle is the hydraulic floor jack. This operation sheet describes the proper procedure for raising and lowering a vehicle with a hydraulic jack. It also describes the use of jack stands.

ACTION STATEMENT:

Raise and lower a vehicle using a hydraulic floor jack.

CONDITIONS:

Within a service shop under simulated work conditions. Given a 3-ton hydraulic floor jack, jack stands, and vehicle.

STANDARDS:

Vehicle raised and lowered without jerky motions and without damage to vehicle or equipment. Hydraulic floor jack and jack stands positioned at proper points on vehicle.

REFERENCE:

Stockel, M.W., & Stockel, M.T. (1984). Auto service and repair. South Holland, IL: Goodheart-Willcox. (pp. 113-114)

PROCEDURE:

1. Determine the proper lifting point on the vehicle from the manufacturer's service manual or owner's manual.

   CAUTION Never try to raise a vehicle by jacking on the engine oil pan, clutch housing, transmission, or other weak component.

2. Roll the floor jack into position using the jack handle. Close the control valve by turning its lever clockwise. Operate the rapid rise foot pump until the jack saddle engages the lifting point (see Figure 1).

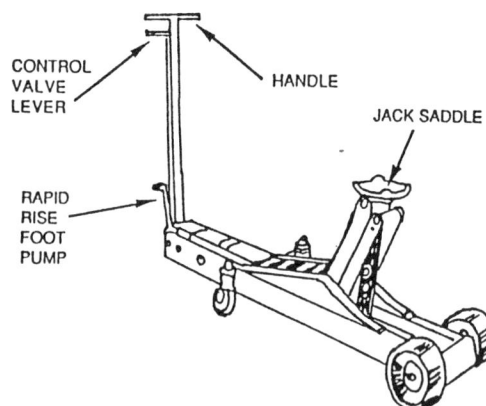

Figure 1. Hydraulic Floor Jack Components

(Continued)

3. Position the jack saddle for lifting, making certain it is firmly engaged. Examine the placement of the jack saddle carefully to prevent shifting of the vehicle during lifting (see Figure 2).

NOTE Always set the parking brake before lifting.

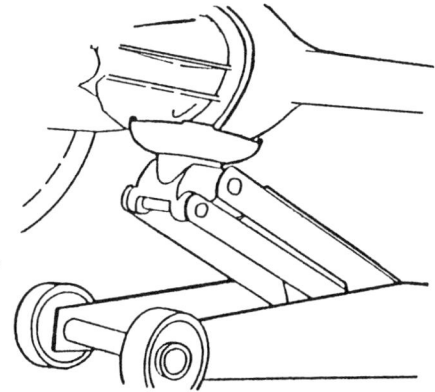

Figure 2. Jack Saddle Properly Positioned Under Differential Housing

Checkpoint

Ask the teacher to check your work before proceeding.

Initials:_____

4. Raise the vehicle to the desired height by pumping the jack handle.

CAUTION Never work underneath a vehicle supported only by a floor jack. If the vehicle fell, you would be seriously injured.

5. Position jack stands in the desired location, usually lifting points. Place them in contact with a unit capable of supporting the load (see Figure 3).

NOTE Do not place jack stands in contact with tapered edges that may cause them to slip.

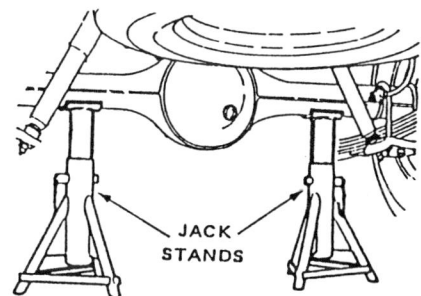

Figure 3. Jack Stands Properly Positioned Under Rear Axle

Checkpoint

Ask the teacher to check your work before proceeding.

Initials:_____

(Continued)

6. Lower the vehicle slowly onto the stands by opening the control valve (turn counter-clockwise). Carefully watch the descent. Allow the jack stands to support the full weight of the load. The hydraulic floor jack may be left in position with a slight lifting pressure to keep it in place. In some cases the floor jack is removed in order to get a clear working area.

   NOTE Jack stands must be properly and securely positioned. Never use concrete blocks, bricks or wood chocks instead of jack stands.

7. Before lowering the vehicle to the ground, remove the jack stands. To remove them, raise the vehicle as described in steps 2 through 4. When the jack stands are free from the weight of the vehicle, remove them from work area.

   CAUTION Inspect the area under the vehicle before lowering. Ensure that there are no tools or equipment that might be damaged and that no one is near the vehicle while it is being lowered.

8. Open the floor jack control valve slowly by turning its lever counterclockwise until the vehicle just begins to lower. Allow it to lower slowly and in a smooth motion to avoid shifting the load and damaging the vehicle.

9. Once the vehicle is on the ground, open the control valve completely, allowing the jack saddle to lower until clear of the vehicle. Pull the hydraulic floor jack from under the vehicle and clear of the area.

APPENDIX 7B

Operation Sheet Headings with Explanations

Page Heading
A heading at the top of the first page. Should include the: (a) program or course number and title, (b) subject matter identification, (c) school name and location, and (d) type of sheet (operation sheet, etc.) as well as its number. When more than one sheet is used, they should be numbered "Page 1 of 2", "Page 2 of 2", etc.

Operation Sheet Title
Name of the operation, which comes from occupational analysis information, preceded by the words "How to." Such a title will help the developer to stick to the topic and the student to know whether the sheet will help with what must be done. An operation sheet titled **HOW TO REPLACE AN ELECTRICAL PLUG** should provide instruction on how to perform the operation on any job task that requires a plug replaced.

Introduction
A "warm-up" statement on the purpose or use of the operation. Should be short, clear and concise. It motivates the student toward an interest in using the sheet and performing the operation. A case may be cited to show the practical application and value of the skill being acquired. Relating the new operation to previous operations helps students link the new skill to what they already know and can do.

Performance Objective
Provides the behavioral action, performance conditions and attainment standards for the operation. Informs students of what is to be learned and what is expected of them.

References
Complete identification of sources for additional information on how to perform the operation. May include optional references for the more ambitious students to use for additional reading.

Tools, Equipment, Furniture, Materials and Supplies
A complete list, in one or two columns, of the items required to carry out the operation. (Not necessary if included in the conditions statement of the performance objective.) This enables students to determine quickly what they need and to make sure everything is ready before they start.

Procedure
The detailed sequential step-by-step procedure for completing the operation, in simple language, and in the proper order. Includes a precise explanation of how to perform each step. The different steps should be set off in distinct numbered paragraphs. Line drawings, diagrams and photographs with captions provide clarification and work well in illustrating step-by-step directions. An illustration often is more instructive than paragraphs of words. It is worth noting that the procedural sequence is not arbitrary but the result of experience and/or an established precedence which reduces the chance for error and results in successful performance.

Note
Precedes important information, which if disregarded, could lead to serious consequences. Use capital letters, boldface type, or underlining for emphasis.

Caution
Identifies safety considerations or precautions to be observed where there is potential danger or the possibility for damage to equipment or to the work. The word caution, in capital letters, boldface type, or underlined, precedes a brief statement concerning the hazard and what to do about it.

Checkpoint
Points in the procedure where students seek teacher assistance or have their progress checked before they perform the next step. Appropriate points (locations) include:
1. Just prior to performing a potentially hazardous step
2. At a quality control point which is important to continued successful performance
3. For verification of a measurement or observation
Provisions should be made on the sheet for the teacher's initials or mark.

(Continued)

Attainment Standards   The acceptable criteria for performance, including, as appropriate, the following categories:
1. Quality, degree of excellence
2. Accuracy, within tolerance limits
3. Number of allowable variations or permissible errors
4. Quantity, rate of production
5. Standards and/or criteria in reference documents
6. Time limit, speed
7. Amount of supervision or assistance to be provided

(Not necessary if included in the standards statement of the performance objective.)

(Continued)

APPENDIX 7C

VTE 112, Automotive Mechanics
Removing and Fitting Wheels

Vocational School, Memphis, TN
Job Sheet Number 10

HOW TO REPLACE A TIRE/WHEEL ASSEMBLY

INTRODUCTION:

Maintenance and repair procedures often call for the removal and replacement of a tire/wheel assembly. Consequently, it is a frequently performed task. Furthermore, there is a possibility for damage to the vehicle and injury to its occupants should this assembly come off on the road. As a result, proficiency in this task is important.

ACTION STATEMENT:

Replace a tire/wheel assembly.

CONDITIONS:

Within a service shop under simulated work conditions, on a full-size 1/2-ton pickup truck. Given a hubcap tool, lug wrench, torque wrench, tire gauge, hydraulic floor jack, jack stand, work order, replacement tire/wheel assembly, and wearing safety glasses and safety shoes.

STANDARDS:

Conical part of lug nuts toward wheel and tightened until they are all torqued, every other one in sequence, to 80-90 ft-lbs. Tire pressure 36+2 psi., and no damage to hubcap or wheel. Process completed within 20 minutes, without assistance.

REFERENCES:

Operation Sheet Number 6 - How To Operate a Hydraulic Floor Jack
Information Sheet Number 4 - Tire Inflation
Hathaway, R.B., & Lindbeck, J.R. (1985). <u>Comprehensive auto mechanics</u>. Peoria, IL: Bennet & McKnight. (pp. 521-523)

PERFORMANCE STEPS:

1. Remove hubcap

   A. Wearing safety glasses and safety shoes, use a hubcap tool to pry the hubcap from the wheel. Be careful not to damage hubcap or wheel.

2. Loosen lug nuts

   A. Use a lug wrench to loosen the lug nuts prior to raising the truck.

   B. Use downward pressure on the lug wrench to loosen the lug nuts by approximately 1/2 a turn.

(Continued)

3. Raise truck

   A. Use a hydraulic floor jack to raise the tire approximately 2" above ground.

   NOTE Before raising the truck, check the manufacturer's recommended lifting points and review Operation Sheet Number 6 - How to Operate a Hydraulic Floor Jack.

   B. Position jack stand ± 1" behind center of lift point.

   Checkpoint

   Ask the teacher to check your work before proceeding.

   Initials:_____

   C. Lower the truck slowly until weight is transferred to the jack stand.

4. Remove and install tire/wheel assemblies

   A. Loosen and remove all lug nuts and place them in a receptacle or upturned hubcap.

   B. Remove tire/wheel assembly from truck taking care not to damage stud threads.

   C. Clean mating surfaces of wheel and wheel hub. Also clean rust, dirt or paint from studs and around bolt holes in wheel.

   D. Replace tire/wheel assembly on hub lifting with legs. Hold in place with one hand while supporting assembly with knee.

   E. Replace all lug nuts on studs with the conical part (tapered end) of the nut toward wheel (see Figure 1). Center wheel on studs and tighten lug nuts by hand until snug.

   F. Use lug wrench to tighten lug nuts gradually, every other one in sequence until all are snug.

   Checkpoint

   Ask the teacher to check your work before proceeding.

   Initials:_____

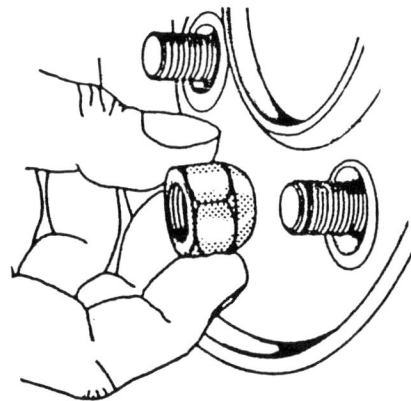

Figure 1. Replace Lug Nuts
With Conical Part Toward the Wheel

5. Lower truck

   A. Remove jack stand and lower truck slowly with no jerky motions.

   (Continued)

6. Torque lug nuts

   A. Use a torque wrench to tighten the lug nuts in accordance with the numbered sequence shown in Figure 2.

   B. All lug nuts must be torqued to 80-90 ft-lbs.

   CAUTION   Tightening the lug nuts in the proper sequence ensures that stress is distributed evenly. Uneven stress could crack a wheel. Overtorquing may cause wheel or hub distortion, runout, and vibration. Undertorquing could allow lug nuts to loosen, resulting in the loss of a wheel.

   Checkpoint

   Ask the teacher to check your work before proceeding.

   Initials:_____

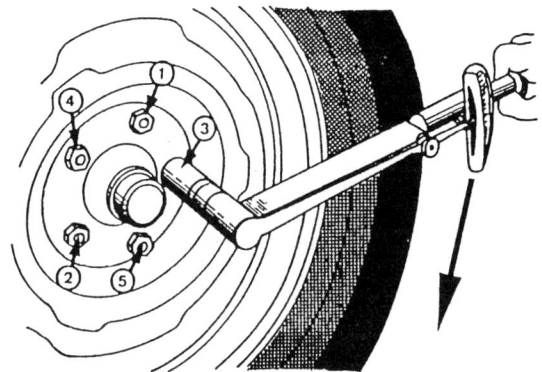

Figure 2. Sequence for Tightening and Torquing Lug Nuts

7. Check tire pressure

   A. Use a tire gauge to ensure proper inflation.

   NOTE   Refer to Information Sheet Number 4 - Tire Inflation

8. Road test truck and make final adjustments

   A. Drive a maximum of 3 miles and inspect to ensure tire pressure is 36+2 psi., all lug nuts remain torqued to 80-90 ft-lbs., and there is no misalignment of tire/wheel assembly.

   B. Replace hubcap by pressing on the edges.

APPENDIX 7D

Manipulative Performance Test

Replacing a Tire/Wheel Assembly on a Full-Size 1/2-Ton Pickup Truck

Student:_____Teacher: _____

Start Time:_____Finish Time:_____ Tester: _____

Results: Pass ____ Fail ____ Tester's Initials: _____ Date: _____

1.0 **TASK STATEMENT** (Behavioral Action)

    1.1   Replace a tire/wheel assembly.

2.0 **PERFORMANCE CONDITIONS**

    2.1   Setting: Service shop, under actual work conditions.

    2.2   Tools: (a) Hubcap tool, (b) Lug wrench, (c) Torque wrench, and (d) Tire gauge.

    2.3   Equipment: (a) Full-size 1/2-ton pickup truck, (b) Hydraulic floor jack, and (c) Jack stand.

    2.4   Materials and Supplies: (a) Work order, and (b) Replacement tire/wheel assembly.

    2.5   Safety Considerations: (a) Wearing safety glasses and safety shoes, (b) Using downward pressure on lug wrench, and (c) Lifting with legs.

3.0 **INITIATING CUE**

    3.1   Receipt of authorized work order.

4.0 **ATTAINMENT STANDARDS**

    4.1   Conical part of lug nuts toward wheel and tightened until they are all torqued, every other one in sequence, to 80-90 ft-lbs. Tire pressure 36+2 psi. and no damage to hubcap or wheel. Process completed within 20 minutes, without assistance.

5.0 **STUDENT DIRECTIONS**

    5.1   The above referenced tools, equipment, materials and supplies shall be used to replace a tire/wheel assembly. Both the process of replacement and the completed replacement (product) will be evaluated by the tester. **All steps must be performed safely and in the prescribed sequence. In addition, all performance must meet standards for the test results to be considered a "pass".**

(Continued)

6.0 ADMINISTRATIVE INSTRUCTIONS

6.1 Tester directions: The student is to demonstrate the ability to replace a tire/wheel assembly on a full-size 1/2-ton pickup truck. Both the process of replacement and the completed replacement (product) shall meet the standards provided herein.

Prior to the test: (a) insure that the referenced tools, equipment, materials and supplies are available; and (b) perform an operational check of the equipment. Give a copy of the first page (Page 1 of 4) to the student(s) so they can review the directions while you read them aloud. Invite the student(s) to ask questions for clarification. After answering all questions, ask the student(s) to return the page before beginning the test. Give the work order to student(s).

Do not provide assistance during the test, but monitor progress to prevent personal injury or damage to the equipment and tire/wheel assembly. Written comments on test administration and student performance may be recorded in the Comments section (item 8.0) on the last page of this test.

6.2 Scoring procedure: Unobtrusively observe the student's performance of each task element/step. Mark the **YES** column if the standard was attained, and **NO** if it was not. Procedural steps in the process are to be rated directly after they are performed. Do not rely on your memory. All standards must be met in order for the test results to be considered a "pass". Enter the start and finish times on the first page and mark the test results, pass or fail; then initial and date your determination.

7.0 CHECKLIST

7.1 (S) Important Sequence: This step must be performed only after the preceding steps.

7.2 (C) Critical Step: Failure to meet the standard for this step will end the test.

Process

TASK ELEMENTS/STEPS	STANDARDS	YES	NO
1. (C) Remove hubcap	• Wearing safety glasses & safety shoes. • Using hubcap tool. • No damage to hubcap or wheel.	☐	☐
2. (C) Loosen lug nuts	• Each nut loosened approximately 1/2 turn. • Using downward pressure on lug wrench.	☐	☐
3. (S,C) Position floor jack	• At manufacturer's recommended lift point. • Parking (emergency) brake is set. • Wheels are blocked.	☐	☐
4. (S) Raise truck	• Tire approximately 2" above ground.	☐	☐

(Continued)

TASK ELEMENTS/STEPS	STANDARDS	YES	NO
5. (S,C) Position jack stand; lower truck	• ± 1" behind center of lift point. • Truck lowered slowly until weight is transferred to jack stand.	☐	☐
6. (S) Remove lug nuts	• All nuts completely removed from studs and placed in receptacle or upturned hubcap.	☐	☐
7. (S,C) Remove and install tire/wheel assemblies	• Clean rust, dirt or paint from studs and around bolt holes in wheel. • Stud threads undamaged. • Lift with legs, holding from bottom of assembly.	☐	☐
8. (S,C) Replace lug nuts	• All nuts replaced. • Conical part of nut toward wheel. • Wheel centered on studs. • Nuts tightened gradually, every other one in sequence until all are snug.	☐	☐
9. (S,C) Raise truck; remove jack stand	• Weight removed from jack stand.	☐	☐
10. (S,C) Lower truck; remove floor jack	• Slowly, with no jerky motions.	☐	☐
11. (C) Torque lug nuts	• Final tightening with torque wrench using numbered sequence shown in Figure 1. • All lug nuts torqued to 80-90 ft-lbs.	☐	☐

Figure 1. Sequence for Tightening and Torquing Lug Nuts

12. (S) Check tire pressure	• 36+2 psi. using tire gauge.	☐	☐
13. (S) Clean and stow tools	• Free of dirt and grease and returned to assigned location.	☐	☐

(Continued)

Product

SCORABLE CHARACTERISTICS	STANDARDS	YES	NO
1. (C) Road test truck and make final adjustments	• Truck driven maximum of 3 miles. • Tire pressure no less than 36+2 psi. • All lug nuts remain torqued 80-90 ft-lbs. • No visible misalignment of tire/wheel assembly.	☐	☐
2. (S) Replace hubcap	• Secure on wheel and undamaged.	☐	☐

8.0 **COMMENTS**

Chapter 8

COGNITIVE ACHIEVEMENT EVALUATION

by

John L. Scott, Associate Professor
Trade and Industrial Education
The University of Georgia
Athens, Georgia

INTRODUCTION

The student evaluation program includes testing, scoring, marking and reporting grades. It is an important part of a comprehensive curriculum guide. This chapter is devoted to evaluating cognitive student achievement. Evaluation of manipulative performance is covered in Chapter 9.

The evaluation portion of an instructional program is more than preparing, administering and scoring tests, and recording grades. A comprehensive evaluation component continuously measures and assesses student accomplishment of all performance objectives. It involves students in the evaluation process, and provides information to them about their strengths and weaknesses. It also provides teachers with feedback information on what instructional strategies work well and where there is need for improvement. The evaluation process requires considerable time and effort to develop measurement instruments and interpret test results for several different purposes. It also requires each teacher to develop an effective record keeping and marking system.

Many occupational teachers feel uncomfortable in their measurement and evaluation role. They are concerned about how to (a) develop tests that measure the important learning outcomes and (b) make the evaluation and grading practices fair to all students. Many would like to improve their measurement and evaluation processes. They often feel inadequately trained to test, evaluate, and report grades required by their schools. Many occupational teachers fear an encounter with students and their parents over their testing, evaluation, and grading practices.

Student evaluation should not be viewed as a dreaded task that teachers must perform. It should be viewed as a vital component of an effective instructional program. Most teachers recognize the many benefits of an effective evaluation system. They see the importance of reporting accurate marks representing student achievement to students, parents, future teachers, and prospective employers.

Occasionally, a teacher can be heard "downplaying" the benefits of an effective evaluation effort. Arguments like the following are typical:

- Employers place little value on student grades in making employment decisions.
- Students don't like teachers who emphasize testing and evaluation.
- It takes too much time away from instruction to construct, administer, and score examinations.
- Written examinations encourage cheating and unhealthy competition.
- Many students can't read or write well enough for the teacher to measure their knowledge of learned content.

The minimum competency testing movement has focused national attention on the need to improve testing to promote learning. The testing movement has primarily applied to measuring and evaluating basic academic skills. However, there is increasing interest in developing minimum competency tests, including performance tests, for use in occupational programs. Occupational teachers, like teachers of other subjects, are being encouraged to spend more time and effort in evaluating student performance. There is the expectation that better testing and evaluation will lead to increased learning and program improvement.

FACTORS TO BE EVALUATED IN AN OCCUPATIONAL PROGRAM

There are many factors to consider in planning and implementing testing and evaluation as an integral part of the instructional program. Some of these are easily understood. Others are not as clear and present measurement problems. A brief review of the major factors follows.

Cognitive Achievement

The student's knowledge and level of understanding of the information necessary to perform an occupational job is an important factor. The usual method of measuring this factor is through written or oral tests. These tests are made up of a variety of different types of items. Examples of test items include multiple-choice, sentence completion, listing, true-false, matching, essay, and modified forms of those just mentioned.

Psychomotor or Manipulative Performance

The ability to perform an actual or simulated work task is a second important evaluation factor. The usual methods of measuring this factor are to (a) observe student performance in following specific work procedures, (b) assess the quality of the completed job, project or work assignment, and (c) measure both work process and product.

Work Habit Development

A third evaluation factor is the level of student work habit development. Work habits include the behaviors of (a) planning for work, (b) following directions, (c) arriving at work on time, and (d) giving an honest day's work. Work habits are usually measured by observation using a rating form that identifies the level of behavior for each work habit.

Interest

A student's interest in training and preparing for a chosen occupational field is another factor to be evaluated. Interests are usually measured through pencil-paper inventories. Another method is through recording information on a rating device such as (a) verbal statements of choice, (b) promoting the program and, (c) volunteering for work-related tasks and assignments.

Attitude

A factor closely related to interest is the student's attitude or feeling toward a training program or chosen occupational area. Attitudes are usually measured by pencil-paper self-report inventories. Sometimes they are also measured by direct questions such as those asked in a structured interview. They also can be measured by observing behavior, using a prepared rating device over a prescribed time period.

Amount of Work Completed

The amount of work that a vocational student completes in a specified time period should be evaluated in occupational programs. The usual method of measuring this factor is by observing and recording information on a progress chart or similar recording device (see Chapter 5). Most vocational teachers use progress charts to record student progress on required learning activities.

Time Required to Complete Training or Work Tasks

Employers expect workers to complete tasks in a standard time period. Therefore, the teacher should evaluate the time required for students to complete learning tasks. The usual method of measurement is to time tasks according to an established timetable for each task. Advisory committee members or prospective employers can establish such time ratings.

Creativity

Another important area for evaluation is the student's ability to solve problems in a unique way or to come up with new ideas or approaches to perform tasks. For example, students may be shown one way to perform a task but should also be challenged to develop another one. The usual method of measurement is to observe student behavior using some type of rating device or record-keeping form.

Safety

A student's attitude, understanding, and practice of safety is another important factor to be evaluated. Measurement methods include performance test items, pencil-paper tests and observational techniques supported by rating devices.

Leadership Development

A final evaluation factor is the development of leadership skills. The use of performance tests, such as the Vocational Industrial Clubs of America Leadership Contest, is one method of measurement. Other tests that use carefully prepared rating and recording forms with stated criteria can also measure leadership development.

DEFINITION OF COGNITIVE STUDENT ASSESSMENT

Instructional program content in occupational education is usually based on identified tasks. The tasks are stated in the form of student performance objectives. These performance objectives describe the intended learning outcomes in terms of specific knowledge, skills, and attitudes needed to obtain employment in a chosen occupational field. Teachers must develop tests to assess learning outcomes in all three learning domains—knowledge (cognitive), skills (psychomotor) and attitudes (affective). The focus of this chapter is on the measurement and evaluation of cognitive learning outcomes. This involves the process of measuring knowledge and the ability to use that knowledge to solve problems relating to a chosen occupational area.

Learning outcomes in the cognitive domain have been divided into six major levels: (a) knowledge, (b) comprehension, (c) application, (d) analysis, (e) synthesis, and (f) evaluation. These learning levels are arranged in order of increasing complexity. Each level has a number of specific learning outcomes to be mastered by students.

A professional test developer would spend considerable time analyzing each performance objective to be included in a test according to the aforementioned levels. Most occupational teachers, however, would probably not be concerned with classifying the learning outcomes of their performance objectives in detail. They may use the cognitive classification only as a guide to ensure that different levels of cognitive behavior are measured by test items. Each teacher must decide which learning outcomes should be taught and tested and the degree of emphasis each should receive in her or his instructional program.

One of the most useful ways to classify performance objectives and test items is to focus on action verbs. Consider the action verb of an objective such as "Interpret diagnostic car computer codes." It is easily recognized as a learning outcome that involves application of cognitive principles and specific procedures to accomplish the task. The following cognitive action verbs are frequently used in occupational programs:

analyze	arrange	assess	calculate
cite	classify	compare	compute
contrast	convert	define	describe
determine	develop	discriminate	emulate
exemplify	explain	follow	identify
implement	initiate	interpret	list
manage	name	point out	prepare
read	record	relate	select
solve	state	transcribe	translate
vary			

Teachers can add terms to the list. They can then utilize it in writing cognitive performance objectives and test items.

TERMS USED IN MEASUREMENT AND EVALUATION

Several terms are frequently misused in evaluating student achievement. Teachers sometimes say to their colleagues, "I must give an evaluation to my sixth period class today." The correct term is "to give a test." A test is an instrument usually constructed by a teacher to obtain measurements of cognitive learning outcomes. Testing is the process of administering an instrument to obtain measurements of learned knowledge. The most common form of testing is pencil-and-paper. This type of test is popular because (a) it can be used to measure many different types of learned behavior and (b) it is fairly easy to administer to a large group of students at one time. Paper-pencil tests help make efficient use of classroom time.

A teacher-made test usually requires no special equipment or training in test administration with the exception of the modern automated test scoring equipment. More information on the qualities and uses of tests will be presented later.

The term *measurement* is the process of collecting and ordering information. It involves assigning numbers or other symbols to objects according to written rules. Anything that exists at all exists in some quantity and can be measured. Measurement refers to the quantity or "how much." An example of a measurement is a test score on a cognitive achievement test which provides information that can be evaluated to answer the question "how much more than?" or "how much less than?"

Evaluation is the process of determining the worth or value of something. Evaluation is being practiced when information obtained through measurement instruments such as achievement tests are used to answer the question of "how good is this?" When occupational teachers administer tests they are measuring only, but when the test scores are compared to statements of quality or standards, evaluation is being practiced.

Assessment is a term that is used in place of evaluation. It involves using information obtained through cognitive measurement to evaluate or form judgments about a learner's cognitive behavior with respect to worth or significance.

There are many other special terms used in measurement and evaluation such as validity, reliability, comprehensiveness, etc. These will be defined when they appear in the information contained later in this chapter.

PURPOSES OF COGNITIVE ACHIEVEMENT EVALUATION

The primary purpose of evaluation is the improvement of learning and instruction. This purpose suggests that student learning will improve as a result of testing and evaluation. It implies that teachers and their instructional programs will also improve as teachers find out what works best in helping students learn.

Other purposes and benefits of cognitive achievement evaluation are:

Motivation: Students are usually more attentive and apply themselves better when they know they will be tested and their performance evaluated. They may become motivated to study for exams because of (a) competition with other students, (b) a desire to improve their knowledge and skills, (c) feelings of guilt and anxiety or the fear of failure, and (d) a need to see how successful they are in learning assigned content.

Diagnosis of capabilities: Teachers who use pretests can provide to students and themselves information about basic prerequisite skills believed to be essential for learning in an occupational program. They also are able to use pretest results to determine what knowledge and skills students already possess in order to focus their instruction better.

Improving teacher and instructional effectiveness: Teachers who use test results are able to modify their instructional program to meet all or certain students' special needs because they know what methods or learning activities produced desirable learning outcomes.

Test taking in an important instructional activity: Preparing for tests causes both teachers and students to review key instructional concepts and points that can be used in solving educational and occupational problems. When students actually take a test, they are provided with an overall review of lesson or unit content and important learning outcomes.

Test results teach important self-evaluative information: When students receive their test results, they learn how others view their level of performance and begin to develop the skills of self-evaluation.

PLANNING TESTS

When planning for a pencil-paper test, the occupational teacher must consider a number of factors.

1. Developing and selecting a sufficient number and type of test items to adequately sample student achievement in a specified time period such as the end of an instructional unit.
2. Determining and selecting the performance objectives to be measured.

3. Analyzing the performance objectives to determine content for test items.
4. Developing a content outline to use in test item construction.
5. Constructing different types of test items and directions for each type.
6. Constructing a table of specifications to guide the selection of test items.

In practice, the beginning occupational teacher spends little time in planning a test. Beginning teachers usually review the instructional materials that were presented in an instructional unit and write items until they reach a predetermined number. Tests constructed in this manner sometimes have too many items measuring some content at the expense of other content.

Teacher-made tests can be improved significantly if some basic procedures and techniques are followed in planning and constructing them. Tests must be planned before they are administered just like lessons are planned before they are presented. Appendix 8A contains a step-by-step process for planning tests.

COGNITIVE ACHIEVEMENT TEST ITEMS

Pencil-paper tests usually are made up of a number of different types of test item formats. There are two major divisions of these formats: (a) supply type questions that require students to generate their own responses or answers and (b) selection type questions that require students to choose from among several possible answers. These item formats also go by other names such as "recall versus recognition" and "constructed response versus identification." They are also known as the "subjective versus the objective" item. Objective items include multiple-choice, true-false, matching, and short answer or completion. The essay item is the only type belonging to the subjective category. The next section is devoted to test item types: their uses, advantages and disadvantages, pointers in constructing items, and pointers in writing clear directions for each item.

True-False Items

The true-false or alternative-response item is widely used by occupational teachers since it is believed to be easily written, administered, and scored. The fact is, good true-false items can be challenging to write. They call for statements that are entirely true or false themselves without qualifying phrases which serve as cues to students. Traditional true-false items are usually written as declarative or situational statements that are either true or false. The student simply responds by reading the statement and making a choice. The true-false example that follows is a traditionally stated item.

EXAMPLE A: T F 1. Class A fires involve electrical equipment.

There are several modified forms of true-false items that increase their usefulness and reduce the probability of students simply guessing the correct answer. One modification requires the students to decide if the statement is true or false. Then, if it is a false statement, the student must indicate what changes are needed to make it true by underlining the appropriate word(s) or phrases(s). In a similar manner, the student is to underline the key word(s) or phrase(s) that makes a true statement true. The previous example is modified to illustrate:

EXAMPLE B: T F 1. Class A fires involve electrical equipment.

(Notice that the problem can be made a true statement by (a) changing A to C or (b) changing electrical equipment to paper, wood, or cloth.)

A second modified true-false item is called the correction type. As before, this type calls for the student to determine if the statement is true or false. If the statement is true, nothing further is done. However, if the statement is false the student must indicate a knowledge of the subject. In this situation the student inserts in blank "A" (_____) the word or letter that makes the statement false and in blank "B" (_____) a substitution for blank "A" to make the statement true. An example follows:

EXAMPLE C: T F 1. Class A fires involve electrical equipment.

A ___A___   B ___C___

A third modified true-false item is the cluster true-false. This item is characterized by a statement followed by a listing of conclusions or reasons. The student is required to indicate by circling the appropriate letter whether or not the statement is true or false. If the statement is false, no additional response is required. If the statement is true, the student indicates whether the conclusion statements are correct or incorrect by circling the "T" for correct statements. The following example shows a cluster-type true-false item:

EXAMPLE D: T F Fire extinguishers are labeled according to the type of fire they are designed to extinguish.

T F 1. They are all labeled with symbols.

T F 2. They are labeled by numbers 1 through 4.

T F 3. They are labeled by letters A, B, and C.

T F 4. They are labeled by individual or a combination of the letters A, B, and C.

The fourth type of modified true-false is an incomplete statement followed by several items that will make it either true or false. The student is to indicate whether each item completes the statement making it true or false. An example follows:

EXAMPLE E: The contents of modern fire extinguishers are comprised of:

T F 1. Carbon tetrachloride.

T F 2. Carbon dioxide.

T F 3. Oxygen.

T F 4. Soda.

T F 5. Halogen.

T F 6. Water.

Uses of True-False Items. True-false items can be used effectively whenever there are only two possible responses, absolutely correct or incorrect. They are useful in measuring achievement at the knowledge and comprehension levels of the cognitive domain. Since they can be completed quickly by students, a large number of items can be written and tested covering a broad base of content. They are particularly effective in measuring factual information such as definition of terms, recall of specific facts, and terminology. The modified forms of true-false items make it possible to measure higher levels of cognitive learning because student reasoning is involved.

Advantages of True-False Items. There are a number of advantages of true-false items over other cognitive achievement measures. These are as follows:

1. They are known and accepted by teachers, students, and parents.
2. They can be used to sample a broad base of content in a short testing period.
3. They can be scored easily and objectively.
4. True-false items are relatively easy to construct with factual information.
5. Items can be used to measure higher levels of cognitive achievement if modified forms are used.
6. Cluster true-false items can be used to check several points concerning a specific concept or principle.
7. They can be quickly constructed and used to create interest in a new unit of instruction.
8. They can provide quick evaluation feedback for teachers.

Limitations of True-False Items. Perhaps the biggest limitation of traditional true-false items is the fifty-fifty chance of guessing the answer correctly. Furthermore, teachers cannot identify the misconceptions students had in mind when they answered items incorrectly. Consequently, true-false items may reveal little real understanding. Some other limitations are:

1. They encourage memorization of facts.
2. It is difficult to write items that are either absolutely correct or incorrect without giving the item away.
3. It is difficult to avoid vagueness, unimportant details, and unneeded clues when writing true-false items.
4. Traditional items are usually limited to measuring only the first two levels of cognitive achievement.
5. Test consistency or reliability is likely to be low unless a large number of items are included. Test reliability is the ability of a test to render essentially the same results when used repeatedly with similar students.
6. Items may measure the student's reading ability rather than knowledge of content.
7. Trivia or minor details receive as much attention in items as important concepts and principles.

Rules for Writing True-False Items. There are a number of rules to consider when writing good true-false items.

1. Write the item on important related course content that contains a single important point, thought, or idea. Keep them as short and simple as possible.
2. Construct statements which are either entirely true or false. Make them positive statements.
3. Avoid using specific clues or determiners such as often, sometimes, always, never, maybe, generally, as a rule, occasionally, all, none, totally, not, etc..
4. Refrain from patterning cues when scattering items such as two true, two false, etc.
5. Construct items so true and false statements are approximately equal in length.
6. Avoid writing items using the personal pronouns such as "you," "me," etc.
7. Exercise care when writing items so later ones do not answer previously written items.
8. Do not write items with specific references or names if possible. For example, "bulls eye shellac is thinned with naptha."
9. Construct the scoring key when writing the items and their origin.
10. State items so the major point is obvious.
11. Avoid lifting items directly from written materials.
12. Construct modified true-false items whenever possible.

Writing Directions for True-False Items. Directions must be simply stated and clearly indicate how students are to respond to each item. For example, if students are to respond by circling the "T" or "F" indicating their choice, they must be directed to do so. Directions also indicate (a) whether or not a guessing factor is involved, (b) the point value of each item, and (c) the total points for each true-false section of the test. Indicate whether students are to write on the test or record their answers on standard, machine-scored answer sheets. Most machined-scored answer sheets require students to completely darken the circle or rectangle under "A" for a true response and follow the same procedure in the space under "B" for a false statement.

Some teachers ask students to write the letters "T" or "F", or words "true" or "false" in the space provided by each numbered item. This practice should be avoided, however, because it requires more student time. It can also be difficult to score because of poor handwriting.

The following are sample directions for each type of true-false item:

EXAMPLE A: Traditional true-false.

Read each statement carefully, then determine if it is true or false. If the statement is true, circle the letter "T"; if false, circle the letter "F." There is no penalty for guessing. Each item is worth one (1) point for a total of ____ possible points.

T F 1. Class A fires involve electrical equipment.

EXAMPLE B: Traditional true-false, machine-scored.

Read each statement carefully, then determine if it is true or false by recording your response on the machine-scored answer sheet. If the statement is true, darken in the space beside each number column under "A." If the statement is false, darken in the space under "B." There is no penalty for guessing. Each item is worth one (1) point for a total of _____ points.

    A   B   C   D   E

1. o   o   o   o   o

EXAMPLE C: Modified true-false.
Read each statement carefully, then determine if the statement is true or false and indicate which word(s) or phrase(s) make the statement true or false. If the statement is true, circle the letter "T"; if false, circle the letter "F." Then underline the word(s) or phrase(s) that make the statement true or false. There is no penalty for guessing. Each item is worth two (2) points for a total of _____ points.
T F 1. Class A fires involve electrical equipment.

EXAMPLE D: Modified true-false correction type.
Read each statement carefully, then determine if the statement is true or false. If the statement is true, circle "T" and do no more; if false, circle the "F"; then insert the word(s) or phrase(s) in blank A that make it false. Then write in the correct information in blank B that will make the statement true. There is no penalty for guessing. Each item is worth two (2) points for a total of _____ points.

T F 1. Class A fires involve electrical equipment.

    A ___A___   B ___C___

EXAMPLE E: Modified true-false cluster, type 1.
Read the main statement carefully and each reason or conclusion which follows it. Then determine if the main statement is true or false. If the statement is true, circle the letter "T"; if false, circle the letter "F" and make no further response. If it is a true statement, circle one or more of the numbered reason(s) which support the choice you made. In some cases there will be only one correct reason, while in others, several or all may be correct. There is no penalty for guessing. Score each question with two (2) points, one point for the correct T/F and one point for the supporting reason.

T F 1. Fire extinguishers are labeled according to the type of fires they are designed to extinguish.
    1. They are labeled with symbols.
    2. They are labeled by numbers 1 through 4.
    3. They are labeled by letters A, B, and C.
    4. They are labeled by individual or a combination of letters A, B and C.

EXAMPLE F: Modified true-false cluster, type 2.
Read each incomplete statement carefully and each of the possible numbered alternatives that may or may not complete the statement correctly. Then indicate which alternatives are true and which are false. If the alternative is true and completes the statement correctly, circle the letter "T"; if the alternative is false circle "F." There is no penalty for guessing. Each item is worth one (1) point for

a total of _____ points.
The contents of all modern fire extinguishers are comprised of:

T F 1. Carbon tetrachloride.

T F 2. Carbon dioxide.

T F 3. Oxygen.

T F 4. Soda.

T F 5. Halogen.

T F 6. Water.

Completion/Short Answer Item

The completion or short answer item requires students to recall specific information and to supply the correct response by (a) completing an incomplete statement or (b) answering a question statement. These items are sometimes called "recall" or "supply" items. There are numerous adaptations or modification of each format. Students may be required to respond with a single word, phrase, sentence, figure, number, symbol, date, etc. These items are written so that students supply a short response rather than an extended one which essay items require.

There are two common formats for completion items. The first is the **incomplete sentence** with a blank or blanks representing a missing word or words. This format is sometimes called "fill in the blank." The second format is the **question statement** which requires students to answer the item. This is done by supplying the word(s) or phrase(s) called for in the question. The following example shows the difference in the two completion item formats.

EXAMPLE A: Incomplete statement.
  __Water__ 1. The type "A" fire extinguisher contains
      _____.

EXAMPLE B: Completion question format.
  __*Water*__ 1. What is the extinguishing agent in a type "A" fire extinguisher?

The example provides a simple recall/incomplete sentence item and a simple recall question item. Completion/short answer items can be constructed to (a) require descriptive information, (b) solve a problem, (c) identify some object or symbol, (d) list specific information (sometimes in order), (e) show relationships or analogies, and (f) complete generalizations with justification. The following examples of completion/short answer items illustrate different possible item formats.

EXAMPLE C: Completion-description type.
Each of the following men made important contributions to occupational education. Identify each of them by writing proper descriptive words in the blank space provided. The first item is answered as an example. Each item is worth one (1) point. Total for this section is _____ points.

Example: 1. Hoke Smith *Co-sponsor of Smith-Hughes Act*

2. Charles Prosser _____

3. Victor Della Voss_____

4. Frank Parsons _____

5. Von Fellenbergh _____

6. Otto Saloman _____

EXAMPLE D: Problem or situation.

Read each of the construction occupation problems given below; then perform the mathematical operations necessary to answer the items correctly. Place your answer in the space provided to the left of each numbered item. Show your calculations on the work sheets provided. Each item is worth one (1) point for a total of _____ points for this section.

_____ 1. A gable roof on a garage is 14'-0" x 30'-0". How many squares of roofing material are required to reroof the building?

_____ 2. A 10'-0" x 12'-0" utility shed is to be constructed with two 3'-0" x 6'-8" doors and no windows. How many 2" x 4" pieces of lumber will be required to frame the walls of this building if standard 16" on-center construction is followed?

_____ 3. How many board feet of lumber are there in three 2" x 8" x 14' pieces?

EXAMPLE E: Identification.

Identify the four types of screwdrivers shown in the pictures below by placing their correct names in the spaces provided for each tool. Each item is worth one (1) point for a total of _____ points for this section of the test.
1. Identify the screwdrivers.

_____   _____   _____   _____

EXAMPLE F: Listing.

List the four strokes of the 4 cycle gasoline engine in the order they occur by writing in the correct information in the numbered spaces below. Each numbered item is worth one (1) point for a total of _____ points for this section of the test.

1. _Intake_____

2. _Compression_____

3. _Power_____

4. _Exhaust_____

EXAMPLE G: Analogies.

This item consists of incomplete analogies on fire protection devices which require you to insert the proper word in the blank space provided to the left of each numbered item. Analogies simply mean that A:B::C:D or that A has the same relationship to B that C has to D. For example 2:4::10:_20_. Each item is worth one (1) point for a total of _____ points on this section.

Infrared detector 1. Ions: ionization detector :: flame: _____ .

Electrical shorts 2. Class A : wood, cloth and paper :: Class B : _____ .

EXAMPLE H: Generalizations and justifications.

Each of the main statements concerning wood technology represents a known fact that is followed by a blank space requiring students to give an example or reason that illustrates or justifies the statement. Write your responses in the space provided to the left of each numbered item.

Laminated beams 1. Some wood products are stronger than similar metal products. Example: _____

Lamination 2. Inferior softwoods such as pine or white woods can now be made stronger than the strongest hardwoods. Reason: _____

Uses of Completion/Short Answer Items. The completion item is useful in testing specific knowledge in an instructional unit that should be remembered. Knowledge in the following categories are examples: terminology, important concepts, classifications, principles, historical events, dates, symbols, methodologies, formulas, contributions, tolerances, specifications, and identifications. Such knowledge can be measured by completion items which virtually eliminate the possibility of guessing. In addition, the completion item can be written to measure nearly all types of vocational content in which accurate information is required to be measured.

The common completion type items are used primarily in measuring the who, what, when, and where type of information at the lower level of the cognitive domain. Through using the variations of completion item formats, teachers can effectively sample a wide range of subject matter and measure higher levels of learning in the cognitive domain. Completion items can be substituted for recognition items like multiple-choice when it is important that students recall information rather than simply recognize it.

Advantages of Completion/Short Answer Items. There are several advantages to completion/short answer items. These are as follows:

1. The completion/short answer item is the best choice when the student's ability to recall specific information is to be measured.

2. Because students must recall important information, guessing is almost eliminated when items are written correctly.

3. Variations of completion items can be used to measure a wide variety of learning outcomes and subject matter content.

4. They are relatively simple to construct.

Limitations of Completion/Short Answer Items. Although completion items offer certain advantages, they also have several limitations. These are as follows:

1. Unless carefully written, completion items tend to measure memorization of trivial facts instead of more important information.

2. Because completion items are relatively easy to construct, they may be overused.
3. Because students must write a response, spelling and writing clarity become a factor in determining the student's intended response, making grading more difficult.
4. Completion items sometimes evoke correct responses that are different than those intended by teachers.
5. Higher-level learning outcomes such as understanding are difficult to measure with the simple recall and completion items.
6. Completion items require longer student response time.
7. Student's ability to read and react at some level of speed can be a factor in completing these items in a given test period.

Rules for Writing Completion/Short Answer Items. While many rules for writing completion items are identical or similar to those for writing other objective test items, they need to be emphasized again.

1. Keep the required responses short — one or two words — when possible.
2. Write completion items so they are correct statements and correctly written.
3. Avoid specific determiners immediately before a blank that may give away the answer (such as a, or an).
4. Refrain from "lifting" items word-for-word from written materials.
5. Write a clear statement and omit only the *important* word or idea.
6. In typing completion items, keep all blanks the same length.
7. Place the blanks indicating important missing words near the end of the statement.
8. To simplify scoring, require students to place their responses to the left of numbered items.
9. When numerical units are to be supplied as part of the answer, such as 20 feet, do not write blanks for the units, (i.e.) "feet," inches, etc.
10. Have each blank call for a single idea.
11. Avoid grammatical clues in other parts of the statement.
12. Avoid mixing incomplete statements and question statements in the same test section.
13. Write completion items in simple language understood by students.
14. Write items based on information that has been presented in assigned reading materials, audio-visual materials or in class.
15. Prepare the scoring key when writing items and indicate their origin. (The item cards or computer file should have this information).
16. Assign the same number of points to each blank.
17. Arrange all completion type items in the same portion of the test.
18. Avoid placing more than one blank in a sentence.

Writing Directions for Completion/Short Answer Items. The directions for the different types of completion/short answer types should be clearly written and simply stated to ensure student understanding. They also should be stated in a manner that facilitates scoring. Therefore, the practice of requiring students to write responses in the statements themselves should be avoided and special blanks should be provided either at the left or right of statements for student responses. As with other items, the point values should be assigned and the total number of points in each section of the test given.

A number of sample directions were provided previously along with sample completion item types. The two most commonly used completion item directions follow:

EXAMPLE A: Directions — incomplete type.
Read each incomplete statement carefully, then indicate your response by placing your answer(s) in the blank space(s) to the left of each numbered item. Incorrect spelling will be noted but no penalty will be assessed. Each blank is worth one (1) point for a total of _____ points.

Ionization   1. The type of fire detector which recognizes a fire in its earliest stages is the _____ type.

EXAMPLE B: Directions — question type.
Read each question statement carefully, then indicate your response by placing your answer in the space provided at the left of each numbered item. Incorrect spelling will be noted but no penalty will be assessed. Each item is worth one (1) point and the total on this portion of the test is _____ points.

Ionization   1. What type of fire detector device senses a fire in its earliest stage?

Matching Items

The matching item is a selection type item that requires students to match two columns of related materials. The common matching item format consists of a list of problem statements in column I called **premises** and a list of related elements in column II called **responses**. The directions tell students what the categories are in columns I and II. The student must indicate the associations or relationships between corresponding column items.

The matching item usually requires students to match such elements as (a) terms and their definitions, (b) causes with effects, (c) tools and their applications, (d) problems with their solutions, (e) questions with their answers, (f) parts with their corresponding units, (g) symbols and their names, (h) descriptive phrases with other phrases, (i) principles with example applications, and (j) characteristics with the units to which they belong.

There are several matching item formats commonly used in occupational education. The following example requires students in a safety class to match terms with their definitions.

EXAMPLE A: Matching item — function with agency.
Match the function in column A with its associated agency in column B by placing the appropriate lettered term in the space provided to the left of its function in column A. No term can be used more than once, but some terms may not be used at all. Each item is worth one (1) point for a total of _____ points.

EXAMPLE:

Column A—Function	Column B—Agency
E 1. A major source of safety educational material in all areas.	A. Occupational Safety and Health Administration.
F 2. Conducts research on safety and health problems and is linked with the center for disease control.	B. American Society for Testing Materials.
D 3. Coordinates the voluntary development of national standards which are used in manufacturing industrial and consumer products.	C. National Fire Protection Association.
G 4. A nonprofit testing institute which provides a service to manufacturer's electrical products.	D. American National Standards Institute.
C 5. Produces the National Electrical Code.	E. National Safety Council.
B 6. The largest source of voluntary consensus standards.	F. National Institute of Occupational Health.
	G. Underwriter's Laboratory.
	H. American Society of Mechanical Engineers.

EXAMPLE B: Matching—characteristics with source.
Match the type of hazard on the left with the sources given on the right. Some hazards will have more than one source given. Each item is worth one (1) point for a total of _____ points.

E 1. Electrical.	A. Misaligned machinery bearings.
C 2. Smoking.	B. Flammable liquid containers not grounded and bonded.
F 3. Friction.	C. Employee's failure to follow smoking regulations.
D 4. Overheated materials.	D. Industrial driers.
B 5. Static sparks.	E. Blocking of fuses.
	F. Inadequately lubricated bearings or shafts.

EXAMPLE C: Modified matching.
For each of the following test characteristics match the type of measurement device that best represents the characteristic. Use only one response, the best one. Each characteristic is worth one (1) point for a total of _____ points.
A. Objective tests.
B. Subjective tests.
C. Performance tests.

____ 1. Gives an extensive test sample.

____ 2. Can be graded objectively and quickly.

____ 3. Is easy to construct but hard to grade.

____ 4. Is hard to construct but easy to grade.

____ 5. Stresses application of knowledge

____ 6. Time-consuming to administer.

____ 7. Best test to measure occupational competence.

____ 8. Efficient for measuring knowledge of facts.

____ 9. Measures organization, writing and creativity.

____ 10. Favors the verbally inclined student.

____ 11. May use a checklist or similar type of recording system.

____ 12. Usually has only a few questions that require longer response on the part of the student.

____ 13. Overemphasizes rote learning.

EXAMPLE D: Modified matching—ordering or ranking type.
If a person is found collapsed on the floor, what is the correct order of first aid steps to follow, according to the American Red Cross? Place the correct number (1-10) indicating the order of each step below.

____ A. Shout for help.

____ B. Position the victim.

____ C. Check for unresponsiveness.

____ D. Check for breathlessness.

____ E. Open the airway.

____ F. Phone the Emergency Medical Service system.

____ G. Begin rescue breathing.

____ H. Check for pulse at the side of the neck.

____ I. Give two full breaths.

____ J. Recheck the pulse.

Uses of Matching Items. As noted in the introduction to this type of item, the matching item can be used to measure the student's ability to indicate relationships or associations between two columns of elements ranging from terms and their definitions to tools and their applications. They are especially useful for measuring the lower level cognitive outcomes involving the who, what, where of subject content. Matching items are very efficient for measuring factual information because a fairly large number of responses can be included in a small space under one set of directions.

Advantages of Matching Items. Matching items have several advantages over other types of objective items. These are as follows:
1. They can be written so they are totally objective and can be easily scored.

2. When matching items are written correctly, they can nearly eliminate the guessing factor.
3. A large number of items can be contained in a small section of the test and completed in a short time period.
4. They can be used to measure associations and relationships of many different things and elements.
5. They can be relatively easy to construct if certain rules are followed.
6. Matching items can also be constructed to use real objects, pictures, drawings, models, and materials instead of using descriptive words to measure knowledge and understanding.

Limitations of Matching Items. In spite of the advantages, matching items have some limiting considerations.
1. Matching items are generally confined to measuring lower levels of the cognitive learning outcomes.
2. Matching items tend to encourage the memorization of facts.
3. Since related or homogeneous content is used to construct matching items, it is difficult to avoid irrelevant clues to correct responses.
4. The student's ability to recognize relationships depends upon reading ability.

Rules for Writing Matching Items. Matching items share common rules for writing with other objective items. There are, however, some unique rules which must be followed in order to construct good items. Note the following rules for writing matching items.
1. For non-machine scored items, as a general rule, include at least seven elements and not more than twelve in any one matching item column.
2. Keep materials within columns related or homogeneous.
3. Write at least three additional elements in column II (responses) than are in column I (premises) to match.
4. Construct matching items so entire item is on one page.
5. Arrange items within columns in logical order.
6. Capitalize the first words of element statements in column I (premises).
7. Construct matching items so longer statements such as definitions are in column I (premises) on the left side of the page.
8. Arrange elements in both columns to avoid any recognizable patterns.
9. Prepare clear, easily understood directions with major column content identified.
10. Prepare a scoring key when writing the matching item.

Writing Directions for Matching Items. The directions must describe what is in the two columns (premises and responses) and how and where students are to make their choices. Directions should indicate if responses can be selected once or more than once and if some choices are not to be selected at all. If only five responses are to be used, the standard machine-scoring answer sheet can be used. If more than five responses are necessary, the student must be directed to respond on the appropriate section of the matching item—usually to the left of each numbered element in column I (premises). Like other test item directions,

the number of points for each numbered element should be indicated as well as the total points for the entire item. The sample directions which follow show poor and better matching item directions.

EXAMPLE A: Poor sample matching item directions.
Listed below are two columns. For each item in column I, there is a word or phrase that matches it in column II. Find the word or phrase that matches the item in column I and place your lettered selection in the space provided to the left of each numbered item in column I.

Notice that the directions **do not** tell the students what the major relationships are between columns I and II. There is also no information provided about using any response only once, more than once, or not at all. Also, there is no point value indicated for elements or the total item.

EXAMPLE B: Better sample matching item directions.
The list on the left in column I describes the functions of different hand tools while the list on the right (column II) contains the names of common hand tools. Match the names of hand tools with their correct functions by writing the letter of the appropriate tool in the blank space to the left of each numbered function. Use each response only once; or not at all. Each item element is worth one (1) point for a total item point value of _____ points.

Other sample directions are shown in the sample matching item types presented earlier.

Multiple-Choice Items

The multiple-choice item consists of an introductory statement or stem which is either in a question or incomplete sentence form. This stem is followed by several possible responses which are sometimes identified by the words "alternatives," "options," "choices," "foils," "distractors," "determiners," and "solutions." These alternatives include the one *best* correct answer along with three or more *plausible* incorrect answers. Plausible incorrect alternatives represent the common mistakes students make related to the concept, problem, or question. The multiple-choice item is commonly used because it can be constructed to measure all levels of learning outcomes in the cognitive domain. Learners prefer the multiple-choice because it is a recognition type item. Teachers prefer it because it is an objective item, easily scored by hand or machine.

As mentioned, the two basic formats for multiple-choice items are the *incomplete sentence* and the *question*. Incomplete statement multiple-choice items are more specific or concise than the question type.

Other format variations are the (a) correct/incorrect type and (b) the *best* answer type which may have correct distractors but there is one choice that is a *best* solution to the problem. The following examples show the various types that can be constructed to measure different learning outcomes in the cognitive domain.

EXAMPLE A: Incomplete sentence type.

_C_ 1. The switch-leg terminal on a front-connected 3-way switch is either colored black or _____.

A. Silver.
B. Brass.
C. Copper.
D. Green.
E. Blue.

EXAMPLE B: Question type.

_B_ 1. What type of safety clothing should be selected for operating power tools and machines that turn?
A. Long sleeve shirt.
B. Short sleeve shirt.
C. Leather sleeves.
D. Leather or fabric gloves.
E. Rubber gloves.

EXAMPLE C: Best answer type.

_D_ 1. The *most* important safeguard against possible injury in a vocational laboratory is:
A. knowing the cause of accidents.
B. operating tools and equipment correctly.
C. knowing how to avoid accidents.
D. having a positive attitude toward safety.
E. having a high level of skill proficiency.

EXAMPLE D: Incorrect statement type.

_A_ 1. Which of the following *is not* generally considered a type of equipment for protecting eyes?
A. Contact lens.
B. Goggles.
C. Face shields.
D. Safety glasses.
E. Welding helmet.

EXAMPLE E: Analogy type.

_B_ 1. In a small air-cooled gasoline engine the ring is to the piston as the bearing is to the:
A. camshaft.
B. crankshaft.
C. valve train.
D. engine block.
E. manifold.

EXAMPLE F: Tool identification type.

_A_ 1. The tool shown in the picture is a(an):
A. ball peen hammer.
B. claw hammer.
C. sledge hammer.
D. riveting hammer.
E. offset hammer.

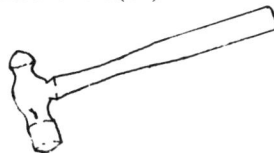

EXAMPLE G: Association type.

_D_ 1. When heat-treating metals, *annealing* is most closely related to:
A. hardening.
B. tempering.
C. strengthening.
D. softening.
E. stressing.

EXAMPLE H: Multiple-choice (true-false) type.

_C_ 1. Which of the following is a false statement regarding general safety practice?
A. Use personal protective equipment appropriate for the job.
B. Keep the work area swept clear of sawdust and clutter.
C. Slow the rotation of power tools like electric drills with your hand before laying them down.
D. Turn off the power switch when a tool is unattended.
E. Know how to operate power tools safely before using them.

EXAMPLE I: Least likely to occur multiple-choice type.

_B_ 1. Which of the following is *least likely* to occur when handling or disposing waste liquids?
A. They may be caustic and burn the skin.
B. They may be ingested.
C. They may give off harmful vapors if inhaled.
D. They may be absorbed through the skin.
E. They may explode.

EXAMPLE J: Multiple-choice calculation type.

_A_ 1. An interior room has two 3'-0" x 6'-8" doors and measures 9'-4" x 12'-6". Approximately how much baseboard trim will be needed?
A. 37 feet.
B. 43 feet.
C. 48 feet.
D. 54 feet.
E. 64 feet.

Example of Multiple-Choice Items for Measuring Learning Levels. The examples that follow show how multiple-choice items can be constructed to measure different levels of cognitive achievement.

EXAMPLE A: Multiple-choice item measuring knowledge.

_A_ 1. Which of the following colors or color combinations are used to indicate caution?
A. Yellow or yellow and black.
B. White or white and black.
C. Orange or orange and black.
D. Red or red and black.
E. Purple or violet.

EXAMPLE B: Multiple-choice item measuring comprehension or understanding.

_B_ 1. What color is used to accent parts of a machine or tool that could cut, crush or otherwise injure an operator?
A. Yellow.
B. Orange.
C. Red.
D. Green.
E. White.

EXAMPLE C: Multiple-choice item measuring application.

_C_ 1. If an electrician wants to wire a room ceiling light so it can be controlled from three door locations, how many three-way switches will be needed?
   A. 0.
   B. 1.
   C. 2.
   D. 3.
   E. 4.

EXAMPLE D: Multiple-choice item measuring analysis.

_B_ 1. The tools "framing square and level" are to carpentry as a "steel rule and surface gauge" are to:
   A. plumbing.
   B. machining.
   C. drafting.
   D. sheet-metal fabricating.
   E. welding.

EXAMPLE E: Multiple-choice item measuring synthesis.

_B_ 1. If an arc weld bead is coarse and there is a large amount of spatter, the most likely cause is:
   A. arc too short.
   B. arc too long.
   C. travel speed too fast.
   D. travel speed too slow.
   E. current set too low.

EXAMPLE F: Multiple-choice item measuring evaluation.

_C_ 1. If welders are attempting to determine what type of steel provided by the spark test method and discover a small stream of sparks, red in color with straw colored streaks near the end of the stream and very few forked spurts, they probably have:
   A. white cast iron.
   B. malleable cast iron.
   C. machine steel.
   D. high-speed steel.
   E. carbon tool steel.

Uses of Multiple-Choice Items. The multiple-choice item is used extensively in professionally developed tests. It is one of the most popular items written by occupational instructors. The multiple-choice question measures all levels of cognitive achievement from simple knowledge learning outcomes to evaluation. It is the most desirable selection or recognition item because a careful analysis of student responses can provide information about common misunderstandings and errors. This information is useful in improving instructional effectiveness and the quality of the test itself. The multiple-choice item can be used to measure what students can recognize. This allows much more information to be measured than is possible with recall items.

The multiple-choice item lends itself extremely well to computerized testing; the distractors and correct responses can be arranged differently by the computer program. This generates a different test format for each student in cases where that is desirable. Also the multiple-choice item can be machine scored. Furthermore, an item analysis or an in-

vestigation into student response patterns can be generated by a computerized scoring machine that provides valuable information to the teacher for improving tests.

Advantages of Multiple-Choice Items. There are a number of advantages of multiple-choice items over other types of test items. These are as follows:
1. They are usually the type of item students prefer because they can recognize the correct response rather than supply it.
2. They can be written to measure all types of subject matter content. In addition, they can be used to measure all levels of cognitive achievement such as the ability to recognize basic facts; as well as interpret, discriminate, analyze, synthesize, apply, and evaluate information.
3. A correctly constructed multiple-choice item reduces the chance of guessing significantly (20 percent possibility of guessing correctly when 5 responses are provided).
4. Multiple-choice items can be objectively scored quickly by individuals as well as by machine scoring devices, thus rendering immediate student test results.
5. Multiple-choice items generally require considerably less student response time than most constructed response items.
6. Multiple-choice items are usually less open to misinterpretation than other test item types.
7. An analysis of student responses on multiple-choice items provides valuable information for the instructor that can be used to improve instruction and student evaluation.

Limitations of Multiple-Choice Items. There are only a few disadvantages or limitations of multiple-choice items. These include the following:
1. They generally require more instructor time and attention to write than other test-item formats.
2. Correctly written multiple-choice items with only one correct or best response and enough plausible distractors are relatively difficult to construct. This is true, particularly for higher levels of cognitive learning outcomes.
3. They require more test space than other items, requiring more paper and increasing test reproduction costs.
4. When constructed to measure higher levels of cognitive achievement, they may measure a student's reading ability rather than the knowledge required to respond to the item correctly.
5. Because multiple-choice items which measure recognition of lower cognitive learning outcomes are relatively easy to construct, teachers must avoid writing too many items testing trivial information.

Rules for Writing Multiple-Choice Items. There probably are more rules to consider when writing multiple-choice items than any other test item formats. Not only must a good stem be constructed but a number of plausible alternatives and a correct response must be written. In the ideal situation, multiple-choice items must be constructed so that the stem clearly presents an important learning task or problem that can be answered correctly only by those students who have learned the desired behavior. The rules which follow should help occupational education teachers construct good multiple-choice items.

1. The stem should clearly state a single, specific problem or pose a question which evokes the correct response from students who have learned the vocational content.

2. The item stem should represent an important concept, principle, or learning outcome that is practical and realistic rather than trivial information.

3. The item stem, distractors and correct alternative should be written as clearly, specifically, and briefly as possible to keep the reading level to a minimum.

4. Select distractors or alternatives that represent the common mistakes or errors students make when they are learning the desired behavior.

5. Write the alternatives as briefly as possible keeping all common wording such as a, an, the, they, etc., in the stem.

6. Develop the item stems in a positive manner and avoid negatively stated item stems, when possible. (If a negative word must be used, underline it.)

7. Construct the correct response that authorities in the occupational field generally consider the only correct one or the best one.

8. Develop the alternatives so they are similar in form. They should be parallel and grammatically consistent with the stem. This is true, particularly when the incomplete sentence stem is used.

9. Avoid using choices such as "none of the above" or "all of the above" when possible. Also avoid selectors like "A and B" or "C and D."

10. Exercise care in giving clues to the correct response such as textbook language, verbal associations, length of alternatives, order or sequence, and grammatical clues.

11. Construct items which measure the definition of terms so that the stem presents the term and the alternatives present the definitions.

12. Position alternatives that involve numbers, dates, or proper names in numerical or alphabetical order.

13. Avoid the common mistake of including the same word(s) in both the stem and one or more alternatives.

14. When possible, construct the choices so each is on a separate line rather than using two lines for four alternatives.

15. Place the appropriate punctuation marks at the end of each alternative and avoid placing a colon at the end of an incomplete sentence stem.

16. When writing a best answer or poorest answer type multiple-choice stem, underline the words *best*, *least*, or *poorest*.

17. Arrange the choices or distractors so that the correct choice is in random order and does not establish patterns.

18. Exercise care so that items are written independently of each other and don't provide answers to other test items included in the examination.

19. Select a multiple-choice format that directs the student to mark the correct choice on a standard answer sheet or to the left or right of each item for easy scoring.

20. Include five choices for each multiple-choice when possible. This provides an acceptable 20 percent guessing factor.

21. When writing incomplete sentence multiple-choice items, construct them so the choices come at the end of the stem rather than constructing blanks in the stem body.

Example Stems for Multiple Choice Items. Occupational teachers sometimes experience difficulty in writing different types of multiple-choice item stems, particularly for higher level learning outcomes. The following list of example stems for learning outcomes can serve as a guide for writing multiple-choice item stems. **NOTE**: The ? mark indicates a missing word or phrase and the marks . . . indicate that the statement continues.

EXAMPLE A: Definitions or meanings of terms and symbols.
  A. The correct meaning for the term ? is . . .
  B. The correct definition for ? is . . .
  C. What means the same as . . .?
  D. Another meaning for the term ? is . . .
  E. Which statement below is the *best* definition for . . .?
  F. The meaning of the term ? is . . .
  G. The symbol ? on a blueprint means . . .

EXAMPLE B: Reasons, purpose and function.
  A. Why is ? done first when . . .?
  B. What is the purpose for . . .?
  C. The most important reason for ? is . . .
  D. What is the function of ? in a . . .?
  E. Which of the following is the *best* reason for . . .?
  F. The function of the ? in a . . .

EXAMPLE C: Specific facts.
  A. What is another name for . . .?
  B. Who is the inventor of . . .?
  C. In what year was . . .?
  D. What is the correct name for . . .?
  E. Which of the following means . . .?
  F. What is the correct setting for . . .?
  G. Who was the first to . . .?
  H. A material is considered ? when . . .
  I. Which machine is used for . . .?
  J. The size of a ? is . . .
  K. Where do you find . . .?
  L. When do you apply . . .?

EXAMPLE D: Relationships, cause and effect.
  A. What is the cause of . . .?
  B. If the ? is set incorrectly, the result will be . . .
  C. What is the effect of . . .?
  D. The result of incorrect ? is . . .
  E. Which of the following results when . . .?
  F. What happens when ? is done?
  G. If ? occurs, then which of the following is true?
  H. Under what conditions will . . .?
  I. ? is to ? as . . .
  J. ? : ? :: ? : . . .
  K. ? belongs to which of the following . . .?

L. Which of the following should be done when . . .?

M. What are the major types of . . .?

EXAMPLE E: Ordering.
A. Which step follows . . .?
B. Which is the first step in . . .?
C. Which is the last step in . . .?
D. Which of the following comes first when . . .?
E. What is the second step when . . .?
F. The procedure which follows *?* is . . .?
G. The best practice to follow after . . .?

EXAMPLE F: Methods and applications.
A. The *best* method of *?* is to . . .
B. What method is used for . . .?
C. What method should be used when . . .?
D. What power tools are needed to . . .?
E. It is *best* to apply *?* in . . .?
F. Which of the following methods should be used when . . .?
G. Which of the following practices is essential when . . .?
H. The method to *?* is to . . .

EXAMPLE G: Principles and rules.
A. A good rule to follow when *?* is to . . .
B. Which statement *best* illustrates the principle of . . .?
C. Which of the following rules apply when . . .?
D. The principle of *?* is *best* stated in which of the . . .?
E. A rule of thumb to follow when *?* is to . . .
F. The principle of *?* is used when . . .
G. The rule to follow when *?* is to . . .
H. Which of the following is an example of the principle of . . .?
I. Which of the following is an *incorrect* rule to follow when . . .?

EXAMPLE H: Standards or criteria.
A. Which is the *most* important standard for evaluating . . .?
B. Which of the following criteria should be used for . . .?
C. What criteria is used to classify types of . . .?
D. The *most* important standard to remember when . . .?
E. The standard for *?* is . . .
F. The standard which must be met in order to *?* is . . .
G. For *?* to meet standards it must . . .

EXAMPLE I: Errors.
A. What principle is violated in the statement . . .?
B. Which of the following is an error when . . .?
C. Which of the statements below is *incorrect* in regard to . . .?
D. The most common error made by *?* is . . .
E. Which error is commonly made when . . .?
F. Which of the following statements contains an error?

EXAMPLE J: Calculations.
A. The number of *?* needed to build a *?* is . . .
B. Which of the following values is equal to . . .?
C. Change the fraction of *?* to a decimal.

D. Find the sum of . . .?
E. Find the square root of . . .?
F. Find the value of . . .?
G. Convert *?* yards to . . .
H. Multiply the values of *?* by . . .?
I. What is the total number of *?* needed to . . .?

Writing Directions for Multiple-Choice Items. Because there are different types of multiple-choice items, it is usually necessary to write specific directions for each item type. These directions should be written in simple, clear terms and contain information about (a) reading item stems and choices, (b) recording responses, and (c) point values for each item and total points for the multiple-choice section of the examination.

EXAMPLE A: Directions for responding to multiple-choice items by circling responses.

In each of the following items, draw a circle around only the one letter selected as the correct or *best* answer. Each item is worth one (1) point. This section is worth _____ points.

EXAMPLE B: Directions for responding to multiple-choice items by placing an X over the correct response.

Each of the items below is an incomplete sentence or question followed by four possible responses of which only one is either the correct or the *best* response. Place an X over the letter indicating your choice. Each item is worth one (1) point. This section is worth _____ points.

EXAMPLE C: Directions for responding to multiple-choice items using an answer sheet.

1. Each item consists of a statement or question followed by five choices of which only one is the *most* correct. Select the *best* response and mark the corresponding letter space on the answer sheet with a No. 2 pencil. Be sure to darken the space completely on the answer sheet and erase any choice changes. Each item is worth one (1) point. This section contains _____ points.

2. Each of the incomplete statements or questions below is followed by four possible completions or answers. Select the *one* which is the *best* and mark the corresponding letter on the answer sheet with a No. 2 pencil. Darken in the space completely and erase any choice changes. Each item is worth one (1) point for a total of _____ points for this section.

EXAMPLE D: Directions for responding to multiple-choice items by placing the letter in the space provided on the examination sheet.

Each of the following is an incomplete statement or question followed by four possible responses of which only *one* is the correct or the *best* choice. Place the letter of your selection on the corresponding blank space to the left of each item number. Each item is worth one (1) point for a total of _____ points on this section.

EXAMPLE E: Directions for association-type, multiple-choice items.

The following groups of words refer to ___?___ . The first word is closely related to another word in the group. Select the word that is related closely to the first word and place the letter in the space provided beside each item number. Each item is worth one (1) point. An example is provided.

_C_ 1. Gauge :
   A. Rule.
   B. Torch.
   C. Pressure.
   D. Tip.
   E. Line.

EXAMPLE F: Directions for analogy type multiple-choice. In the following items, determine the relationship between the first two parts of the item. Apply this relationship to the third and fourth parts. Select your choice on the basis of the relationship existing between the first two parts. Place the letter of your choice in the space provided to the left of each item number. Each item is worth one (1) point for a total of _____ points on this section. The item which follows serves as an example.

_B_ 1. Square : four :: triangle : ___?___
   A. Two.
   B. Three.
   C. Four.
   D. Five.
   E. Six.

EXAMPLE G: Directions for reverse multiple-choice items. Each of the questions or incomplete statements below is followed by four possible responses. All but *one* of these choices is correct. Select the one that is wrong or false and place the letter of your choice in the space provided to the left of each item number. Each item is worth one (1) point for a total of _____ points on this section. The following item serves as an example.

_D_ 1. Nichrome wire is used in making electric
   A. Toasters.
   B. Heaters.
   C. Heating pads.
   D. Light bulbs.
   E. Thermostats.

Essay Items

The essay item is probably the oldest written test item and one of the easiest to construct. This type of item requires students to read and understand the question or problem. Students are required to supply or create, organize and write the expected response. There are two major types of essay items, the restricted or closed response type and the extended or open-ended response type.

Restricted or Closed Response Type. The restricted or closed response essay item limits the student's response to certain desired answers. These include listing procedural steps for a task, providing reasons for an occurrence, or describing a process. This type of item usually requires the student to recall and supply a given number of responses and sometimes to place them in logical or sequential order.

The normal student response is usually limited to several sentences or a paragraph or two. Seldom would a restricted-response essay type require answers of a full page or more. The following examples show one item limited by content and one by the item format.

EXAMPLE A: Restricted-response item limited by content.
   1. Discuss the four strokes of a four-cycle gasoline engine.

EXAMPLE B: Restricted-response item limited by content and format.
   1. Discuss the strokes of a four-cycle gasoline engine and describe the positions of valves and pistons.

Extended or Open-ended Response. The second major essay type, the extended or open-ended response item, provides students with freedom to determine the appropriate factual information to include in their response. They also have opportunity to make personal judgments required to answer the item and to organize and present their responses in their own way. While the question stem may impose some limitation such as the length of responses in terms of page space or time given for each item, there is usually no limitation on the item content or the form of response. Students are free to show their abilities, to sort out, and to combine ideas into new and unique response patterns.

EXAMPLE A: Extended or open-ended response items.
   1. There has been a heated debate over automobile passenger restraining devices such as shoulder straps, lap belts and inflatable air bags. Describe each of these restraining devices and their function. Then prepare a table showing the advantages and disadvantages of each type according to characteristics of your choice. Finally, indicate your restraining system choice and explain why you favor it over others.

EXAMPLE B: Extended response or open-ended essay item.
   1. A customer brings in a lawn mower that is not working properly. The complaint is hard starting. When it does start it runs for only a few seconds. Write a trouble-shooting evaluation of the probable causes of the mower engine malfunction. Then choosing which of these is the most likely cause, describe how you would repair the engine. Also, make an estimate of the cost involved so you can discuss it with the customer before beginning any repairs.

Uses of Essay Items. The essay item can be used for a variety of purposes. It is the best choice when measuring higher levels of cognitive learning outcomes. This is particularly true when the responses are to be supplied by the student. Essay items are most useful when measuring student performance on the learning levels of application, analysis, synthesis and evaluation. These items can be used to promote thinking and studying content in a manner that leads to creating, organizing, evaluating, and applying ideas to solve problems. Their use also enables teachers to evaluate students' writing abilities, skills, knowledge, handwriting, and use of vocabulary, spelling, and sentence structure.

Advantages of Essay Items. The essay item has several advantages over other types of test items. One is that it can be used to measure learning outcomes which are difficult to measure with other test item formats. For example, when teachers want to measure a student's ability to solve problems or to express themselves in writing, the essay item is an appropriate choice. The use of essay items provides feedback about student performance. Essays show the extent to which student understands material and requires student to put forth more effort in studying, which helps in retention of learned material. Also, this type of question can be used as motivation to improve writing and communicating skills. These abilities are becoming more important for many workers in our changing work roles.

Occupational teachers also find writing essay items fairly easy and fast. They do, however, recognize the difficulty scoring them. For this reason, occupational teachers tend to use the restricted type of essay items. Establishing criteria or standards for grading is easier.

Limitations of Essay Items. Essay items also have their limitations. Since they usually are time-consuming to complete, only a small sampling of content can be included in a test. This means that more testing must be done or only a limited sample of student learning outcomes are measured. Other important material may never be included in an examination.

Another major limitation is the student's ability to respond to essay items in writing. Students who have good writing skills may have a poor understanding of content but receive good marks on essay items because of their written expression. On the other hand, students who may have a good understanding of a concept or process may receive poor marks on essay items because of an inability to express themselves well in writing.

One other major limitation of essay items is the difficulty of scoring them in a fair, impartial manner. Unless teachers identify acceptable student responses for each essay item, they may be influenced by the range of these responses. They may then formulate their marking system according to how students performed instead of how they should have performed.

Another difficulty of objectively scoring essay items is the large amount of time it takes to evaluate and mark responses. Teachers have a tendency to read the first group of student responses carefully. As time goes on, however, they speed up the evaluation process in order to complete all papers in a given time period. Papers graded last receive less attention.

Rules for Writing Essay Items. There are a number of suggestions or rules for constructing and scoring essay items. These are:

1. Choose content from the objectives to be measured which cannot be adequately measured by objective test items.
2. Analyze each learning outcome to determine precisely what performance should be measured. When possible, limit essay items to one concept or idea.
3. Write the question so that the intended student response is clear but does not simply ask students to recall memorized information. Do not ask students to "list" or "enumerate." Use such words as "explain," "discuss,"

"describe," "illustrate," "define," "evaluate," "compare," "contrast," "develop," and "tell how."

4. Write directions which call for the desired response without giving clues. Be sure to include the point value for each item constructed.
5. Prepare the answer key as you write the items. Indicate the source of each item and the correct response. Decide whether only the content of the student response will be evaluated. The teacher may decide to include other criteria such as spelling, sentence structure, and the like.
6. Avoid giving students choices among items on a test.
7. Avoid open-book tests.
8. Arrange items on a test in order of increasing difficulty or complexity.
9. Inform students in advance of an examination about the type of items that will be included.
10. In grading, evaluate all students' responses on one item before proceeding to evaluate other items. Take every precaution to avoid knowing whose test paper is being evaluated and scored. This can be accomplished by having students place names on a cover sheet which is turned over before evaluation. Papers can also be placed in random order.
11. Avoid placing point values on sentence structure, writing ability, vocabulary, and spelling (unless it is an important component of the learning outcome). This does not mean that poor performance on these components should be ignored. They should be marked in order to improve student written communication skills. Nevertheless they should not take away from a student's performance on the main learning outcome called for in the essay question.
12. Set aside a sufficient amount of time to evaluate items carefully and conscientiously.
13. When possible, have at least two people evaluate and score the items. This is particularly important on major tests which are used in future decision making, i.e., grade promotion, remedial decisions, etc.

Writing Directions for Essay Items. The directions for essay items must indicate clearly what students are to do in as few words as possible. They must include what will or will not be counted in scoring and what the point value will be for each item. For example, a student may be asked to describe a process and to give examples or illustrations of certain parts of the process. The following directions are commonly used to guide student responses.

EXAMPLE A: Directions for essay item.

Directions: The following are essay questions which require you to (a) decide what response is required, (b) outline your response, and (c) write your response in complete sentence and paragraph form. Correct spelling and use of occupational terms will count in the final score. The point value for each of these items corresponds to major informational points and each item has a specified point value for a total of _____ points on this section of the exam. (Sentences should be grammatically correct and legibly written; however, no points will be deducted for error in these factors.)

1. A building supply salesperson is asked for advice on what wood and type of fasteners to use to build a picnic table. Describe what type of wood and fasteners to use and why. Be sure to include the cost factor of materials in your response. Point value of five (5).

ADMINISTERING TESTS

A common mistake of occupational teachers is to assume (a) that students know how to take tests, (b) that they will observe behavior rules during a test, and (c) that they can and will read the general test and specific item category directions. Another error is teachers' failure to prepare the facilities and test materials in advance of giving the test.

Good Test Administration Procedures

The test items are written. A master copy of the test is prepared with general test item directions and specific directions for each item type. Is the teacher's job completed? Not yet. There is the matter of choosing a duplication method that will produce clean, easy-to-read copies. The teacher must also prepare separate answer sheets if students will not be recording answers directly on tests or papers. A sufficient number of copies should be duplicated so there are extras for future testing. Then too, it is necessary to duplicate answer keys, as well as to maintain a master test file.

It is important to prepare students for examinations. Give them prior notice regarding content of the test and the types of items to be included in the test. Announce the test day well in advance. Avoid scheduling examinations the day before or after holidays or major school events or on days that interfere with religious services for students.

It is good practice to review tips on test-taking with students prior to major exams that weigh heavily in the grading system. Explain to them:
1. How to respond after reading test items. Consider (a) selecting the answer believed to be correct, (b) finding the number and question on the answer-sheet, and (c) using the pencil provided to respond by circling, marking through or darkening in the appropriate space.
2. How to achieve the best possible score. Consider:
   a. Do not spend too much time on any one question.
   b. Answer all of the questions you are sure of first; then go back and attempt to answer the remaining ones.
3. Following directions. Here indicate that the student supply all the required information called for in the directions for each item type.
4. How to study for tests. Here consider such tips as following the PQRST system of (a) Previewing, (b) Questioning, (c) Reading, (d) Studying, and (e) Testing reading materials, when studying for test.

Prior to the examination, prepare the test booklets or papers for distribution. Also prepare other needed test materials such as lap boards, extra pencils, answer keys, and folders in which to place completed examinations. Arrange seating for maximum spacing between students. This will reduce the temptation to look at someone else's work. Regulate the temperature and lighting to optimal conditions.

At the beginning of the testing session, assign seats and request students to remove all books, notes, and other materials from desks or tables. Remind them to sharpen pencils and obtain any other instruments such as protractors, rules, and calculators required for the test. Indicate the amount of time they have for the test and the procedure for asking questions. Also tell them how they are to turn in their completed test materials. It is very important for the teacher to communicate test procedures clearly and in a friendly, supportive manner. Avoid a "get even" or threatening tone of voice. Distribute test papers face down and ask students to leave them so until all have received a copy. Read the directions and signal to start.

During the test, answer student's questions in a quiet manner. Circulate quietly about the room without attracting attention. When exams are completed, check to see that students have placed their names on the test and completed all pages.

When completed, place all exams in a file folder and store them in a secure place. Try to score the exam before the following class day so results can be reported. This gives students immediate feedback about their performance.

At the next class, if possible, review the test results with students in an encouraging manner. Point out common errors made on the test and suggest how to overcome them. Never use poor test performance to punish or humiliate students. Remember, testing is a valuable learning experience and learning from mistakes is an important part of improving performance in any endeavor.

An important consideration in administering tests is to provide alternate testing situations for special needs students who cannot demonstrate achievement in traditional test-taking situations. This may require the use of alternate testing procedures such as (a) open-book tests, (b) teacher read test items, (c) small group tests, (d) take-home tests, (e) oral tests, (f) increased length of time to complete tests, (g) decreased number of test items, (h) having students respond orally to test items and record responses on tape recorders, and (i) reducing reading level of test items.

SCORING TESTS

It is important to score tests as soon as possible after they are given. Then feedback information can be provided to students in a timely fashion. Scoring is defined as the process of (a) checking completed tests to determine whether or not each item is correct and (b) assigning a numerical score which is usually the raw score or number of items a student answered correctly. Other scores can be assigned to communicate test results that are statistically determined. These can be standard scores, percentiles, or percentages. Such scores are infrequently used by classroom teachers except when reporting student standardized test performance.

Scoring procedures for classroom tests usually involve hand scoring test booklets or answer sheets. More sophisticated procedures might include feeding answer sheets into a modern optical test scanning machine to determine raw or converted scores. Scoring procedures can also be made more complex if teachers elect to assign weights to different item types or employ correction for guessing processes. Most occupational teachers prefer to use simple scoring procedures that provide raw scores.

Answer keys or a listing of correct or acceptable responses must be prepared for each item included in a test. One method of developing a master key is to write the correct response on the actual student test booklet or answer sheet, using a colored pen or pencil. Scoring is performed by comparing the key responses with each student response. Then mark the incorrect response with the correct response or place an "X" or "✓" mark beside each incorrect numbered or lettered item.

A second method of preparing a scoring key requires a heavy paper or cardstock. On it, is developed a strip key containing correct responses placed in corresponding spaces in the test booklet or answer key.

Strip keys can be easily constructed by cutting the response sections of each page of a test and mounting them on cardstock or poster board. The strip key is then laid beside each page of a student's test booklet or answer sheet and scoring is performed by comparing the two responses. A strip key saves time because the teacher needn't turn pages of the master key.

When separate answer sheets are used, it is desirable to construct a scoring stencil. This device is simply a copy of the answer sheet with holes punched or response lines cut out where correct answers should appear. It is essential to check each student's answer sheet to ensure that only one response was marked because any item marked more than once must be scored as incorrect.

Regardless of the type of scoring key used, it is good practice to mark each item that is answered incorrectly and to mark through the correct answers on multiple-choice items. If time permits, the correct response should also be written below completion item spaces with a colored pen. Providing correct responses in writing helps the student to correct errors and to avoid the confusion which results when reviewing test results orally with students.

An increasing number of schools are providing optical scanning test scoring machines. One example is the "scan-tron" machine which reads specially prepared test answer sheets and provides raw scores, and other useful data such as derived scores and test item analysis results. Occupational teachers should inquire into whether scoring machines are available in their schools. These devices should be used in testing programs to save valuable teacher time.

Essay items present unique scoring problems because each student response is typically different. Therefore, subjectivity is a very real factor that must be controlled. It is important to analyze each essay item and to write down the specific segments of each item accompanied by their point values. Decisions also have to be made as to whether or not points will be assigned to essay items on written communication skills such as grammar, spelling and punctuation. Teachers should follow the practice of scoring each student's identical numbered item in succession before advancing to a different essay item.

Short-answer or completion items, like essay items, must be carefully planned. Students have some freedom of expression and may not use the precise wording expected by the teacher. Occasionally teachers may choose to award partial credit for short-answer item responses when warranted. Scoring short-answer items and essay items provide teachers with the opportunity to identify what students have learned. Also, they can see the content areas in which students are having problems. This information has implications for needed changes in the instructional program.

Inexperienced teachers may take the easy way out of scoring written tests and have students score the tests by exchanging papers. This practice should be avoided since it is impossible to eliminate the possibility of students changing other students responses. Furthermore, it also can be considered a form of invasion of the student's right to privacy. Another poor practice is to give student-written tests to student aids or to family members to correct. This deprives the teacher of the opportunity to analyze the test for strengths and weaknesses. It may also introduce unwanted subjectivity if the test includes short-answer or essay items. It is best for teachers to score their own tests, thereby ensuring accuracy, guaranteeing confidentiality, and obtaining important information from total student test performance.

GRADING

After student tests are scored they must be evaluated. This usually results in the assignment of letter grades or marks used (a) to communicate how one student's performance compares to other students' performance on a test or (b) how a student's performance compares to a specified performance standard related to a job. This may be thought of as the criterion in the case of criterion-referenced testing. Student grades earned on written tests, performance tests, quizzes, activities, special assignments, participation in class and vocational student organization activities are recorded in a grading book. They are then converted into a predetermined grading system that is in compliance with the overall school grading policy. A summary report like a grade slip or report card is then given to the student. Sometimes it is sent home for parents to review how the student performed in a specified grading period. It is important that grades are based on student achievement and not on student behavior or misbehavior. Ideally, the evaluation and marking system should be based on the amount of progress made by students toward prescribed outcomes, and the quality of work produced. This evaluation is compared to the assessed abilities, interests needs, and effort of each student.

An evaluation and grading system should include (a) the factors to be evaluated, (b) the criteria for each factor, (c) the methods that will be used to evaluate each factor and (d) the way that grades will be determined.

Many factors should be considered when evaluating vocational student progress and included in the grading system. These include:

1. Task or competency performance.

2. Performance on written tests and quizzes measuring cognitive achievement.
3. Work habit development.
4. Attitude and personal growth.
5. Daily class effort.
6. Quality of homework and outside assignments.
7. Safe work behavior.
8. Completed products or projects.
9. Vocational student organization participation.

Experienced occupational teachers include many factors in their evaluation and grading systems. They have found that grading systems comprised of a variety of factors provide incentive for students to develop proficiencies in the three major areas required by most employers: (a) skill performance, (b) theory or understanding required to satisfactorily complete work tasks, and (c) work attitude and habits required.

Characteristics of the Grading System. There are important characteristics to consider in establishing a grading system for an occupational program. The system should:
1. Accurately reflect the competencies developed.
2. Be based on each student's capabilities and achievement level.
3. Enhance student self-concept.
4. Include the multiple grading factors of student effort, progress, and achievement.
5. Reflect both quality and quantity of work completed.
6. Be easily understood by students, parents, and teachers.
7. Include student involvement in the grading system.
8. Be flexible enough to accommodate the changing needs of students.
9. Be individualized in order to reduce anxiety and competition over grades.
10. Encourage students to accept increasing responsibility for their achievement.
11. Reduce the teacher's burden of determining grades.
12. Operate as a continuous process so students can assess their progress in relation to goals and objectives.
13. Comply with school system grading policy.

Grading Techniques. Occupational teachers must develop a fair and impartial system for arriving at grades for all students. Few teachers simply award a grade of "pass" or "fail." Even if they do, they must have a basis for arriving at their decision. Most occupational teachers are required to grade students on a five-factor scale which is communicated either as grades or points that stand for levels of performance. An example of this five-factor scale is shown in Figure 8-1.

Letter	Points	Status
A	4	Excellent
B	3	Good
C	2	Fair
D	1	Poor
F	0	Failure

Figure 8-1. A five-factor scale.

Vocational teachers can use a number of techniques to determine student grades. One is to grade student work as either satisfactory or unsatisfactory. If student work is graded as satisfactory in relation to predetermined performance standards, the student is able to continue to the next learning experience. If student work is graded unsatisfactory, the student must repeat the activity after receiving additional remedial learning experiences.

Satisfactory and unsatisfactory grades can be converted to a locally mandated five-factor grading system of A, B, C, D, and F. Nevertheless, one must also consider the many factors of achievement such as (a) quality of work performed, (b) relative importance of the work, (c) quantity of work performed, and (d) completion time for the activities.

The pass/fail system is similar to the satisfactory/unsatisfactory system. Student performance at the "D" level is considered to be unsatisfactory.

Another popular grading technique is to include skill reports or competency checklists along with the school's official report card. Employers especially like skill or competency information included with student performance records.

Finally, there is performance contracting. In this technique, a contract is jointly developed between the student and teacher which identifies specific activities to be completed by the student with specified criteria for each. The student's grade is determined by evaluating contracted performance in relation to established criteria.

Marking Systems. Two marking systems are often used by vocational teachers. One is the *point* system and the other, the *averaging* system.

Point System. In the point system each factor to be evaluated is awarded a certain number of points. The total of these possible point values is the maximum a student can earn in a given marking period. These factors might include written or cognitive achievement tests, safety tests, classroom and laboratory behavior, required notebooks, and skill or performance tests. Each is awarded a certain number of points. Figure 8-2 shows a point system for determining grades.

In establishing a point system, occupational teachers should first review the grading and marking system established for the school. Next, the teacher should talk with peer teachers to gather information required to set point values for each factor to be evaluated in a marking period. Higher point values are usually assigned to factors considered to be the most important. The teacher will also need to determine the point values required for each letter grade.

Experienced teachers have developed fair and appropriate point system values by trial and error over several years of practice. There are, however, several mathematical procedures that can be used to set the point limits for letter grade conversion tables. The point system described in Figure 8-2 shows the lower limit of the D level to be 200 points.

To obtain a good distribution of marks between the upper and lower limits (a) subtract the lower limit of the D mark from the lower limit of the A mark and (b) divide this value by three to determine the point values for the B and

Factor to be Evaluated	Point Value	Student Points
Skill performance (10 tests @ 40 points each)	400	320
Written exams (2 exams @ 100 points each)	200	165
Safety/work habit development (10 observations @ 15 points each)	150	134
Attitude and effort (10 observations @ 5 points each)	50	43
Completed notebook (100 points)	100	86
Outside assignments, i.e., Vocational Student Organization participation (5 evaluations @ 20 points each)	100	79
Total	1000	827

Point/Grade Conversion Chart

Points	Grade	Student Grade
800-1000	A	827 out of 1000
600- 799	B	827 = A
400- 599	C	
200- 399	D	
0- 199	F	

Figure 8-2. Point system for determining grades.

Factors to be Evaluated	Points	Weight	Weighted Points	Percentage of Total Weighted Points
Skill performance (10 tests @ 40 points each)	400	.15	60	60
Written exams (2 exams @ 100 points each)	200	.10	20	20
Safety/work habits (10 ratings @ 15 points each)	150	.05	7.5	7.5
Attitude/effort (10 ratings @ 5 points each)	50	.05	2.5	2.5
Completed notebook (100 points)	100	.05	5	5
Outside assignment/ Vocational Student Organization participation	100	.05	5	5
Total	1000		100	100

Point Conversion Chart

90-100	A
80-89	B
70-79	C
60-69	D
Below 59	F

Figure 8-3. Weighted point system for determining grades.

C grades. Note the example point values of 800 − 200 = 600, and 600 ÷ 3 = 200. To determine the lower limit of the C mark add 200 to the D mark. To determine the lower level of the B mark, add 200 to the C mark.

A second method of determining point limits is similar to the one just described only it uses a different mathematical procedure. In the example described, the upper level or maximum point value was 1000 points. To establish the lower limit of each letter mark, simply divide the total possible points by 5 which yields a value of 200 points. The distribution of points between each letter mark then is 200 points. Total points (1000) ÷ 5 (letter grades) = 200 (points between letter grades).

Weighted Point System. Another type of marking system is the weighted point system for determining grades. This system is based on the principle that some evaluation factors are more important and, thus, should carry more points than others. One common factor usually weighted higher in occupational education programs is task performance. Figure 8-3 shows a typical weighted point system for determining grades.

Occupational teachers who choose the weighted point system for determining grades can (a) arbitrarily assign weights or (b) assign them on the basis of percentage of total weighted points. This can be calculated by converting weighted points on a 100-point scale, which reflects the desired percentage value. Weights can then be determined by dividing the weighted points by the total points assigned to each factor. For example, skill performance was given a percentage weight of 60 in the weighted point system (described in Figure 8-3) or a weight of 60. The weight value was calculated by dividing 60 by 400 which yields a weight of .15. To determine a given student's weighted point value

for any factor, multiply the total points earned by the assigned weight. It is sometimes desirable to avoid small numbers by multiplying by a value of 2 to convert the 100 point scale to 200.

Figure 8-4 is a sample of student scores from the point system for determining grades presented in Figure 8-3.

	Points Earned		Weight		Converted Points
1. Skill performance	320	×	.15	=	48
2. Written exams	165	×	.10	=	16.5
3. Safety/work habits	134	×	.05	=	6.7
4. Attitude/effort	43	×	.05	=	2.15
5. Completed notebook	86	×	.05	=	4.3
6. Outside assignment/VSO's	79	×	.05	=	3.95
					81.60

Figure 8-4. Sample of student's scores using the weighted point system.

By calculating the students grade in the weighted point system grade curriculum process, it can be found that the student earned weighted points of 48, 16.5, 6.7, 2.15, 4.3 and 3.95 or total weighted points of 81.60. The student earns a grade of "B" in the weighted point system rather than a grade of "A" as was assigned in the traditional point system because different weights were assigned evaluation factors. Note that the student's total points in the weighted system were 81.6 and total points in the traditional point system were 827.

Averaging System for Determining Grades. The most frequently used system for determining student grades in a given marking period, is the averaging system. Each factor to be measured such as written and skill performance, is evaluated against a common base (highest achievement as 100%) and given a relative percentage weight in relation to other factors. The total is averaged and the final student grade is determined by comparing it to the school's marking system such as 90% to 100% equals an A grade; 80% to 89% equals a B grade and so forth. Figure 8-5 is a sample averaging system for determining grades.

Evaluation Factor	Relative Weight	Maximum Points
Skill performance (10 tests @ 30 points each)	40%	300
Written exams (2 exams @ 100 points each)	15%	200
Safety/work habits (10 ratings @ 10 points each)	5%	100
Attitude/effort (10 ratings @ 5 points each)	5%	50
Completed notebook (one evaluation, 50 points)	5%	50
Outside assignments (5 evaluations, 10 points each)	5%	50
One final examination	25%	250
Total	100%	1000

Figure 8-5. Averaging system for determining grades.

An example of one student's performance should help clarify how the averaging system works. In order to calculate a factor such as the two written exams, calculate point values for each test by converting the total point values to the 100% scale. This is easy for the two written tests because the total possible points for each was 100 and the student's total points is simply 100 minus the number the student answered incorrectly for each test. If the student missed 14 items, the score would be 86.

Suppose that the total points for an evaluation factor do not equal 100 as in the case of the 10 performance tests, each worth 30 points. A point conversion to the 100% scale must be made. This is easily accomplished; simply divide the assigned total point value into 100. For example, the actual point value for each performance test is 3.33. This is derived by dividing 30 into 100.

To calculate the student's total point value for each performance test multiply earned points by point value. Suppose that the student had 24 out of 30 points. Converted to the 100% scale (24 × 3.33 = 79.92). The student's converted percentage point value is 79.92.

The teacher will calculate the converted point value for each performance test and then total all the performance test totals. To arrive at the final point value for all performance tests, the teacher must divide the total points earned in performance tests by the number of tests. If the actual total points earned by a student in performance tests

was 843, the student's actual point total for performance tests is 843 ÷ 10 or 84.3 points. To determine the actual point value for performance test, the teacher must multiply the assigned weight which was 40 in the sample averaging system or 84.3 × 40 = 337.2 converted points.

A summary of a given student's factors is shown below, Figure 8-6.

Factor	Weighted Values
Skill performance tests	337.2
Written tests	183
Safety/work habits	89
Attitude/effort	46
Completed notebook	44
Outside assignments	46
Final examination	210
Total	955.2

Grading Scale	Example Student Grade
890-1000 points = A	Student earned 955 points resulting in a grade of ''A''
790- 889 points = B	
690- 790 points = C	
590- 689 points = D	
Below 590 points = F	

Figure 8-6. Summary of student's factors.

Reporting Grades. Student achievement is reported in many different ways by school systems. The vocational teacher must learn how the grades are to be reported and report the information accurately and in a timely manner. Most schools use the traditional student report cards which usually contain grades, percentages, pass/fail and satisfactory/unsatisfactory ratings of student achievement in relation to identified subject areas or competencies. Some school systems also require that vocational competency lists and certificates be provided along with traditional report cards to provide a more detailed report of what capabilities a student has demonstrated. The vocational teacher can usually secure information about student grading and reporting procedures in the faculty handbooks available in most schools.

SUMMARY

Preparing and implementing the evaluation component of an instructional program is a time-consuming, continuous and sometimes difficult responsibility for most teachers. It is especially challenging for new teachers who have not had instruction in how to prepare tests, administer and score them, and mark and grade them so they are consistent with the school's evaluation policies. The material presented in this resource should serve to (a) increase the competency of occupational teachers to identify factors to be evaluated, (b) develop systematic procedures for selecting and writing test items and their directions, (c) improve their ability to administer and score tests, and (d) establish fair and defensible procedures for determining and reporting student grades.

APPENDIX 8A
SIX-STEP PROCESS FOR PLANNING TESTS

In planning tests, occupational teachers must develop and select a sufficient number and type of test items to adequately sample learning outcomes taught in an instructional time period. Typically, teachers prepare tests at the end of an instructional unit. When units are small or when time allotted for testing is limited, tests are prepared to cover content presented in several units. It is usually impossible to include all of the test items that should be written to cover lesson content on any one test. Teachers must carefully select an adequate sample of items to measure each important learning outcome.

Teachers must also select test items that measure different levels of learning outcomes in the cognitive domain. All too often, teachers develop unit tests by going through their lesson plans, text reading assignments and other assigned resources, and choosing content that is important to them without much thought about levels of learning or the make-up of tests. Teachers usually have in mind how many items they want to include on a test and when they reach the magic number, they quit writing items and construct the tests. This method of test construction is like a carpenter building a house without a blueprint or plan; simply building the house from memory until the materials run out. Imagine what the finished house would look like!

Tests constructed without adequate planning are often poor measurement devices. They contain trivial or unimportant items and emphasize recall and sometimes understanding with few, if any, items on higher learning behaviors (like the ability to analyze a situation or to apply knowledge to solve realistic occupational problems). In addition, tests constructed in this manner often contain too many test items measuring one content area at the expense of few or no items measuring other important content. Is it any wonder students sometimes remark to teachers, "You asked a lot of questions in the area I did not understand or study"?

Teacher-made tests can be improved significantly if some basic procedures and techniques are followed in planning and constructing tests. The six-step process for planning tests which follows is recommended.

1. Test Specifications

Develop some initial test specifications which address the following questions:
1. What is the purpose of the test?
2. What performance objectives will be measured?
3. How much time will be consumed by the test?
4. When and how will the test be administered?
5. What types of measures should be used (pencil-paper test, performance test or both) and their item types and formats?
6. What is the total number of points on the test?
7. What equipment and materials are available for testing and test duplication?

8. What should be included in the directions for the test?

This list of questions is not all inclusive. However, it does contain many of the factors teachers must consider before they begin constructing a measuring instrument.

2. Determine Performance Objectives

Select the appropriate performance objectives to be used as a basis for developing test items or selecting already prepared ones.

The most commonly used basis for test item selection and/or development is the objectives taught in unit of instruction. List them on a sheet of paper; then establish the percentage value or degree of emphasis each of these objectives should receive in the unit test. The results of this process as shown in Figure 8A-1, can be used as a rough guide for selecting items from a test item bank or for developing new items to include on a unit test.

3. Analyze Performance Objectives

Analyze the measurable behaviors described in the performance objectives. Some performance objectives are not specific enough to identify all the content which should be

STEM: Given a worksheet activity, student will be able to:	
OBJECTIVES	**EMPHASIS**
1. Demonstrate knowledge and understanding of true-false item formats and construct test items of this type which meet the criteria presented in your readings. Level of knowledge and understanding must be at the 70% criterion level or higher.	15%
2. Demonstrate knowledge and understanding of short answer/completion test item formats and construct test items of this type which meet the criteria presented in your readings. Level of knowledge and understanding must be at the 70% criterion level or higher.	20%
3. Demonstrate knowledge and understanding of multiple-choice item formats and construct test items of this type which meet the criteria presented in your readings. Level of knowledge and understanding must be at the 70% criterion level or higher.	30%
4. Demonstrate knowledge and understanding of matching item formats and construct test items of this type which meet the criteria presented in your readings. Level of knowledge and understanding must be at the 70% criterion level or higher.	20%
5. Demonstrate knowledge and understanding of short answer essay item formats and construct test items of this type which meet the criteria presented in your readings. Level of knowledge and understanding must be at the 70% criterion level or higher.	15%
TOTAL EMPHASIS	100%

Figure 8A-1. Sample objectives and level of emphasis for preparing a test on test item formats.

measured through test items. In many cases, the measurable behavior component of a performance objective is an occupational task. Analyze the task to determine what steps and key points of information are necessary for students to master.

There are several different task analysis formats for occupational programs. The sample task analysis format shown in Figure 8A-2 was adapted from the format used by the Vocational-Technical Education Consortium of States (V-TECS) in analyzing tasks for constructing test items.

The procedure for analyzing tasks using the recording sheet shown in Figure 8A-2 is easy. The teacher must identify the task from either the objective or a task listing contained in the school's programs or course of study. All necessary title information, such as the name of the program, course title and number, unit title and number, lesson title and number

TASK ANALYSIS RECORDING SHEET

PROGRAM: _____ COURSE/NO. _____

UNIT/NO. _____ LESSON/NO. _____

PERFORMANCE OBJECTIVE: _____

_____

_____

Sequenced Steps	Tools, Equipment, Materials	Key Information Points	Supporting Resources	Safety Precautions Work Habits

Figure 8A-2. Performance objective task analysis format used to identify content for constructing test items.

and task title, should be entered in the spaces provided. The performance objective should also be entered.

Next, the teacher lists the steps required for the student to complete the task or the steps demonstrated to the student by the teacher. It is important for teachers to break down the task into steps a beginner can perform and not steps that only a skilled worker can follow. Skilled workers sometimes learn short cuts which may eliminate certain steps, which, if followed by the learner, make it difficult to complete the task safely.

With the task steps identified, complete the balance of the information required. Include the identification of tools, equipment and material involved in each step; key points of information; supporting resources like textbook assignments, handouts, and mediated materials; and any safety and work habits which must be observed in completing the tasks. The V-TECS catalogs are one excellent source for task analysis information.

4. Develop a Content Outline

The performance objectives, often containing tasks as their measurable behavior, were analyzed in the previous step to identify a number of content topics. The performance objectives specify the type of response students are expected to make relative to subject matter topics. It is helpful to construct a content outline for each unit to be included on the test. This is accomplished using the data contained in the task analysis recording sheet.

Figure 8A-3 shows a sample content outline for types of test item formats. The amount of detail to include in the outline is up to each teacher. It is important, however, to identify the essential information that will provide a solid source of test item content to adequately sample the subject matter taught.

5. Construct Test Items

Construct test items of different types to measure the subject-matter content identified in the performance objectives, task analysis recording sheets and content outline. Test items can be written on index cards, 8 1/2 x 11 inch sheets, or they can be entered directly into a computer test development program.

The traditional practice is to write test items on either 3 x 5 inch or 5 x 8 inch index cards. Use colored cards, if available, to separate categories. It is essential to determine the types of information to record on the cards.

First construct a *name of course* card. This card should have large print and may contain information on how this course is sequenced with other courses in an instructional program. The name of the course card is sometimes placed on the outside of the card file drawer or can be located anywhere inside the drawer as a header.

The next card would contain one or more sets of general directions for tests. Related to this card are other cards which contain directions for each type of test item format which should be prepared in advance.

The next cards are header cards which should be lettered or typed in large, bold print indicating the name of each test item format like **TRUE-FALSE, COMPLETION,** etc. The actual test item cards must be prepared next and filed in numerical order. It is very desirable to print the format information on the cards ahead of writing test items so that the amount of time needed to complete each card is minimal. Figure 8A-4 shows a sample format card (front and back).

The front of the test item card contains the file code and test item code which should be developed so that item source data can easily be recognized by code letters and numbers. For example, a true-false item on a testing course could be coded as follows:

Course = T (testing course)   ITEM CODE: T441155
Unit = 4 (fourth unit)
Lesson = 4 (lesson four)
Item = 1 (true-false)
Item no. = 15 (item number in blank)
Source = 5 (reference number 5)

The file code is necessary to store and retrieve the item from a file drawer. The file code for an example coded item is as follows:

Drawer = A (file drawer A)   FILE CODE: AT4115
Course = T (testing course)
Unit = 4 (fourth unit)

CONTENT OUTLINE

I. True-False Items
  A. Types of true-false items
    1. Traditional
    2. Clustered
    3. Modified
  B. Uses of true-false items
  C. Advantages and disadvantages
  D. Points in constructing true-false items
  E. Writing directions for true-false items
II. Short Answer/Completion
  A. Types of short answer/completion items
    1. Fill-in-the-blanks (completion)
    2. Identification
    3. Definition
  B. Uses of short answer/completion
  C. Advantages and disadvantages
  D. Points in constructing short answer/completion
  E. Writing directions for short answer/completion items
III. Multiple-Choice Items
  A. Types of multiple-choice items
    1. Incomplete sesntence
    2. Question
    3. Best alternative
    4. Pictorial identification
  B. Uses of multiple-choice items
  C. Advantages and disadvantages
  D. Points in constructing multiple-choice items
  E. Writing directions for multiple-choice
IV. Matching Items
  A. Types of matching items
    1. Traditional stems and alternatives
    2. Modified
  B. Uses of matching items
  C. Advantages and disadvantages
  D. Points in constructing matching items
  E. Writing directions for matching items
V. Short Answer/Essay
  A. Types of essay items
    1. Closed or restricted
    2. Open or extended
  B. Uses of essay items
  C. Advantages and disadvantages
  D. Points in constructing essay items
  E. Writing directions for essay items

Figure 8A-3. Content outline for cognitive achievement item types.

Item type = 1 (true-false)

Item no. = 15 (item number 15 in bank)

The arrangement of test file cards can be decided by the teacher. One common arrangement is to file cards in the order of (a) course, (b) unit, (c) item type (true-false), (d) item type directions, and (e) sequentially numbered test items. A good tip is to use different colored cards for each type of item. It helps locate and refile cards. If colored cards are not available, markers can be used to color white cards in some fashion. For example, color the top edge of all cards containing (true-false) items red.

A second method for building test items is to use 8 1/2 x 11 inch colored paper which has been formatted with desirable information in the same manner as cards except both sides of the sheet can be used, sample item sheet is shown in Figure 8A-5.

The other method of building test items is to build a test item bank using a microcomputer software package on test development. There are several such programs available for different types of computers. These computer programs are recorded on floppy disks and have written manuals telling the operator how to code and write test items on the computer. The ones available at present are menu driven and are very easy for teachers to use, even when computer skills are limited.

6. Construct Table of Specifications

A table of specifications is a blueprint for selecting test items. It is a matrix with two different categories of information, one listed across the top and a second listed down

FRONT

```
TRUE-FALSE:              FILE CODE _____

                         ITEM CODE _____




ITEM:






ANSWER:
```

BACK

```
COURSE NO./TITLE:

UNIT NO./TITLE:

LESSON NO./TITLE:

SUBJECT:

LEARNING TYPE:



SOURCE OF ITEM/PAGE NO:



DATE WRITTEN/AUTHOR:

DATE REVISED/AUTHOR:


REMARKS:
```

Figure 8A-4. Sample test item card.

TEST ITEM SHEET

```
Item Code:_____              File Code:_____

Course Title/No. _____

Unit Title/No. _____

Lesson Title/No. _____

Item Subject _____

Learning Type: ☐ Knowledge ☐ Skill ☐ Attitude/Work Habit
               ☐ Perceptions

Learning Level _____

Item Type: ☐ True-False ☐ Completion ☐ Multiple-Choice
           ☐ Matching ☐ Essay ☐ Performance
           ☐ Other _____

Source/No. _____

Item:




Answer:




Remarks: Difficulty index _____  Discrimination index_____

Date prepared _____  Author initial _____

Date revised _____   Author initial _____
```

Figure 8A-5. Sample test item building sheet.

the left side, forming a chart or table. There are at least two different ways to construct the table for guiding test item selection. The first type, shown in Figure 8A-6, is a table of specifications to measure performance objectives. The performance objectives for types of test items are entered down the left side. The degree of emphasis placed on the objective during instruction, along with four different learning types and item totals, are placed across the top. The cells for each objective and learning type contain (a) numbers representing the degree of emphasis expressed as a percentage and (b) the number of items to be written for each type of learn-

ing outcome. The bottom of the table contains a listing of the total number of items to be written to measure achievement classified by learning types. The example in Figure 8A-6 is an incomplete table of specifications for an actual test. It is totaled for only two performance objectives, however.

It should be noted that construction of a table of specification as described here is sometimes difficult for the beginning teacher. In this case, the teacher could simply use the listed objectives and percentage emphases shown in the sample table, Figure 8A-6, and identify the total number of items, skipping the identification of the number of items

TYPES AND LEVELS OF LEARNING						
OBJECTIVES	EMPHASIS	KNOWING	UNDERSTANDING	PERFORMING	FEELING	ITEM TOTAL
1. Demonstrate knowledge and understanding of true-false item formats and construct test items of this type which meet the criteria presented in your readings. Level of knowledge and understanding must be at the 70% criterion level or higher.	15%	3	5	2	1	11
2. Demonstrate knowledge and understanding of short answer/completion test item formats and construct test items of this type which meet the criteria presented in your readings. Level of knowledge and understanding must be at the 70% criterion level or higher.	20%	4	6	2	1	13
(Continue OBJECTIVES)						
TOTAL % ITEMS	100%	7	11	4	2	24

Figure 8A-6. Sample table of specifications for performance objectives on types of test items.

OBJECTIVES UNIT #_____ UNIT TITLE_____	NO. OF ITEMS
1. Demonstrate knowledge and understanding of true-false item formats and construct test items of this type which meet the criteria presented in your readings. Level of knowledge and understanding must be at the 70% criterion level or higher.	11
2. . . .	
3. . . .	

CONTENT TOPICS UNIT #_____ UNIT TITLE_____	NO. OF ITEMS
1. True-False	
A. Types	3
B. Uses	3
C. Advantages and disadvantages	3
D. Points of constructing	3
E. Writing directions	2
F. Writing items	3
2. . . .	
3. . . .	

Figure 8A-7. Simplified sample table of specifications formats for performance objectives and course/unit content.

for each learning type. A sample of an abbreviated table of specification using objectives and course/unit content is shown in Figure 8A-7.

There is another type of table of specifications. It can be constructed when specific performance objectives are not written for an instructional program. This type of table of specification lists course content down the left side of the table with learning types listed across the top. Using the content outline information contained in Figure 8A-3, an example content table of specifications is shown in Figure 8A-8.

CONTENT	RELATIVE EMPHASIS	KNOWING	UNDERSTANDING	PERFORMING	FEELING	ITEM TOTAL
I. True-False	15%					
A. Types of true-false items						
1. Traditional		1				1
2. Clustered		1				1
3. Modified		1				1
B. Uses of true-false items			3			3
C. Advantages and disadvantages			3		1	3
D. Points in constructing items			3			3
E. Writing directions				2		2
F. Writing items				3		3
II. Short Answer/Completion	20%					
A. Types of short answer/completion items						
1. Completion		2				2
2. Identification		2				2
3. Definition		2				2
B. Uses of items			3			3
C. Advantages and disadvantages			3		1	4
D. Points in constructing items			3			3
E. Writing directions				2		2
F. Writing items				3		3
TOTAL ITEMS	35%	9	18	10	2	40

Figure 8A-8. *Sample table of specifications for selecting test items based on course unit content.*

Chapter 9

MANIPULATIVE PERFORMANCE TESTS

by

Clifton P. Campbell
Professor, Technological and Adult Education
The University of Tennessee
Knoxville, Tennessee

INTRODUCTION

The basic nature of occupational education is learning by doing for the purpose of doing. For this and other reasons, testing should focus on the observable, measurable, and definable actions taking place. This can be done by using performance tests which objectively evaluate task proficiency against predetermined attainment standards.

Performance tests differ markedly from the popular true-false, multiple-choice, and matching tests used to measure knowledge and compare students with one another. While they have a purpose, these "written tests" cannot determine whether a student performs a manipulative task with the proficiency required for success on the job. Apart from assigning grades and checking learning progress, written tests have limited use; they lack predictive validity, even when they are found to be reliable.

Research in occupational education, as well as in medicine and law, has shown only a slight relationship or connection between grades and on-the-job performance. Furthermore, employers view task performance deficiencies as barriers to productivity, quality control, and, in the end, marketplace success. Consequently, they are concerned with closing the gap between what graduates know and what they can do. A point worth noting is the agreement among experts that requiring students to demonstrate task proficiency is the significant difference between the competency-based and the conventional approach to teaching.

Accountability, the driving force behind competency-based occupational education, is greatly increased when performance tests are used to evaluate hands-on psychomotor skills. This task-relevant method of testing also serves to improve the management control of laboratory and field-based courses and programs.

Manipulative performance tests are derived from job tasks. They provide the most direct, complete, and realistic method of testing a student's ability to perform tasks under workplace requirements. As a result, they should be devel-oped and used primarily for those tasks considered essential to adequate job performance.

The behavioral action, conditions, and standards of these tests imitate, when possible, actual task performance. Because of this, they clearly distinguish whether, and how well, a student can perform.

Ideally, a manipulative performance test evaluates task proficiency using actual equipment under realistic work conditions and standards. These tests are a means of keeping instruction consistent with job requirements. They serve as a connecting link between job tasks and learning objectives.

BENEFITS

Once an occupational (job) analysis has been performed and the tasks have been identified and described (see Chapter 2), performance tests can be developed. The manipulative performance test (MPT), as the title shows, involves actual performance (doing) by a student. It is said to be a criterion-referenced competency test. This is because the MPT provides a direct and realistic method for measuring job task proficiency against attainment standards criterion. An important advantage of MPTs is their relationship to "real life" task performance. See Appendix 9A at the end of this chapter for a sample MPT.

Complex psychomotor behaviors, such as those involved in operating or repairing equipment, can be evaluated in an objective and meaningful way with this kind of test.

On the basis of MPT results, a course or program is revised to improve its effectiveness. Thus, MPTs can be used to assess course and program effectiveness as well as student competence. Thoroughly developed MPTs are beneficial to occupational education because they:

1. Provide a more objective, valid, and reliable measure of each student's ability to perform a manipulative job task than can be obtained by any other practical means. MPTs accurately discriminate between individuals who can meet attainment standards and those who cannot.

Bluffing is impossible and the advantages of being "test wise" or lucky at guessing are eliminated.

2. Reveal specific difficulties and weaknesses in knowledge and skills so that prescriptive remediation can be provided to correct learning deficiencies.

3. Determine whether a student can transfer what was learned in order to perform a manipulative task correctly. In addition, they reveal whether the student can handle the pressure of actual task performance under workplace conditions which may be stressful.

4. Serve as a benchmark for controlling the quality of instructional programs. When students pass the test they are certifiable as job ready and the teaching effort can be considered successful. Moreover, they provide authoritative information on the maintenance, over time, of quality instruction.

5. Facilitate proper placement when students change schools or transfer into a related program. (This is called horizontal articulation.)

6. Document student competence for advanced standing in a senior level institution or apprenticeship program. (This is called vertical articulation.)

7. Provide behaviorally written performance objectives, and are adaptable for secondary use as job sheets.

These and other benefits justify the investment of resources necessary to develop, validate, and administer performance tests.

CONTENT AND PREDICTIVE VALIDITY

MPTs are criterion-referenced tests and, as such, should have both content and predictive validity. Content validity can be established by comparing checklist items to the task statement, performance conditions, and attainment standards (performance objective). See Appendix 9A for an example of an MPT. If the checklist items measure what the performance objective calls for, the test has content validity.

Content validity is self-evident when the entire task is tested just as it is performed on the job. In such cases, the MPT is identical to—not merely representative of—the skill being measured. For example, one task of an "over-the-road" truck driver is to fill out a logbook on vehicle operation. The MPT for this task is identical to the task, its performance conditions and attainment standards. In this case, the test would have a high degree of content validity.

Predictive validity is concerned with the relationship between test performance and, later, successful task performance on the job. An MPT will have high predictive validity if, over the course of time, those who passed it could perform the task on the job and all those who failed could not.

In the following case, test performance is limited to a road test course. Even though this MPT is only representative of actual task performance, predictive validity probably would still be reasonably high. That is, students who pass the MPT probably can perform the task on the job. Those who fail probably cannot.

Another task of an "over-the-road" truck driver is to drive a truck pulling a trailer. The MPT requires driving over a road test course under a variety of conditions in compliance with the attainment standards.

TASK STATEMENT (Behavioral action):
   Drive a truck with a trailer
PERFORMANCE CONDITIONS:
   Over-the-road test course consisting of an interstate highway and city streets, given a truck with standard transmission pulling a trailer, observing all safety procedures and traffic laws.
ATTAINMENT STANDARDS:
   According to standard operating procedures, using proper gears and shifting without a grinding sound, using mirrors when passing vehicles and backing up, keeping both hands on the steering wheel, turning corners without going over the curb, using proper brake action to slow down and stop, completing the road test course within eight hours with the tester riding in the truck providing only minimum supervision

Properly developed paper and pencil tests are suitable for measuring those tasks that are actually done by using paper and pencil in a "real-world" situation. Instances of this include (a) filling out a logbook on vehicle operation, (b) developing a site plan for a specific structure when given a topographical map, and (c) preparing a profit and loss statement from a worksheet. When paper and pencil are used in "real-world" task performance, the MPT should, likewise, be a paper and pencil test.

Reliability and objectivity are discussed later. It is worth noting here, however, that a reliable MPT is one that gives consistent results. Further, careful attention to content validity greatly improves objectivity. Reliability and objectivity will not be a problem if the practices provided under the heading Scoring Procedures are followed.

Physical Fidelity

Physical fidelity has to do with how well the behavioral action, conditions, cues, and standards of the MPT approximate those of the actual task. In the example, filling out a logbook, the MPT is identical to performing an "over-the-road" truck driver task. This test has the highest possible physical fidelity. See illustration "A" in Figure 9-1. In the other example, drive a truck with a trailer, the MPT has lower but still reasonably high physical fidelity. This is because test performance is on a road test course which will not be identical to actual performance conditions such as driving on ice or snow-covered roads in a high wind. This is like "B" in Figure 9-1. When it would be extremely hazard-

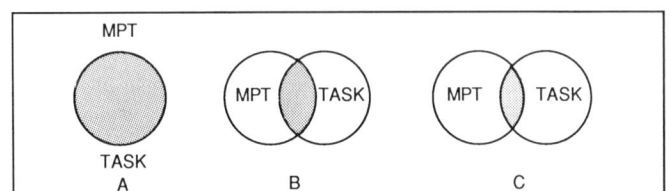

Figure 9-1. Degrees of physical fidelity.

ous to test task performance, the MPT has to be different from the actual task. The physical fidelity will, of necessity, be lower. This is like "C" in Figure 9-1.

Unfortunately, having high physical fidelity does not ensure that predictive validity will be high. However, if evidence of predictive validity is not available, one must often settle for high physical fidelity.

UNITARY AND MULTIPLE TASKS

Another factor that affects test construction is whether the task is unitary or multiple. A unitary task is one that is always performed in the same way with exactly the same inputs. This step-by-step sequence is diagramed below:

$$1 \rightarrow 2 \rightarrow 3 \rightarrow 4 \rightarrow 5 \rightarrow 6 \text{ etc.}$$

A multiple task is one that has several possible inputs. There are two types of multiple tasks. One is always performed by following essentially the same procedure. The following is a case in point.

A task requiring the multiplication of a three-digit number by a three-digit number is a multiple task. The multiplication is always performed by following fundamentally the same procedures. However, there are 810,000 possible inputs (combinations of the two three-digit numbers).

In this case, it would be unreasonable to test all possible inputs to make sure a student knows how to do each of them. For unitary tasks, the test can measure the total, whereas for multiple tasks, a truly representative sample must be taken.

The second type of multiple task is one in which the inputs vary. Here the task is performed differently depending on the input. This means the input is a cue that determines the appropriate response. For example:

One task performed by a police officer is to apprehend those suspected of committing a crime. The procedure for performing this task depends, for the most part, on the inputs (cues). Answers to questions in the following checklist will determine how the task is performed.
1. Is the suspect armed?
2. Is the suspect intoxicated or on drugs?
3. Is the suspect in a vehicle or on foot?
4. Is the suspect alone, with a few others, or in a crowd?
5. Is the police officer alone or with others?
6. Is the police officer in a vehicle or on foot?

As with the first type of multiple task, the test for this task cannot measure the total task. Consequently, it must test a sample of the possible variations. However, for this type of task, the test must do more than measure the *adequacy* of the performance. It must also measure the *appropriateness*; that is, whether the performance was the correct response to the particular inputs (cues).

TEST DEVELOPMENT

The makeup or composition of an MPT may vary to suit a particular need. Figure 9-2 provides a useful format. This worksheet has blank spaces to fill in the following key information.
1. Job title and task number.
2. Statement of the task (behavioral action to be taken).
3. Performance conditions under which the test is to be administered.
4. Initiating cue(s).
5. Attainment standards which are a measure of the adequacy of performance
6. Administrative instructions which include directions to both the student and teacher or other tester.
7. Scoring procedures.
8. Performance measure checklist which contains the task elements/steps that are the actions which make up the total performance and/or the scorable characteristics for a product.
9. Comments (a brief description of observed behavior that appeared significant for evaluation and feedback purposes).

The information called for in items one and two is rather straightforward. A full discussion of the other items is presented later in this chapter.

It is not always feasible to duplicate every aspect of a task in a test. For this reason, the procedure for developing an MPT is basically one of (a) considering in what ways the test must be different from the task because of various testing constraints, and (b) constructing a test that is the best compromise.

As shown in Figure 9-3, there are eight procedural steps in developing an MPT. A recommended approach to following this step-by-step procedure is to work on one manipulative task at a time and determine (a) testing constraints, (b) if product, process, or both should be measured, (c) performance conditions, (d) initiating cues, (e) attainment standards, and (f) if the entire task or part of it will be tested. Then develop the test along with its scoring procedure. Take the next task and repeat the procedure.

The first determinations should be considered tentative. After repeating this procedure for a few tasks it is advisable to go back and make revisions as appropriate. When several of the tests have been developed, they should be validated or verified.

TESTING CONSTRAINTS

If constraints such as (a) money, (b) facilities and equipment, (c) personnel, (d) time, (e) extreme hazard, and (f) legal and ethical considerations did not exist, every MPT would imitate the task it intends to measure. That is, the test would consist of observing the student performing the task under job performance conditions and noting whether or not the standards were attained. For example, the test for "clean a typewriter" ought to be identical to task performance. Since resource and other constraints do exist, it may not be possible or reasonable to duplicate in a test situation all that is called for in task performance at the workplace.

Test Development Worksheet

1. JOB TITLE _____ TASK NO._____

2. TASK STATEMENT (Behavioral action)

   _____

3. PERFORMANCE CONDITIONS (Identify those conditions under which the test is
   to be administered that would make a difference in performance)

   3.1 Setting: _____

   3.2 ____ Actual equipment under actual work conditions

        ____ Actual equipment under simulated work conditions

        ____ Simulator, Trainer, or Mockup

   3.3 Tools: _____

   3.4 Equipment: _____

   3.5 Materials and Supplies: _____

   3.6 References: _____

   3.7 Safety Considerations: _____

   3.8 Personnel Reqd: _____

   3.9 Other: _____

4. INITIATING CUE(S) _____

5. ATTAINMENT STANDARDS (A measure of the adequacy of performance)

   5.1 100% of all process task elements/steps completed to standards

   5.2 100% of all product scorable characteristics completed to standards

   5.3 Time requirement/limit: _____

   5.4 Other: _____

6. ADMINISTRATIVE INSTRUCTIONS

   6.1 Directions to Student: _____

        _____

   6.2 Directions for Teacher/Tester: _____

        _____

(Continued)

Figure 9-2. Test development worksheet.

7. SCORING PROCEDURES _____

_____

8. PERFORMANCE MEASURE CHECKLIST (Place an (S) or (C) to the left of task elements/steps and scorable characteristics. Include a performance rating scale or space for initials)

    (S) Important Sequence: This step must be performed only after the preceding step(s).

    (C) Critical Step: Failure to meet the standard for this step or characteristic results in test failure.

    8.1 Process

TASK ELEMENTS/STEPS **STANDARDS** **SCALE/INITIALS**

    8.2 Product

SCORABLE CHARACTERISTICS **STANDARDS** **SCALE/INITIALS**

9. COMMENTS _____

_____

Figure 9-2. (Continued)

INPUT

Manipulative Task
Selected For
Instruction

Step 1

Determine
Testing
Constraints

Step 2

Determine If
Product, Process
Or Both Should
Be Measured

Step 3

Determine
Performance
Conditions

Step 4

Determine
Initiating
Cues

Step 5

Determine
Attainment
Standards

Step 6

Determine If All
Or Part Of The Task
Will Be Tested

Step 7

Develop Scoring
Procedure
And Test

Step 8

Validate Or
Verify Test

Test Ready
For Use

OUTPUT

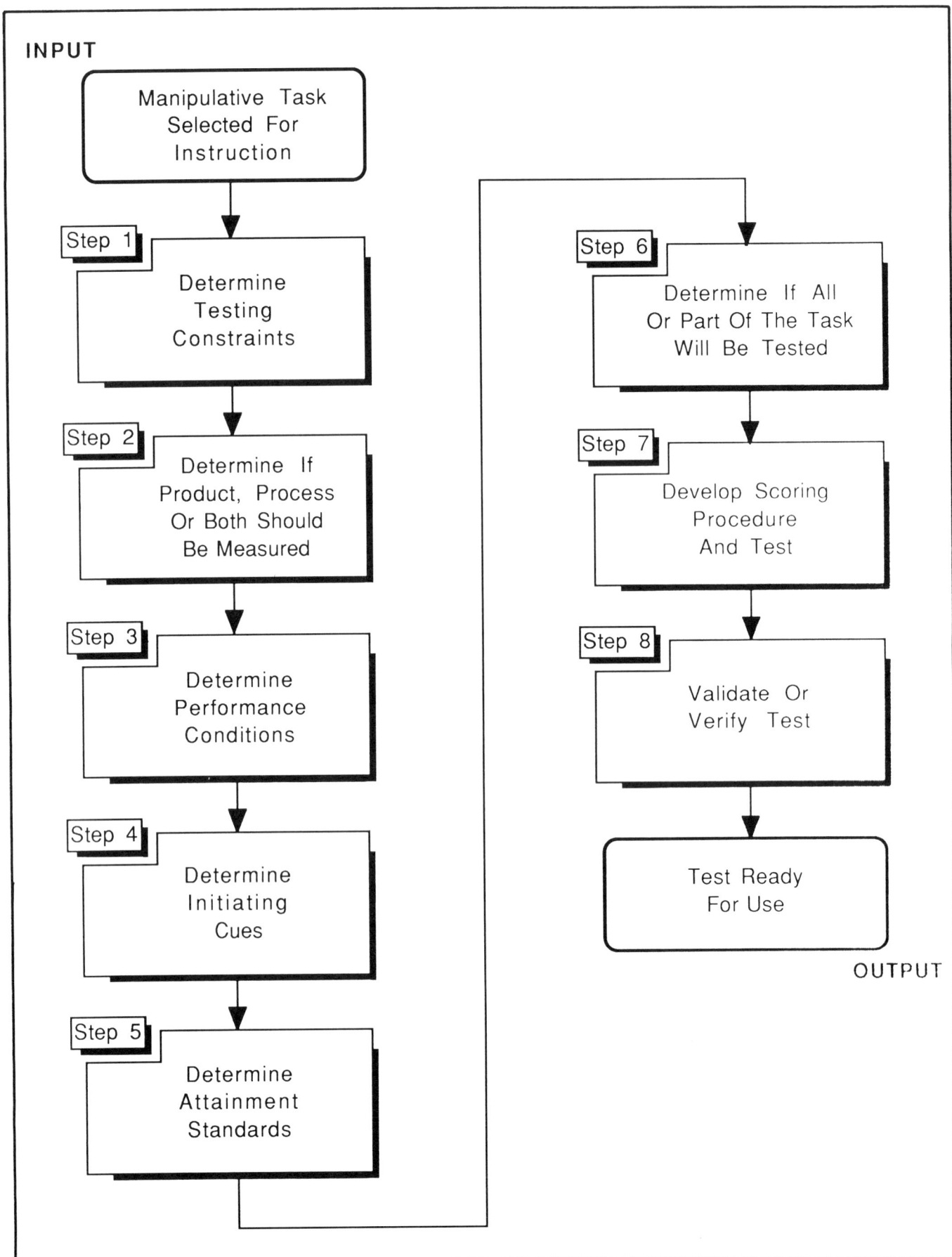

Figure 9-3. Developing a Manipulative Performance Test.

The first step in developing MPTs that have high predictive validity, high physical fidelity, or both, is to review the task to determine testing constraints. The following constraints can force a change from a higher to a lower physical fidelity test. They are, for the most part, interrelated. For example, money, facilities and equipment, personnel, and time are often different aspects of the same problem.

Money

The first constraint is usually one of economics. Costs are an important factor in developing and administering any test. They must be kept within reasonable limits. The following example illustrates this point.

In most cases, cost would prohibit having a demolition specialist destroy a building to measure task proficiency. There are other more practical means of testing this task. If the task specifies demolishing a building, the test may need to be modified so the building is not actually demolished, but the student demonstrates the process and procedures up to but not including the actual demolition. Simulation is another alternative that should be considered.

Facilities and Equipment

Often job-relevant facilities and actual equipment are not available to support test administration. This is especially true for specialized facilities and sophisticated equipment. An example of an equipment availability constraint might involve a course or program on computer troubleshooting. Computer downtime may be too costly and disruptive for testing use.

When testing would tax facilities or equipment beyond reasonable limits, it may be necessary to test only those tasks which would cause the least disruption. The remainder of the tasks might be tested using simulation.

Personnel

The availability of additional or support personnel may also impose a constraint on performance testing. This can occur when teamwork or more than one individual is required to perform a task under normal conditions in the job environment. The following situation clarifies this point.

If machine operation requires two individuals, and only one student is available for the test, someone trained in the other machine functions will be required before the test can be administered. Should the second individual, a staff worker or another student not be available, there will be insufficient personnel to conduct the test under normal operating conditions.

When this situation occurs, it would be preferable to schedule the test for two students simultaneously. Although individual performance is usually tested, multiple or even team performance can be evaluated.

Time

The practical constraint of time availability is easily understood. Often the situation is such that it is impractical to test the entire task in the time available.

In general, some time constraint must be placed on test administration. This and the time standard for task performance limit the amount of time that can reasonably be spent on each test. If performance of some of the tasks requires more time than is available for testing, the MPT should be constructed using a sample of the critical task elements.

As was pointed out before, constraints are interrelated in most cases. The practical constraint in the example of computer troubleshooting was categorized under equipment availability, but it could also be categorized under money.

Considering the limitations of money, facilities and equipment, personnel, time, safety requirements, and other factors, obtaining the highest possible physical fidelity is not always practical. In such cases, the test developed must be viewed as the best possible trade-off with reality. Nevertheless, the teacher must carefully weigh how critical it is to duplicate in the test situation the conditions and standards of the workplace, then decide whether full realism is possible. This is important because, without full realism, some degree of relevance is likely to be lost.

SIMULATION

When it is decided that the conditions and standards of the workplace cannot be duplicated in the test situation, a substitute approach must be developed. This is one of the most challenging aspects of the test development process. Here a teacher's inventiveness is needed in devising a testing situation that is as similar as possible to task performance on the job.

Too often this problem causes teachers to resort to tests using true-false and multiple-choice items which measure knowledge but do not even approximate activities that are "task-like." This is an approach that, in most cases, should be rejected out of hand. A viable option for testing task relevant skill and knowledge is simulation.

Broadly defined, *simulation* is any change from reality, an imitation. It is a testing situation that recreates, with as much fidelity as possible, the conditions encountered in the workplace. Both research and experience have shown a positive relationship between performing a task under simulated conditions and performing it under actual workplace conditions. Moreover, the low risk to students and equipment provides a strong argument for using simulation, particularly when complicated and expensive equipment are used on the job and in the laboratory or field.

An imitation of the entire environment ranging from facilities and weather conditions to equipment, including sounds and smells to name a few, is critical in quality simulation. The closer the simulation is to the actual environment of the job, the better students perform under actual conditions as employees.

If a test cannot be administered under "real-world" conditions, some form of simulation may be necessary. When deciding whether or not to use simulation, the following factors should be considered: (a) the effects of reduced physical fidelity; (b) the effect on productivity when actual equipment or facilities are used for testing, (c) the potential dangers to students or damage to equipment, (d) the cost of materials, supplies, and equipment used under workplace conditions, and (e) the efficiency of simulation.

MEASURE PRODUCT AND/OR PROCESS

Task performance standards are based on a product, a process, or both. The end product is the most obvious task output; it is observable and can be physically examined. A welded steel pipe is a product of task performance.

The other output of task performance is the completion of procedural steps (process). Occasionally the process itself leaves no record. The skills involved (for instance, in safe driving) can be evaluated only by direct observation of the student's performance.

In some cases, both product and process must be examined as task output. See Appendix 9A for an example. Many tests evaluate processes that result in products in order to provide feedback on (a) process errors which affect the product or (b) related policies and procedures.

In certain cases, the processes or procedures in performing a task may be critical in that they ensure personnel safety or prevent damage to tools, equipment, or materials. For example, a driver arrives at destination B from point A as required by the task, but in the process, violates traffic laws or causes an accident. In such a case, product evaluation alone would be inadequate.

The MPT will usually measure the same factors (product, process, or both) that are used as a basis for the task standard. It may be necessary, however, to incorporate some form of simulation such as the mannequin used in the test documentation shown in Figure 9-4. Here the task of performing mouth-to-mouth resuscitation is evaluated based on successful completion of each procedural step using a cardiopulmonary resuscitation (CPR) mannequin instead of a victim.

PERFORMANCE CONDITIONS

Conditions communicate prerequisite requirements that exist for task performance. They include the: (a) environment (setting) in which the performance must be demonstrated, (b) tools, equipment, furniture, materials and supplies, (c) references, special instructions and job performance aids, (d) special physical demands, (e) safety, and (f) other considerations such as additional or support personnel needed to accomplish a task. Figure 9-5 provides examples of performance conditions for each of these items.

There are two kinds of conditions, constant and variable. Both kinds are illustrated in the following task.

TASK STATEMENT (Behavioral action):
    Fabricate stair and landing handrails.
CONSTANT CONDITIONS:
  1. Given a detail drawing.
  2. Using production tools and equipment.
  3. Wearing protective apparel and following safe working procedures.

VARIABLE CONDITIONS:
  1. All sizes and kinds of metal pipe (carbon steel, aluminum, etc.).
  2. All handrail shapes.
  3. All types of settings (both inside and outside) and weather (rain, snow, ice, wind, etc.).

If variable conditions, such as the weather (an environmental condition), had been left out, the test would be imprecise. Yet it is virtually impossible to combine all the variable conditions especially when factors such as the weather cannot be controlled.

Constraints usually prevent using all the variable conditions identified. As a result, the teacher has little choice but to use a sample of them. Those constant and variable conditions that influence task performance need to be included in the test. This is especially true whenever it will help to communicate any differences in task performance created by such conditions.

After the conditions under which the task is performed have been identified, they should be reviewed. The job performance aid presented in Figure 9-6 can be used to make sure that (a) all the items which are necessary in the statement of performance conditions are in fact included and (b) all those that do not affect task performance have been deleted. The resulting statement of conditions will consist of only those conditions which make a difference in the performance of the task and, therefore, must be in the test.

INITIATING CUES

A cue is a signal to perform an action. For example, a school bell at eight o'clock is a cue (signal) to begin class. To initiate means to start or cause the beginning of. Initiating cues are defined as "things in one's surroundings which convey an awareness through any of the senses (smell, taste, touch, hearing, sight) and cause an individual to begin performing an appropriate action." The sight of steaming coolant on a machine lathe initiates (triggers) the action of adjusting the feed rate or cutting speed. See Figure 9-7.

For some tasks there may be more than one initiating cue. Some of the cues that would initiate the task "change a flat tire" are:
1. A loud "bang."
2. Difficulty in steering.
3. Sound of rubber flapping on the pavement.
4. Sight of a flat tire.

In certain instances, a cue may appear to initiate several different tasks. If the temperature gauge or light in a vehicle shows the engine to be overheated, there might be a need to (a) add coolant, (b) repair a leaking radiator, (c) replace a broken water hose or fan belt, (d) replace the radiator cap, thermostat, or water pump. An initiating cue which appears to start several different tasks may really start a troubleshooting procedure. For this initiating cue a series of checks are performed. If you saw that the fan belt was broken, you would replace it. Thus, an initiating cue could start a troubleshooting check which would produce one or more other initiating cues to start replacement or repair tasks.

Task Statement	Performance Conditions	Initiating Cue	Attainment Standards
Perform mouth-to-mouth resuscitation on an adult.	Victim lying face down on the floor. CPR mannequin used as victim.	Tester says: "You enter this room and discover the victim lying face down on the floor. You are alone. Proceed with the actions you deem necessary."	Each step performed in sequence, according to approved procedures, victim revived, without assistance.

Process (Procedural steps)

1. OVERVIEW THE SCENE
   Look for clues to indicate cause of victim's condition. (None noted.) Determine by position of body, and any other evidence, if there is a possible neck fracture. (None noted.)

2. DETERMINE LEVEL OF CONSCIOUSNESS
   Gently shake victim's shoulder. Simultaneously shout "Are you ok?" (No response from victim.) Call out - "Help!"

3. REPOSITION VICTIM
   Gently straighten victim by placing arm on the side to which the victim will be turned along victim's head. Place victim's other arm down by the side toward the feet. Straighten legs. Support victim's head and neck with one hand. Use other hand to roll victim as a unit toward the rescuer, until victim is flat on his or her back. Move the arm of the victim that was supporting head to along his or her side.

4. OPEN VICTIM'S AIRWAY
   Kneel beside victim's shoulder. Place upper hand on victim's forehead and lower hand on chin. Lift chin until upper and lower teeth of victim are almost together.

5. LOOK, LISTEN AND FEEL
   Lean over victim, facing feet, placing ear directly over mouth and nose. Look at victim's chest to check for rising and falling indication of breathing. Listen for breathing sounds. Feel for breath exhalations on ear or cheek.

6. PINCH NOSE SHUT
   Pinch victim's nostrils shut keeping one hand on forehead to prevent air leakage. Maintain pressure on forehead to keep head tilted.

(Continued)

Figure 9-4. Test documentation.

7. SEAL MOUTH, GIVE TWO QUICK BREATHS
   Take deep breath, make tight seal with mouth over victim's mouth. Give two full breaths at 1 - 1.5 seconds per breath. There should be a 4 - 7 second interval between breaths. Check rise and fall of chest as air enters and exits.

8. CHECK CAROTID PULSE
   Pause and check victim's carotid pulse for at least five seconds. Using index and middle fingers of chin hand, find victim's trachea. Then, slide fingers into the groove of the neck where carotid artery may be palpated.

> Tester says:
> "You have a pulse, but
> no breathing."

9. CONTINUE RESCUE BREATHING
   Pinch victim's nostrils shut, maintain open airway and deliver one breath every five seconds (12 per minute).

> Tester says:
> "Victim is revived, you
> are now relieved."

Items to be Considered in a Statement of Performance Conditions		Examples of Conditions	
1.	Environment	1.1	outside on a hot sunny day
		1.2	under extreme pressure and/or anxiety
		1.3	in an air-conditioned office
		1.4	in a noisy factory
		1.5	in a garage with poor lighting and ventilation
2.	Tools, equipment, furniture, materials, and supplies	2.1	using a hand-held calculator
		2.2	using a claw hammer
		2.3	given a sheet of problems and a pencil
		2.4	using a ladder and scaffold
		2.5	using an oral thermometer
		2.6	using a grinder
		2.7	with a standard transmission
3.	References, special instructions, and job performance aids	3.1	using a procedural guide
		3.2	with the help of a checklist
		3.3	given technical manuals
4.	Special physical demands	4.1	crowded working conditions
		4.2	prolonged physical exertion
		4.3	kneeling or squatting
		4.4	unusually cramped position
		4.5	while lying down
5.	Safety considerations	5.1	wearing safety shoes
		5.2	given toxic fumes
		5.3	wearing clean room overalls
		5.4	wearing welding gloves and a welding helmet with ultraviolet shield
		5.5	wearing an air-purifying respirator

Note. In considering the applicability of different items in the statement of performance conditions, the major question to be answered is, "Does it affect task performance?"

Figure 9-5. Specifying performance conditions.

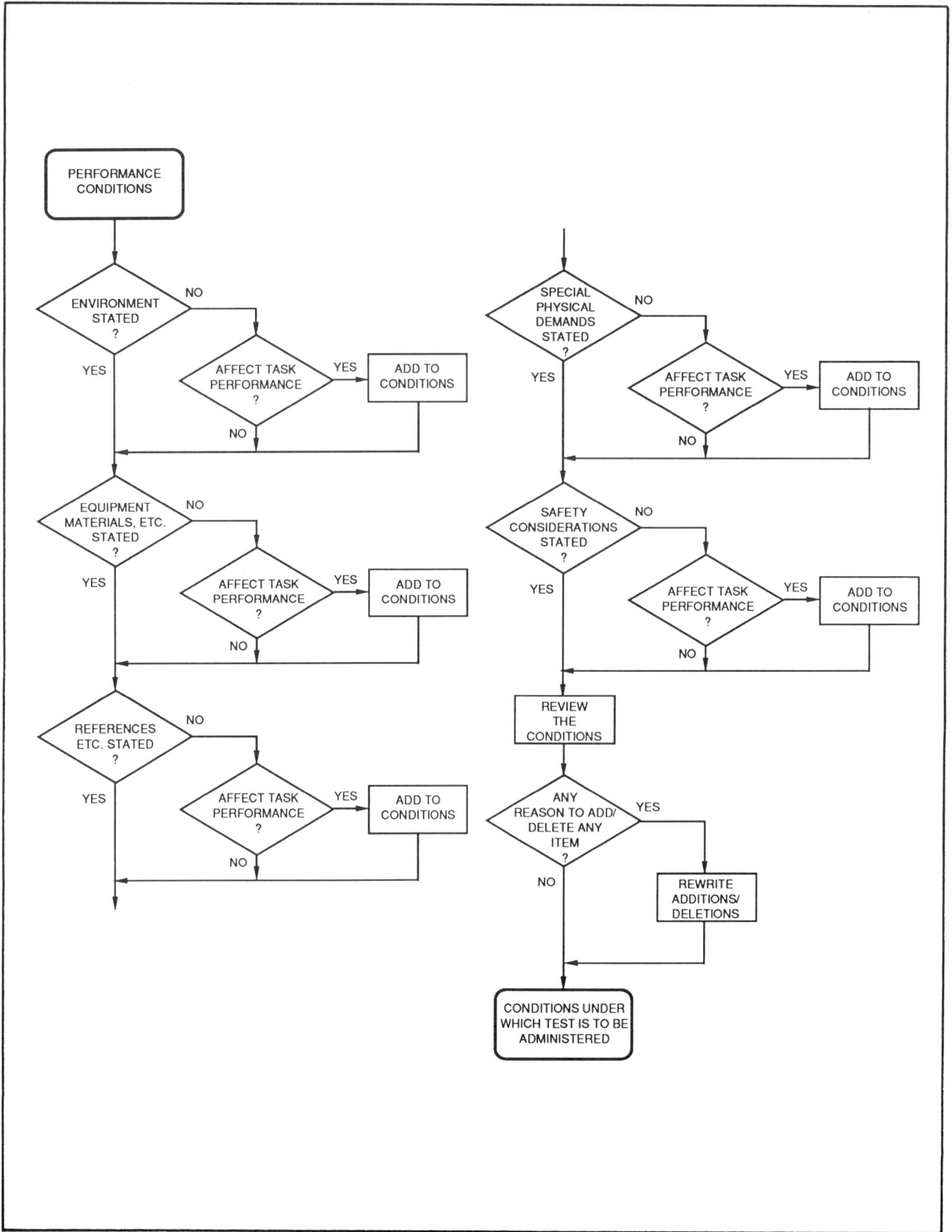

Figure 9-6. Job performance aid for editing performance conditions.

CUES

Steaming coolant

Shoulder is produced ragged

Cutting noise changes to an intermittent rumble or vibrating whine

Chips begin to smoke

Chips become ragged

Vibrating hand-wheel

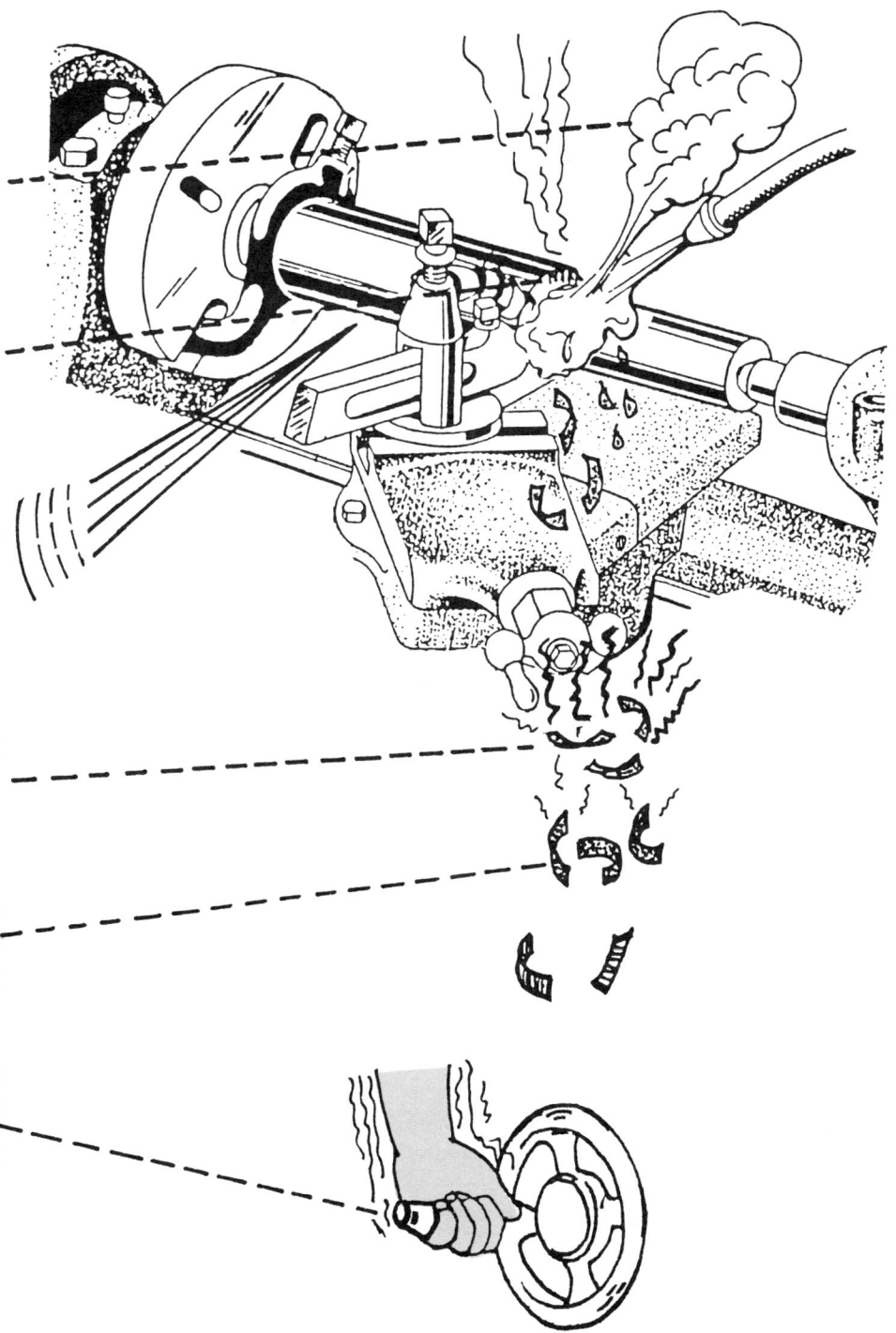

Figure 9-7. Cues which stimulate a sensory awareness of the need to perform an action.

It is useful to know what cues cause an individual to begin performing a task, yet they are seldom stated in documents which list and describe the tasks. As a result, the teacher may have some difficulty writing them. When this is the case, workers can be interviewed to discover exactly what the initiating cues are.

Often the initiating cues used in tests are different from those that prompt or signal a worker to begin performing a task. See Figure 9-4. This is frequently the situation even though it reduces physical fidelity. The following is a case in point.

The initiating cue for a nurse to perform mouth-to-mouth resuscitation would be that the victim is unconscious and breathing has stopped. However, this is an unrealistic test cue. While changing the cue reduces test fidelity, probably the best that could be done would be to use a cue such as having the tester say, "You enter this room and discover the victim lying face down on the floor. You are alone. Proceed with the actions you deem necessary."

Test cues may be spoken, as in this example, or written. Entries made on forms, such as a work order, can be used effectively.

Insofar as constraints permit, the *critical* initiating cues should be realistic. A critical cue is one for which the proper response determines success or failure in performing the task. For example:

The task, "repair malfunctioning equipment," could be such that the actual repair is relatively simple when the student knows what to fix. The critical part of the task might be determining what needs repair. In this example, if the initiating cue were having the tester say, "Assume the equipment needs a new switch," the test would have very low fidelity and probably very low predictive validity. This is because the cue initiated the wrong action. The proper response includes a troubleshooting procedure.

ATTAINMENT STANDARDS

When providing feedback to students about their performance, teachers need to avoid generalized reactions such as "this is not good enough!" Such a response is neither fair nor functional to the improvement of performance. Students ought to know the standards against which their performance will be rated so they can also determine whether the necessary proficiency level has been attained.

For this and other reasons, the criteria for attainment standards must be defined in observable and measurable terms. As such they need to describe the level of proficiency required for successful task performance, based on the applicable categories in the following list.

1. Quality, degree of excellence.
2. Accuracy, within tolerance limits.
3. Number of allowable variations or permissible errors.
4. Quantity, rate of production.
5. Standard(s) or criteria identified in reference documents.

6. Time limit, speed of performance.
7. Amount of supervision or assistance to be provided.

Fig. 9-8 provides examples of how to state observable and measurable criteria for the seven attainment standards categories.

These examples are useful in preparing attainment standards which are complete and unmistakably clear. In reference to Category Five in the list, the preferred treatment is to provide the standard or criterion as well as cite the source document. However, when the standard or criterion is lengthy or well-known to the students and tester, a source reference alone will suffice.

Depending on the *job entry task performance standards of the workplace and/or occupation*, as determined through occupational (job) analysis or by on-the-job workers, various combinations of the appropriate criteria are used. These criteria specify the necessary level of proficiency. The job entry performance standards are usually less than those expected of an experienced worker. Even so, it may be advisable to make an additional allowance for the fact that students are engaged in a learning process.

For example, a maximum time limit may be specified in order for the student to attain the accuracy criterion of the intended workplace and/or occupation. On the other hand, a student ought to demonstrate the accuracy and speed required on the job if the task is considered important by the employer and it (a) is not taught on the job, and (b) must be performed well soon after being employed. This is particularly true when no grace period for improving proficiency through practice is provided.

Historically, teachers have established attainment standards for the tasks they teach. Often these standards represent their personal perception, which may or may not be valid. This happens most often when there is no verifiable "real-world" requirement. As a result, an inappropriate criterion, such as a time limit, may be specified. The following situation illustrates this point.

The task "clean a typewriter" may be required of a secretary. However, if the time limit, "within fifteen minutes," is included in an MPT, it will set a criterion which is not implied in task performance. It might be troublesome if the secretary took an hour to perform the task correctly, but what if it required only half an hour? To the statistician that means being off by a factor of 100%, but to the secretary, it may be only a minor problem. Unless there are job requirements for a specific criterion, it should not be included in the attainment standard. In the case of cleaning a typewriter, it would be necessary to do a time and motion study to discover a fifteen-minute procedure, when most secretaries could learn to perform the task correctly in thirty minutes.

In some tasks the criterion of time is of little consequence and should not be included. In others it is critical and may even be set in a "flat rate manual." Consequently, if speed is important, a reasonable time limit should be stated. The student must practice enough to complete the task within that time limit.

Attainment Standards Categories		Examples of Criterion	
1.	Quality, degree of excellence	1.1	such that the seam will not split when the two pieces of material are jerked sharply
		1.2	at least seven practice plates will pass the free bend test with no visible damage to the weldment
		1.3	with <u>no</u> uncorrected errors
2.	Accuracy, within tolerance limits	2.1	within one-half of one degree as compared with the instructor's reading
		2.2	with a tolerance of $\pm$ 0.001 inch as measured by a micrometer
		2.3	no more than 2 inches in diameter and no less than 1 inch
3.	Number of allowable variations or permissible errors	3.1	with no more than two noncritical errors
		3.2	with no more than one of the total items not meeting "standards"
		3.3	missing no more than one reading/recording within a two-hour period
		3.4	two out of three products must meet all criteria
		3.5	not more than two indications of porosity for every three inches of weld metal
4.	Quantity, rate of production	4.1	at the rate of 25 per hour
		4.2	not less than 10 cubic yards of earth must be excavated and dumped in 15 minutes
		4.3	minimum output, 10 pages per hour

(Continued)

Figure 9-8. Specifying criteria for attainment standards.

5.	Standard(s) or criteria identified in reference documents	5.1	in accordance with the criteria set forth in XXX.X
		5.2	within limitations of the standards listed in MIL-STD-1379A
		5.3	based on the criteria specified in ASA document 1.6.3
		5.4	according to approved clinical procedures
6.	Time limit, speed of performance	6.1	completed within three hours
		6.2	ready for return to customer within 24 hours of drop-off
		6.3	malfunctions must be identified within 20 minutes
7.	Amount of supervision or assistance to be provided	7.1	without assistance
		7.2	with minimum supervision

Note. The criterion examples are not intended to be relevant to any specific job.

The introduction of inappropriate criteria in attainment standards to make the test more difficult or challenging must be avoided. Although, when there are no clear-cut verifiable workplace attainment standards, the alternative is to begin with best-estimate criteria agreed to by incumbent workers. Later, by testing and verifying against on-the-job performance, estimates are changed. Caution is necessary when setting standards because unnecessarily high attainment criteria are costly in training. Furthermore, they may be of questionable value in decision making.

Attainment standards may relate to the process or product of performance or a combination of both. Process standards include the required step-by-step procedures to be followed and usually a time limit. Product standards describe the adequacy of the end product and include criteria for judging its acceptability.

Standards relating to procedures require that certain steps be followed in the performance of the task. If these steps are omitted or done out of order *when sequence is important*, then the student does not meet standards. The assumption is that there is no such thing as performing skills partially right.

Permissible deviations or allowable variations in quality, quantity, and time measures need to be included in the performance criteria. Tests may also allow a student to vary the sequence in which certain steps of a procedure are performed. This is the case when the sequence of step performance is not important.

Some standards include requirements related to the final product. Occasionally, procedures followed in turning out or producing the end product may be less important than the adequacy of the product itself. If procedures are followed correctly, however, the chances that the product will meet attainment standards should be improved.

It is helpful to have a model, exhibit, or photograph of the acceptable end product which can be used for clarification and comparison. This example, along with a checklist that includes each criterion used to measure acceptability, can help in the evaluation process. It is useful when showing a student where the deficiencies are and in helping to develop an understanding of the proficiency required for successful performance.

As mentioned, both process and product can be used to measure task performance. For example, if the product is a paved road, it might be examined directly and compared to the standard for scorable characteristics such as (a) bank slope, (b) ditch slope, (c) shoulder, (d) crown, and (e) appropriate pavement. See Figure 9-9.

The same paved road could be measured on each procedural step in the process of construction. Figure 9-10 shows a portion of a process scale for rating proficiency.

Another class of attainment standards are highly qualitative, such as those for a sales presentation. The level of proficiency required for a successful oral presentation is difficult to break down into criteria that can be objectively scored on a right-wrong basis.

Qualitative task performances must be evaluated carefully. This is critical in order to avoid measuring only the less important parts of the task that are more easily scored. Even though evaluation of these tasks is mostly judgmental and qualitative, a quantitatively measurable standard for performance measurement purposes should be derived.

After the task performance standards are identified, they should be reviewed. The job performance aid presented in Figure 9-11 can be used to make sure that all seven categories, which may be included in the attainment standard, have been considered. The resulting attainment standards are those which describe the level of proficiency required for successful task performance and, therefore, must be included in the test.

TESTING THE WHOLE TASK OR PART

The decision to test the entire task or part of it depends mainly on whether it is a unitary or a multiple task. For unitary tasks, those that are always performed in the same way, the entire task is tested.

The behavioral action, conditions, cues, standards, and constraints previously identified provide guidance in determining what can be done realistically. If the entire task can be tested, it ought to be. If not, a part-task test should be developed that will accurately predict job performance.

Alternate Forms

When there are a number of possible actions, conditions, or cues, the teacher must decide (a) whether or not they are all equally likely to occur and (b) if there is the same importance attached to the occurrence of each one. In cases where they are equal, each one should be included in an alternate form of the test. When the likelihood of occurrence or their importance is unequal, a sampling plan should reflect this.

Alternate forms are equal but different versions of the test. Developing alternate forms makes it possible to include the important variables without making any single MPT too long to administer. In the following case, alternate forms of an MPT can be developed to include "striking" a representative sample of the mortar joints.

If the task included the element or step of striking (shaping) mortar joints between masonry units such as brick or block, there would be nine joint finishes to select from. However, the most durable and the most effective joints, in terms of moisture resistance, are the (a) concave, (b) V-shaped, and (c) weathered joints.

In this case, a predetermined number of randomly selected mortar joints could be used. Consequently, no one would know, until the test was administered, which joint would be tested.

This raises the question: Why not initially select the most durable and most effective mortar joints and include them in three alternate forms of the test? The reason is that one of the uses of MPTs is to serve as a basis for the development and control of instruction. This means the course or program would be designed to teach students to perform successfully only one-third of the mortar joints used. Even if the others were taught, there would be no way to know they had been learned since they would not be tested.

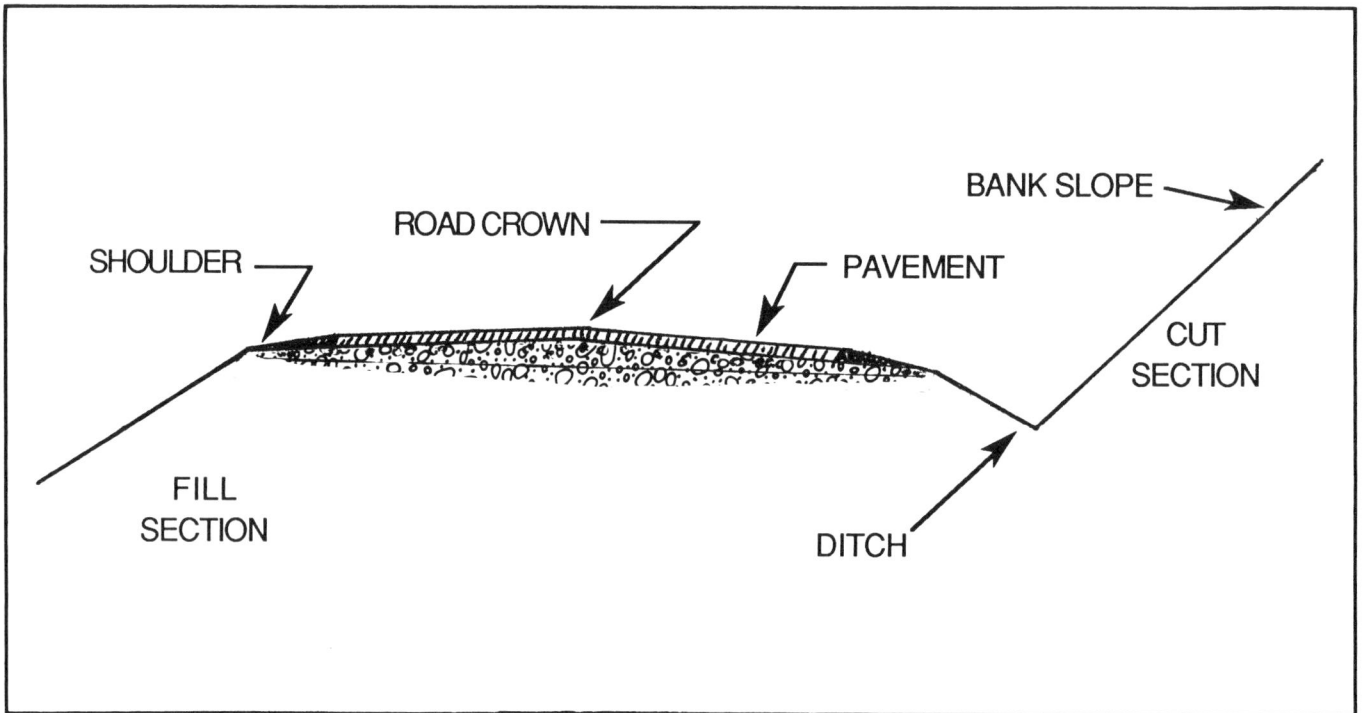

Figure 9-9. Product scale for rating proficiency.

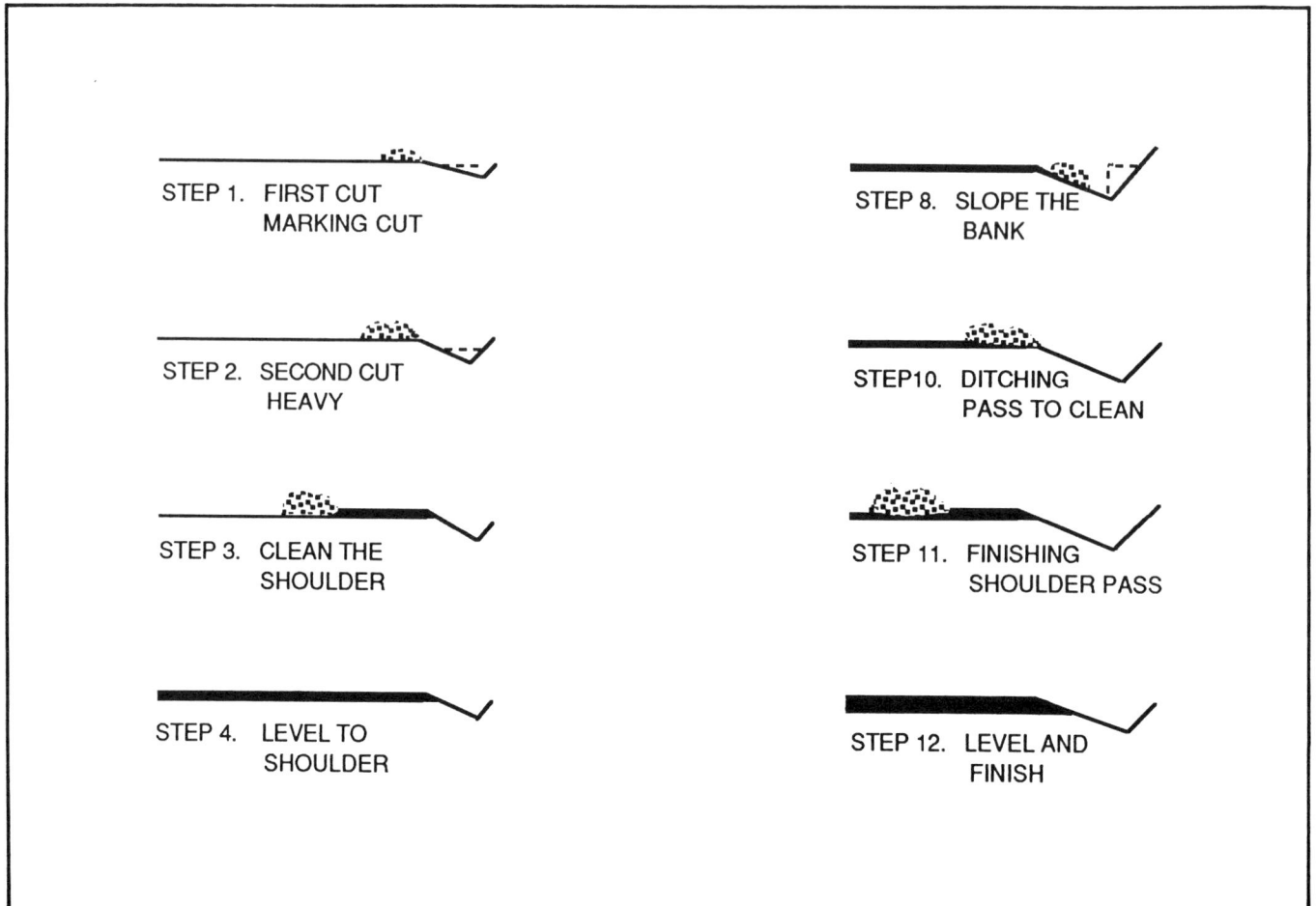

Figure 9-10. Part of a process scale for rating proficiency.

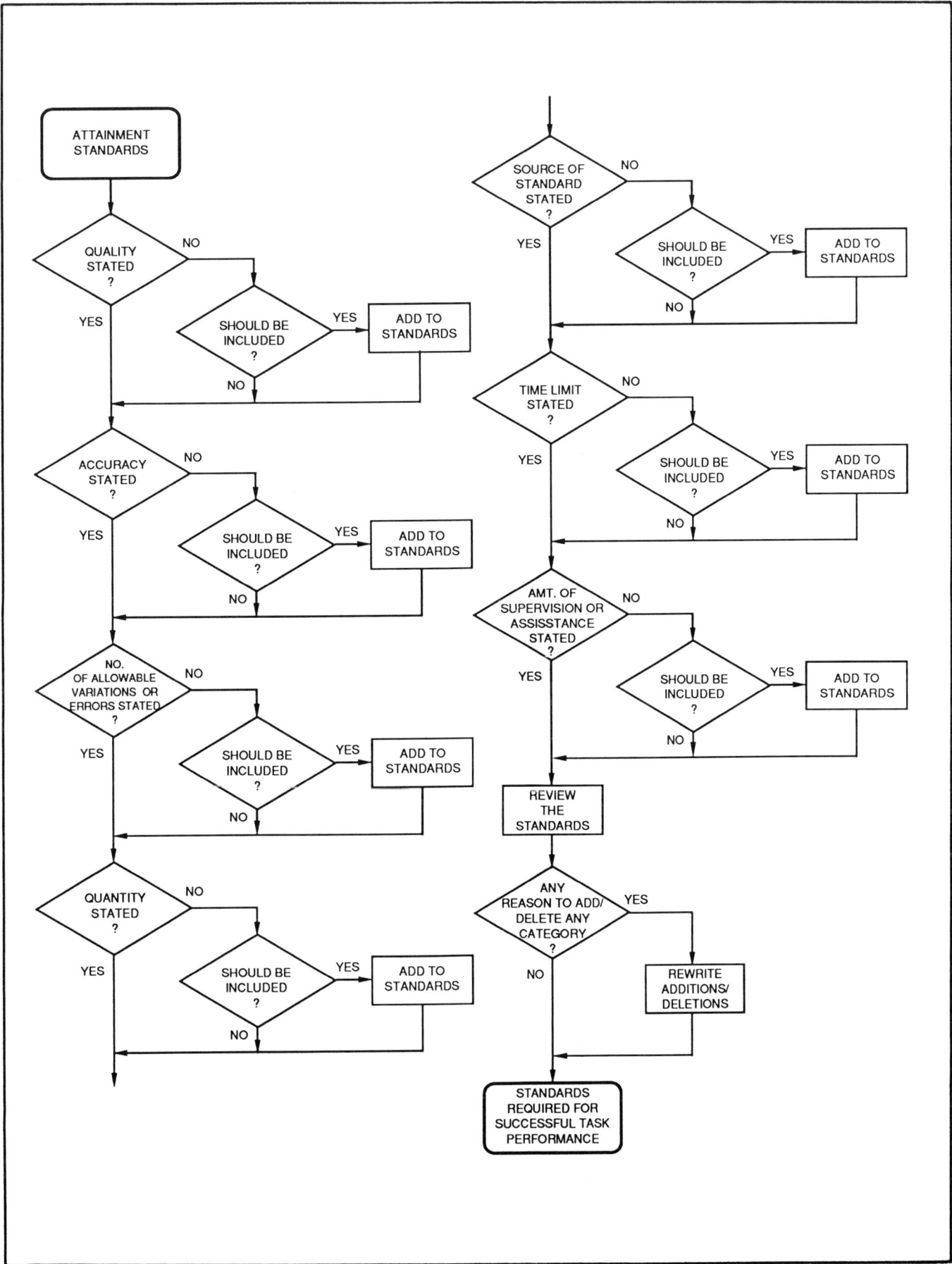

Figure 9-11. Job performance aid for editing attainment standards.

SCORING PROCEDURES

Scoring procedures used during the measurement of task performance need to be reliable and objective. Reliability means that evaluation of task performance will be consistent from one occasion to the next, and that different testers will evaluate the student the same way in any given testing situation. Objective scoring means that ratings are not influenced by the personal bias of the tester or inappropriate factors such as the tendency to be either generous or "hard" on the student.

Reliable and objective (unbiased) scoring procedures include (a) the use of clear and precise attainment standards which are the same for every student and (b) orientation on proper test administration for testers.

Another important consideration is whether task performance should be rated as it occurs as a process or whether the focus is on a tangible result, a product. Process evaluation is necessarily the choice for performances that yield no tangible product. For example, the steps followed by a nurse performing mouth-to-mouth resuscitation (see Figure 9-4) can be rated in terms of the observed proficiency. No product is produced, however.

For those performances where the natural result is a product, it is advantageous to focus on evaluating that product. The tangible product constitutes a permanent record that can be unhurriedly and repeatedly examined in as much detail as necessary. By contrast, a process is transient and must be observed as it occurs. The distinction between product and process evaluation is clarified in Figure 9-12.

Developing scoring procedures involves determining the most appropriate way to record the adequacy of the product, processes or both. Following are guidelines in the form of discussions of techniques for scoring products as well as processes and various types of rating instruments. Test scoring procedures can be based on these guidelines.

Product Rating

The content validity of an MPT generally increases when product ratings are included. This is because of the quantitative standards which can be identified. Since the product, unlike the performance, is a tangible object, product rating is usually more objective and reliable. Additionally, it is usually faster and easier to examine a machined workpiece than it is to rate the process used in machining that product. This is true because precision measuring tools such as a micrometer can be used to objectively measure the end product.

In developing a scoring procedure for a product, all characteristics that distinguish an acceptable product from an unsatisfactory one are identified and described as accurately and specifically as possible.

When the product is to be measured by some type of tool, the characteristics to be measured, such as the shape, must be communicated to the tester along with specific instructions for making the measurement. In addition to measuring tools there are other product rating aids such as templates, overlays, meters, etc. It is possible to examine a product on the basis of observable and measurable criteria and then decide if the standards for successful performance were met.

Process Rating

An effective scoring procedure for process measurement provides the tester with a detailed step-by-step description of the process by which the task is performed. The task elements/steps and required attainment standards are usually prepared in checklist form. The teacher, or some other tester, observes the student's performance and checks whether each step was performed satisfactorily. Item 8.1 on Figure 9-2 suggests a performance checklist format for process rating.

Each task element and step on a performance checklist is labeled when sequence is important and when the step is critical. This is done by placing an "S" before steps which must be performed only after the preceding steps and a "C" before critical steps where failure to meet standards will result in test failure. The interdependence of steps means that an error early in the sequence may have a marked effect on the outcome. Some steps are labeled with both an "S" and a "C." Refer to the procedural checklist on pages 3 and 4 of Appendix 9A.

Regardless of whether the output of tested task performance is a process or product, some form of rating instrument is used. The following sections discuss some of these instruments.

Checklists

This "laundry list" approach to presenting task elements and steps facilitates the recording of observations. It also assures consideration of all important aspects of the performance. Checklists reduce the scoring activity to one of matching or comparing student performance with attainment standards. This makes rating the *acceptability of performance* relatively easy. Moreover, checklists eliminate the need to rely on memory when *rating the ability to perform a set of procedural steps*.

A well-formatted checklist is easy to follow and permits a thorough evaluation. It enables the tester to observe and rate the student on each step without missing any of the ongoing test performance.

Separating the performance into observable task elements/steps greatly reduces the potential for rating errors. Also, the identification of any deficiencies is made easier. The diagnostic information provided on individual students facilitates formal feedback and prescriptive remediation. Such remediation may include an alternative learning activity, tutorial help, and additional practice before retesting.

As a detailed and formal record of student achievement, checklists like the one shown in item 6.0 of Appendix 9A, are used to document competence for vertical articulation (advanced standing in a senior level institution or apprenticeable trade). They also help facilitate proper placement when students change schools or transfer into a related occupational program.

As mentioned, separating the performance into specific procedural steps reduces rating errors. Additionally, when

Output	Evaluation	Examples
	Product	
1. A product which is observable and tangible.	1. The end-product displays success or failure. It can be examined directly and compared to the attainment standards.	1.1 Filled out log book 1.2 Machined workpiece 1.3 Assembled item 1.4 Typed paragraph 1.5 Welded steel pipe
	Process	
2. A procedure which is observable but transient.	2. The performance must be observed and (a) rated directly after it occurs, or (b) recorded by some means, e.g. video tape for later rating.	2.1 Safe driving 2.2 Hiking 2.3 Apprehending a suspect 2.4 Mouth-to-mouth resuscitation

Figure 9-12. Performance evaluation by means of a product or process.

the procedural steps have an observable and measurable attainment standard with only two possible ratings (yes or no), the chance for rating errors or bias is further reduced. Consequently, reliability and objectivity are improved. The more specific the steps and the more precise the attainment standards, the higher the reliability will be.

Rating Scales

Rating scales are somewhat similar to checklists; however, instead of marking "yes" or "no," the teacher rates the degree to which a student exhibits the performance or behavior under observation. Rating scales should be confined to behavioral actions where enough opportunity for observation exists. A lack of multiple observations can reduce both the accuracy and reliability of the evaluation.

Rating scales are uniquely appropriate for evaluating behaviors such as (a) work habits, (b) attitudes, (c) judgment, (d) dependability, and (e) ability to work with others. These behaviors are somewhat difficult to define or describe. In addition to this problem there are seven common rating errors which need to be taken into account.

1. *Contrast error*—rating of students in the opposite direction from the teacher's own perceived ability on a given item.
2. *Error of central tendency*—hesitancy to give extreme ratings, tending to group ratings close to the center of the scale.
3. *Error of leniency*—tendency to rate students known well or liked higher than they should be rated.
4. *Error of standards*—tendency to overrate or underrate because of differences in standards among individual teachers.
5. *Halo effect*—rating too high or too low because of a general impression of a student that has little or nothing to do with the behavior under observation.
6. *Logical error*—giving similar ratings for behaviors that seem related in the mind of the individual making the error.
7. *Proximity error*—making similar ratings for items adjacent on the rating form.

Despite these possible errors, rating scales may be the most effective method available for evaluating certain behaviors. Their usefulness improves when the teacher knows that rating errors exist and takes steps to counteract them.

The two types of rating scales used most frequently in occupational education are the numerical and descriptive scales. A numerical scale divides performance or behavior into a fixed number of points. These points are generally numbered and a qualitative word(s) is used to give each one meaning. The number of points on the scale depends primarily on the teacher's ability to differentiate between them. Most individuals can make at least five differentiations, but even with training only about nine are made reliably. As a result, most numerical scales contain three to seven points. Figure 9-13 shows a four-point numerical scale for rating behaviors.

The descriptive scale uses words or phrases to indicate levels of ability. Figure 9-14 shows a descriptive scale for rating a truck driver. It uses five different words to describe levels of ability. A good choice of words or phrases helps reduce rating errors.

The degrees of performance can vary to suit the occasion. For example, suppose a teacher wants to rate the driving ability of an entire class. All the students satisfy performance requirements, but there is a need to know the degree to which each is better than satisfactory. Additionally, the teacher wants to spark initiative and increase performance quality. By utilizing a descriptive scale, the teacher uses a frame of reference. Here the lowest rating possible is labeled "acceptable."

Semantics is a disadvantage in using descriptive scales. An "excellent truck driver" does not mean the same thing to everyone. Another disadvantage is the difficulty in selecting words and short phrases which describe degrees of performance that are equally spaced in the mind of the tester. When the scale shown in Figure 9-14 is used, some may feel there is more distance between "excellent" and "superior" than between "acceptable" and "fair."

The validity of rating scales cannot be established absolutely unless they include the attainment standards with which the performance is to be compared.

Cutoff Points

When it is impractical to insist on a perfect test score, a cutoff point (dividing line between pass and fail) must be determined. The more complex the skill and the more varied the procedure or product, the greater the danger of designating a "fail" as a "pass" or vice versa.

Establishing cutoff points is a complex matter since there are no universally applicable methods for determining them. Decisions should be reached only after careful consideration of the generally acceptable attainment standards for the tasks. A recommended guideline is that when the consequences of passing one incompetent student are severe, the cutoff point should be set high. In general, cutoffs are useful when:

1. Mastery of the task is not expected but a suitable level of performance (success threshold) can be specified.
2. Mastery is possible but factors other than competence (such as careless errors) affect the score.

Once a cutoff point has been established, test results should be monitored for their meaningfulness in decision making. It is only through constant reappraisal that appropriate cutoff scores can be maintained.

VALIDATION OR VERIFICATION

Regardless of the care a teacher takes in developing, reviewing, and editing an MPT, students may still encounter difficulties with the test and testing situation. Thus the MPT needs to be tried out to determine if unforeseen problems exist. Following the tryout, students are asked to comment on the strengths and weaknesses of the MPT and to make recommendations for its improvement. After all the problems are identified and the necessary modifications are made, the MPT is said to be validated. That is, the students

NAME: ______________________ SSN: __________

DIRECTIONS: Rate each item by circling the number which best describes the degree of observed behavior. The numbers have the following meanings.

1 - Unsatisfactory 2 - Satisfactory 3 - Good 4 - Excellent

1. Industry: Earnest, steady effort, day in and day out 1 2 3 4
2. Cooperation: Willingness to work with others 1 2 3 4
3. Initiative: Ability to plan and direct own work 1 2 3 4
4. Flexibility: When faced with change 1 2 3 4
5. Responsibility: Willingness with which assignments are accepted and performed 1 2 3 4

REMARKS:

Figure 9-13. Numerical scale for rating behaviors.

DIRECTIONS: Place a mark in the box above the word that most accurately describes the truck driver's level of ability.

☐	☐	☐	☐	☐
ACCEPTABLE	FAIR	GOOD	EXCELLENT	SUPERIOR

Figure 9-14. Descriptive scale for rating a truck driver.

who pass the test are those who can perform the task on the job.

MPTs are validated at the workplace when resources permit. If this is done, validation is similar to an occupational (job) analysis performed using the observation technique. Experienced workers are observed performing the task. Their performance is compared with the attainment standards on the MPT checklist or rating scale.

In situations where there are constraints which cannot be overcome, tests are "verified" rather than validated. Incumbent workers, with up-to-date knowledge and skills, are asked to verify the attainment standards, add any missing performance conditions, task elements, or steps, and delete unnecessary ones. They also ensure that the test is technically accurate and consistent with current procedures.

Tryout

The following activities are completed in preparation for conducting a validation tryout.

1. Write student directions and administrative instructions. They must be complete, clear and easily understood; yet they must be reduced to the simplest terms. See Appendix 9A pages 1 and 3.
2. Set the test aside for a day and then edit it. This cooling off period makes it easier to catch composition and grammatical errors.
3. Ask colleagues or others who have the necessary expertise and experience to examine and edit the test. Constructive critics will identify problems which should be corrected before the tryout.
4. Collect all the references and items of equipment, tools, materials, supplies, etc., for administering the test.
5. Perform an operational check on the power-operated equipment.
6. Select students to participate in the tryout. Those chosen for the individual trials should have high aptitudes. Students selected for the small-group trial should represent all those who will take the test (target population).
7. If external testers are to be used, orient them on how to administer the test and observe student performance objectively.

The tryout is conducted in steps. Begin with five individual trials. During each trial, closely observe a single student and tactfully question her or him during the test. Carefully record trouble spots and how much time the student takes. This can be done efficiently by (a) making notes on a copy of the test, (b) using a form designed for this purpose, or (c) dictating into a portable tape recorder. Patterns of error and difficulty, which emerge during successive trials, show where modifications are necessary.

Once the necessary modifications are made and the test appears to be effective, a small-group trial is started. There are no rules for deciding how many students should be in the group. Even so, five to ten may be as many as can be tested at any one time. When detailed information is necessary, a smaller group is preferable. This small-group trial is a check on the success (or failure) of the modifications made. It may also uncover further difficulties. After the small-group trial, revise estimates of time requirements made on the basis of individual performance to reflect average completion time. The cycle of testing and MPT modification is continued until all the significant problems are identified and corrected.

Students participating in the tryout should be told at the outset that the purpose is to help identify problems, not to test their proficiency. They need to understand that if errors are made or difficulties are encountered, it is probably a reflection on the test, not on their ability. Furthermore, once difficulties are identified, the students can make suggestions on how to eliminate them.

The following checklist can be used as a guide for getting information concerning the test.

☐ 1. Are the directions clear and understandable? To make sure, ask the tester and students to explain their understanding of the directions. Emphasize that this process is necessary as a protection against misunderstanding.

☐ 2. Did the students ask for any clarifications? Instructions can be written to answer frequently asked questions.

☐ 3. Were there any accidents?

☐ 4. Were there any breakdowns or damage to tools and equipment?

☐ 5. Was there a shortage of materials and supplies?

☐ 6. If the test is given in a series of stations, were there

any problems in maintaining a smooth flow of students from one test station to the next, or in restoring the stations to pretest conditions for the next student?
- ☐ 7. Did any testing situation occur which may invalidate the results?
- ☐ 8. Did any actions or comments by the tester confuse the students?

Problems uncovered during the tryout provide the basis for a group debriefing. During the debriefing, general agreement can be reached as to what beneficial modifications need to be made. For more detailed procedural information on individual and small-group trials, see Chapter 7.

SUMMARY

Several factors influence the choice between written and manipulative performance tests. First, the task to be learned, when specified in behavioral terms, will suggest how attainment ought to be measured. Apart from being influenced by the action verb used in the task statement, the test should measure precisely what was taught and learned. Asking students to answer questions about a manipulative task instead of having them perform it is not a valid measurement of learning.

Second, performance tests provide a valid and objective measure of student competence that is not biased due to gender, race or other factors. Because of the importance test scores have on a student's future, concern is often raised about test bias.

Third, the proposed use of the information will also affect the choice between written and performance tests. For providing feedback to students, improving individual attainment and enhancing program accountability, MPTs provide a sound and worthwhile technique. Nevertheless, considerable effort is involved in their development and validation.

In addition to pointing out the developmental effort required, uninformed and novice teachers may argue against using performance tests because they take considerable time to administer. This is true especially when only a few students can be tested at a time. However, the problem can be avoided, while simultaneously enhancing program credibility, by involving external testers.

Craft advisory committee members, retirees who are experts in the specialization, workers from the public and private sectors, and other capable volunteers can effectively augment the program by serving as testers. Even paraprofessionals or senior-level students can be used in some cases. This is possible because MPTs are developed in such a way that test administration need no longer be the exclusive responsibility of the teacher.

One additional benefit of MPTs is the potential for adapting them for a secondary purpose. Because of their content and format, MPTs can be made to suit instructional purposes by changing them into *job sheets*. Chapter 7 describes the preparation and use of job sheets, as well as the other forms of instruction sheets.

Since the job sheet is used to facilitate instruction in performing a task and the MPT requires the same performance as that taught, it is clear that a carefully developed MPT is perfectly suited for this secondary purpose. Of course, there is a need for modifications since the MPT is designed to record observed performance.

Among the usual modifications is the need to provide additional instruction and appropriate illustrations for those procedural steps where clarification and elaboration are needed. A good way to identify the need for illustrations and additional explanation is to try the MPT "as is." Supplemental wording and the incorporation of illustrations will depend on information obtained through student trials.

This multiple application of MPT documentation has the added advantage of providing complete public disclosure on the tasks to be learned and performed. Additionally, students who use the job sheet, while learning how to perform a task to standards, can check their own performance capabilities prior to testing. As a result, they are in a good position to perform the task again so that competency can be certified.

There is no need to debate the issue of "teaching the test," or "giving the test away" because it is irrelevant in competency-based education. This is true especially when one remembers that the task, its conditions, and its standards, are identified and described through occupational (job) analysis. Given the need to perform the task for success on the job, it is obvious that both teaching and testing ought to be performance oriented, and that competency is based on proper instruction and opportunities for appropriate practice.

Some teachers tend to evaluate the student's learning activity and certify competence based on this first experience. This is the case, particularly when a product is produced. Evaluating the first experience creates a problem since teachers normally provide guidance, prompts, and other forms of help to facilitate learning. Surely it is evident that at least a second performance, without teacher help, is necessary for certifying competence. Once the principle of evaluating unassisted performance is accepted, the value of using MPTs for testing and their adaptation for instructional purposes becomes apparent.

In conclusion, it must be pointed out that MPTs for a course or program can be developed over a period of time. Often, time doesn't permit the preparation of all MPTs either before or during the first course or program offering. A teacher may be able, however, to get a good start and continue the effort over the years.

APPENDIX 9A

Pipe Welding Test

Student: _____ Tester: _____

Results: Pass ____ Fail ____ Tester's Initials: _____ Date: _____

1.0 **TASK STATEMENT** (Behavioral action)

    1.1 Prepare, weld and inspect pipe.

2.0 **PERFORMANCE CONDITIONS**

    2.1 Setting: Welding shop, actual equipment under simulated work conditions.

    2.2 Tools: (a) Slag chipping hammer, (b) Wire brush, (c) Tape measure, (d) Ball peen hammer, (e) Steel stamps, (f) Double-cut file, (g) Protractor, (h) Combination gauge, and (i) Flashlight.

    2.3 Equipment: (a) Safety glasses, (b) Welding gloves, (c) Face shield for grinding, (d) Bench vice, (e) C-clamps, (f) Portable disc grinder, (g) Metal cutting band saw, (h) Oxy-fuel cutting equipment, (i) Welding helmet with ultraviolet shield, and (j) Welding machine with volt and amp meters, leads, and ground.

    2.4 Materials and Supplies: (a) Carbon steel pipe, and (b) Electrodes.

    2.5 References: (a) American Welding Society (AWS) Structural Welding Code D1.1, herein referred to as the Code, and (b) Welding Procedure Specification, herein referred to as the WPS, see Attachment A, Page 2 of 5.

3.0 **ATTAINMENT STANDARDS**

    3.1 In accordance with the qualitative as well as other requirements of the Code and the WPS, to be completed within seven hours, without assistance.

4.0 **STUDENT DIRECTIONS**

    4.1 The attached WPS, the above referenced tools, equipment, and materials and supplies shall be used to prepare, weld and inspect carbon steel pipe. The preparation, welding and inspection of test coupons will be evaluated by the tester using the Code and the WPS. Completed coupons will be inspected and tested under Code paragraphs 5.26 through 5.28. Steps must be performed safely and in the proper sequence. All performance must meet standards for the test results to be considered a "pass".

(Continued)

APPENDIX 9A

WELDING PROCEDURE QUALIFICATION TEST RECORD

PROCEDURE SPECIFICATION

Material specification ___A 106   Grade B___
Welding process ___Shielded Metal Arc Welding (SMAW)___
Manual or machine ___MANUAL___
Position of welding ___6G___
Filler metal specification ___E-7018___
Filler metal classification ___SFA 5.1___
Weld metal grade* ___N/A___
Shielding gas ___N/A___ Flow rate ___N/A___
Single or multiple pass ___Multiple___
Single or multiple arc ___Single___
Welding current ___20-25___
Welding progression ___Upward___
Preheat temperature ___60___
Postheat treatment ___N/A___
Welder's name ___Phil Collins, Stencil C___

*Applicable when filler metal has no
 AWS classification.

VISUAL INSPECTION (9.25.1)

Appearance ___Acceptable___
Undercut ___None___
Piping porosity ___None___

Test date ___1 January 19___
Witnessed by ___Tim Hatcher___

GROOVE WELD TEST RESULTS

Reduced-section tension tests
Tensile strength, psi
1. ___78,300___
2. ___77,800___

Guided-bend tests (2 root-, 2 face-, or 4 side-bend)

	Root		Face
1.	OK	1.	OK
2.	OK	2.	OK

Radiographic-ultrasonic examination

RT report no. _____
UT report no. _____

FILLET WELD TEST RESULTS

Minimum size multiple pass Macroetch
1. ___ 3. ___
2. ___

Maximum size single pass Macroetch
1. ___ 3. ___
2. ___

All-weld-metal tension test

Tensile strength, psi _____
Yield point/strength, psi _____
Elongation in 2 in., % _____
Laboratory test no. _____

WELDING PROCEDURE

Pass No.	Elect. size	Welding current Amperes	Volts	Speed of travel	Joint detail
ALL	1/8"	80-150	20-25	2-8 IPM	30° 1/8 INCH MAX. 1/8 INCH MAX. 6" DIA. SCHEDULE 80 STL. PIPE

We, the undersigned, certify that the statements in this record are correct and that the test welds were prepared, welded, and tested in accordance with the requirements of 4E and 5B of AWS D1.1, (_____) Structural Welding Code.
year

Procedure no. _____
Revision no. ___0___

Manufacturer or contractor ___TAE Corporation___
Authorized by ___C.P. Campbell___
Date ___1 January 19___

(Continued)

5.0 ADMINISTRATIVE INSTRUCTIONS

5.1 Tester Directions: This test is based upon the criteria referenced in the Code and the WPS. The student is to demonstrate the ability to perform welding skills and produce sound welds by preparing, welding and inspecting test coupons from carbon steel pipe. Test coupons shall be inspected and tested in accordance with AWS D1.1, paragraphs 5.26, 5.27, and 5.28. The WPS is to be utilized for those task elements/steps not specified in the Code.

Prior to the test: (a) insure that the referenced tools, equipment, and materials and supplies are available; and (b) perform an operational check of the equipment. Give a copy of the first page to the student(s) and read the directions aloud. Answer all questions before beginning the test.

Do not provide assistance during the test, but monitor progress to prevent personal injury or equipment damage. Written comments on test administration and student performance may be recorded in the Comments section on the last page of this test.

5.2 Scoring Procedure: Unobtrusively observe the student's performance of each task element/step. Mark the **YES** column if the standard was attained, and **NO** if it was not. Procedural steps in the process are to be rated directly after they are performed. Do not rely on your memory. All standards must be met in order for the test results to be considered a "pass". Mark the results, pass or fail, on the first page and initial your determination.

6.0 CHECKLIST

6.1 (S) Important Sequence: This step must be performed only after the preceding steps.

6.2 (C) Critical Step: Failure to meet the standard for this step will end the test.

Process

TASK ELEMENTS/STEPS	STANDARDS	YES	NO
1. Select Base Material	• As referenced in the WPS: 6" diameter schedule 80 ASTM A 106 Grade B carbon steel pipe.	—	—
2. (S,C) Cut pipe to length	• Two pieces, minimum 3" long.	—	—
3. (S,C) Prepare pipe end	• Beveled ends to 30 degree (37 1/2 degree maximum) angles. • Maximum land thickness 1/8".	—	—
4. (S,C) Tack & maintain root opening	• Maximum root opening 1/8".	—	—
5. (C) Stamp welder identification	• Stamped assigned identifier steel stencil stamp adjacent to weld every 6" of linear weld.	—	—

(Continued)

TASK ELEMENTS/STEPS	STANDARDS	YES NO
6. (S,C) Position assembly for welding	◉ 6G (inclined fixed) 45 degree angle, plus/minus 5 degrees.	__ __
7. (C) Select type & size of filler material	◉ As referenced in the WPS: Electrode SFA 5.1, F-4 1/8" diameter.	__ __
8. (C) Select amperage & current	◉ As referenced in the WPS: direct current, reverse polarity, 80-150 amperes.	__ __
9. (S,C) Maintain welding progression	◉ As referenced in WPS: Upward or Uphand progression.	__ __
10. (S,C) Clean & visually inspect root pass prior to deposition of subsequent passes	◉ As referenced in the Code paragraph 5.28.5.4: There shall be no evidence of (a) cracks, (b) incomplete fusion, or (c) inadequate joint penetration. ◉ Maximum root surface concavity shall be 1/16" with 1/8" maximum melt-thru, provided the total weld thickness is equal to or greater than that of the base material.	__ __
11. (S,C) Clean & visually inspect each pass, & complete weld	◉ As referenced in the Code paragraph 5.28.5: (a) there shall be no cracks; (b) all craters shall be filled to the full cross section of the weld; (c) face of the weld shall be at least flush with outside surface of the pipe; and (d) the weld shall merge smoothly with the base material. ◉ Undercut shall not exceed 1/64". ◉ Weld reinforcement shall not exceed 1/8".	__ __

Product

SCORABLE CHARACTERISTICS	STANDARDS	YES NO
1. (C) Guided bend tests	◉ In accordance with the criterion set forth in the Code: (1) Root, face & side bend welds & heat-affected zones shall be within the bent portion of the specimen after testing.	__ __

(Continued)

SCORABLE CHARACTERISTICS	STANDARDS	YES NO
	(2) Guided bend specimens shall have no open defects exceeding 1/8", measured in any direction on the convex surface of the specimen after bending, except that cracks occurring on the corners during testing shall not be considered, unless there is definite evidence that they result from slag inclusions or other internal defects.	— —

7.0 **COMMENTS**

202 Improving Vocational Curriculum

Chapter 10

SAFETY AND LIABILITY

by

Richard K. Crosby, Professor
Occupational Education
The University of Louisville
Louisville, Kentucky

INTRODUCTION

Safety is one element of instruction that remains constant. Job descriptions, tasks, and procedures may change, but safety is and will always be a very important part of the curriculum. It is the responsibility of every occupational teacher to include those things in the curriculum guide that facilitate safety when working with tools, machinery, and materials. This responsibility requires teachers to be sure that the curriculum guide contains appropriate content to continually teach, reinforce, and evaluate safety. Every part of the curriculum guide must include items that give safety a high priority in instruction.

STUDENTS

Students have a wide range of abilities, needs, and interests. They may be very capable, average, or below average. Students may cooperate with the teacher or be difficult to teach. Student's interests may parallel the course or program offering. Some students enroll at the urging of friends. Others are there through direct placement by school personnel. For these and other reasons, it is difficult to determine how students will react to the teacher, the content of the program, or the instruction. The curriculum must take into consideration a variety of student characteristics, actions, and reactions. There may not be a second chance to modify instruction to ensure the safety of students.

Most students new to an occupational program lack skills and knowledge necessary in the training area. They have been accustomed to trying, failing, and trying again in other school subjects. This approach may result in success or walking away and allowing someone else to assume responsibility. Of course, such behavior cannot be allowed in an occupational program. The curriculum must be structured so students learn to accomplish all tasks safely. They must learn to assume responsibilities for safe actions in completing assigned tasks. Students must learn to change their attitudes about safe working procedures.

Along with being able to work safely, students must develop attitudes which keep them safe throughout the training program. Many times students enter programs with the attitude that safety is for someone else; nothing can or will happen to them. Also, they tend to believe that they have the ability to operate machinery and equipment with which they are unfamiliar. These attitudes must be changed. Students must learn to think about safety continuously and to act safely in all training situations.

An important goal in the instructional program is to keep students free from accidents and injury while they are enrolled. Much of the curriculum guide is designed so that students learn how to be safe in all aspects of instruction. A long-term goal is to develop a safety consciousness that helps students act safely in school, when away from school, and on the job. This requires careful preparation of the curriculum guide so that students are taught to assume responsibility for their actions, as well as to understand why safe procedures must be followed.

TEACHER

Student safety in a training program depends, to a large extent, on the ability of the teacher. The teacher must understand why safety is important and accept safety as a focus of instruction. From the moment students enter a laboratory until the time they leave, safety must be considered. This is accomplished by the development of a complete curriculum guide that includes safety instruction throughout the entire document. If safety guards are required on a machine, the teacher must include complete and thorough safety instruction about safety guards. If a safety lesson is needed, the teacher develops and includes the lesson in the curriculum guide. For every item in the curriculum guide, the teacher must ask, "Is there some safety principle that should and could be taught effectively at this point?" A teacher with a positive attitude about safety and dedication to a safe learning environment can develop a complete safety program. This prepares students to be safe in school and on the job.

FACILITY

Safety instruction, as stipulated in the curriculum guide, must be matched with a laboratory that is planned with safety as an important consideration. The laboratory must meet federal, state, and local standards. Safety guards must be on machines. Personal protective equipment must be available in sufficient quantities for use by all. Hand tools must be in proper locations and stored safely. All areas of the laboratory must be clean, well organized, and maintained to make instruction as safe as possible. These physical features aid the teacher in ensuring that the curriculum guide is complete with safety instruction.

SCHOOL POLICIES

The beginning of the course or program is an important time for the teacher to implement safety. Students typically want to get started using all the tools and equipment in the training area as soon as possible. To deal with this situation, students are told that the teacher must give permission before any tools or equipment are used. This is followed by instruction that focuses on safety and allows students to participate in activities that encourage safety practices.

School policies are a starting point for instruction. These policies ought to be presented to students, discussed, and enforced throughout the school year. They are also the basis for developing other more specific rules.

Figure 10-1 provides examples of school safety policies. A number of these rules are designed to prevent tripping, falling, fires, and smoke contamination. Other rules dictate appropriate clothing, standards for hair length, and eye protection requirements. A rule prohibiting "horseplay," one of the leading causes of accidents, is listed.

Rules, such as those in Figure 10-1, are found in manuals issued to students the first week of school. The teacher should go over the rules carefully to be sure students know what they must do to be safe. Since the rules are very general, it is necessary to explain how they relate to student well-being. It should be noted that many of the rules will be observed only if the teacher provides adequate supervision.

Some schools have separate policies for the use of machinery in laboratories. These policies should be used with specific rules that have been developed for individual machines. Figure 10-2 displays a sampling of machine-use policies.

GUIDELINES FOR DEVELOPING RULES

It is necessary to include both general and specific safety rules in the curriculum guide. These rules relate to machinery, activities, materials, conduct, and procedures that are particular to a course or program.

Some of the general rules listed in the student manual apply to the program and should be included in the curriculum guide. Also, rules from other programs can be

---

A. BUILDING
1. Smoking is strictly prohibited anywhere in the building.
2. No littering of:
   a. break area
   b. halls
   c. classrooms
   d. shop area
   e. building grounds
   f. bathrooms
3. All aisles, work areas, and floors will be kept clear of any loose material, grease, and other waste material that might cause tripping or falling.
4. Work areas, machinery, and floors will be cleaned or swept daily before the end of class.
5. First aid kits shall be kept adequately supplied. All first aid areas shall be properly marked or color coded.
6. There is a place for everything and everything must be in its place.

B. STUDENT BEHAVIOR
1. Students shall display proper behavior in classroom and shop areas, outside the building, and on school buses.
2. Avoid horseplay anywhere on school property.
3. No loitering is permitted inside or outside the building.
4. No one will leave the classroom, shop area, and/or school property without permission and signing out.
5. Students will provide evidence that they have accident insurance coverage.
6. Each student will be assigned a specific job and is expected to continue working at that job throughout the period. Students will not wander throughout the laboratory.
7. Students are to remain at work until the cleanup bell rings.
8. Sitting on desks or tables is not permitted.
9. All students must provide coveralls or work clothes suitable for laboratory work.
10. Students with long hair must wear a tightly fitting cap or hair net when operating any machine having exposed revolving parts.

C. OTHER SAFETY POLICIES
1. Each student will wear safety glasses, goggles, or face shield when required by the task to be accomplished.
2. All safety rules and policies are posted on the bulletin board.
3. Fire drill procedures are posted with all fire exits marked. Fire drills are practiced regularly.

Figure 10-1. Examples of school policies.

---

1. **Instruction for using machine tools**
   Before a student is permitted to operate a machine, the teacher must give a written examination covering the essential technical knowledge and safe practices involved in use of the machine. Records showing the satisfactory completion of the examination must be kept on file.

2. **Supervision of students in a laboratory or classroom**
   The teacher must remain in the laboratory or classroom area at all times when students are present.

3. **Authorization to operate certain machines**
   The occupational teacher, with the approval of the principal, may request authorization from parents to instruct specified students on the operation of machines considered especially hazardous. The approval will be given under the following conditions and restrictions.
   The student must have demonstrated reliability and stability during one semester of instruction in the laboratory. The student must be 16 years of age or older. The operation of these machines must be a necessary part of the instructional program in the course.

4. **Prohibiting certain students to use machines**
   The teacher of any occupational class may prohibit a student from using certain machines. When this occurs, the teacher will discuss the reasons for this action with the student.

5. **Guards on machinery**
   The guards that have been installed on any machine and that are defined as a part of the machine when it was inspected and approved may not be removed while such machine is being used by students.

Figure 10-2. Policies regarding machine use.

---

found and utilized. There may be rules from this publication that can be modified and used. Often rules are needed that are not found elsewhere. These rules must be developed, placed in the curriculum guide, and posted. The following suggestions will help develop and implement safety rules.

1. Write rules so they are clear and easily understood by students. This may require involving students in the writing and evaluation of the rules.
2. Select rules that are essential to student safety. If rules are selected that are of little concern to students and teacher, they might be ignored.
3. Make as few rules as possible. The fewer rules, the easier it will be to enforce them.
4. Enforce all rules. A rule, once adopted, must be worthy of enforcement. Make a plan for enforcement that is understood by students.
5. The teacher must follow the same rules as students. If she or he does not, the students will also probably fail to follow them.
6. Keep rules uppermost in the instruction for the whole training program. Rules are not something to be looked at once and forgotten. They must be presented, enforced, discussed, and re-discussed frequently. Students must recognize that the rules are part of the instructional program. Be sure to include the necessary rules in the curriculum guide.
7. Students should be rewarded for following the rules. The teacher will usually call attention to broken rules. Also, something positive should be said when rules are followed. Positive reinforcement will cause students to become more eager to follow the rules.

---

1. Horseplay, running, and throwing of objects are dangerous practices in the laboratory and are forbidden at all times.
2. Students are to operate only those machines for which they have received instruction and permission to operate.
3. All students are responsible for cleaning up after themselves.
4. When using machines or hand tools, direct all your attention to the job you are performing.
5. Loose clothing, jewelry, and gloves are not to be worn while operating any power equipment.
6. Avoid talking to any student who is operating a machine or performing work.
7. Eye protection must be worn when demanded by the task to be accomplished.
8. Do not lean on machines.
9. Make repairs on laboratory equipment only when permission has been given. Do not tamper with laboratory equipment.
10. If the equipment is not operating properly, shut it off and tell the teacher at once.
11. Cloths and rags containing flammable materials are to be placed in a covered metal container.
12. Only one student is to operate any one piece of equipment. Two students are not permitted to be within the marked safety zone of any piece of equipment.
13. All machine adjustments should be made when the machine is stopped.
14. When in doubt ask the teacher. Do not depend on other students for advice.

I have read and understand these guidelines set forth by the teacher. It is understood that I am to cooperate fully.

SIGNATURE OF STUDENT_____

DATE _____

Figure 10-3. Sample of general rules.

GENERAL RULES

It is important for students in an occupational program to conduct themselves in the appropriate manner. Figure 10-3 indicates examples of general safety rules to include in a curriculum guide. One way to ensure that students have read and understood the rule requirements is to have them sign a statement to that effect. Note such a statement at the bottom of Figure 10-3.

SAFETY RULES FOR MACHINERY

Along with school policies and general rules, it may be necessary to teach rules for particular machinery. This is especially true where machinery plays a very important part, such as in carpentry, machine shop, sheet metal, and printing. Figure 10-4 is an example of safety instructions for using the circular saw. The teacher must be sure to include all

---

1. Thoroughly examine the machine visually before turning on the power.
2. The guard must be kept down over the work while machine is being operated.
3. The saw blade must not be raised above the table to a height more than 1/8 in. above the thickness of the stock.
4. The usual position for the operator is at the left of the blade. **Never** stand directly behind the blade when feeding stock.
5. A push stick must be used when ripping pieces of lumber of 5 in. or less in width.
6. The clearance block must be fastened to the fence when cutting off short pieces of stock.
7. The fence must not be adjusted until the saw blade has completely stopped.
8. Fingers must be kept clear of the saw track and hands must never cross the saw line in advance of the end of the board while machine is in operation.
9. All special setups, dado heads, and molding heads must be inspected by the teacher before power is turned on.
10. Students must never attempt to clear away scraps close to the saw blade with their fingers. If necessary, to remove them, they should be pushed away with a stick at least two feet long.
11. The dado head and molding head must be taken off the saw after use.
12. When helping to "tailoff" the saw, students must never pull on the board being ripped. They should hold the board up and allow the operator to push stock through saw.
13. Re-sawing must not be done on a circular saw without the teacher's permission.
14. Cylindrical stock must not be cut on the circular saw.
15. Never lower pieces of stock down over the saw blade.
16. Ripping stock without using the ripping fence or crosscutting stock without using the miter gauge is extremely dangerous and absolutely forbidden.
17. Check that no fence or setup will be in line of saw before starting work or turning on power.
18. Before turning on power, be sure that the saw blade on the tilting arbor will clear on both sides.
19. Do not do any angle cutting with tilt in arbor without special permission from the teacher.
20. Stock that is warped so that it will not rest solidly upon the saw table should not be ripped. Stock which is "cupped" but otherwise straight may be sawed with the concave side down.
21. Plan ahead so that everything necessary (push stick, helper, etc.) will be available when needed.

I, the undersigned, have read and understand these safety rules.

SIGNATURE OF STUDENT _____DATE_____

SIGNATURE OF PARENT_____DATE_____

Figure 10-4. Safety rules for a circular saw.

aspects of safety using the saw. Also, a space is left at the end of the form for the student and parent to sign. Parental understanding is important when trying to communicate safety instructions. Giving parents the opportunity to

understand what is required in the operation of a machine may prevent problems.

The teacher may combine safety rules for a particular machine with descriptions of what could occur if they are not followed. This idea is used during instruction by providing such information before or during operation of a machine. An example of the safety instruction for an engine lathe, with related descriptions, is shown in Figure 10-5.

In some occupations it is necessary to enforce safety rules relating to both the tasks of the trade and materials used to accomplish those tasks. Appendix 10A shows a listing of safety rules for a welding program.

HAND TOOL SAFETY

It is also important to include hand tool safety in the curriculum guide. More persons are injured each year with hand tools than with machine equipment. While the injuries may be less serious than machine-related injuries, they are a more persistent safety problem.

Hand tool safety should be included with other training instruction. If students develop safe work habits with hand tools, they will become more aware of other aspects of

---

1. Use the engine lathe only after the following items are inspected and approved.
    a. The adjustments of the lathe are checked by turning the work over by hand.
    b. The tool post is set as close as possible to left side of compound rest.
    c. The carriage is run back to determine if the complete cut can be made without hitting the lathe dog or chuck.
    d. The chuck key is removed.
    e. The guards are in place.
2. Put hands in the correct position when adjusting the tool bit with a wrench.
CAUTION:
    The hands must not pass over the cutting tool, the work, and parts of the lathe when the tool post and tool holder are tightened. Injuries occur when the lathe operator is careless about how the hands are placed on the wrench.
3. Use a brush to remove metal cuttings and chips.
CAUTION:
    Shavings are sharp and can cut the hands. Those close to the tool bit may be hot enough to cause blisters. Avoid cuts and blisters by using a brush.
4. Always stop the lathe when changing or setting the tool bit.
5. Never throw in the back gears when changing or setting the tool bit.
6. Shift the feed screw to neutral when the work being done in the lathe does not require its use.
7. Do not touch revolving work with the hands.
CAUTION:
    Students with no experience in metalworking often want to touch the work with their fingers. Sharp ridges and burrs can cause serious cuts when touching. Metal shavings should not be cleaned out of a hole with the fingers. No work should be touched with the machine running.
8. Oil should never be wiped from knurled stock with the fingers.
CAUTION:
    Sharp burrs left by a knurling tool will cut the skin. Once the lathe has stopped, remove oil with a cloth.
9. Wear eye protection with side shields for all lathe work.
CAUTION:
    Cast iron is especially dangerous, because the scrap does not curl up in a continuous piece but breaks into small chips. These fly off and might become lodged in the eye.
10. Do not lean on the lathe.
CAUTION:
    It is convenient to lean against the lathe. Also, there may be a long wait for a cut and leaning against the lathe seems natural. However, this practice may result in clothing being caught or the body may be caught by moving parts. This could result in very serious injury.
11. Stand with your face a safe distance from the work.
CAUTION:
    Students find the action of the cutting tools to be interesting and often lean over the work to watch the work more closely. It is not safe to put your face near the work, because chips and shavings, may fly toward your face.
12. Cloths and waste must be kept away from the work.
CAUTION:
    A wiping cloth is convenient for wiping oil from hands and from the work. The cloth should not touch the revolving work or moving parts of the machine. The cloth could become tangled in the moving parts and could draw the operator's hands into the machinery with the cloth. This is a frequent accident in the shop and great care should be taken to ensure that the cloth is not caught in the machinery.

Figure 10-5. Safety rules for the engine lathe.

General Safety Rules

1. **Do not** use pliers for cutting hardened wire unless the pliers are specifically manufactured for this purpose.
2. **Never** expose pliers to excessive heat. This will draw the temper and ruin the tool.
3. **Do not** attempt to repair pliers that are cracked, broken, sprung, or have nicked cutting blades.
4. **Never** extend the length of handles to secure greater leverage. Use larger pliers or a bolt cutter.
5. Always cut at right angles. **Never** rock the tool from side to side or bend wire back and forth against the cutting blades.
6. Pliers **should not** be used on nuts or bolts. A wrench will do a better job with less risk of damage to the fastener.
7. Oil pliers occasionally. A drop of oil at the hinge will lengthen tool life and ensure easy operation.
8. **Never** use pliers as a hammer. Never hammer on the handles. They may crack and break, or blades may become nicked.
9. Wear safety glasses while cutting wire or other objects to protect against being struck by loose material.
10. Be sure you know the proper use of the various kinds of pliers.
11. Ordinary plastic-dipped pliers are designed for comfort, not for protection against electrical shock.
12. Be careful to avoid dropping pliers on hard surfaces. Damaged pliers are unsafe.

Safety Rules for Specific Pliers

1. Bend stiff wire using appropriate pliers.
2. Pry or twist materials with appropriate tool.
3. Use end nippers for cutting off wires. **Do not** use them to cut nails or bolts.

Figure 10-6. Safety in using pliers.

---

1. An oral warning from the teacher will be given to any student for a safety violation.
2. Any student committing the same safety violation twice, will receive a written warning. Copies of the warning will be sent to the parents as well as to the principal's office.
3. Any student committing the same safety violation three times, will be sent to the principal's office with a recommendation that he or she be removed permanently from the course.

Figure 10-7. A safety enforcement policy.

safety. Hand tool safety handouts can be developed for wrenches, socket wrenches, pliers, screwdrivers, striking tools, hammering tools, snips, clamps, vises, etc. The sample handout in Figure 10-6 shows rules that could be included in the curriculum guide.

ENFORCING RULES

Compliance with safety rules is a must in order to maintain safe instruction. The student must understand the rules and the consequences of failing to follow them. Figure 10-7 is an example of a safety rule enforcement procedure used at a vocational school.

DOCUMENTATION OF SAFETY INSTRUCTIONS

One way to indicate that students have read and understood safety instructions is to have them sign a safety pledge. Refer to Figure 10-8.

It may be to a teacher's advantage to let the parents know what the student is doing and to point out the dangers associated with machine operation. Figure 10-9 is an addition to a pledge, allowing involvement of the parents. A parent's signature is proof that he or she is aware the child is using machines.

Some instructors have students earn permission cards to operate machines. This creates student competition to learn how to operate machines safely and become the first "licensed" machine operator. Figure 10-10 is an example of a permission card that may be used to motivate students.

I have read the safety instructions regarding the operation of the following power-driven machines. I fully understand the importance of the rules and regulations, and I am aware that the violation of any one of them is likely to cause injury to myself and others.

(Teacher's Name) has demonstrated to me the proper method of using each listed machine and has pointed out the danger of violating any of the safety instructions. (Teacher's name) has taught me how to avoid injury by observing the safety instructions and using the machines properly.

I have demonstrated my ability to use each of the machines listed in the safety record in the presence of (Teacher's Name). I passed with 100% accuracy the written test covering the material listed in the safety record.

I understand how to avoid injury through the proper use of the machine. I am confident that I can operate this machine without injury to myself and others.

I have read the above statements and promise to observe the safety instruction and to follow the instruction given in the demonstrations. I understand that if I use a machine, I do so at my own risk.

STUDENT SIGNATURE_____DATE_____

TEACHER SIGNATURE_____DATE_____

Figure 10-8. Example of a safety pledge.

(Note: The pledge content, such as in Figure 10-8, is listed here)

I have passed the tests covering safety in the shop and have demonstrated my ability to use the following machines:

NAME OF MACHINE	DATE	STUDENT'S SIGNATURE	TEACHER'S INITIALS
1.			
2.			
3.			
4.			
5.			

(List as many machines as needed)

I promise to observe the safety instructions and to follow the instructions given in the demonstration. I may use the machines only after I have been properly instructed in their safe use and have had the approval of the teacher.

SCHOOL _____SIGNED _____
(student)

DATE _____SIGNED _____
(teacher)

PARENT OR GUARDIAN:
This form is being sent home for your review and signature to allow you to see your child's progress. Upon return, it will be placed in his or her course records for future reference.

DATE _____SIGNED _____
(parent or guardian)

Figure 10-9. Acknowledgement of safety instruction and pledge.

Front of Card

PERMISSION TO USE MACHINES
_____has studied the safety information, satisfactorily passed the test on school laboratory safety, has observed the teacher's demonstration, and has used the machine identified on the back of the card under teacher supervision.

DATE_____

Back of Card

_____has my permission

to operate the _____

SIGNED_____
(parent or guardian)

SIGNED_____
(teacher)

DATE_____

Figure 10-10. Permission card.

This card certifies that

_____

has successfully passed the operating and safety tests of the machines checked below:

DATE _____   _____
teacher

_____Radial Arm Saw   _____Belt/Disk

_____Bandsaw   _____Circular Saw

Figure 10-11. Permission card to use machines.

Figure 10-11 is a permission card popular with teachers. This card has an advantage over other cards because it lists more than one machine.

Figure 10-12 shows a parental permit slip. This form gives parents the opportunity to list the doctor preferred in case of an accident. Before adopting this slip, teachers should investigate school policy to check the procedures required for calling a physician.

Name _____

has my permission to operate the machines and tools in the laboratory

for the year 19_____ -19_____

In case of an accident we prefer medical treatment be received from:

DR./HOSPITAL _____

ADDRESS _____

_____

PHONE _____

Figure 10-12. Parent's permit slip.

MACHINE OPERATOR'S LICENSE

STUDENT'S NAME _____

CIRCULAR SAW

_____	Rip	_____	Crosscut
_____	Groove	_____	Rabbet
_____	Dado	_____	Resaw
_____	Miter	_____	Cut Tenons
_____	Taper	_____	Spline Miter
_____	Slip Feather Miter	_____	Bevel

CIRCULAR SAW

_____	Chamfer	_____	Cut Molding
_____	Tongue & Groove		

OTHER MACHINES

_____	Jig Saw	_____	Sander
_____	Drill Press	_____	_____
_____	_____	_____	_____
_____	_____	_____	_____

BAND SAW

_____	Rip	_____	Crosscut
_____	Bevel	_____	Chamfer
_____	Stop Chamfer	_____	Taper
_____	Multiple Saw	_____	Compound Saw
_____	Miter	_____	Saw Curves
_____	Resaw	_____	Coil Blade

Figure 10-13. Machine operator's license.

On some machines it is necessary to give approval for specific operations. Figure 10-13 is an approval form that is used as an operator's license. Calling the form a license gives students an incentive to qualify for all operations. The teacher initials the form before each operation and fills in the date when the student qualified for a particular operation.

SAFETY TESTS

A teacher needs to be sure students know the safe way to operate equipment. Tests are a way to determine whether or not students understand what has been presented. Once administered, scored, and discussed, tests are kept on file as evidence of student progress. In most cases, the student must attain 100% accuracy on a machine-related test before being allowed to operate that machine.

The teacher decides the type of test to be used. There are a variety from which to choose. Figure 10-14 shows a multiple-choice test. This is a good type to use.

True or false questions are also used for safety tests. This type takes less time to read and complete than others. This is an advantage for students who have reading problems. True-false items are quickly scored and can be promptly returned to students. By reviewing their corrected safety tests, students can learn and retain a large portion of the information.

One problem with the true-false test is that students have a 50% chance of answering correctly by guessing. This factor is a disadvantage when used only for grading purposes and presents concern about the knowledge students actual-

Directions: Each of the following is an incomplete statement followed by four possible responses of which only *one* is correct or the *best* choice. Place the letter of your selection on the corresponding blank space to the left of each item number. Each item is worth one (1) point, for a total of five (5) points in this section.

_____ 1. The blueprint machine must be connected to a voltage source of:
    A. 24 volts.
    B. 115 volts.
    C. 220 volts.
    D. 480 volts.

_____ 2. 115 volts is:
    A. a low and safe level.
    B. dangerous to humans.
    C. of no concern to operators.
    D. not a safety factor.

_____ 3. Inhaling ammonia vapors from the print machine can cause:
    A. coughing.
    B. dizziness.
    C. sneezing.
    D. unconsciousness.

_____ 4. If the paper jams in the rollers:
    A. pull paper back through feed rollers.
    B. call the teacher.
    C. keep machine running.
    D. ask a classmate for help.

_____ 5. If the machine doesn't sound right:
    A. keep going until the machine breaks down.
    B. ignore the noise and keep working.
    C. make a note of the problem.
    D. call the teacher.

Figure 10-14. Multiple-choice safety test.

Directions: Read each statement carefully, then determine if it is true or false. If the statement is true, circle the letter "T"; if false, circle the letter "F". There is no penalty for guessing. Each item is worth one (1) point, for a total of six (6) points.

Safety and the Portable Electric Hand Drill

T F 1. The cable of a drill must be checked for frayed wires before using.

T F 2. New drills are safe to use while standing in water.

T F 3. The chuck key must be removed from the chuck before operating the drill.

T F 4. The operator of a drill may put as much pressure on the drill as necessary.

T F 5. Overheating of a drill is normal.

T F 6. Sparking of the drill must be reported to the teacher.

Figure 10-15. True or false safety test.

Directions: For each of the following statements, place an "S" if the statement represents a safe act or a "U" if the statement represents an unsafe act. Use only one of the two responses (the best one). Each of the statements is worth one (1) point, for a total of fifteen (15) points.

_____ 1. To hold stock in a vise when drilling holes with the drill press.

_____ 2. To brush chips away from the moving drill with the forefinger.

_____ 3. To keep long hair away from the drill press spindle by keeping it tied back or covered.

_____ 4. To leave a key in the drill press chuck.

_____ 5. To wear eye protection.

_____ 6. To keep the long end of material being drilled to the left of the operator.

_____ 7. To wear loose-fitting clothes while operating a drill press.

_____ 8. To talk to someone while operating the drill press.

_____ 9. To use caution when you must reach around a revolving bit.

_____ 10. To use dull drill bits.

_____ 11. To force the drill through the work as fast as possible.

_____ 12. To operate the drill at top speed on all types of work.

_____ 13. To try to stop a piece of work caught on the drill bit.

_____ 14. To wear gloves to protect yourself from burns.

_____ 15. To drill into a container that may have contained gasoline or inflammable liquids or materials

I have taken the above exam and have correctly answered the questions. I have successfully demonstrated the safe operation of the drill press with my teacher's supervision. I promise to conduct myself in such a fashion that I will not create hazards that may cause injury to others or myself while working in the laboratory.

SIGNED: _____ (student)

_____ (teacher)

_____ (date)

Figure 10-16. Drill press safety test.

ly have about safety. Figure 10-15 shows several true or false questions from a safety test.

One problem common to both true-false and multiple-choice questions is that students who respond incorrectly may believe their answers to be correct. The negative effect of this belief is lessened by using a type of test that allows a discussion after students select their choice for an answer. Figure 10-16 is an example of a test of this type. Note that a statement for the student to sign is at the bottom of the page. After this test is taken and corrected, it is discussed and filed for future reference.

It may be better to give tests designed to be discussed. The test in Figure 10-17 requires students to write out their answers. These responses are discussed with the students afterward.

LESSON PLANS ON SAFETY

Occupational teachers typically have many years of work experience and have dealt with safety in all aspects of their work. This safety experience is used to determine when and how instructional activities will be offered. The teacher must take every opportunity available to teach and reinforce safety. Entire safety lessons may need to be taught on one topic. The teacher should also incorporate safety at key points in skill lessons that deal with the use of machines, tools, or procedures. Whatever the lesson, the instructor must always discuss the safe way of performing tasks.

It is necessary to establish safety consciousness early in a course or program. Students who are unskilled or unfamiliar with the proper ways to conduct themselves must learn enough safety to start hands-on activities.

Figure 10-18 is a sample lesson plan for safety in a graphic arts program. Note that the Preparation stage deals with safety while getting attention, creating interest, and explaining why the lesson is important. Many aspects of safety are covered. Step B of the Presentation stage addresses horseplay, reporting accidents, safety in working alone, slipping, security, ventilation, and lighting. Other steps in the presentation discuss safety glasses, the use of chemicals, fire

Directions: The test items that follow are essay questions which require you to decide what response is needed and to outline your response in complete sentences and paragraphs, using correct spelling and occupational terms involved. Sentence structure and legible written expression should be neat and grammatically correct; however, no points will be deducted for error in these factors. The point value for each of these items corresponds to major content information, and each item has a specified point value for a total of 14 points on this section of the exam.

1. Describe how to clamp angle iron in a vise for sawing.
2. Describe how to clamp 1/4" x 1" stock in a vise.
3. What is the shortest length of stock that can be safely cut with the saw?
4. Does the saw cut on the pull or push stroke? Why?
5. How do you replace a blade after the cut in the stock has been started?
6. Does aluminum, brass, or mild steel require more pressure on the saw?
7. Why is it necessary to use cutting lubricant?

Figure 10-17. Power hacksaw safety test.

TEACHER: Dean Tucker
LESSON TITLE: Safety in the Print Shop
AIM: To instill the importance of being safety conscious.
TEACHING AIDS: Booklet "Safety in Your Future," handout sheets 2A and 2B, transparencies 13-2 through 13-15.
MATERIALS: Fire Extinguisher, safety glasses
REFERENCES: *Safety in the Print Shop*

I. PREPARATION (of the learner)
    A. The print shop has valuable equipment and should be protected against damage, but this concern is secondary to personal safety.
    B. Safe practices mean increased income and material security.
    C. During this lesson you will learn many aspects of safety in printing.

II. PRESENTATION

Instructional Topics   Key Points

    A. Safety tour of shop
    B. General shop safety
        1. No "horseplay."
        2. Every injury, no matter how slight, must be reported.
        3. Never work alone in laboratory or darkroom.
        4. Adequate lighting and ventilation.
        5. Floors clear.
        6. Doors unlocked.
    C. Personal safety
        1. Wear approved safety glasses when mixing chemicals.
        2. Never mix chemicals near eyes or face.
        3. Wash thoroughly after handling chemicals.
        4. Wear proper apparel.
    D. Fire safety
        1. Location of fire extinguishers

            a. Tell how to use.
            b. Demonstrate.
            c. Explain where fire extinguishers are located.
        2. No smoking in laboratory or darkroom.
    E. Machine safety
        1. Paper cutter is dangerous.
            a. Always work alone.
            b. Proper procedure.
            c. Never disconnect safety devices.
        2. Presses.
            a. Cylinder gaps.
            b. Gears.
            c. Delivery.
            d. Cylinders and rollers.
        3. Folding machines.
            a. Rollers.
            b. Making adjustments.
    F. Other shop areas
        1. Glass table tops.
        2. Staplers-stitchers.
        3. Paper drill.
        4. Small tools.
    G. Safety foreman
        1. Discuss "Daily Safety Checklists."
        2. Job responsibilities.

III. APPLICATION (drills, questions, analogies, oral questions, or assignments)
    A. What is the primary goal of a lab safety program?
    B. Should you work in the darkroom alone?
    C. What accidents should be reported?

IV. TESTS (final check on student's comprehension)
    Safety test (All students must pass with a 100% accuracy before they are allowed to operate any machine.)

Figure 10-18. Safety in a graphic arts shop.

prevention, cuts, machine hazards, and many other items of safety. The Testing stage requires each student to pass a safety test with 100% accuracy. The lesson covers many necessary safety items in the laboratory and requires students to know various safety items in preparation for hands-on activities.

Safety is included in all lesson plans at the points where it is a concern. The safety questions, phrases, and statements, to be repeated exactly as written, are located in the "Key Points" section of the presentation. These safety items relate to a variety of safety topics and are written so the teacher will not forget to use the statements. Figure 10-19 lists a number of statements found in lesson plans developed by occupational teachers.

Occasionally, a safety topic becomes large enough to develop into a lesson. An example of this might be a general safety lesson about electricity (see Appendix 10B). Note in the lesson that the preparation, presentation, and application stages all focus directly on learning the hazards involved in working with electricity. Since faulty electrical situations can lead to accidents, the entire lesson is on safety. It is suggested that this lesson be used, with revision, to deal with the topic of general electrical safety in the laboratory or on the job in all occupational programs.

Safety should be included in lesson plans when teaching how to operate equipment. In some cases, it may be necessary to focus on safety for machine or equipment use by developing a safety lesson specifically for that piece of equipment. Appendix 10C shows a safety lesson plan to be used for instruction with a specific piece of equipment.

Figure 10-6 presents a list of safety rules for hand tools as a necessary item in instruction. Should hand tool safety be taught in separate lessons? This decision depends upon how much safety is involved with hand tools in a program and whether or not the teacher can deal with the safety in lessons related to the use of each specific tool. Appendix 10D covers part of a lesson plan for teaching about hand tool safety.

Instruction sheets are used to supplement instruction. See Figure 10-20.

SAFETY COMMITTEE

The Vocational Industrial Clubs of America (VICA) encourages safety by promoting safety committees in all Trade and Industrial (T&I) education programs. While working toward the VICA safety competition, the committee should support the safety efforts of the school. Competing safety

Caution:
Emphasize how to stop the machine quickly.
Make sure the splitter guard is in place when ripping stock.
Use a push stick when ripping narrow stock.
Wear eye protection.
Wear a face shield.
Do not use machine without permission from teacher.
Disconnect machine from power before replacing paper disk.
Check on-off switch before connecting machine to power.
Clamp workpiece in vise.
Do not reach over saw while it is in operation.
Do not feel work for smoothness while machine is running.
Check to be sure no hot metal is left in the work area.
Do not weld without gloves.
Do not saw in reverse direction.

Figure 10-19. Safety key points.

programs must comply with regulations for the United States Skill Olympics (USSO) competition. Refer to the USSO regulations early in the school year.

The safety committee should become active in September. It should have a chairperson, secretary, and at least five members. Plan to have at least one regular meeting a month.

The committee needs to plan a safety program for the school year. A number of activities may be selected. An activity may run during an entire year or part of a year. Documenting what occurs in planning and carrying out activities is necessary if the school plans to enter the VICA safety competition.

It is suggested that the committee select a number of VICA safety activities from the following five categories. More than one activity can be selected from one category. A well-rounded safety program will be selected from the following categories:

1. **Vocational Shop/Laboratory Safety Survey**
   A. Describe all aspects of implementing the survey, including planning, conducting, and final reporting.
   B. Describe any action taken as a result of identifying possible hazards in the school shop or laboratory from the survey.
   C. A separate survey and description must be completed for each occupational area covered.
2. **Machine and Equipment Safety**
   A. Describe in detail the safety instruction provided in a selected vocational shop/laboratory regarding the operation of all power machines and equipment as well as general safety instruction. Included in the description should be the demonstrations, copies of safety rules, listing of audiovisuals used and other pertinent information.
3. **Environmental Safety**
   A. Inspect and describe the physical condition of the shop/laboratory including the positive conditions as well as those that are potential hazards. Consideration should be given to floor surface, obstructions, lighting, furniture, fire, chemical, electrical, radiation, mechanical, asbestos, heat, dust, and other hazards.
   B. Describe what action (if any) was taken or future

MATERIALS: Soldering iron
Soldering gun
Solder wick
Two (2) mounted terminal strips with unsoldered mounted components
A terminal strip with good solder joints
Directions: Complete the following procedures. Obtain all necessary materials to complete the instruction sheet.
PROCEDURE:

1. Wear safety glasses when completing this task. Molten solder is harmful to the eyes.
2. Solder the components on one of the terminal strips by using the soldering iron.
   NOTE: Be sure to place the iron in the correct position in an approved holder. Burns can result from improperly placed irons.
3. Solder the components on the second terminal strip using the soldering gun.
   NOTE: Place the gun so the tip is not in a position to burn clothing and/or skin.
4. Compare the solder connections on both strips with a sample furnished by the teacher.
5. When checking your connections be sure
   a. there is not too little or too much solder on the connection.
   b. the solder joint is shiny and free of materials.
6. Remove solder from components on the terminal strip lugs.
   NOTE: When components are desoldered, there is the danger that molten solder will splatter. This is why safety glasses are so important. Also, clothing that covers the arms may prevent burns from the solder.
7. Continue to solder and desolder until you are satisfied your solder connections meet the checks listed in Step 5. Proceed to Step 8.
8. When excess solder is removed, heat each connection with an iron/gun and remove the component lead from the terminal strip lug. Removing the component so it can be used again indicates you have used proper desoldering techniques.
   NOTE: Pulling on components to remove them from the terminal strip can cause solder to splatter. Observe the note after Step 6. Avoid accidents from splattering solder.
9. Return all materials to storage.

Figure 10-20. Soldering and desoldering terminal strips.

action planned as the result of your investigation.
4. **Industrial Site or Plant**
   A. Inspection: Make arrangements for a class safety visit of an industrial, business, or construction site. The purpose will be to:
      1. Learn firsthand what are the safety concerns of employers and employees.
      2. Observe an actual place of business in operation from a safety point of view.
      3. Compare the safety concepts taught in the classroom to those encountered in the workplace.
      4. Describe in detail the planning, site visit, and your general observations regarding safety as practiced in the workplace.
5. **Develop a safety program/activity in one of the following areas and document all activities**
   A. Safety in lifting and moving heavy objects.
   B. Heat stress and industrial respiratory safety.
   C. Indoor air pollution safety.
   D. Industrial hygiene.

E. Industrial protective clothing.

F. Occupational vehicle driving.

G. Plant/school building safety.

H. Other industrial or occupational safety concerns as identified by the chapter safety committee.

Note: There must be a total of four safety activities documented in the safety entry selected from the five categories listed above. Two activities may be selected from one area. Three areas of safety must be covered. Any entry omitting a major section as identified on the rating sheet will automatically be disqualified.*

The safety project book describes the activities of the committee and is used in the VICA safety competition. The book is also helpful for publicizing your safety program during open houses and other educational activities. Some hints for developing a quality project book are:

1. Take and use color photos.

2. Include appreciation letters in the book.

3. Include newspaper clippings on events.

4. Include events listed in the school newspaper.

5. Include safety inspection check sheets for each shop inspection. Supplement this with "before" and "after" photos.

6. Include accurate minutes of monthly safety committee meetings. Use a standard form which includes a meeting date, length of meeting, summary of meeting, and actions taken. Have minutes signed by the safety chairman and secretary.

7. Make a written abstract of all safety events. Report all *positive* results.

8. Solicit letters which applaud the club's safety efforts.

9. Mount all materials in an attractive manner.

   A. Double-check spelling on all material in the scrapbook.

   B. Use thin cardboard rather than soft sheets.

   C. Use plastic or lamination protectors on pages.

   D. Have a good table of contents.

   E. Type captions on a contrasting color of paper.

   F. Follow one basic style of lettering.

   G. Organize materials in scrapbook by USSO regulations.

   H. Follow a like format throughout.

   I. Think of artistic ways to place page numbers.

   J. Publicize the safety programs.

   K. Make sure judges can understand all details of your program.

   L. Use neat lettering and typing.

   M. Do not put commercial brochures in the booklet.

   N. Shadow the photos with colored paper.

   O. Trim some photos and display materials in unusual shapes.

   P. Offset sheets and photos with contrasting colors.

R. Use sheets with attractive borders.

10. Check to ensure compliance with all regulations.

   A. Indicate single-section or multiple-section entry on front cover.

   B. Place all materials in an official VICA Safety Project book.

   C. There are no secondary or postsecondary designations.

   D. Limit book to 3" in thickness, including the cover.

   E. Plan to use both sides of the sheets.

   F. Do not alter the cover of the project book.

   G. Organize materials as follows:

      1) Title page with name of school.

      2) Table of Contents and page numbers.

      3) The Introduction.

         a) A description of how and why the VICA club decided that safety was going to be a major emphasis in your yearly program of work.

         b) Documentation as to how the specific areas of safety were to be a major emphasis in the yearly program of work.

      4) Calendar of events or program of work for the club year.

      5) Minutes of all official club business meetings that set the stage and give direction or support the safety committees.

      6) Safety Project #1 - Title and page number.
      Safety Project #2 - Title and page number.
      Safety Project #3 - Title and page number.
      Safety Project #4 - Title and page number.

LIABILITY

A good safety program is essential in order to provide a safe learning environment. The responsibility for providing a safe environment is shared by the school and teacher. The school provides the facility, and the teacher ensures that it is used properly. Because of the nature of their positions, teachers must continuously be responsible to provide the safest possible environment for student learning.

The possibility for accidents and subsequent liability must be considered in occupational programs. Students who are inexperienced and often immature are taught skills that require the use of potentially dangerous machines, hand tool procedures, and processes. When a student is involved in a serious accident, parents may bring suit to recover damages for the injury. Teachers need to be aware that legal consequences may result from student injury. Teachers must strive to reduce the possibility of negative consequences from legal involvement. This requires careful planning and implementation of instruction, including a complete and well-planned curriculum guide that focuses on safety.

Occupational teachers are vulnerable to being involved in legal actions resulting from accidents. Student injuries resulting in court cases are on the increase. Juries are awarding large sums of money to those that bring suit. Occupational teachers and school districts are being named as defendants in liability suits. Sometimes teachers are

---

*Reprinted from *VICA U.S. Skill Olympics Regulations and Technical Standards* by permission of the Vocational Industrial Clubs of America, Inc. This publication is available in original form from VICA, Inc., P.O. Box 3000, Leesburg, VA 22075. Copyright 1993 by the Vocational Industrial Clubs of America, Inc.

cleared; at other times they are found negligent. Teachers must pay attention to this factor and do what is necessary to avoid being found negligent. Teachers are at risk for legal costs and judgments as well as for damage to their professional reputation.

Negligence

School insurance may cover judgments against teachers. However, teachers should not assume they are protected in all situations of liability. Teachers should find out how much insurance coverage they have and what their insurance covers.

A major concern for occupational teachers is the extent to which they may be held liable for damage awards by a court. Injured students may initiate a civil action to collect compensation for the injuries they have suffered. The laws regarding liability differ from state to state. Every teacher should be aware of liability laws and how they apply in certain situations. The discussion in this section is general and may or may not apply to a given state, depending on how the laws are written. However, the general principles discussed are accepted as necessary to offer safe instruction and usually apply to most state laws.

Elements of Negligence. It is generally accepted that the responsibility to students is shared by the teacher and the school. The injured student may blame the teacher for an unsafe situation in the learning area. The teacher may be found negligent; that is, the teacher did not carry out a responsibility to protect the student from injury. Three elements appear in many state laws to support a case of negligence:

1. The teacher had a responsibility (duty) in a particular situation.
2. The teacher did or did not act in the appropriate manner.
3. The breach of duty is the proximate cause of the injury.

All three elements are usually necessary to substantiate a claim. The injured party must carry the burden of proof in showing negligence on the part of another.

A major item to be determined in any case is whether the law recognizes an obligation on the part of a teacher to act in a prudent manner to meet a realistic standard for the benefit of a student. In a learning situation, teachers and administrators have a duty to exercise care and supervision for the safety of students under their supervision. The law in most states recognizes that persons entrusted with children have a special responsibility to supervise them.

A second item is to determine what the standard of care is for the relationship between the teacher and student. The traditional standard is to determine whether the teacher exercised the same standard of care as another reasonable person might under the same circumstances. For the teacher, this standard is usually the degree of care that a parent would observe in a comparable circumstance.

It is important to note that teachers are not expected to be ensurers of safety, nor are they liable for injuries simply because the injuries happened in a laboratory learning situa-

tion. Injuries sometimes happen without negligence. That is, the accident could not have been foreseen and therefore avoided by the exercise of reasonable precautions. This implies that the teacher must take reasonable care so the student is not harmed. The teacher must anticipate students' safety when they are performing an activity. It is important to note that the teacher is required to act in the same manner as a reasonable person of ordinary intelligence and foresight would have acted under the same circumstances.

The third item to consider is whether the injury was the natural and probable result of the teacher acting or failing to act as an ordinary person would have acted under the same or similar circumstances. The answer to this question will depend upon the circumstances surrounding the incident.

Importance of Supervision. The maintenance of supervision is very important in order to lessen the possibility of being held liable. It is difficult to define how much supervision is needed, since care and adequate supervision of students depends upon such circumstances as the number and mental ability of the students, as well as the activities in which they are involved. In cases where students are left without supervision, the court will often seek to determine whether some alternative means of supervision could have been provided. Also, consideration is generally given to the responsibility of the administration under the rules and guidelines of the school board. The general rule is that the individual teacher is responsible for supervision in the classroom and laboratory at all times. It is inadvisable for the teacher to be absent from a classroom or laboratory where he or she is responsible for supervising.

Since there are dangerous tools, equipment, and working conditions in occupational programs, the teacher must anticipate harm to students. In determining whether or not the teacher had exercised reasonable care, it would be necessary to ascertain what had occurred in the instruction. The court would probably look at:

- The extent of instruction on safety precautions.
- Whether the teacher had observed the student using the machine after the demonstration.
- Whether the teacher was routinely correcting improper procedures.
- Whether there had been any periodic observation following corrective action.
- The history of how well the student had followed instructions in using equipment.

With such apparent dangers in occupational programs, occupational teachers must give significant attention to the safety of students.

Another factor to consider is the general industrial safety standards for machine use. The court will probably probe the standards that exist in industry and compare these standards with those being followed in the instructional program. This situation applies particularly to the use of safety guards. Machine guards must be used by both students and teachers. New machines must be equipped with safety guards, and instruction should always contain references to using safety guards whenever operating equipment.

SAFETY GUIDELINES

Over the years, there have been some general principles which occupational educators have followed. The following guidelines are essential to maintaining safe instruction and minimizing possibilities for liability action:

1. Remain in the laboratory or class whenever students are there.
2. Never leave unqualified instructors in charge of the shop.
3. Do not conduct unsupervised after-hour work sessions.
4. Avoid sending students on errands during class periods.
5. Do not allow students to leave the school grounds without permission from the administration.
6. Do not permit the use of faulty machines, tools, equipment, or facilities.
7. Never permit the use of machines without safety guards.
8. Do not allow students from other classes to pass through your shop/classroom or mingle with your students.
9. Never allow poor housekeeping.
10. Do not permit students to wear unsafe clothing and accessories.
11. Avoid requiring all students to use power equipment. Some are not capable of using the equipment, and others may be fearful.
12. Never allow the use of equipment without proper instruction.

The development and implementation of the curriculum guide plays an important part in teaching and documenting safety. In a liability suit, teachers are usually required to show evidence of teaching and testing safety. The curriculum guide with safety rules, lesson plans, tests, licenses, and other items discussed in this chapter can provide evidence that the teacher did plan for a complete safety program that ensures the safety of all students. Also, the teacher must show that the curriculum guide was followed and the plan implemented. These two elements of instruction should provide safe training and minimize the possibility of teacher liability.

SUMMARY

Safety is a very important part of instruction. It becomes more important as students work with machines and materials that have the potential to cripple or result in fatal injuries. Safety must be addressed from the first day students arrive at a training site until the day they leave. Both information and hands-on activities should be provided. Safety discussions should be a part of all instructional activities in which the teacher is involved. The many examples provide a wealth of materials that can assist in organizing a comprehensive program to offer a safe training environment.

APPENDIX 10A

WELDING LABORATORY SAFETY

It is very important that safety precautions be observed at all times in welding because of the constant danger from open flames, highly flammable gas, sparks, and electrical shock.

Welding operations should be carried on in a restricted and ventilated area as far as possible from any paint spraying.

Students must be instructed in safe work habits when using all types of welding equipment. They must be taught to use all the safety devices at all times.

BURNS

Welding demands that special clothing/apparel and protective clothing/apparel be worn by the student.
1. Wear woolen clothing rather than cotton or synthetic.
2. Avoid wearing trousers with cuffs — they trap sparks.
3. Wear high, leather shoes or leggings rather than low, cloth shoes.
4. Button shirts to the neck.
5. Wear hats or caps to prevent hair burns.
6. Wear leather gloves without loose cuffs.
7. Always use goggles and eye shields with the proper protective glass that will filter out harmful ultraviolet or infrared rays. These should be used by both welders and observers.
8. When hammering scale or chipping, wear goggles with clear glass to protect the eyes.
9. In arc welding, it is necessary to protect the skin as well as the eyes from the harmful rays.
10. Pay attention to hot metal until it is cool, or mark it hot if it is left where others might touch it.
11. Beware of touching or picking up items lying about the shop. Many things that are hot may not appear so.
12. Melt the filler rod at one end only. This will prevent people from picking it up by the hot end.
13. Dispose of all combustible or explosive materials around the welding area.
14. Use soapy water to detect gas leaks. They may cause explosion or fire. Acetylene fires can best be extinguished with:
    a. carbon dioxide extinguishers.
    b. wet cloths.
    c. wet blankets.
    d. wet sand.
    e. dry lime.
15. If clothing is on fire, use a fire blanket. Place the blanket about the neck first to keep the fire from the face.

OXYACETYLENE WELDING EQUIPMENT

1. Store cylinders away from all fire.
2. Store cylinders away from places of sudden temperature changes, such as radiators and steam pipes.
3. Do not store more than 2000 cubic feet of fuel gas in any one row.
4. Carry leaky cylinders outdoors where gas can escape in safety.
5. Do not use oil or grease on oxygen or acetylene connections. Oil and oxygen will ignite.
6. Never open tank valves until certain that regulator valves are closed. When the regulator is not used, the adjusting screw should be screwed out until the diaphragm is free.
7. Never use a hammer to open valves on cylinder.
8. Never hammer oxygen or acetylene regulators.
9. Do not store cylinders in room where temperature is more than 80 degrees.
10. Do not adjust, alter, change, build, or do any experimental work on cylinders, regulators, torches, or other gas equipment.
11. Never attempt to weld a closed or jacketed tank, vessel, or container without a vent for air; even then, great care should be used not to get gas in tank. If for any reason you should get gas in tank, be sure to aerate the tank.
12. Before lighting torch, be positive that hose, tanks, or any inflammable material will not be exposed to heat, flame, or sparks.
13. Beware of high acetylene pressure. Under no condition should acetylene gas be used when the pressure is greater than 15 pounds per sq. in. (Acetylene gas when compressed to more than 15 pounds becomes highly explosive.)

14. Never screw the regulator screw in tight against the regulator — this will spoil the diaphragm. Check tank pressure if hose pressure drops — as regulator tank is probably empty.
15. Open valves only one-quarter turn so they can be closed quickly.
16. Handle tanks carefully. Damage may cause explosion or dangerous gas leaks.
17. Store tanks in upright position to prevent acetylene from running out.
18. Keep hose or line pressure at 15 pounds per square inch.
19. Use water seals at outlet end of the manifold to prevent flashback from the torch reaching the supply.
20. Fasten full and empty cylinders to stationary objects to prevent them from falling.

OXYGEN CYLINDER

1. Store cylinders away from combustible materials.
2. Store in upright position.
3. Store cylinders away from areas where there may be sudden changes in temperature.
4. Handle tanks carefully.
5. Protect valves with safety caps when the cylinders are not in use.
6. Remove tanks with leaks to outdoors to allow the gas to escape.
7. Open valves slowly so as not to damage gauges and regulators.
8. Always use regulators to maintain uniform pressure.
9. Clean all dirt and dust from tank valves before attaching the regulators.
10. Inspect regulator connection for dust and dirt before attaching regulator.
11. Open tank valves with care. Stand to one side, so that in case of a failure, particles will not strike the body.
12. Do not force regulators on tank valves.
13. Tighten regulator sufficiently to prevent leakage. Leakage may cause an explosion.
14. Turn out or release adjusting screws when equipment is not in use or when cylinders are being changed.
15. Operate low pressure gauges at pressures not exceeding half the gauge reading.
16. Report creeping regulators to teacher. The maximum creep allowed is equal to the number of pounds of pressure needed for the size of a tip.
17. Mark the cylinder with arrows to show direction to turn the pressure "off" and "on."

HOSES

1. Use only red welding hose for acetylene.
2. Use only black or green hose for oxygen.
3. Use only hoses in good condition. Report all worn or charred hose to teacher.
4. Protect hose as much as possible against stray sparks and hot metal.
5. Do not kink or tangle hose; coil it neatly.
6. Keep all connections tight between cylinders, apparatus, hose, and piping.
7. Keep connections working freely.
8. Use connections for acetylene hoses that have left hand threads and for oxygen hoses that have right hand threads.

WELDING TORCHES

1. Never leave torch valve open.
2. Never cut or weld too close to concrete; put fire brick next to your work.
3. Do not use torch as a hammer, crowbar, wedge, or any other purpose than for welding.
4. Check torches for leaks before using them.
5. Never use torch that leaks.
6. Turn off torch each time you leave it, even for short periods of time.
7. Never use tip that gets hot.
8. When gas in a hose becomes ignited, turn off oxygen needle valve first.

9. Do not use matches or cigarette lighters to light torches; always use friction lighters or stationary pilot flame.
10. Do not hold welding or cutting tip too close to your work. This will cause flashback in your torch.

CUTTING TORCHES

1. Do not use cutting torches where flame or sparks from cutting might start a fire.
2. Move flammable materials out of danger zone or take work to safe place.
3. Use sheet metal guards or sheet asbestos to confine slag molten metal.

ELECTRIC WELDING MACHINES

1. Protect other persons from arc with shield. Warn them about looking at the flash.
2. Check cables to see that there is no chance of a short circuit because of poor insulation.
3. Be sure water is flowing to cool points properly.
4. Do not weld dirty or rusty material.
5. Turn off both electricity and water when leaving a spot welder.

APPENDIX 10B

ELECTRICAL HAZARDS

TEACHER'S LESSON PLAN
Related Technical Information

TEACHER: S. Bundy
SUBJECT: Electrical Hazards
AIM: To learn the hazards involved in working with electricity.
TEACHING AIDS: Transparencies 8-1, 8-2, 8-3, 8-4, 8-5
MATERIALS: Insulated tools and safety equipment
REFERENCES: *Accident Prevention Manual for Shop Teachers*, pp. 34 - 76
                National Safety Council Handbook, pp. 13-15

I. PREPARATION (of the learner)
   A. Failure to understand the danger of electrical energy is the cause of many accidents.
   B. Many men, women, and children each year are victims of electrical shock and burns.
   C. Electricity is not to be feared but is to be respected.
   D. The greater knowledge we have concerning the theory of electricity, the better prepared we become to avoid electrical hazards.
   E. With this knowledge, we can avoid accidents by taking the necessary safety precautions.

II. PRESENTATION (of the skills)
   Operations or Steps   Key Points
   A. Voltage, current,   A.
      and resistance   1. High voltage (550 volts and above) is very dangerous.
                             2. Low voltage (50 volts and above) can often be dangerous.
                             3. Most fatal accidents occur from 115 volt house circuits.
                             4. The current flow (amperes) is also a big factor in how severe a shock or burn may be.
                             5. The resistance of the human body varies among individuals.
                             6. Any electrical circuit should be considered a potential hazard,

B. Results of body   B.
   contact with   1. Nerve shock occurs when current flows through some part of the body.
   electrical energy   2. Severe burns are often left where the current enters and leaves the body.
                            3. Physical injuries are sometimes a primary result of shock.

C. The amount of   C.
   current flowing   1. Resistance of the skin and clothing.
   through the body   2. Insulating qualities of the surrounding area.
                            3. Amount of voltage and current in the circuit.
                            4. Resistance of dry skin (100,000 to 600,000 ohms).
                            5. Resistance of wet skin.

D. Path or course   D.
   of electricity   1. Passage through vital organ causes muscular spasms.
   through the body   2. Passage from head to foot is most dangerous.
                            3. Passage from arm to arm may cause breathing to stop.
                            4. Give results of other pathways.

E. Duration of shock   E.
                            1. Sometimes victim is knocked away.
                            2. Victim may be frozen in contact with electricity due to contraction of muscles.
                            3. Long contact will cause some of the body organs to stop functioning.

F. Type of electrical   F.
   energy   1. DC considered less hazardous from shock standpoint.
                            2. DC causes more severe burns than AC.
                            3. Low frequency AC more dangerous than high frequency.

G. Physical condition   G.
   of the victim   1. Diseased organs more easily affect chest muscles and cause breathing to stop.
                            2. May stop heart action and circulation of blood.
                            3. Severe burns may result.
                            4. Wounds caused by arcing electrical current are usually severe and slow to heal.

H. Injuries resulting   H.
   from shock and   1. Falls from ladders, platforms, poles, etc.
   secondary shock   2. Accidental starting of machines.

I. Causes of electrical   I.
   accidents   1. Unsafe conditions.
                            2. Unsafe practices.
                            3. Combination of both.
                            4. Lack of knowledge of danger.

regardless of the amount of voltage or amperage.

III. APPLICATION (practice by learner under close supervision)
   A. What amount of voltage might be considered dangerous?
   B. What four results might be caused by body contact with electrical energy?
   C. How does electrical shock affect the muscles?
   D. What path of current flow through the body is the most dangerous?
   E. What are some causes of electrical shock?

IV. TEST: Checkup
   Safety test No.1 to follow lesson

APPENDIX 10C

CIRCULAR SAW SAFETY

TEACHER'S LESSON PLAN   UNIT_____
Safety Lesson

TEACHER: R.N. Jones
SUBJECT: Circular Saw Safety
AIM (purpose):   To each overall safety techniques in circular saw operation.

TEACHING AIDS:
MATERIALS: Stanley Chart "Clear Scraps with Push Stick"
                  NSC Posters 43, 16, 32
REFERENCES: *Woodworking with Machines*, pp. 70-132.

I. PREPARATION (of the learner)
   A. Power machinery represents a hazard because of the terrific rate of speed.
   B. An error of a single second may result in a serious accident.
   C. Although guards are designed to protect operator, they are not foolproof if the operator does not use them correctly.
   D. Get into the habit of paying strict attention to your machine while working.
   E. Attention given now may save you from later injury.

II. PRESENTATION (of the information)

Instructional Topics	Key Points
A. Circular saw operation is a one person job.	A. 1. Don't allow others to throw switch. 2. Don't help with stock unless requested. 3. Help needed only in "tailing off."
B. Adjust blade to 1/8" above stock.	B. 1. Less likely to contact blade. 2. Exception: hollow ground blade.
C. Always stand to one side.	C. 1. Danger of kickback. 2. Frequent pinching. NOTE: Assume correct position *NSC Poster #43
D. Never attempt freehand cuts.	D. 1. Stock will be thrown back. 2. Point out purpose of fence. 3. "Scare" can be a hazard. NOTE: On stopped saw, place partially sawed block. Demonstrate possibility of "throw back."
E. Never cross-cut against fence.	E. 1. Stock is pinched and thrown out. 2. Fence for ripping only. 3. Miter gauge for cross cutting. 4. Use a clearance block. NOTE: On stopped saw, place small block between fence and blade.
F. Check clearance of miter gauge when table is tilted.	F. 1. Make sure gauge works freely. 2. Miter gauge can be used only on left when table is tilted. NOTE: Move miter gauge in slots while table is tilted. 3. Use poster #32.
G. Don't clear scraps with fingers.	G. 1. Wait until saw stops. 2. Never reach over saw. 3. Use push stick. NOTE: Demonstrate.
H. Long stock requires assistance.	H. 1. Show Stanley chart. 2. Assistance needed for "tailing off." 3. Don't allow helper to pull or tilt board.

4. Operator must be in complete control.
5. Use roller support if help is not available.

I. Use push stick on narrow stock.	I. 1. Dangerous to use fingers. 2. 4" or less, use push stick. 3. Narrow stock, use featherboard. 4. Demonstrate. NOTE: Show scars on push stick; say "This could happen to your fingers."
J. Check fence before ripping.	J. 1. Check lock on both ends. 2. Check fence alignment. 3. Check anti-kickback fingers. 4. Demonstrate. 5. Measure alignment, front and back.
K. Turn off power immediately if saw doesn't sound right.	K. 1. Call teacher. 2. Blade may be loose, reversed. 3. Motor may need repair.
L. Avoid distractions.	L. 1. Don't look around while operating. 2. Never talk to machine operator. NOTE: Cite example of accident which occurred because of distraction.
M. Stay with machine.	M. 1. Turn off power and remain until saw blade stops, or else someone may be injured. 2. True for all machines in shop.
N. Remove guard only with special permission.	N. 1. Only a few operations can't be done with the guard in place. 2. These will be explained later. 3. 95% of accidents occur when guard is not being used.

III. APPLICATION (Drill, illustrations, analogies, oral questions or assignments)
ORAL QUESTIONS
   A. What is a clearance block, and how is it used?
   B. Why shouldn't the operator cross-cut against the fence?
   C. What safety precaution should you observe when ripping narrow stock?
   D. Why are freehand cuts dangerous?
   E. What is the purpose of standing to one side when cutting?

IV. TEST (final check on students' comprehension of material presented)
   A. Written safety test on circular saw next Tuesday.
   B. Performance test can be taken only by those getting a perfect score on written test.

Suggested Reading for Student: Chapter 14 in text, "Jointers"
The next lesson is: Unit 6—Lesson 5, "Operation of the Jointer"

APPENDIX 10D

TEACHER'S LESSON PLAN   UNIT_____
Related Technical Information

TEACHER: J. Butcher
SUBJECT: Hand Tool Safety
AIM: To practice safe use of hand tools
TEACHING AIDS: Tools, safety devices as called for
MATERIALS: Transparencies 3-1, 3-2, 3-3
REFERENCES: *Residential Electrician*, pp. 9-12

I. PREPARATION (of the learner)
   A. Safety is everyone's job. For this reason, it is essential that all employees understand the nature of accidents and be familiar with hand tool safety, precautions, and safe practice.

B. Tools are expensive items and should be properly cared for at all times.

II. PRESENTATION (of the information)

Instructional Topics	Key Points
A. Wood handles	A.
	1. Splintered handles on hammers, sledges, hatchets, axes, picks, or shovels can be dangerous. Taping is a makeshift effort. Handle should be replaced.
B. Loose or missing wedges	B.
	1. Head coming off can cause serious injury. Never use the back of an ax as a maul (hammer).
C. Pointed or edge tools	C.
	1. If dull, should not be used until sharpened.
	2. When handing to anyone, pass handle first.
	3. Should be stored and handled in a way that prevents injury to personnel and damage to tools.
D. Tools with tangs	D.
	1. Should always be used with a handle.
	2. Tang can pierce hand.
E. Chisels, screwdrivers, files, and rasps	E.
	1. Made of hard, brittle metal; should never be used for prying or hammering.
	2. Blade of screwdriver should be kept square and flat.
	3. Select screwdriver that fits in slot of screw.
F. Driver tools	F.
	4. Never use metal handled screwdriver in electrical work.
	1. Mushroomed head must be dressed before using.
	2. If a particle of steel flies into eye, see doctor immediately. (Steel will rust after 4 hours.)
	3. When driving ground rods, use tongs or other suitable device.
G. Grinding wheel	G.
	1. Use goggles.
	2. Do not stand directly in front of machine at start.
	3. Keep rest close to wheel.
H. Portable drill	H.
	1. Use both hands.
	2. Keep hands clear of bit and chuck when using drill press.
	3. Use proper jig to hold the work.
	4. Never wear gloves when drilling small objects.
I. Electrician's knife	I.
	1. Use a closable knife for skinning wire.
	2. Work knife away from you.
	3. Avoid use of hooked cable knives or long pointed knives.

III. APPLICATION (Drills, illustrations, analogies, oral questions or assignments. Inspect and demonstrate proper use of tools.)

IV. CHECKUP (or test) (Final check on students' comprehension of material presented).

Test tomorrow. Hand tool safety

Suggested Reading for Student: *Residential Electricity,* pp. 16-18.
Next lesson is: Working Safely with Electrical Equipment

Chapter 11

SELF-DIRECTED LEARNING

by

Walter S. Ramey, Assistant Professor
Virginia Commonwealth University
Richmond, Virginia

INTRODUCTION

Teachers realize that not all students learn or develop skills at the same rate. Progress within a class is often hampered by the vast differences in the abilities of the students. Because of these unique circumstances, the teacher has difficulty in covering the material to be taught. To overcome these obstacles, teachers look for additional tools that will help students develop the occupational skills needed.

Many occupational education teachers have found that by using modules in their instructional program they can:

1. Accommodate different rates of learning.
2. Conserve teacher and student time.
3. Improve student achievement levels.
4. Encourage independent learning.
5. Promote creative ability.

THE MODULE PLAN—SEQUENCING

A *module*, sometimes called a *learning activity package* (LAP), provides a self-directed learning experience for the student. It is usually associated with an individual competency or a group of competencies. When modules are joined and properly sequenced, they form the basis for a self-contained learning system. Such a system would be the outcome of an occupational analysis where the objectives have been sequenced to facilitate the learning process.

Figure 11-1 illustrates the proper sequencing of objectives, module content, and unit organization for a food service program.

This sequence relates to three sections: Unit 1, Clean and Sanitize; Unit 2, Weights and Measurements; and Unit 3, Beverages. Unit 1 includes two modules, one with three objectives and one with only one. Units 2 and 3 have only one module each but contain multiple objectives. Within each unit, objectives are identified and placed in a logical teaching order. The objectives are then grouped to fit into modules. The modules now form a part of a modular learning system.

As a rule, it is best to place no more than five objectives in any one module. Also, a module title should be limited to six words that describe what the student is going to do. The title should be written using the present verb form (*e.g.*), "Wash Dishes" or "Make and Pour Beverages." Appendix 11C, Auto Mechanics—Program Sequence.

MODULE CONTENT

Module content will vary with a particular task or competency. Some modules contain all the necessary information, directions, and materials needed for completing the assignment. Others may direct the student to references, resources, or tools, and contain only the directions for completing the task. It is not uncommon for teachers to refer to "modules" that they have constructed or assembled that are not truly modules. However, if these materials work and serve a purpose within the program, they, too, can be self-directed learning experiences.

Whatever module system is used, the following suggestions may improve the instructional delivery:

1. Use a variety of teaching and evaluation methods.
2. Avoid assignments that require only reading with a written response.
3. Monitor the work of each student.
4. Mix group instruction and assignments with module packets.
5. Remediate an unattained learning activity by assigning another activity that is similar to the first one attempted.

CONSTRUCTING A MODULE

Normally, a module will have a title page, an introduction, a performance objective, assigned reference materials,

MODULE NO.	UNIT AND MODULE TITLE	V-TECS OBJECTIVE NO.	OBJECTIVE	SUGGESTED SEQUENCE
	**Program Sequence-Food Preparation I**
UNIT 1	CLEAN AND SANITIZE			
FP-6	Clean Equipment and Work Areas	89	Clean and care for equipment. Practice safety techniques when using, cleaning, and caring for equipment.	1
		90	Clean and sanitize kitchen blocks.	
		91	Clean floors, windows, counters, and tables. Practice personal sanitation.	
FP-7	Wash Dishes	92	Wash dishes, glasses, silverware, trays, pots, and pans by hand and by machine.	2
UNIT 2	WEIGHTS AND MEASUREMENTS			
FP-8	Weigh and measure	2	Increase and decrease recipes.	3
		32	Weigh and measure staple items and ingredients.	
UNIT 3	BEVERAGES			
FP-10	Make and Pour Beverages	24	Pour juices and beverages.	4
		33	Brew tea.	
		59	Make coffee.	

Figure 11-1. Proper sequencing of objectives and module content will help improve the learning process.

specific learning activities, and the teacher's final checklist or evaluation. Modules can be very elaborate or elementary in their construction and content. One thing to remember is that a module should be concerned with only a single concept or segment of the subject matter being taught. It is an attempt to present an individualized activity that will teach only one concept before moving to another.

Modules should present a variety of activities and instructional media. When these activities are well defined and executed, students will be comfortable with the modules. They will become both actively and personally involved in the learning process. When constructing modules, place the emphasis on the individual and develop content appropriate to the performance objective.

Figure 11-1 addresses the program sequence and the grouping of objectives for identifying modules. This is often associated with curriculum analysis as presented in previous chapters. Once the analysis is completed, the construction of a module begins.

COMPONENTS OF A SELF-DIRECTED LEARNING MODULE

There are several models which can be used as patterns for designing modules. Between the essential module components and the potential number of components lies a wide range of choices for the teacher.

The essential components of any module, however, may resemble any well organized instructional sequence:
1. Present an objective.
2. Determine student knowledge.
3. Provide instructional activities.
4. Posttest to measure achievement.

The outline of a more complex module is presented in Figure 11-2. This outline contains features that are potentially useful, but not always necessary in achieving a particular objective.

The final organization of a module, complete with supporting learning activities, could appear as in Figure 11-2. However, some teachers visualize a structure or format like Figure 11-3. Here the module is a part of a self-contained learning system that utilizes modules or learning activity packages (LAPS).

In this system, several modules provide instruction for a group of related competencies. When all modules have been completed, the student will have attained the identified competencies for the course or program.

The quality and correct format of a module is much like the old saying about beauty: it lies in the eyes of the beholder. Therefore, another example of a module format is shown in Figure 11-4. This example combines features of several formats and provides a more complete structure along with a suggested order for development. All essential elements are shown in this module. However, the design may be modified to meet specific needs identified by the teacher.

Module Format

Title page
- A. Name of module
- B. Unit number
- C. Purpose (one or two sentences)

Introduction
- A. Short paragraph introducing topic
- B. Performance (objective(s)
- C. Module directions
- D. Pretest (optional)

Study materials
- A. Short study materials (may include directions to read other materials)
- B. May be followed by tests or check-out activities

Learning activities
- A. Things to do
- B. Assignments, games, other activities
- C. Self-check tests

Teacher's final test
- A. Based on entire module
- B. Scored by the teacher
- C. Reflects the module's performance objective(s)

Figure 11-2. An outline for a complex module.

Self-Contained Learning System Sequence

1.	MODULE INTRODUCTION	The student carefully reviews the Module Introduction, Directions, Enabling Objectives, and Performance Objectives.
2.	PRETEST	The student completes Module Pretest. If the established minimum score is obtained, the student proceeds to Step 7; if not, the student proceeds to Step 3.
3.	INTRODUCTION OF CONTENT	The instructional content of the Module is introduced to the student.
4.	EVALUATION OF CONTENT UNDERSTANDING	The student completes a response sheet which assesses understanding of the content introduced in Step 3. If the established minimum score is obtained, the student proceeds to Step 5; if not, the student reviews content until it is understood.
5.	APPLICATION OF CONTENT	The student completes an activity designed to apply the content identified in Step 4. Activities may include research assignments, project completion, or performance of "hands-on" tasks. When specified standards of performance are met, the student proceeds to Step 6.
6.	POSTTEST	The student completes the posttest. If the established minimum score is obtained, the student proceeds to Step 7; if not, Steps 3 through 5 are reviewed until the minimum score is obtained.
7.	NEXT MODULE	Steps 1 through 6 are continued for each successive module until all system modules have been completed.

Figure 11-3. A format for a LAP module.

WRITING THE MODULE

The task of writing a module is best explained as completing the component parts outlined in Figure 11-4. The order of development indicated in this topical outline provides a framework for discussing the following 12 items.

1. **Objectives**

   A terminal or performance objective should be stated in performance terms. It should have a condition(s), a behavior(s), and a criterion-referenced measure(s) or standard(s) for the desired performance. The objective addresses one concept, a related section or a component of the instructional unit. It is a statement describing what is to be done, the conditions under which the work or task will be performed, and the standard(s) by which the performance will be evaluated. For a particular module the performance objective or the terminal objective is the task the student will be expected to perform upon completion of the assignment or on the job. *An enabling objective* is a statement of the knowledge, skill, or attitude the student must develop to reach the terminal objective. A learning activity should be designed to achieve each enabling objective in a module. Enabling objectives may contain only condition(s) and behavior(s).

2. **Prerequisites** are competencies the module writer considers essential before the student proceeds with the work involved. Often there are no prerequisites required. Previously learned knowledge or skill is appropriate for determining the level of readiness suitable for performing an assigned task.

3. **Pretest** varies from a written test or simply the teacher's judgment. In either case, the purpose is to determine

Developing a Module

Order of Development		Finished Order
12	*Cover Page*	1
7	Title	
10	Table of Contents	
2	Prerequisites	
4	*Introduction* Answer the question "WHY"	2
9	*Directions for the Module*	3
3	Pretest	
1	*Objectives* Terminal Enabling	4
5	*Learning Activities* Procedure/assignment sheet Information sheet Laboratory worksheet Others	5
6	*Check-Out Activities* Criterion referenced measure	6
11	*Teacher's Final Checklist*	7
8	*References* Credits Resources	8

Figure 11-4. An alternate module format.

if the student is capable of completing the module's objectives.

There are many cases where it will be unnecessary to pretest. However, there are situations where the pretest can determine the necessity for completing the module at all. In such situations the pretest would be used to identify a level of competence that would allow the student to bypass a particular module. See Figure 11-3. In any event, the teacher must determine the practicality of a pretest.

4. **An introduction** states the purpose of the module. It should also identify the knowledge or skill to be developed and present a few well-directed motivational sentences to assist in goal setting.

5. **Learning activities** are selected or designed by the teacher to address the performance and the enabling objectives. Quite often the activities or study materials needed are readily available within the shop or classroom. Also, a review of the other chapters in this book could be helpful, especially those dealing with the development of instruction sheets. See Figure 11-4, *Learning Activities.* Usually the activities needed to teach a skill or competency are self-evident because of the subject area content and the teacher's experience. Whatever approach is taken in teaching the task, the design of the activity should be such that the student will be able to master the skill or content at a self-determined rate of progress.

6. **Check-out activities** should be designed to engage the student in a self-evaluation exercise. Properly constructed, this section prepares the student for the final evaluation of the performance. Without entering into a formal testing situation, this activity saves the teacher time and actively involves the student in self-evaluation. This activity is critical to the learning process.

Check-out activities are based on the criterion-referenced measure. Usually it is an outline of the procedure followed in meeting the standards. Often based upon the performance guide, it provides for a review of the activity and serves as an exercise for corrective practice. It helps the student build confidence and prepare for the teacher's evaluation.

7. **Title** should consist of no more than six words. As shown in Figure 11-1 the title should reflect what the student is going to do. Titles should use the present tense of the verb, such as "Wash Dishes."

Most teachers using modules have established a coding system. The code is associated with the *Unit* and *Objective* number in a filing system that is discussed in Chapter 12. Whatever the coding system, the number should be used in the heading of all sheets.

In Figure 11-1, each module has been identified by a code for filing and other identification purposes. Such a record allows both the teacher and student to locate modules quickly!

8. **References** and other resources used in the development of the module should be identified for future use. They are a critical component of the module for identifying

special resource needs of the student.

9. **Directions for the module** set the stage and tell the student how to use the module. They may identify prerequisites and provide a brief review of previous learning experiences associated with the work at hand. Directions should lead the student to the objective and into the learning activities. It is best to present the directions in a straightforward manner.

10. **A table of contents** may or may not be needed. Module content and complexity will determine this. If the module is self-explanatory, the table of contents can be eliminated. Common sense should prevail. If it is needed, put it in. Put yourself in the user's place as you decide.

11. **The teacher's final checklist** can take different forms, depending on the activities involved and what the teacher feels is necessary for instructional management. If the nature of the posttest requires a formal test setting, formal administration of the test should be included here. If the student's efforts result in a product to be evaluated, an evaluation checklist, based upon the performance guide, should be included. If the final evaluation involves acknowledging the accomplishment of the learning activities, the evaluation instrument may be represented by a checklist indicating that the procedure was or was not accomplished. This checklist may also indicate the student's grade or proficiency level.

All posttests or evaluative instruments must reflect the criterion-referenced measures associated with the performance objective. Without this, the module would not be competency-based.

12. **The cover page** presents the module's title, the author's name, the class, and the school where the module will be used. If the module has been coded, the code number should be conveniently placed for reference purposes.

Sometimes a little creativity on the part of the teacher can set the stage for an improved learning situation. However, in most cases, the typical cover page carries the title and introduces the learning activity.

Assembling the Module

Figure 11-4, *Developing a Module,* presents three thoughts: (1), the outline of a completed module, (2), the suggested order for developing the content, and (3), the finished order for the assembled module.

When a teacher is writing a module for classroom or shop use, the procedure outlined in Figure 11-4 can be of significant help. It enables the teacher to think in logical steps and build upon the performance objective.

A preprinted format is suggested for module development. The worksheet in Appendix A was designed for this purpose. However, the order of development presented in Figure 11-4 ought to be followed. Begin with Item 1, *Objectives,* and continue through Item 12, *Cover Page.*

Module Format and Examples

The appendices show a module format and several examples of modules. As was stated earlier, modules can take different forms. They are designed, not for the teacher, but for the student. The teacher designing or developing them must determine their complexity.

Appendix A describes the functional components of a module. The developmental order for writing a module is presented in Figure 11-4, *Developing a Module*. Combining these two resources can simplify the writing of a module.

Reviewing Appendices B and C will provide an additional perspective regarding module construction. Appendix B provides an example of a module used with beginning masonry students. Appendix C shows a partial program sequence that includes a selected module from that sequence. Each of the examples serves a distinct purpose in the educational process. They were designed for different levels of instruction.

The worksheet and sample modules can provide ideas for developing instructional materials.

APPENDIX 11A

WORKSHEET FOR DEVELOPING A MODULE

Module No. _____

Objective No. _____

Module Title
Use present verb form
Six words or less

Introduction
Purpose of the module
Knowledge or skill to be developed
Motivational statements
Approximately 75 to 100 words

Directions
Set the stage
State prerequisites needed
Lead student through the module

Performance Objective
The performance objective should be taken from the program sequence, V-TECS catalog, or other reference when possible. Otherwise it must be written by the teacher. It should be assigned a number for use with the module. All performance objectives have a *condition*, a *behavior*, and a *standard.*

Enabling Objectives
Enabling objectives are related to the performance objective. They are usually a statement of a desired behavior. Each enabling objective should be addressed in the learning activities.

Learning Activities
Similar to instruction sheets, especially the assignment sheet
May embody the job, operation, and the information sheet(s)

May direct the student to a reference or prescribe the procedure for completing a task
Number each activity

Check-Out Activities
Check-out activities provide a means for the student to perform a self-check prior to submitting to the teacher's final checklist. Check-out activities are basically a test over the material assigned for each learning activity. These activities should reflect the criterion referenced measure or standard in the performance objective.
Directions for performing the check-out activities should be simple, direct, and reflect the performance objective.

TEACHER'S FINAL CHECKLIST

The teacher's final checklist should be stated in the past tense for each item in the list. It should be derived from the performance and enabling objectives and the learning activities. The teacher must indicate either approval (+) or disapproval (−) of each item listed. Space should be provided at the bottom of the sheet for the teacher's comments and, if appropriate, the grade assigned.

Item No.	Checklist Item	+ −

(+) = approved   (−) = not approved

Comments

Grade Assigned _____

APPENDIX 11B

JOINTING MASONRY WORK

by Donn M. deKraft
Amelia-Nottoway
Vocational Center
Jetersville, Virginia

Photographs
by
Chesterfield Technical Center
Chesterfield, Virginia

Module No. ___M-1___

JOINTING MASONRY WORK

Introduction
One of the most important skills required of a mason is that of jointing or striking work. This process is simple, but very important. It should be taught at the start of masonry training.
Jointing work is done for two reasons (a) to seal the mortar joints by compressing the mortar into the bricks and (b) to enhance the appearance of the work. The first reason is the more important of the two because pressing the mortar into the joints will make it waterproof and will help the masonry resist weather much longer.

Directions
You have just learned how to lay up a brick wall. Now you will learn how to finish all head and bed joints by JOINTING.
Read the performance objective and enabling objectives, then proceed with the learning activities and checkout activities.
After practicing the steps prescribed in this module, you will be able to correctly joint head and bed joints in a wall and score well on a test at the end of the module.

Performance Objective
Given the necessary tools and a "just built" brick wall, the student will joint all assigned head and bed joints in the wall and score 100% on a test on jointing masonry work.

Enabling Objectives

Following assigned readings the student will:

1. Identify the masonry tools needed for jointing a green wall.
2. Demonstrate the proper use of the sled runner.
3. Demonstrate the proper use of the hand jointer.
4. Demonstrate the proper use of the mason's trowel in cutting mortar tags.
5. Demonstrate the proper use of the masonry brush in brushing brick work.

LEARNING ACTIVITIES

No.	Activity

1. Study Learning Activity No. 1, *Tools and Materials Needed for Jointing Work.* Notify your teacher that you can identify the masonry tools needed for jointing and request your designated wall area for jointing.
2. Read Learning Activity No. 2, *Using the Sled Runner,* and practice striking bed joints.
3. Read Learning Activity No. 3, *Using the Hand Jointer,* and practice striking the head joints.
4. Read Learning Activity No. 4, *Using the Mason's Trowel,* and practice cutting the mortar tags from the wall.
5. Read Learning Activity No. 5, *Using the Masonry Brush,* and complete your assignment by brushing your work.
6. Proceed to the Check-Out Activities.

LEARNING ACTIVITY NO. 1
TOOLS AND MATERIALS NEEDED FOR JOINTING WORK

The masonry tools pictured below are used in jointing brick and block work. Jointing is important when building structures, such as the brick wall pictured below, because it protects the mortar joints and improves the appearance.

Tools
1. Hand jointer—used for striking head joints
2. Sled runner—used for striking bed joints
3. Mason's trowel—used for cutting tags from the wall
4. Mason's brush—used for brushing tags from the wall

1. Hand jointer

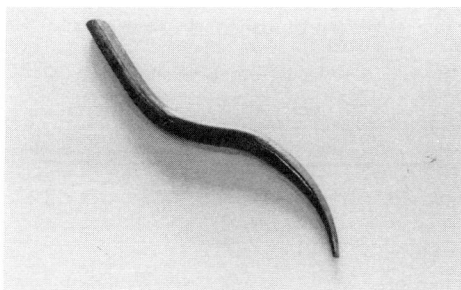

2. Sled runner

3. Mason's trowel

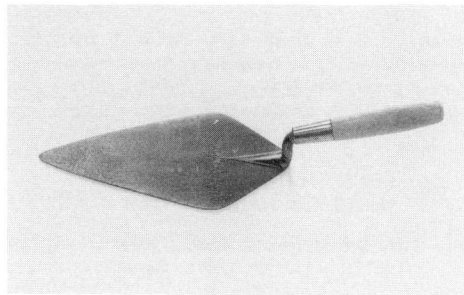

4. Mason's brush

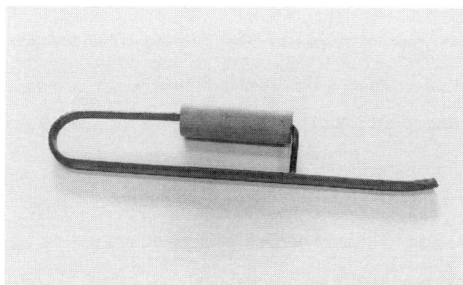

5. "Green" or just build masonry wall

LEARNING ACTIVITY NO. 2
USING THE SLED RUNNER

Hold the sled runner in your right or left hand as shown in Figure 1. Always strike the bed (horizontal) joints first as they tend to dry out much quicker than the head (vertical) joints.

To begin striking bed joints, stand with the wall to your left (right) side and, with the runner in your right (left) hand, begin moving the

Figure 1. Using the sled runner.

runner back and forth with a smooth motion in the joint. Be careful not to let the runner jump out of the joint, as this will cause a crooked joint. Be sure not to cut the joint too deeply. Remember to keep all the joints neat and straight as shown in Figure 1. After jointing the bed joints, check to see if any have been missed.

LEARNING ACTIVITY NO. 3
USING THE HAND JOINTER

Now that you have jointed the bed joints, you are ready to practice jointing the head joints. Hold the hand jointer between your thumb and fingers, as shown in Figure 2. Notice how your thumb is in the middle of the jointer with one end straight up.

Pull the jointer downward to strike a neat joint but do not cut too deeply into the mortar. After striking all of the head joints, check to see that none have been missed.

Figure 2. Using the hand jointer.

LEARNING ACTIVITY NO. 4
USING THE MASON'S TROWEL

Now take the mason's trowel. Holding it as shown in Figure 3, cut all the mortar tags from the wall. Mortar tags are the excess mortar that is left on the wall after using the sled runner. Cut the tags by turning the trowel on an angle as pictured and following the bed joint. After cutting the tags, check to see that none have been missed.

Figure 3. Using the mason's trowel.

LEARNING ACTIVITY NO. 5
USING THE MASONRY BRUSH

Now that you have jointed all the head and bed joints and cut off all the tags, the last step is to brush the wall. Holding the masonry brush as shown in Figure 4, brush lightly following the bed joints. When this has been done, make a final check to see if anything has been

overlooked. When you are satisfied with your work, complete the Check-Out Activity. You have now finished the lesson. Call your teacher to evaluate your work and to arrange for you to take the final test on "Jointing Masonry."

When you are ready, take the test starting below.

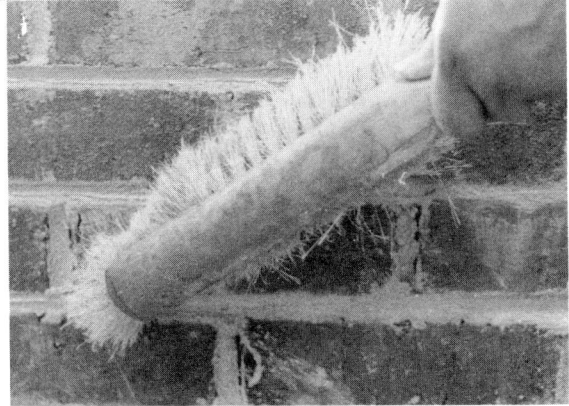

Figure 4. Using the masonry brush.

CHECK-OUT ACTIVITIES

STATEMENT OF DIRECTIONS Read each of the activities below and identify the quality of your jointing on the green wall. When you can answer "yes" to each of the statements, you are ready for the final Check-Out Activity.

Number	Check-Out Activities	Yes	No

I have completed the learning activities, and I:
1. Can identify the four masonry tools used in jointing brick and block work.
2. Can use the sled runner in striking bed joints keeping all joints neat and straight.
3. Can strike head joints neatly and accurately with the hand jointer.
4. Can remove mortar tags with the mason's trowel as instructed.
5. Can use the masonry brush to finish masonry work.
6. Have reviewed the information sheets on jointing, and I am ready to take the written test on jointing masonry.

Name _____

Module No. ___M-1___

FINAL TEST
JOINTING MASONRY

1. The most important reason for jointing masonry work is to _____ the mortar joints.

2. The second most important reason for jointing work is to make the work _____.

3. The tool used to strike bed joints is called a(an) _____.

4. The tool used to strike head joints is called a(an) _____.

5. Joints that tend to dry out more quickly are called _____.

6. When striking the bed joints, the sled runner is usually held in the _____ hand.

7. The runner should be run through each joint with a _____ motion.

8. The hand jointer should be pulled in a _____ motion to strike the head joints.

9. After jointing all work, cut the _____ with a trowel.

10. The last step in jointing, before final inspection, is to _____ the entire wall.

Name _____

Module No. _____M-1_____

ANSWER SHEET

FINAL TEST
JOINTING MASONRY

1. The most important reason for jointing masonry work is to _____SEAL_____ the mortar joints.

2. The second most important reason for jointing work is to make the work ____"LOOK GOOD"____ .

3. The tool used to strike bed joints is called a _____SLED RUNNER_____ .

4. The tool used to strike head joints is called a _____HAND_____ _____JOINTER_____ .

5. Joints that tend to dry out more quickly are called _____BED_____ _____JOINTS_____ .

6. When striking the bed joints, the sled runner is usually held in the _____RIGHT_____ hand.

7. The runner should be run through each joint with a _____SMOOTH_____ motion.

8. The hand jointer should be pulled in a _____DOWNWARD_____ motion to strike the head joints.

9. After jointing all work, cut the _____TAGS_____ with a trowel.

10. The last step in jointing, before final inspection, is to _____BRUSH_____ the entire wall.

Module No. _____M-1_____

TEACHER'S FINAL CHECKLIST

Directions: After each item, circle the level of the student's accomplishment. A (+) indicates quality work, a (0) represents acceptable work, and a (−) indicates that the work is unacceptable.

CHECKLIST ITEMS

The student:

1. Correctly identified the masonry tools used in jointing and explained their use.	+	0	−
2. Demonstrated the correct use of the sled runner. All joints were straight and neat.	+	0	−
3. Demonstrated striking head joints neatly and accurately with the hand jointer.	+	0	−
4. Demonstrated the correct removal of mortar tags by using the mason's trowel.	+	0	−
5. Demonstrated the correct use of the masonry brush in jointing masonry work.	+	0	−
6. Scored 100% on the final test on "Jointing Masonry."	+	0	−

Teacher's Comments:

Grade Assigned: _____

Name _____

APPENDIX 11C

AUTO MECHANICS UNIT VII

PROGRAM SEQUENCE
MAINTAIN AND REPAIR THE COOLING SYSTEM

SAMPLE MODULE
MODULE AM—77
LOCATE COOLANT LEAKS

by

Steven D. Dimmett
Chesterfield Technical Center
Chesterfield, Virginia

AUTO MECHANICS

PROGRAM SEQUENCE

UNIT VII: Maintain and Repair the Cooling System

MODULE NO.	UNIT AND MODULE TITLE	V-TECS OBJECTIVE NO.	OBJECTIVE	SUGGESTED SEQUENCE
AM-71	Learn about the engine cooling system	N/A N/A N/A	Describe the types of cooling systems. Identify the cooling system components and explain their functions. Explain the liquid cooling systems process of heat transfer.	1
AM-72	Know the symptoms of system failure	N/A N/A N/A N/A	List causes of and explain remedies for overheated coolant. List causes of and explain remedies for coolant that does not reach operating temperature. List causes of and explain remedies for blocked coolant flow. List causes of and explain remedies for coolant leakage.	2 (Sequence 3 and 4 have been eliminated to save space)
AM-75	Inspect and replace fan belts	N/A N/A 130	List bad belt conditions and their causes. Inspect and recognize bad fan belts. Adjust and replace a fan belt.	5
AM-76	Inspect and replace cooling system hoses	N/A N/A 135 136	List bad hose conditions and their causes. Inspect and recognize bad radiator and heater hoses. Inspect for and replace a bad heater hose. Inspect for and replace a bad radiator hose.	6
AM-77	Locate coolant leaks	N/A 128 132 N/A 131	Visually inspect cooling system for external coolant leaks. Inspect overflow tank for leakage and proper operation. Pressure test cooling system to locate external coolant leaks. Perform pressure test to isolate internal engine coolant leaks. Chemically test cooling system to detect an internal engine coolant leak.	7

MODULE NO. AM-77

LOCATE COOLANT LEAKS

by

Steven D. Dimmett
Auto Mechanics
Chesterfield Technical Center
Chesterfield, Virginia

Module No. AM-77

LOCATE COOLANT LEAKS

Introduction

An overheated engine can lead to damage of internal engine parts. Overheating may be caused by a low coolant level resulting from a leak in the cooling system. As an automotive technician, part of your job will involve the detection and repair of such leaks. However, before a leak can be repaired it must be found. Therefore, it is important that you master the procedures for leak detection before moving on to the repair of cooling systems leaks.

Most leaks are easily found, but others are hard to locate and require special detection procedures.

Directions

1. Prerequisite—mastery of material in module AM-72, "Know the Symptoms of Cooling System Failure."
2. Read and understand the performance objectives.
3. Study the procedures in the "Learning Activities" section of this module.
4. Complete the "Check-Out Activities" by performing the task procedure.
5. Have your work evaluated by the teacher using the "Teacher's Final Checklist.'

Performance Objective

Given a vehicle with a liquid cooling system that leaks and the appropriate test equipment, conduct (a) a visual inspection for external leaks, (b) a pressure test for external and internal leaks, and (c) a chemical combustion test for internal engine coolant leaks. The results of all tests are to be properly identified and recorded for inspection during the teacher's final checklist. All tests are to be conducted in a safe and professional manner.

Enabling Objectives

The student will be able to:

1. Explain the operation of the liquid cooling system.
2. Visually inspect it for leakage.
3. Properly and safely affix the pressure tester to the cooling system.
4. Explain the principle of the Combustion Leak Detector.
5. Install and use the device in a testing situation.

LEARNING ACTIVITIES

Directions

Follow the outline and procedures presented for locating leaks in the cooling system.

I. Review material from AM-72, "Know the Symptoms of Cooling System Failure."
II. Follow the procedure outlined below for locating cooling system leaks.
  A. Visually inspect cooling system for signs of coolant leakage.
    1. Position vehicle in service bay, set parking brake and turn off engine.
    2. Set a drain pan under dripping coolant.
    3. Let engine cool down until it reaches a touchable temperature.
      a. A hot engine surface and engine coolant can cause burns.
      b. DO NOT remove radiator cap! Hot, pressurized coolant could burn your skin and eyes.

4. Disconnect negative battery cable so vehicle is not accidentally started while you have your hands in and around the engine fan!
5. Remember that leaking coolant invariably runs downward due to the effects of gravity.
6. Inspect for signs of coolant leakage:
  a. In depressions on top of engine and from freeze plugs
  b. On the underside of radiator and heater hoses
  c. Down the face of the firewall (engine side)
  d. From the heater core cover inside the passenger compartment (front, passenger side)
  e. Along radiator tank seams.
7. Inspect for discoloration of metal parts, especially on the radiator, caused by chemical reaction of the coolant with copper. Discolorations of a blue-green or brown color will be apparent.
8. Check for leakage from the coolant recovery tank. Proper operation of the coolant recovery tank can only be checked by removing the radiator cap when the engine has cooled down! Remove the cap. If the radiator is full of coolant, up to the top of the radiator neck, the tank is functioning correctly for it allows the coolant to enter the radiator. If the radiator is not full, check the operation of the vacuum valve in the radiator cap. The proper operation of the cap depends on the coolant level being between the add and full marks in the coolant recovery tank. Check for leaks first.

B. Pressure test the cooling system for external and internal leaks. If the source of the leak is not found through a visual examination of the cooling system, proceed to pressure test. The pressure test should be conducted under cold engine conditions first. Follow with a test under operating temperature conditions. The procedure is followed because some leaks may or may not occur under operating temperature conditions. Heat and pressure developed in the cooling system will sometimes seal off a leak. The reverse can also take place. Contraction of coolant and metal parts in a cold engine can temporarily stop a leak. To test:

1. Remove radiator cap and attach pressure tester to radiator neck. Engine must be cool.
2. Increase the pressure on the cooling system up to the pressure rating of the radiator cap, or to the vehicle manufacturer's specifications, if available. Pump tester until the needle on the tester's dial gauge indicates that the proper pressure has been reached.
3. If pressure remains steady for two to three minutes, the system has no leak with the engine cold.
4. If the pressure drops there is a leak and the escaping pressure will force more coolant out of the system.
5. With pressure still sufficient to continue forcing coolant out of the system, look for the source of the leak. Sometimes the sound of escaping coolant will lead you to the location of the leak.
6. Search for possible leakage at the sites listed in AM-72.
7. If no leakage was evident under cold engine pressure testing conditions, or if the exact location of the leak is not certain, try pressure testing under normal engine operating conditions.
8. Remove pressure tester and refill cooling system, reconnect battery, reconnect pressure tester and start engine.
9. Reestablish pressure on the cooling system and operate the engine until normal operating temperatures are reached.
10. Once the operating temperature is reached, shut off the

the engine and disconnect negative battery cable.

11. Again, search for leaks at the sites covered in AM-72.

C. If the source of coolant loss cannot be found, leakage may be occurring on the inside of the engine. Some believe water in the oil is evidence enough of an internal leak. By itself, however, traces of water in the oil are not a sufficient indicator to prove coolant leakage past a blown head gasket or cracked water jacket. An accumulation of moisture through condensation could give the same indication.

It is important, therefore, to be able to use an accurate testing method. Either of two procedures can be followed. One involves the pressure tester and the other a chemical and an instrument called a combustion leak detector.

Since an internal coolant leak involves a blown head gasket or a crack in the water jacket that surrounds the cylinders and combustion chambers, the escaping combustion and/or exhaust gases can help locate the leak. This is exactly the principle under which the chemical and pressure tester methods operate, although the way they indicate a leak is different. A coolant leak is indicated with the pressure tester as the escaping gases cause an increase in the system pressure.

Detection with the chemical method is, however, more accurate and dramatic. In this case, escaping gases diffuse through the coolant, entering the combustion leak detector. A chemical in the tester is blue in color, and immediately turns yellow in the presence of combustion or exhaust gases.

1. To use the pressure tester:
   a. Affix the pressure tester to radiator and apply eight to ten lb. of pressure.
   b. Start the engine and allow it to idle.
   c. If pressure increases on the dial gauge, there is an internal coolant leak somewhere in the engine.
   d. To isolate the cylinder that has the coolant leak, alternately release the pressure on the tester, pump it back up to eight to ten pounds, and remove a spark plug wire from a spark plug. Ground the plug wire and watch for an increase in pressure. The cylinder that causes the increase in pressure is the one with the leak.
   e. On V-8 and V-6 engines, remove the spark plug wires from one bank or the other to isolate the leak to one side of the engine. Once the leak has been determined to be on the left or right side of the engine, follow the procedure of removing one plug wire at a time and testing each cylinder till the leak is isolated.

2. The chemical method of internal leak detection follows the same process of elimination:
   a. Start the engine and bring it to operating temperature; then allow it to idle.
   b. Fill the radiator bringing the coolant level to 3 in. below the radiator neck.
   c. Pour the chemical into the combustion leak detector filling it to the yellow line.
   d. Press the rubber cone-shaped end of the detector into the mouth of the radiator and hold firmly.
   e. Affix the suction bulb to the top of the detector, squeeze and release the bulb for three minutes to pressurize the cooling system. This pressure will help force leaking combustion gases up through the coolant into the detector where they react with the chemical.
   f. An internal coolant leak, is indicated by a change in the chemical's color. Use the process of elimination to isolate the leak to one cylinder, or, in some cases, two adjacent cylinders. That process is exactly the same as with the pressure tester method except that you are looking for a change in the chemical's color rather than an increase in pressure as each cylinder is tested. Caution: be sure to use fresh chemical with each cylinder testing even if just a slight yellowing has occurred. The results will be more accurate.

D. Decide upon and begin an appropriate procedure to repair the leak. Repair procedures for various coolant leaks are given in subsequent modules.

CHECKOUT ACTIVITY

Directions:

Using the automobile provided, check the liquid cooling system for leaks. Inspection should involve a visual check of the system for external leaks, a pressure test for external and internal leaks, and a chemical combustion test for internal leaks. The results of your inspection and tests are to be recorded on the *Summary of Results* form. When complete, the recorded data are to be turned in to your teacher for evaluation.

Module No. AM-77

SUMMARY OF RESULTS

Inspections Conducted	No. of Leaks Found	Location of Leaks
1. Visual inspection for external leaks.		
2. Pressure test for internal and external leaks. a. Cold engine b. Under operating temperature		
3. Pressure/chemical combustion test for internal leaks a. Pressure tester method b. Chemical method		

Name _____

Module No. AM-77

TEACHER'S FINAL CHECKLIST

The marks assigned indicate that the teacher has reviewed the performance in completing the objectives of this module and has found that the work performed is:

Acceptable _____   Unacceptable _____

The criteria used for evaluating the performance and the assignment of a grade is based upon the numerical scale below.

4 = excellent	The average of the points given in the
3 = good	categories shown shall constitute the
2 = average	evaluation for completion of this
1 = poor	module. An average mark less than *2*
I = incomplete	will not be acceptable.

Area of Concern	Points	Comments
1. Followed safety precautions and worked in a professional manner	_____	
2. Followed prescribed procedure	_____	
3. Found all coolant leaks Actual number of leaks (_____) compared to number found by student (_____) = _____%	_____	
AVERAGE SCORE	_____	

Name _____

Chapter 12

ORGANIZING CURRICULUM GUIDE COMPONENTS

by

Lester G. Duenk, Professor
Vocational Industrial Education
Virginia Tech
Blacksburg, Virginia

INTRODUCTION

This chapter is composed of a series of explanatory pages and forms which, when completed by the teacher, will comprise a personal curriculum guide. One blank unit guide is contained in the entire curriculum guide format to serve as a model for all unit guides which follow.

The exact format and sequence to follow in curriculum guide design will vary considerably among localities, states, and federal agencies. The main thing to keep in mind is that the content described in this text should be contained in a logical, cumulative order. Local school districts may require a specified format for the curriculum guide or for its various segments. Unit guides are always developed as separate components but the organization, content, and sequence may differ from one locality to another. There are many variations of lesson plans, instruction sheets, and competency list designs. The primary consideration is that teachers develop an organized systematic approach with which they feel comfortable.

The use of purchased curriculum guides is recommended only as supplementary resource material. Materials that conform to the exact needs of a particular instructional situation are available in abundance from State Departments of Education, consortiums, businesses, industries, and commercial sources. Space, facilities, cost, student level, and content will all vary greatly, making it important for teachers to plan personal curriculum guides to fit their own unique situations. Furthermore, effective teachers will find teaching more satisfying when they put their own personal effort into the design of their courses or programs.

EXPLANATION OF CURRICULUM FORMS

The forms that are included in this chapter are for you to duplicate in order to assemble your customized curriculum guide. The full-page forms may be reproduced, allowing you to develop specific courses or programs.

Beginning teachers, especially, would do well to use this system as an aid to planning, thus assuring that all aspects of good instruction are covered. As teachers gain experience and develop more course or program material, these forms can be refined into an even more useful instrument.

There are 32 pages of forms in all. The forms are presented in sequence with the first 12 pages being used to assemble the course or program guide. The next 13 forms are intended for the development of the individual units or lessons. The last three forms relate to testing and evaluation, laboratory management, and supplementary course materials that do not fit elsewhere.

The following forms are provided:

Course Guide Forms
1. Cover Sheet
2. Table of Contents
3. Introduction
4. Course Philosophy
5. Objectives for the Course
6. Occupational Description
7. Curriculum Resource Materials
8. Audiovisual Resource Materials
9. Units of Instruction
10. Program/Course Outline
11. Individual Competency Record
12. General Safety and Conduct Rules

Unit Guide Forms
13. Cover Page for Unit Guide
14. Unit Task Titles and Performance Objectives
15. Unit Lesson Plan Title Breakdown
16. Unit Safety Precautions
17. Laboratory/Classroom Rules for This Unit
18. Instructors Unit Lesson Plan Manipulative Skills (3 pages)

19. Instructors Unit Lesson Plan Technical Information (3 pages)
20. Unit Test, Performance Rating Scales
21. Unit Instruction Sheets
22. Unit Safety Materials
23. Learning Modules for Unit
24. Unit Appendix
25. End of Unit Guide

Supplemental Forms

26. Course Evaluation
27. Laboratory Management Materials
28. Appendix for Curriculum Guide

This chapter contains only one set of form masters for each unit title. Occupational education courses will vary considerably in the number of units needed. Generally there are from 5 to 15 units in a curriculum guide.

Note also that this sample unit guide contains only one manipulative skill lesson plan and one related technical in-formation lesson plan. The units that you prepare should contain a completed lesson plan for each lesson title listed in the lesson plan title breakdown for the unit.

The first priority is to complete forms 9 through 21. The other items can be added as the curriculum guide is developed.

Special Instructions appear on many of the forms. These provide guidance on the types of information or topics that should be included on the particular page as you build your curriculum guide. When the forms in this chapter are duplicated, cover these Special Instructions with a plain white sheet of paper. This will provide you with a useful blank form acceptable for your finished guide. The boxed directions are not intended to become a part of your finished guide.

The format included in this chapter will become the basis for planning a strong instructional program. By completing the forms and following the teaching plan, the quality of instruction should improve and the amount of learning taking place should increase.

Cover Sheet

Table of Contents

┌─ *Special Instructions* ─────────────────────────────────┐

Plan the topics for the table of contents by studying the chapters preceding. It may be advisable to make a rough copy at first that can be refined as you proceed through the curriculum guide writing process. Do not use page numbers at first, as it will be necessary to add and revise material. A tab arrangement is satisfactory for locating the various sections.

└───── *Cover this boxed information when duplicating forms* ─────┘

Introduction

Special Instructions

Describe here the need for competency based education, purpose of this guide; how it was developed; type of community, school, student; and other factors that will orient the reader to the course or program.

Cover this boxed information when duplicating forms

Course Philosophy

┌─ *Special Instructions* ─────────────────────────────────────┐

State here the course philosophy, program philosophy, and school philosophy in terms of belief statements. This may be written in paragraph or listing form.

└────── *Cover this boxed information when duplicating forms* ──────┘

Objectives for the Course

Special Instructions ———————————

List the national objectives of education, general vocational education objectives, school objectives, and program or course objectives. The program or course objectives should be limited to 5-25 broad statements that will cover the entire course. Refer to these objectives when writing performance objectives for the individual unit guides.

——————— **Cover this boxed information when duplicating forms** ———————

Occupational Description

Related Areas of Employment
(Include D.O.T. numbers for each occupation)

Curriculum Resource Materials

Title	Description	Year	No. of Pages	Source

Audio Visual Resource Materials

Type (videos, slides, transparencies, etc.)	Title	Unit	Available From

Units of Instruction

Unit 1 _____

Unit 2 _____

Unit 3 _____

Unit 4 _____

Unit 5 _____

Unit 6 _____

Unit 7 _____

Unit 8 _____

Unit 9 _____

Unit 10 _____

Unit 11 _____

Unit 12 _____

Unit 13 _____

Unit 14 _____

Unit 15 _____

Unit 16 _____

Unit 17 _____

Unit 18 _____

Unit 19 _____

Unit 20 _____

Unit 21 _____

Unit 22 _____

Unit 23 _____

Unit 24 _____

Unit 25 _____

Program/Course Outline

Develop the course outline by listing the major course units as numbered headings. Place the content of each unit in outline form below each unit title. This outline is generally kept on file by the school administrator. Use an outline form as follows:

I. _____

    A. _____

        1. _____

        2. _____

    B. _____

    C. _____

        1. _____

        2. _____

        3. _____

        4. _____

    D. _____

        1. _____

        2. _____

    E. _____

II. _____

    A. _____

    B. _____

        1. _____

        2. _____

    C. _____

        1. _____

        2. _____

        3. _____

    D. _____

        1. _____

        2. _____

Individual Competency Record

┌─ *Special Instructions* ─────────────────────────────────

    Individual competency records are required in most occupational programs. The format varies widely; however, the main type of information to include on the individual competency record is:

1. *Student name, course, and level.*
2. *Unit titles with required tasks.*
3. *Student ratings.*
4. *A scale which describes the meaning of ratings.*

You may want to use the form below as a model:

STUDENT'S NAME: _____ SCHOOL _____

ADDRESS: _____ SS# _____

PHONE: _____ DATE OF BIRTH: _____ SEX: _____ AGE: _____

ENROLLMENT DATE: COMPLETION DATE: TOTAL HOURS: GRADE:

SHOP COMPETENCIES

DIRECTIONS: Evaluate the student using the rating scale below. Check the appropriate number to indicate the degree of competency. The rating for each of the tasks should reflect job readiness rather than the grade earned in the class.

RATING SCALE

4 - Skilled—can work independently with no supervision.
3 - Moderately skilled—can perform job completely with limited supervision.
2 - Limited skill—requires instruction.
1 - No exposure—no experience or knowledge in this area.

I. ORIENTATION

4 3 2 1 _____
4 3 2 1 _____
4 3 2 1 _____
4 3 2 1 _____

II. JOB PLANNING AND LAYOUT

4 3 2 1 _____
4 3 2 1 _____
4 3 2 1 _____
4 3 2 1 _____
4 3 2 1 _____
4 3 2 1 _____
4 3 2 1 _____
4 3 2 1 _____

(Continue to fit your curriculum)

Instructor's Comments: _____

_____
_____
_____
_____
_____

── *Cover this boxed information when duplicating forms* ──

General Safety and Conduct Rules

┌─ *Special Instructions* ─────────────────────────────────┐

    List the safety and conduct rules that apply to the whole course. Specific rules may differ for each unit and will appear in the beginning section of each unit guide.

└──── ***Cover this boxed information when duplicating forms*** ────┘

Cover Page Unit Guide for

Unit No._____ Title_____

Unit Task Titles and Performance Objectives

Unit No._____ Title_____

Task Number	Title of Task	Performance Objectives

Unit Lesson Plan Title Breakdown

Unit No._____ Title _____

Number	"Doing" Lesson Titles	Reference Code	Number	"Knowing" Lesson Titles	Reference Code

Unit Safety Precautions

Unit No._____ Title _____

Special Instructions _____

    List here only the safety precautions that are new for this unit. General safety precautions or those that were taught in previous units may be reviewed.

Cover this boxed information when duplicating forms

Laboratory/Classroom Rules For This Unit

Unit No._____ Title _____

Special Instructions ———————————————————

List here only the laboratory/classroom rules that are new for this unit. General student conduct rules or those that were taught in previous units may be reviewed.

——— **Cover this boxed information when duplicating forms** ———

Instructor's Unit Lesson Plan
Manipulative Skills

Instructor: _____   Unit_____

Lesson Title: _____   Lesson Number _____

Objective(s): _____

_____

Tools and Equipment: _____

Materials: _____

Teaching Aids: _____

References:_____

I. PREPARATION (of the learner):

II. PRESENTATION (of the skills):

Steps	Key Points (things to remember to do or say)

(continued)

Instructor's Unit Lesson Plan
(continued)

II. PRESENTATION (of the skills):

Steps	**Key Points** (things to remember to do or say)

Instructor's Unit Lesson Plan
(continued)

II. PRESENTATION (of the skills):

Steps	Key Points (things to remember to do or say)

III. APPLICATION (practice by learner under close supervision)

IV. CHECK UP (or test performance of skill to acceptable standards)

Suggested Reading for Student:

The Next Lesson Is:

Instructor's Unit Lesson Plan
Technical Information

Instructor: _____   Unit_____

Lesson Title: _____   Lesson Number _____

Objective(s): _____

_____

Tools and Equipment: _____

Materials: _____

Teaching Aids: _____

References:_____

I. PREPARATION (of the learner):

II. PRESENTATION (of the knowledge):

Topics	Key Points (things to remember to do or say)

Instructor's Unit Lesson Plan
(continued)

II. PRESENTATION (of the knowledge):

Topics	Key Points (things to remember to do or say)

(continued)

Instructor's Unit Lesson Plan
(continued)

II. PRESENTATION (of the knowledge):

Topics	Key Points (things to remember to do or say)

III. APPLICATION (drills, illustrations, analogies, oral questions, or assignments)

IV. CHECK UP (or test is a final check on students comprehension of material presented)

Suggested Reading for Student:

The Next Lesson Is:

Unit Tests, Performance Rating Scales

┌─ *Special Instructions* ──────────────────────────┐

Include here self-check tests, regular tests, performance rating, and manipulative performance tests. If tests fit with particular lessons, attach to the lesson plans. Duplicate copies for student use. Include scoring keys.

└──── **Cover this boxed information when duplicating forms** ────┘

Unit Instruction Sheets

Special Instructions

Include here all job sheets, assignment sheets, operation sheets, information sheets, and other types discussed in chapter 7.
Note: If an instruction sheet is used with a specific lesson, attach it to the lesson plan. Place here only those materials that can be used with various lessons throughout the unit.

Cover this boxed information when duplicating forms

Unit Safety Materials

Special Instructions

   Place here any unit safety materials other than the safety rules at the beginning of the unit.

Cover this boxed information when duplicating forms

Learning Modules For Unit

Title Page:

Name of module
Unit number
Purpose

Introduction:

Performance objectives
Module directions

Study materials and learning activities:

Module evaluation:

Unit Appendix

Special Instructions

Place here drawings, charts, journal articles and other materials that will supplement the lessons and activities in the unit.

Cover this boxed information when duplicating forms

End Of Unit Guide

┌─ *Special Instructions* ─────────────────────────

This is the end of the unit guide. The remaining materials refer to the entire course rather than a single unit. Plan a unit guide for each of the units. It is a good idea to set up the entire expanding file unit guide system initially. As materials are developed or located, place them in the appropriate files. Eventually, through a process of developing, revising, and gathering new materials from various sources, an entire curriculum guide is formulated. Remember that it is necessary to have a loose-leaf notebook copy of the curriculum guide, with all materials organized cumulatively, as well as a filing system that complements this document.

└─ **Cover this boxed information when duplicating forms** ─

Course Evaluation

Special Instructions

Place here any evaluation materials that do not belong in specific unit guides.

These might include:

1. Semester tests.
2. Final course evaluation.
3. Methods of arriving at periodic and final grades.
4. Copies of student report cards.
5. Other evaluation materials.

Cover this boxed information when duplicating forms

Laboratory Management Materials

Special Instructions

Include here such items as:
1. *Progress checklists.*
2. *Progress charts.*
3. *Student personnel plans.*
4. *Machine use arrangements.*
5. *Locker assignment forms.*
6. *Stock sheets.*
7. *Student account records.*
8. *Live work agreements.*
9. *Maintenance program information.*
10. *Tool and equipment inventories.*
11. *Other laboratory management materials.*

Cover this boxed information when duplicating forms

Appendix For Curriculum Guide

Special Instructions

Place here any supplementary course materials that serve as aids to instruction. These materials should be placed in the unit appendix if they do not pertain to a particular unit. Place such materials here only if they apply to the entire course.

You may organize these materials into areas such as: safety, school regulations, youth group information, advisory committees, self-study materials, regulations (state and local), etc.

Cover this boxed information when duplicating forms

INDEX

A

Achievement evaluation, cognitive, 145-171
Administering tests, cognitive achievement evaluation, 161
Affective, cognitive, and psychomotor competencies, 72
Alphabetical filing, 76
Analysis, and industry, 7-9
Analysis, occupational, 7-17
Analysis breakdown system, 15
Analysis charts, 15-17
Assignment sheet, 116, 119
  editing sample, 120
  review sample, 121
  sample, 118
Attainment standards, 186, 189
Attainment standards, specifying criteria sample chart, 187, 188
Audiovisual and curriculum materials sources, 30-50
Averaging system, 165

C

Cardinal principles of secondary education, 55
Checklists, 192, 194
Circular saw safety, appendix 10C, 217
Clarification of objectives example, appendix 4B, 63, 64
Class sessions, 5
Cognitive, psychomotor, and affective competencies, 72
Cognitive achievement, 145, 146
Cognitive achievement evaluation, 145-171
  administering tests, 161
  definition of cognitive student assessment, 146, 147
  factors to be evaluated, 145, 146
  grading, 162-165
  measurement and evaluation terms, 147
  planning tests, 147, 148
  purposes of, 147
  scoring tests, 161, 162
  test items, 148-161
Cognitive student assessment, definition, 146, 147
Colleges and universities, curriculum and audiovisual materials sources, 36, 37
Commercial publishers, curriculum and audiovisual materials sources, 47-50
Community type, curriculum guide introduction, 51, 52
Competency list, 61
Competency list sample, 60

Competency record, individualized, 67-78
Completion/short answer items, cognitive achievement evaluation, 150-152
Computer database search, 26-30
  LABORDOC database, 29, 30
  NTIS database, 29
  RIVE database, 29
  TRAINET database, 29
  training and development alert, 29
  training media database, 29
  VECM database, 29
Conduct rules and general safety, 61
Contacts, personal, 25, 26
Course guide forms, 231-244
Course objectives, writing, 8, 9
Course of study, 3
Course outline, 3
Course outline for industrial electricity, appendix 4D, 65, 66
Course syllabus, 3, 4
Cues, sample chart, 185
Curriculum,
  development, 2, 3
  documentation, 3, 4
  educational programs, 1, 2
  major groupings, 2
Curriculum and audiovisual materials sources, 30-50
  colleges and universities, 36, 37
  commercial publishers, 47-50
  curriculum consortiums, 33
  international organizations, 30, 31
  manufacturers, 46, 47
  national organizations, 31, 32
  professional associations and unions, 42-44
  regional curriculum coordination centers, 32, 33
  state departments of education, 38-42
  state resources, 37, 38
  trade organizations, 44-46
  U.S. government agencies, 35, 36
  U.S. Military, 33-35
Curriculum consortiums, 33
Curriculum coordination centers, regional, 32, 33
Curriculum formats, 4, 5
  class sessions, 5
  formal/descriptive method, 4
  modules of instruction, 4, 5